COLD TIMES

How to Prepare for the Mini Ice Age

by

Anita Bailey, PhD

AUCTORITAS PUBLISHING LLC
Springfield, MO 65803
2017

DEDICATION

For Rick

CONTENTS

A CONSIDERATION

We're not discussing the end of the world, of course;
we're talking events like those that can be found repeated many
times in the histories of other failing civilizations.
That said, my guess is that some of those discontinuities
are going to be harsh ones. Those who brace themselves
for serious trouble and reduce their vulnerabilities
to a brittle and dysfunctional system
will be more likely to come through in one piece.

---*John Michael Greer, December 28, 2016*
http://thearchdruidreport.blogspot.com/

History teaches us the mistakes we are going to make.
- Jean Bodin

1 THE NEW REALITY

I wrote this during the final months of 2016 through the autumn of 2017. As it went to publication, there was early snow in the upper Midwest, frozen unharvested grain crops in Russia, and foot-deep hail in Spain. Earlier in the spring, Kansas farmers lost 40% of their wheat crop to flooding and frost – California's tomato crops are dropping by millions of tons, and Florida's citrus crops were decimated by hurricanes. America's crippled and dying "legacy" media rarely report it.

This is the time you knew was coming.

You knew, and I knew, because we are the children of the long-ago survivors of similar planetary phenomena. Our ancestors survived every past Mini Ice Age cold time – Dalton, Maunder, Wolf, Middle Ages, Sporer, Roman – and every actual 10,000-year glaciated full-on Ice Age, as well. The subconscious awareness of this coming time is written in our genes, stored in a dusty section near the 'thrifty genes' that make gaining weight easy and 'anxiety genes' that trigger the tendency to store up things.

Just as birds flock together and start heading south when the seasons are about to change, and caterpillars build cocoons when their development reaches a specific stage, we too are biologically programmed for survival through Cold Times. Many of the social changes happening around the entire world are part of the genetic responses triggered by whispered advance warning of the coming

Cold. Humankind's historical behaviors will be our behaviors and our descendant's behaviors, as well, because what our ancestors did is the root of persistence and written in our survivor's genetic program.

This is significant in a way we only sense – biology, as they say, is destiny. But it is critically important to remember that biology's subtle signals are not the same as *determinism,* the inability to alter biological programming, and nowhere near the same as *knowledge.* The common-sense know-how to deal with aberrant weather comes from cultural learning and personal experience, often passed along as word-of-mouth and inexplicable 'family traditions'. Those strange family traditions arose in response to some previous hard time, lingering on in passed-along actions. Thanks to sociopathic social controllers and several generations of great weather with good times, that knowledge has been all-but erased from modern awareness. Even the librarians who should have known to store our collective wisdom on paper and in safe places, didn't.

Historically, Cold Times start with erratic and unusual weather. Ancient documents record frosts in midsummer that destroyed warm-weather crops, for example. Over time, weather becomes more difficult to predict. Flooding destroys farmland, crops, and towns. Winters get colder and snow lasts longer; spring comes late, summers are unusually wet, winter hits before the summer's crops are harvested. Lakes and rivers freeze, and thaw late. Glaciers grow down valleys at 150 feet *a day.*

As harvests fail, people starve and clamor to their neighbors for supplies. Desperation triggers crime and wars break out. Distress and hunger wear down immunity, and epidemics rage. One out of every three children born dies before the age of 5; one of the remaining two dies before reproducing. Cities shrink and coalesce around strong men, while far rural areas become increasingly isolated. Gangs and robbers, unable to provide for their own, prey on unwary travelers and out-of-the-way dwellings. Some areas depopulate and become wilderness, just as Rome's once-great structures fell and became rough pasture to nomadic shepherds and their flocks. Over centuries, weather improves and stabilizes, bumper crops again are harvested, more infants survive to adulthood, populations increase, cities rebuild, and the cycle of forgetting starts over.

One of the great failures of imagination of our age is the unfailing faith in the religion of progress. This faith creates a blindness to the simple reality: there is no salvation in human works. Technology is a tool, what amounts to a hammer. Humans make technology; a hammer has no abilities greater than the one who wields it. Technological advancement *will not save us.*

Remember, every dead ancient culture had its technology. Romans, Egyptians, and Mayans created buildings that have lasted thousands of years -- ours are poor copies and will not stand that long. Aztecs, Peruvians, Persians, and the Algonquin cultivated the first of the great crops that are now mainstays around the world, including turkeys, potatoes, wheat, and corn – we, with all of our high tech have destroyed the genetics of the ancient crops by inserting genes that makes subsequent generations infertile or dependent on another manufactured product. The Renaissance in Europe led to the creation of beauty and art that modern humans can appreciate but not duplicate. Both China and India developed medical arts based in entirely different, and often more effective, systems than used in the West today – herbalism, energy fields, and dietary essentials will still be healing humankind long after modern antibiotics are a dusty memory.

Each great civilization rises with its own skills and focus, trusts those talents to override reality forever, and fails as it becomes blinded by its own success. We are mites riding the back of the elephant. Mites with hubris, to be sure, but mites nevertheless.

The New Reality

We are now at the leading edge of this world-wide change. Socially, mankind is turning away from the great overriding systems (banks, governments, pharma and medical conglomerate, conventional media, political powers, industry), everything that is in the hands of unseen giants. This appears as an "awakening" on a global scale. I suspect this occurs cyclically, as underscored by economist Martin Armstrong's cycle discoveries, and may be an effect that is genetically programmed when certain cosmic conditions come about. A percentage of people simply know that the times are changing, even as the sun's energetic output decreases and the entire planet destabilizes and becomes cooler.

The now-visible effects of this new reality include:
- the sudden appearance of tornados in places they have previously been unknown;
- snow falling in the tropics and the deserts of Northern Africa where it has not been seen in recorded history;
- hail storms so heavy that "rivers" of ice a foot deep run through streets and in canals;
- rain "bombs", coming down like a waterfall so forceful that a year's worth of rain falls in an hour;
- intense heat followed by a frost followed again by heat;
- 100-year or 1000-year floods in the same place *every year;*
- snows falling months early or late, or multiple feet deeper than before;
- strange atmospheric phenomena: mesospheric "bores" that light up the sky in waves, purple skies;
- iridescent "noctilucent" clouds;
- aurora visible in the tropics, and atmospheric electric "light columns" and "sprites" flitting where they have never been seen;
- lightning killing herds of animals and crowds of people;
- eerie sounds like groaning or trumpets coming from the sky;
- jet stream wildly out of position;
- arctic cold pouring down into tropical regions at the same time heat waves are melting tundra;
- an increase in volcanic eruptions, affecting travel and weather and local crops;
- the onset of swarms of earthquakes, bigger quakes, and quakes in regions that haven't known them in the past.

Meanwhile, sunspots all but disappear, and earth's magnetic field weakens. This will affect our generations in a way that is profoundly different than when this type of solar downturn happened in the past -- because *today's electronics and electric grid are unprepared for the newly incoming ionized blasts and electromagnetic surges.* This doesn't even count the fragile state of our national economies, or the widespread cultural disarray going on worldwide. And we have created a social structure that is 100% dependent on the grid functioning normally.

The key concept of this coming Cold Time is *adaptability*. Those things we have taken as "predictable" – that April 15th is the last frost day and it's safe to plant tender tomatoes, for example – will seem charmingly naïve in a few decades. The weather and planetary rhythms that were routine during the development of modern agriculture and seed-strains will turn into wild oscillations, unpredictable from year to year. Farmers struggle and fail, and food "suddenly" becomes a serious issue – first in nations that import a large percentage of their grains, and then in the formerly rich nations, who then can barely feed their own.

It's going to hurt; there is no doubt. As during *every* previous cycle, people will die prematurely. Cold, floods, and bizarre weather extremes will kill directly – they already are. Diseases of malnutrition will break out and uncontrollable epidemics rage. The social stressors will trigger wars and civil violence – and there will be starvation on a scale that is nearly unimaginable, some because of politics and some from sheer privation. Empires will fall, cultures will contract into tight knots, and some will disappear entirely. The historical details may vary, but the big picture remains the same with each Cold Time.

The point of this book, though, is not to convince you that the climate is chilling, social structures are failing, or that you will have to adapt and prepare to meet those changes. You already know that part. This book's purpose is:
- to provide a foundation for understanding how the Cold Time will affect every aspect of your existence;
- to provide a structure for survival in a physical environment that is significantly different from the one in which you were raised;
- and to give you a framework of knowledge and skill on which you can create your own decisions and choices.

Framework & Assumptions

In the coming Cold Time, basic human nature and needs will still continue. A primary need is accurate information. There's no value to 'information' that panders to political correctness or a false sense of security.

I will give you the best info that I have, but this won't be a research thesis -- I've written hundreds of them -- with references for each assertion. I'm not trying to prove this in that way, merely give you a starting point for your *own* research. The internet is working and libraries are open – gather what you need so that you have it later when the internet is just a memory. Print it out, or buy paper books. Paper can last hundreds of years; your e-reader won't.

Also, keep in mind that *no one* has the answers you need for your unique situation – this book is merely a set of suggestions for things that have worked for others in the past. If you want you to survive through the calamities that await us in the coming years, *you must turn your brain on and take responsibility for **every** aspect of your life.* You simply **cannot** place your wellbeing in the hands of strangers, even well-meaning strangers. No one cares as much about you and yours as *you.*

Resistance to Change

The most common resistance to making serious life changes, especially moving to a rural area, is often a practical one: money. Your job's in City X, you're living paycheck to paycheck already – how can you save enough to buy another place? How will you make any money to cover land payments?

Some people are not financially stuck – any resistance to change comes from their worldview, not their finances. No amount of money will protect these people from what lies ahead, if they persist in their closed minds. A big 401K will not save you, and neither will those 'great contacts' at the brokerage. These will be among the first things that are swept away in the early Cold Waves.

Those who are financially stuck – the good, hardworking people who see what is coming – will have to decide what is really important. Many of these live in houses that are excessively large and expensive to heat and cool, or waste money every month on a rental when the same money could have bought a little piece of land. Many drive cars with monthly payments, or worse yet with a lease, when they could have bought an older vehicle for much less and no payments. Many have useless money wasters – daily coffee bought on the way to work ($80 per month?), cable service of any kind (waste of time, money, and mind), meals eaten "out" instead of prepared at home for a fraction of the price, weekly or monthly nail or hair parlor visits, gym fees (what's wrong with jogging around the block for free?).

Resistance comes from the dying legacy media – the people whose personal and corporate incomes depend on you and everyone else continuing to "buy" their so-called news and their advertiser's products. There are already multiple outlets now doubling down on the global warming agenda – yes, they are actually saying that even though we "might" see something like the Maunder Minimum cold (because they can no longer deny the sun's lack of sunspots), man-made global warming will nullify the effects.

That's right: man-made global warming is more powerful than the sun and will "protect" us from the coming Age of Ice! If that's the case, they should be *encouraging* **more** polluting cars, **more** smoke stacks, **more** carbon dioxide aerosols! But, of course, logic is not the media's strong point; it is *taxes* that will save us from excess planetary heat. Even so, the dying media's inability to grasp the critical nature of this Cold Time will leave their followers helpless. It's sad.

The Spouse

One way to measure the potential outcome of any plan, is to test the willingness of both partners in a marriage to aim toward the same goals. Spouses who pull together, tend to accomplish what they want. Those who pull in opposite directions, fail. Simple as that.

What if the spouse doesn't buy into your preparedness concerns? You have exactly three options:

1. Have a serious sit-down "we have to do this and this is why" meeting and get the spouse onboard. Make a PowerPoint – really. Use YouTube websites from Adapt 2030, Oppenheimer Ranch, and Ice Age Farmer, who are easily understood and provide convincing evidence.
2. Do all the prepping yourself and hide it from your spouse (not recommended, since dishonesty weakens the relationship).
3. Recognize that the spouse was not a good match for you

and divorce, amicably. Or forget about prepping entirely.

Work together, work alone, or move on. Those are your choices.

Your Level of Skill

Many people who buy preparedness books are just starting out learning readiness and survival skills. More often than not, these beginners can't differentiate between genuine knowledge from someone who has "been there done that", and someone who is a keyboard commando who merely passes along whatever they read on the 'net....or the outright rip-offs selling inadequate storage food or cheap gadgets.

I have "been there done that" (see my author info at the end of the book) on prepping, small farming, search and rescue, health care, growing and storing food, and et cetera. I will be speaking from hard-won experience, making a lot of mistakes, and passing along the benefit of my trials. That's why I'm able to give it to you straight.

Throughout this book it's assumed that you already know something about life and about doing things on your own – because I can't tell you how to be a responsible adult. That's beyond the scope of this book.

It's also unrealistic to imagine that you can start from a "typical" suburban or urban lifestyle, and move immediately to a self-sufficient one. You will NOT be able to grow all your own food during your first season as a gardener. It's unrealistic even if everything stays the way it is now. If you are downsized unexpectedly and facing foreclosure on your home, you will have to learn *really fast*. We don't want it to get to that, because at that point any failure could be a mortal one.

The ideal, of course, is that you start from a position of strength and stability, and merely add new knowledge and skills. That's the ideal, but you do what you have to do. It will take you several *years* at the very least to become a decent food grower, for example. Begin where you are, right now. You don't have several years.

Support

Unless you develop an independent social group now, such as an extended family, that meets all its own needs in vegetables, fruits, grains, meats, fiber, building supplies, future relationships, child-raising, arts and music, classical education, mechanics, health care, electricity, and repairs of all kinds, you will still have to learn to trade/barter with an outside community. When times get hard, families, whether blood relatives or simply like-minded individuals, will come together for mutual support. And, your group will interact with other groups. This is what humans have done since the beginning of time.

Historically, the largest group of people who can live together in self-supplying mutual assurance, before bureaucratic social systems start developing, is about 140 individuals. Hutterite religious communities keep this as the cap number, and when they reach this size, the community divides. In a group this size, there is generally sufficient labor and ability to cover all the basic needs of everyone. Each person will recognize all other members. Each person will have "close" friends and relations, and more distant ones – but everyone will know everyone else, as well as everyone else's personal details, skills, quirks, and talents.

There's good sides to this: it tends to keep everyone honest, and strangers stand out. The down side is that there is reduced privacy. Almost everything becomes public knowledge, eventually. That's why it promotes honesty.

Assume, therefore, that you must either provide the place, or go to another place, where your group can live for at least the next several generations, until 2060, possibly longer. Life will *never* return to "normal" as it was at, say, 2015. That time is done forever.

Clearly, you will have to do some serious thinking about this – you won't survive the Cold Time holding a 9-to-5 job at a cubicle or living in an apartment or suburban home, no matter how tactically it is outfitted. If you choose to stay there, you, your spouse, and your children risk succumbing, right there.

Grid and Power

Also, a major portion of our framework in this book, is that we cannot assume that the electrical grid, propane, gasoline, or diesel will continue to be available at a reasonable price -- or even exist at all. Generators, solar, or wind power can be a temporary, gap-filling option as the system devolves, but eventually your people will have to live as our ancestors did, that is, without it.

Electricity and gas/diesel machinery have been enormous "force multipliers" – one man with a tractor could plow a field in a day that would have taken a week with a horse-drawn plow; one woman could bake bread and wash a household's laundry in a couple hours instead of a taking a day or longer. Without those tools, physical labor and skill once again come into their own. Ideally, you will have sufficient backup resources so that your transition to more hand-labor will be gradual, over several years. Additionally, having a group working together hoeing vegetables or hanging laundry promotes bonding and solidarity while lightening the load for each contributor.

Geological Upheaval

John Casey makes a remarkable case for the correlation of low sunspots (as occurred during each solar minimum of the past) and the *increase* in earthquakes and volcanos. His book, *Upheaval*, graphically connects major quakes in the US over the past several hundred years with solar minima; there's other indications the same is true of the rest of the world.

Many reports from the past indicate that major volcanic eruptions helped worsen the climate by sending up clouds of dust that blocked the sun.

The combination of poor cold weather, with further reduced sunlight because of high volcanic particulates in the upper atmosphere, along with the risk of being hit by a major quake...well, "interesting times". A great earthquake on New Madrid would not only shake the entire Midwest and much of the northeast and east coast, it also could break every oil and gas pipeline that crosses the Mississippi *and* bring down railroad and highway bridges. The loss of food and heating supplies during a northeast winter would be unthinkably devastating.

Even so, since historically solar minima are associated with increased major earthquakes and volcanic eruptions, it would be foolish to ignore the possibilities.

Specialization

Part of our assumed framework is that each member of your group will have specific skills or natural orientation toward certain interests: music, for example, or healing arts. Initially, group members will arrive with the unspoken personal assumption that they will *specialize* in their preferred discipline.

However, over time everyone becomes a *generalist*, with multiple duties that contribute to the group's function and survival. The doctor can also be a gardener. The artist is also the bread maker. The machinist is also part of the security team. Each person who is a current specialist can likewise become a teacher of the next generation, taking on one or more "students" in an apprenticeship model so that their skills are passed along.

Division of Labor

Division of labor within our framework is also assumed. This arises in part from innate biology, and in part because life simply works more efficiently with work divided among those who can best do it. Men, in general, excel at skills involving equipment and machines; women, in general, shine in person-centered activities.

However, many productive jobs in a self-sufficient setting can be done by any sensible person, including children. There is no reason to treat the very young or very old like incompetents or invalids – feeding chickens, collecting eggs, cleaning livestock pens, hoeing weeds, stringing and shelling beans, mending clothing, and so on can be done by those with little physical stamina, mental acuity, or high level skills.

Everyone contributes; there are no free rides.

Family Primacy

Along with division of labor, is the primacy is family life – that is, a male and female partner as the stable foundation from which a home is developed, and in which children are raised and the elderly are cared for. With division of labor, the wife is able to attend to child-rearing and education, as well as making and repairing clothing, cooking healthful meals, caring for small livestock, keeping the stoves fed, canning and storing food, and maintaining family discipline, all critically important activities that require a huge investment of energy and skill. The husband takes care of large livestock, heavy labor, equipment construction and repairs, security and defense, and other outside chores, also critically important. Each of these are valuable full-time jobs that *together* accomplish the many tasks that keep a homestead running.

Although all various permutations of human relationships are possible (male/male, female/female, male/female/female, female/male/male, etc.), social stability is stronger with the traditional relationship – that's why it is traditional, because it worked for long term survival. Open gay and lesbian relationships historically flourish within civilizations that are past their peak, and are a marker of that stage.

Children

Young civilizations require high levels of reproduction in order to grow. Collapsing civilizations require children in order to care for the parents in their old age, since there is no longer a social safety net to do that job. Today's parents who took little interest in their children's growing years will find that their children take little interest in their aging years, and no one else will, either. Sterile unions have no future. Consider how many members of the celibate Shaker religion you know. Hint: none. They died out a hundred years ago, childless.

Therefore, family must be encouraged within the group social community itself, because family is the foundation from which the group, community, society, and the future itself eventually springs. Childless couples can take on orphaned children, as they have in other Cold Times. There will be many who need homes.

After the current generation is gone, there will be many fewer people who postpone childbearing or who choose voluntary sterility. Children are practical immortality, and the future of your clan.

Shared Purpose

Unity of purpose is a critical element in a group's survival, and some basis for that will be assumed in your group as well. This unity may be as simple, and primal, as blood-ties – that is, a family, tribe, clan, or other kin-relationship that results in members favoring relatives over outsiders. This is a basic *us*-vs-*them* condition. In addition, unity of purpose can extend to group survival in order to propagate an idea, belief, or skill – say, a religiously-based order such as the Amish; or a clan that is formed around, for example, moonshine production or metal working.

Each group passes along its unifying concept to the next generation, and that becomes a deeper unifier to succeeding descendants.

Ideally, a unifier would include elements of blood-kinship PLUS a universally-needed skill or product that is marketable within and outside the group such as food production, or herbal medical knowledge, or construction skills, or even mercenary defenders, though rogue warriors have limited lifespans and tend not to reproduce successfully. As time goes by, make an effort to have your group "known" regionally as providers of some valuable service. Then, your wider community, reliant on your service, will help protect you when the inevitable marauders come through.

Value

All things have some value to someone. Generally today, we determine value by comparing to currency, that is, my object is worth X dollars. This pound of coffee is worth $15. That car is worth $20,000. That loaf of bread is worth $4. Price, however, is NOT the same as value, true value. If you are desperately hungry, you might be willing to trade your car for a loaf of bread; the bread has greater value to you than the car.

During the Weimar Germany hyperinflation in the 1920s, starving people traded gold and diamond jewelry, mink coats, fine art, and concert-quality grand pianos, for a bag of potatoes. A bag of potatoes.

So, what is the *real value* of object X? *Only what someone else is willing to pay for it.*

The real question is: what are the items that retain value, no matter what is going on in the world? The real answer is: *food, water, shelter, security.* Extras include: medicine, ammo, distilled liquor, marijuana, and tobacco. Sex, too, but that only has value to someone who isn't getting any otherwise -- another reason to encourage devoted family structures.

Keep in mind: anything written on paper is only as good as the paper. That applies to stocks, bonds, mining certificates, contracts, licenses, registrations, gold shares, and even paper dollars themselves. After a collapse has run its course, historically gold and silver value return as tokens for trade. But always remember: real value is in *food, water, shelter, security.* Everything else is just a tool to achieve that end.

This Century and Beyond

One of the biggest assumptions I make in this book is largely unprovable – until it happens or it doesn't. It is the assumption that we are heading into what is effectively a mini-ice age, a period of global cooling initiated by changes in the sun's energetic output and resulting changes in earth's magnetic shielding and climate. It might be worse and convert to a millennia-long ice age, but it won't matter for planning since the needs are the same.

Secondary to that, and possibly connected via some mechanism of which we are largely unaware, are a set of changes in both human perception and behavior. It's a switch from reliance on large-scale governance to local control along with a generalized failure of the economic and financial system. Once again, Martin Armstrong has observed this as a repeating cyclical pattern in human behavior going back thousands of years within multiple nation's histories.

There are also strong indications that the solar changes initiate increased volcanic activity and stronger earthquakes. Author John Casey has made a good case correlating solar output lows with very large and destructive earthquakes in the United States.

Teasing out which effect leads and which follows is quite the challenge. I suspect that solar energetic changes affect humankind in ways we don't understand, and those properties also impact planetary climate and geography as well. In our historical past, climate and geographic changes caused crop loss, which in turn caused famine, which caused disease, which caused populations to die off and survivors to migrate – which generated wars, which initiated regime changes. When sun and climate stabilized, people settled down, formed cities and nations, built and grew, and assumed it would always be that way.

Infrastructure

Today, we have the additional problems of an enormous and complex society that is built on a fragile energy infrastructure, and on accounting principles – that is, the philosophy of "just in time" (JIT). These are the greatest weaknesses in our culture today, and the very large seeds that will inevitably lead to our social destruction, whether now or later.

The energy infrastructure – by which, I mean the electrical generating architecture of power plants and the extensive powerline grid that distributes that power – is itself a large centralized system of power governance. It is rather like the central government, reaching over great distances into our homes, and controlling our day and our behavior. Like the federal government, it requires enormous financial and manpower inputs to sustain itself....both of which are now drawn to their physical limits

Meanwhile, the variety of upgrades and even routine maintenance that it requires to keep pace with society's energy needs, is simply not being done. Temporary patches have kept power flowing from ancient, inefficient, centralized plants, but without the expenditure of *more* non-existent funds, the situation proceeds exactly where it is obvious that it is heading. At the very least, brown-outs and power-down days are in our near future. We are one terrorist attack on a critical substation, or one hard solar coronal mass ejection (CME), or high altitude nuke-generated electromagnetic pulse (EMP) away from "lights out," permanently.

Our system of fossil fuel extraction and distribution is also in *extremis,* having utilized all the easily-pumped surface oil. Today's attempt to pull the dregs by fracking has its own unintended consequences – earthquakes directly underneath large fracking operations in Oklahoma, where there is no plate boundary and consequently shouldn't be quakes, according to current seismic theory; and in California, Colorado, and elsewhere. At some point, the financial and energy cost of fracking will exceed the value of the return, and then it will be done. No, ethanol is not the answer, and neither is solar or wind power which return less power than they consume to create and deliver. Neither are electric or hybrid cars. Where does the electricity for the hybrids come from, again?

JIT represents another oil/electric/computer/internet/truck/ delivery/communications structure that was designed to increase efficiency and reduce the need for on-premises warehousing and the associated costs. When the JIT system works as it was intended, an in-store purchase of, say, toothpaste, goes through several systems. It is recorded at the cash register computer, sent immediately to the store's main computer, then out to the conglomerate's central computer, then to the company regional warehouse, and a tube of toothpaste is pulled from storage and packed onto a pallet for *today's* shipment back to that very store where it was sold. Additionally, a new order for one more tube of toothpaste is sent to the manufacturer's center, and they begin the process of generating more toothpaste.

It is an incredible symphony of buying and selling going on at a million stores nationwide, for *literally* billions and billions of products every hour of every day. Without a fully-functioning computer/internet interface, AND an active grid, AND a functioning financial system to buy products with, AND diesel and running trucks, AND an unobstructed highway system, *JIT breaks down.* That's why when something as commonplace as a big predicted weather front moves into an area, store shelves are picked clean – the JIT system has taken a hit, and resupply cannot be done on time to keep product on the shelves.

The underlying false premise for both our energy infrastructure and JIT is that *things will continue as they are now.* There is no backup plan for any significant interruption to the systems. Typically, there is about 3 days of food ready to roll in any given city. In a shutdown of any element in the chain of the JIT system, everything stops. That's where the saying, *We are 72 hours away from starvation,* came from – 3 days, stores are empty, and you are on your own. JIT must work perfectly all the time...or it doesn't work at all.

Fragility Plus

Without getting into further details of industrial agriculture, where 50,000 chickens can die in a *single* chicken-raising house, on a farm with, perhaps, a dozen similar houses due to something as simple as a blocked air vent; consider how fragile this system has become. A hurricane like Katrina, Sandy, or Harvey which is expected, followed, predicted, and with days to prepare for – can virtually immobilize an entire region. Years later, parts of Katrina's path remains a desolate and unlivable area. And that was just a hurricane, a weather event that is extreme but understood, with a wealthy and intact nation surrounding and able to come to the rescue.

Now, imagine something like a Hurricane Katrina or Harvey in terms of its ability to destroy power lines, make roads impassable, cut off internet and cell phones, and strand people without food, heat, or shelter – say, a blizzard that wraps the entire northern third of the United States in ice. Now, imagine it remains frozen for a mere 6 weeks. Streets and homes and businesses, wheat fields and livestock, buried under 15 feet of hard snow in sub-zero cold. Trucks do not roll. Food is not delivered. Water mains freeze and rupture. Homes and skyscrapers burn as warming fires made from busted furniture get out of control; firetrucks cannot get to the site, and there is no water to pump to control the blazes. Livestock and crops die in the fields.

In 6 weeks, when it begins to thaw, the number of dead is a national horror. The blame is concentrated on political appointee supervisors or agency heads, banks and insurance companies fail, investment monies move to warmer climates, research papers are written, authorities explain what happened and how to make everything better, knowledgeable speakers reassure a shaken public, the economic disaster is swallowed like bad medicine, and people try to go on. The following year, it happens again. And again the year after, this time in the spring when corn fields are planted and apple trees are in bloom.

That is the arrival of the Cold Times.

Not only is this nation unprepared, it *cannot* get prepared. We have structured our entire system, our existence, on *it will all work as it always has.* There is no national plan, no direction, and no public will to prepare...although there are plenty of independent researchers and journalists and preppers who are shouting the news from any venue that will let them.

The Cold Times will continue at least until your grandchildren have passed on from old age, perhaps longer. The things you do now, the plans you put in place, the sacrifices you make, and your foresight, will affect your descendants a hundred generations into the future – just as your ancestors' day to day choices during every past Cold Time and ice age, led to your life today. Choose wisely.

If you can only afford one reference, the best I've ever seen on every aspect of simple living is:

> *Gene Logsdon's Practical Skills: A Revival of Forgotten Crafts, Techniques, and Traditions,* by Gene Logsdon. Published by Rodale, 1985 – reprinted 2016. Get two copies because you will wear the first one out.

2 THE TRANSITION TO COLD

There are two questions that form the foundation to most people's concerns about the coming ice age:

1. When?
2. How bad?

In reality, these are crystal ball questions; there is no one answer that can cover every person's experience. Just as a regional ice storm affects everyone *in some way* – some severely as pipes break and falling tree branches crush their car, others with mere inconvenience of having to fuel a generator to keep their home lit and warm – so, too will the coming Cold Times. The information here provided will necessarily be general as to individuals, but specific as to the Big Picture.

My personal preference is to take steps to insure against the greatest risk – by doing so, all lesser risks are covered, as well. There is profound peace and security in knowing that all your bases are covered.

When?

In the simplest terms, the next ice age has already started. The winter of 2016-2017 began with greater snow and cold over large parts of the Northern Hemisphere, going down into the tropics, than has been seen in decades, centuries, or since any records were kept. Coffee-growing regions known for their warm climates, such as Myanmar and parts of Brazil, have lost young trees and crops to unseasonable cold. California had enough rain and snow during an 11-day period to refill all the reservoirs emptied by a decade of drought and cause panicky evacuations below overloaded under-maintained dams. Unheard-of category-5 hurricane force winds, 175 mph, battered the mountains covered with 60 feet of snow. In parts of Asia, dry season was interrupted by rains so heavy that rivers over-flooded banks and inundated cities and crops standing in fields. In the great Australian desert, a year's worth of rain fell in three days. Snow fell in New Zealand in mid-summer and dozens of their glaciers grew inexplicably larger.

Already, food prices are going up significantly. In the United Kingdom, fresh vegetables were rationed when crops from southern Europe were destroyed by unexpected snow and cold. Grains suitable for humans to eat are rising in price. Crops have been degraded so much that they are only good for livestock feeds. Even *oatmeal,* once among the least-expensive foods you could find, has already jumped almost 20% in a year. Anyone who shops has seen the abrupt and unhappy price increases that are already hitting our populace. It's harder in Third World countries, where impoverished people have no extra money to pay for higher-priced foods.

The winter of 2017-2018 should convince anyone who has been on the fence – but it will be almost too late to start preparing by then. By 2022, no one will doubt.

When? Now. It will get worse.

How bad?

If we consider this answer on a planet-wide basis, the answer is *it will be worse than you can imagine.* For many people, it will be as bad as it can get – just as Katrina was as bad as the folks who stayed behind could conceive of, including watching loved ones die.

On an individual basis, it will vary from "death" to "hardly knew it happened." Some of the sad outcomes will be from poor luck – getting stuck in a snowbank when an unpredicted blizzard strikes – and some from poor planning.

That one element, planning, can mitigate much of the downside, excluding effects of bad luck. Planning, plus sensible awareness of your region's trends, political structure, cohesiveness, and the general health of your clan as we head into this time. Here's a mental exercise that can help you visualize your own "how bad?" outcome:

Write down the answers to these questions:

1. Is your home or go-to location in a flood plain, in a dam's spillway, in the path of a volcano's probable zone, near a major earthquake fault, within sight of a major highway, within 25 miles of a city of 100,000 or more, or in a suburb?
2. At two meals per day per person, how long would all the food you have *right now* last?
3. At 2 gallons of water per day per person, how long would your *existing* supply (count the water in your water heater and holding tanks) last?
4. Do you have enough stored *alternative* heat sources (kerosene stove, propane heater, wood heat stove with dry wood stocks, etc.) to last through a 6-month winter?
5. Do you have enough seeds to plant a half acre of mixed nutritious food crops for each person in your group? If you don't know how much seed that would be, the answer is "no".
6. Can you raise one steer yearly or 7 goats or 90 rabbits or 90 chickens for each 3 people in your group?
7. How many people outside your "in group" know about your existing supplies? The best answer is "zero".
8. For those in your group who require medication, how long would their *existing* supply last?
9. Could your group *immediately* field a competent perimeter observation and defense team?

The way you answer those questions will tell you exactly "how bad" it could be for you and yours. If you've got all this covered fairly completely, you're likely to have a relatively easy experience going forward. If your level of preparedness falls short, it is time to work seriously toward getting it done.

Stages of Transition

There are three primary stages leading to the full-on effects of the coming mini ice age. These are identified by the perception of the situation that most people will hold. There's no specific length to each stage, and it is likely that there will be some fluidity between the borders of each stage. Different regions, even different households, go through these at their own rates, as well.

Early Stage: Awakening

We are well into the awakening of awareness of the coming mini ice age. The unbelievably severe weather in the winter of 2016-2017 was an eye-opener for many who were on the fence about the reality of climate chill, and those who endorsed the fanciful concept that people control planetary weather by raising taxes. The proof is there, the cold is affecting the entire planet. The coming winters will sweep the rest of the sleepers into full awakening.

In the Awakening stage, prices for foods and other supplies begin to rise, and there will be shortages of some items, enough to be talked about. The grid within regions will go down abruptly, and there will be brownouts during the aftermath of storms and freezes. This is the natural consequence of severe weather. Some media will ignore this, and some will play it as ordinary seasonal variance. It is not, of course.

There will be enough "normal" that it will be possible to keep the normalcy bias going for a while. Summers will still be bright, flowers will grow, ATMs will work, there will be rush hour traffic jams.

During this phase, if you have never grown a garden and put-by your own food, you *must*. You have to experience the entire process, from seed to table, to understand what it requires from you. If you have never stored food and vital supplies, you *must*. You have to learn your own methods of record-keeping and the rate at which you use your supplies and what the best storage methods might be.

If you have not already done so, this is the last opportunity to stock freeze dried staples, toilet paper, building and plumbing supplies, repair equipment, extra batteries, lightbulbs, all the things that make life comfortable....plus those things that make it survivable when the power is out, such as backup solar, generator, and fuel. Stock a personal library of paper books that have repair, construction, sewing, military, and medical information. Do not count on others to take care of you and yours. Sell unnecessary toys and cancel time-wasting subscriptions like cable, use the money for supplies. The more you know, the more skills you have, the more *things* you use routinely and have extras set aside, the less stress and worry you will face as the next stage of the transition is felt.

Middle Stage: Zen-Slap

There is an old Japanese Zen *koan*, or teaching story, that tells about the young student who asks the elderly Zen master, "What is Zen?" The old master immediately slaps the student across the face and strolls away. Confused by this response, the student goes to another master and asks, "What is Zen?" The next master punches him in the nose, and goes back to carrying water. When the student moves to the third master with the same question, that master stomps him on the toe.

As absurd as that seems, that *is* the answer. Zen is "reality", without words, without barriers, and without illusions. There isn't anything quite as real as being slapped, punched, or stomped!

The Zen-slap of the mini ice age is when it is here, and virtually everyone recognizes it. It is that moment when each person knows, absolutely knows in their gut, that whatever is happening at that moment is the *new normal, and they are not ready.*

In this stage, the irregular, changeable, seriously cold weather is here to stay. Your employer's business gets washed away during the flood and they will not rebuild, so your job is gone. The supermarket is STILL out of fresh veggies, and they don't know when the next shipment will be. The box of oatmeal that cost $2.50 a couple years ago, now costs $12. People drop their dogs out on lonely country roads, hoping the kindly farmer will take them in, and Farmer Brown regrets having to shoot feral packs of hungry pets that are trying to kill his goats.

At that point, if you don't have a particular item in your possession – coffee, toilet paper, nails, writing paper, caulk for a broken window pane, seeds or fertilizer for your garden – you won't be able to find it easily, or at all. You may have to pay what today is an exorbitant price for some "luxury" things – chocolate or whiskey, for example – or do without. New economies will develop on a local scale....the elite at the top won't experience these struggles and won't even imagine that they happen, but everyone around you will know the experience quite well. Farmer's markets will become more important, and "seasonal eating" will be more than a fad.

Late Stage: Hang On

At this point, your primary goal is no longer to "thrive" – it is to "survive". Being comfortable in your home, being able to acquire the things you need or even those you merely want, being able to adapt to changing circumstances, having enough to eat, staying warm and staying healthy, will be the signs of a *good life*.

Creativity and the old skills such as sewing, repairing, making-do, manual labor, will have made a stunning comeback. Food will become a daily conversation piece: people will exchange recipes and eggs, share garden seeds and harvests with friends: your excess zucchini for my extra cucumbers. At the same time, many will "hold their cards close to their vests", and you'll only know how well they are doing by how thin they are.

Health care will be herbal, at home, and more-or-less natural. There will still be antibiotics, but they'll be expensive, hard to find, and not always terribly helpful due to antibiotic resistance, weakened immunity, and how late in the disease process these are used. People will die from things that were easily treated in the past – strep throat, accidents, pneumonia, a cut on the hand that gets infected. Old disease makes a sudden comeback (measles, mumps, and rubella already are), and forgotten diseases related to poor hygiene show up: typhoid, cholera, dysentery, boils, tuberculosis.

There will still be a national economy and technology, but fewer people will participate in it, and those who do will be concentrated in population centers. Food and clothing will be available in these places, but more expensive as a portion of total income. Society will go on even though with fewer participants, and quite a few people who are independent-minded will have moved to the country for a less socially-dependent lifestyle.

Problems that befall individual households will have to be solved on the local level. If a tree branch crashes through your roof, it will be up to you, yours, your neighbors, and friends to repair it. If someone's home catches fire, they will need help to find a place to live or help to rebuild. All solutions will become local. FEMA, National Guard, DHS, and whatever imaginary other agencies exist, simply will not be able to resolve the hundreds of thousands of problems that develop.

Home break-ins, raids that empty your garden, poaching of pets and livestock, lawlessness, violence, robbery, crime, the dead laying in the street – this is part of it, too.

This will be the new normal. Make your plans accordingly.

> But remember – even when the weather has made existence more challenging, the sun will still come out, flowers will bloom, people will fall in love and marry, children will be born. Celebrations of life will have deep meaning. It is not the end of the world, just the end of the generations-long warm spell.

COLD TIMES

3 PLACE

The most basic aspect of your primary preparation for Cold Times is where you live. Clearly, keeping warm will be an enormous part of this process; preparation and protection from weather extremes – for us, for our livestock, our food stores and our crops -- figures into this very heavily. Commonplace modern homes and trailers will fail in the time to come, so the sooner adjustments are made for the coming intense cold, the easier your transition will be.

But first, your location.

Several reports indicate that zones north of 30 degrees latitude in the Northern Hemisphere (and south of 30° in the Southern Hemisphere) will not be reliable growing regions as the weather turns. You can plot your location utilizing online maps, or if you've got a paper map of the world, or a globe, that 30° level is easy to pinpoint. Most of the US is in the cold zone above that, except for south Texas and lower Florida. So is Europe, China, Japan, and Russia. These areas are likely to be progressively less reliable for the currently-grown crops. The zone between 30° and 40° north latitude (south in the southern hemisphere), will probably be livable but severely limited by unstable weather. Above 40° latitude will be the realm of polar bears, wolves, and not much else – although in past Cold Times, coastal Alaska was actually relatively warm and green.

Major crops currently grown above 30° latitude includes corn, wheat (both spring and winter), soybeans, and potatoes. Rice is usually produced in "lowland" flood zone farms in the US's currently-warmer regions only a little north of the 30 degree zone.

Beef, chicken, and hogs are also above the line.

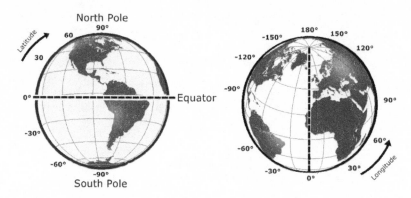

Image created by Trestudios.com

Ultimately, this means that food prices *must* go up, since food production will concentrate closer to the equator – which means creating farms where none currently exist, both costly AND time sensitive because it takes years. It also means your ability to produce your own food in the northern parts of the US and in Canada will be limited by weather extremes – not impossible, just much more challenging than it is now.

My home is at about 36° north latitude, well within the cold zone but certainly not into the worst parts of it. We already have four very different seasons, with moderately cold winters and hot, humid summers. Spring and fall are generally mild and pleasant.

It is likely that during the Cold Time, winters for us will get colder, wetter, snowier, and longer. Summers may become mild with some spiking hot or freezing periods. Spring and fall will probably be cool to frosty, with high flood risks, but otherwise okay. Our growing season will likely shorten from 6 months to 4, with the risk of the loss of warmth-loving crops in both late spring and early fall. It would be as if we moved 700 miles north today.

Best Place Scenario

The easiest and clearest way to envision the place you need to be living, in order to weather the Cold Times, is to describe it. Some elements may not be understandable until you've gone through the rest of the book and internalized the rationale – just recognize that there is a big picture that will make sense when we close in the final chapter.

Land

Avoid: anywhere below a dam, downwind of nuclear reactors and military facilities, known missile silos, regions with a history of rioting, major highways or rivers, population density, areas already known for extremely cold winters.

Figure that you will need 5 acres for each adult you expect to be living with you. If you have an extended family of 20, that would be a minimum requirement for 100 acres. About half of the land, at least, should be crop, pasture, or hay land, with the rest in woods.

You *must* have free, available year-round water sources, such as rivers, ponds, swamps, streams, or artesian wells. None of these should be major, named waterways (which will either be highly controlled or overrun). If your area is already prone to dry spells, make sure you can put water-holding tanks, cisterns, or new ponds into place to sustain you through the dry periods. Keep in mind that some currently dry areas won't be in the coming years.

The woods will provide heating fuel, building materials, some degree of protection from wind and snow, water-holding capacities, access to tree nuts or other wild forage, and an area that can be home to native animals for occasional harvest as a food source.

Ideal home sites are situated below the tops of hills and above any possible risk of flooding, sheltered from prevailing wind, and facing into the south for winter sun (in the southern hemisphere, that would be north-facing). In addition, clear lines-of-sight surrounding the area will help with the defensive positions, which we'll discuss in a later chapter. Trees and landscaping must be 20 to 40 feet from the house to reduce risk from fire and falling limbs. We are discussing a time when home insurance is just a memory, and the Fire Department is "you".

Minimize potential risks.

Neighbors

Unless we are surrounded by family, we have little control over who lives around us. We do have the capacity to *know* our neighbors, though, and be willing to recognize who might be an ally and who needs to be handled with kid gloves.

Neighbors are the people who will need your help and will help you when you require some assistance. They can support defense of your area; become trading-partners so that chores and products can be exchanged; and, as time passes, neighbors will be the people who your clan suffers with, celebrates with, marries and has children with. It is to you and your group's advantage to cultivate the good ones, and find a way to remove the trouble-makers.

Buildings, Structures

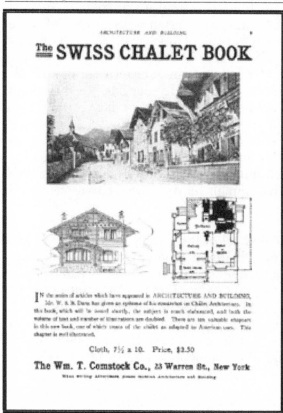

Today's typical stick-built home is poorly constructed to withstand weather extremes. Mobile homes and RV trailers are worse. They are nothing but a light wood frame with a metal or fiber skin, and a set of fiber interior panels. Without exterior heat sources (electric, propane, or natural gas) and air conditioning, these are unlivable spaces even today and will be death traps when the Cold arrives.

We cannot assume

that general weather patterns will remain as they are today: regions that have never had a tornado, now report repeated incidents. Rain pours down like a river from the sky in other areas, creating intense pressure on buildings and causing roofs and ceilings to collapse. These changes are in addition to the effects caused by heavy snow loads and extreme spring water run off as the snow melts.

The Swiss have thousands of years of experience living in a glaciated and frozen climate, and their architecture reflects that. The structures are squatty, and built to be able to carry heavy snow weights, generally utilizing enormous log-beams for structural elements. Many are constructed with heavy stonework around the base to act as a water repellant zone. A second story allowed access even during snow so deep that the ground-level was covered. The roof line extends away from the walls, so that the snow, icicles, and water runoff falls away from the walls and reduces water intrusion into the house. Windows are relatively small to facilitate heat retention. The walls are considerably thicker than conventional homes – greater volume in the wall means better insulation and heat retention. Finally, chimneys provide the ability to build fires and cook meals – some home's masonry chimneys generate heat from the entire stone heater structure, making wood use more efficient.

Looking at other cultures that have adapted well to extreme cold, provides good examples of how to survive in lean circumstances. The Vikings, professionals at living in severe cold,  built "long houses" – low, long, narrow structures that were sturdy enough to hold up under snow loads, and shed the ice and snow readily.

Most important for our perspective isn't the sod-type roof, but the fact that this one appears to have been built into the hillside or soil-work was packed around the exterior. The surrounding soil helps retain heat. Notice the chimney has a propped up stone cover that will keep snow from entering the top. The front entrance leads to a covered "porch" or "mudroom" type arrangement, so that the actual entry door is both covered and out of the wind and weather. Tiny vents are visible to the top right end of the building, which would have let in a little light and fresh air.

The downside of many of these structures is that wood is a major part of the interior, the walls, ceiling and sides – highly flammable. With open fires for heat and light, the risk of torching the place was always present. For our purposes, and long-term safety, stone or concrete makes a safer building material.

Which brings us to the modern equivalent of the Icelandic Viking long house, the *underground house*. Notice the remarkable similarities to the previous image -- placement of the door, the covered chimney, the earthwork surrounding the walls and back – clearly demonstrating than the ancient design doesn't require much in the way of "modern" improvements.

The heat retention of this home would be excellent. A somewhat more-covered "porch" area could provide better weather resilience and would keep blowing snow and rain from entering each time the door was opened – and, of course, the large windows would generate some heat loss. But double-paned and insulated glass could compensate by providing better lighting than our forebears had. Heavy curtains could retain heat at night, too.

This type of building is commonly called "earth sheltered". There are multiple online sites and many books that have plans and guidelines galore, so there's no lack of existing information that won't need to be repeated here. Just think "mass".

The critical elements of earth sheltered design are keeping the walls protected from water infiltration by waterproofing and drainage lines, allowing light into the interior, and making sure there is adequate fresh air entering the structure – particularly if a fireplace or stove is used for heat and cooking. This could be an ideal location for a rocket-type mass heater, which is adequate for cooking and outstanding for heating an underground space.

The ultimate earth-sheltered design is likely humankind's oldest dwelling space: a cave. If you are fortunate enough to own land with a cave on it, do not overlook the possibilities of converting that into a livable space. Modification to prevent flooding and to assure ventilation might be significantly less expensive than retrofitting an existing dwelling, or building something new. Plus, caves tend to maintain steady temperatures year-around, a real benefit during cold spells.

Caves, also, are naturally resistant to marauders, may have additional "rooms" so that there is some level of privacy, and can act as cool storage for food and other provisions or even a home for small livestock. Some caves may have free-moving water, seasonal streams, or other easy-water accesses. You may have to divert an in-cave stream during times of heavy rain or snow, a more costly and time-consuming project, but possibly worthwhile.

Be sure there are at least 3 separate, disguised exits, in case the main entryway is blocked or attacked – even bunnies make extra exits from their burrows.

Using Passive Heat

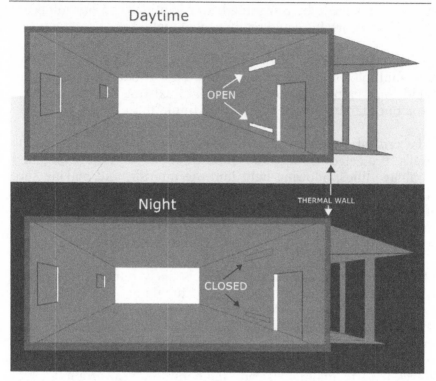

In a cold time, any means to collect heat that requires little effort is a valuable tool as well as a time and human energy-saver. In the chapter on growing food in cool climates, we'll see the benefits of heat-retaining walled gardens on extending the growing season, but here we are looking at an example of the "Trombe Wall".

This is merely a masonry or other heat-retaining mass (water and cob will work, too) that is situated to receive full sun during the winter day, but with an overhanging roof that limits summer time sun. Set behind heavy glass windows situated on the right in this image, the low winter sun shines on the wall all day, and utilizes floor and ceiling vents in the wall to move air into the interior of the home. At night the vents are closed, and the heat built up during the day stays inside the house.

The glassed area also receives reflected heat from the Trombe wall after the sun has gone down. Imagine, too, that the glassed area has a dark, heat-retaining floor of dark concrete, stone, or tile, and that low fast-growing cool tolerant plants (kale, lettuce, bok choi, etc.) are situated in planters to receive mid-day sun. Now, place heavy curtains that can be drawn over the windows at night to keep heat inside that glassed area, and you have both a means to "passively" warm your home *and* grow a small winter greens garden indoors. This is the idea behind "earthship" homes.

The "mass" of the Trombe wall, plus the heating rays of the sun, combine to provide a level of comfort within any dwelling. However, even the best Trombe wall is limited. When the sun is obscured by clouds or during snow storms, the wall neither retains nor radiates heat.

When you are thinking about being prepared for intense cold, consider how you can utilize natural means to increase, retain, and magnify the heat that already exists. More in later chapters. Including efficient wood-burning stoves that do not require fans or other technological additions is part of that picture. Siting a dwelling so that it is sheltered from the fiercest seasonal storms, and so that summer breezes blow through, or so that unwanted heat rises outside easily, are part of that consideration as well.

Today's systems for heating and cooling have all but erased the once-intimate structural awareness of natural placement for buildings. Most new construction, especially of office towers and academic settings, are created as architectural art, fully dependent on air conditioning (windows don't open), continuous grid power, and pressure systems that lift columns of water to upper stories. When the Cold Times fully arrive, when the economy makes electricity too expensive to maintain, when all the human constructs we have built our society around no longer function at adequate capacity, then the reliance on the old ways – gravity, air flow, mass – will return again.

Retrofitting

It is probable that many readers of this book already have a city, suburban, or residential home and would prefer to remain there.

I caution you to think carefully about where you will be when the Cold is upon us.   No suburban residence will survive social calamity, fires that rage through when firemen are busy protecting their own, and the general failure of civility that lays ahead. There is no benefit to beating around the bush and softening that reality.

Access to five acres per adult means a rural setting but proximity to a city can be part of that picture. It just shouldn't be easy to get to or find your home, so do not be on a major highway. "Three turns" from the main road are your minimum goal, according to survival blogger James Wesley Rawles: a side road off a side road, off a side road. The less "curb appeal", the better!

Even given that, it is extremely unlikely that you already have a Cold Times-ready home. Therefore, retrofitting is probably going to be a part of your near-term plans. Retrofitting is making the changes in a residence to conform to a new standard. The new standard your home needs to conform to is: intense snowload, extreme cold, no electricity, no gas or propane, no water mains, no police or fire department, sited well above flood plains, and probable presence of dependent visitors/family.

If you prepare for the worst case, even if power and society remains intact, you will be ready for any scenario and doubly ready for any commonplace downturn, illness, or job loss. That's a win-win. This chapter will consider the "intense snowload and extreme cold" retrofit, and the rest will be dealt with in the remainder of the book.

Snowload

Today, a light fluffy snow weighs about 7 pounds per cubic foot. A heavy, compacted snow can weigh 20 pounds per cubic foot. So, if a pleasant light snowfall puts a mere 12 inches of snow on 1000 square feet of your small house's roof, that's *7000 pounds,* close to 4 tons, additional weight over your head. Two feet of snow puts 14,000 pounds on your roof, walls, and foundation – 7 tons.

Now, imagine 12 inches of heavy dense snow, 20 pounds per cubic foot. That's *20,000 pounds*, bearing down on your 2x4 wall studs, and pressing your roof's beams into those walls. Suppose you have 24" of heavy snow built up over several days to 40,000 pounds. That is *20 tons,* sitting on your roof, more than 40 pounds on each square foot of roof.

In Minnesota, where heavy snowfall is the routine during winter, the minimum legal requirement is that a roof support 35 pounds per square foot. Compare that number with, say, 3 feet of heavy snow falling. Parts of Italy received over 5 feet of snow in one storm in early 2017; parts of China received 15 feet! Hundreds of buildings collapsed under snow in Oregon, Colorado, and Washington during the 2016-2017 winter. Fifteen feet of light snow would weigh over 100 pounds per square foot; heavy snow would be over 300 pounds per square foot. Even in Minnesota, that amount of snow would crush houses.

In 2016, the rule of thumb for heavy snow loads, was to climb on up there and shovel the snow off your roof. Sounds like a lot of fun, during a blizzard. Naturally, of course, that will pile snow around your home's walls as you dump it off the roof. Will your walls stand up well to tons of pressure against them? How will your walls tolerate all that water melting out of the snow beside them?

Too Much Roof Snow

One of the simplest ways to check if your roof is undergoing stress, is to go outside and visually examine it under snow weight. If any sags are visible, you have a problem. Next, visit the attic and the basement. Look for sagging, bowing, or dripping, especially if pipes are bent or bowed. Listen for pops or cracking sounds.

Check that all doors and windows open as easily as usual. Any sticking, especially if doors or windows are jammed shut, means your house has actually shifted under the weight of the snow already. Stuck doors and windows combined with popping and cracking sounds means: *get out right now.* Do not go back inside until the snow is gone, and a structural engineer has said it's safe.

If structural engineers are absent, then you're on your own and need to reinforce what you have OR build something new. Don't use it until it has been made safe, or you risk having yourself and family crushed to death.

A Stronger Roof

One relatively simple but not necessarily inexpensive method to strengthen the structure over your head, is to build a second roof above your existing home. If you live in a location that has stringent codes, you will probably find it nearly impossible to get a building permit for something this uncommon. However, if you are in a rural area, or society has devolved so far that regulations no longer are enforced, this is a do-it-yourself (DIY) project that can preserve your residence and improve your comfort in the time to come.

A standard roof supports weight by a combination of structural elements. Rafters are the beams that extend from the peak of the roof to the top of the wall at the top plate. At the peak, rafters from both sides of the sloping roof join to a central "ridge beam".

Each rafter is joined to its twin on the opposite slope of the roof by a collar tie, placed about a third of the way up the rafter length. At the level of the top plate, each rafter is met by a ceiling joist that crosses to the opposite twin rafter. This is the absolute minimum structural layout in standard construction. More solidly constructed roofs are also possible, but require stronger wall construction to support the weight.

The strength of the structure arises from the rafter "base" [B] or width, and from the rafter "height" [H], the depth. So a rafter beam that is, say, 2" wide and is 6" in depth, has a base of 2" and height of 6". The length of the rafter can vary – 10, 12, 14, 16 feet are not uncommon.

There's lots of ways to build a roof, so I'm including a few ideas here. Use what you have or what you can improvise, and aim toward strength and stability.

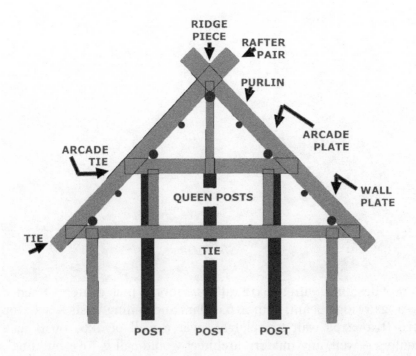

Usually, rafters are placed on 16" centers. An important point is that the closer together the rafters are placed, the greater overall roof strength as each individual rafter bears a lighter load. Increasing the rafter base and height also increases the resistance to bending under weight -- as long as the walls are beefy enough to hold up the total weight. The formal calculation is $BH^3/12[length]$ = Moment of Inertia (MOI, inertial resistance to bending). Higher MOI means greater strength

The slope of a "typical modern" roof is commonly 5:12, that is, it rises 5 inches for every 12 inches of length. If you build a steeper roof, say, 7:12, snow is a bit more likely to slip off, and so is anyone working on that roof.

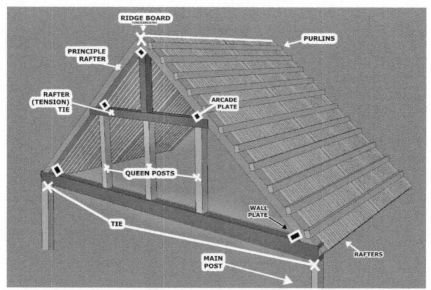

A roof designed with 2x6x12 rafters, set on 8 inch centers attached to a 2x6 ridge beam, with 2x6 collars and ceiling joists – set atop 4x6 (two 2x6s wall top plates), over a wall of 2x6s on 8 inch centers – well, any modern architect would call it "overbuilding". But the physics of that construction would provide tremendous load-bearing capacity and withstand enormous snowloads.

Even a mobile home could be retrofitted with this type of design, making an ordinarily flimsy frame into a sturdy permanent structure. Think of retrofitting a mobile home as building a new exterior for an existing home – place the new walls at 8"-12" outward from the current walls on a wide concrete or stone foundation, inset windows deeply where ones already are.

Use that space between the old and new walls as insulating space – get the heaviest, thickest insulating rolls and double them up. Or fill the space with reinforced stonework or concrete, both of which are insulating as well as providing resistance to fire, hail, and ballistic weapons.

Finish the exterior with stonework in thick mortar to provide resistance to water and strength against both snow and wind pressure.

When is "over- building" a sensible choice?

Fill the space above the old roof with the thickest insulating materials, and fill the attic below the old roof, as well. Insulate the floor and around the exterior walls with a good 12" of material, too. Make sure you use wire mesh at edges to discourage squirrel, raccoon, rats and mice from moving in.

Keep your costs down by using as much recycled and "found" materials as you can. If you live on stony land, you have free building materials everywhere. Steel beams could be utilized, as well, although the construction method requires welding skills.

A-Frame, Sturdy and Comparatively Inexpensive

A-frame construction is rather like building a roof without deep walls, basically a steeply pitched roof connected to a base or to a floor-level wall. It is probably one of the most inexpensive dwellings to build, even using purchased materials, because siding is minimal (it's mostly roof), and has very good resistance to external snow *and* wind loads, depending on how sturdily it is built.

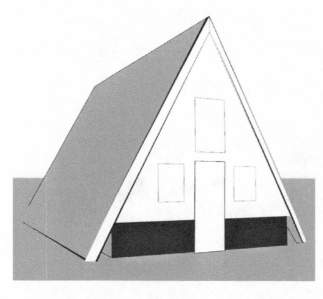

The peaked area can be used as a type of loft; space is reduced here, obviously. Second story windows can be utilized as exits if snow is too deep to get out the doors.

Drawbacks of A-frames are the reduced interior light and lack of windows on the sides – not as much of a problem if we're dealing with maintaining interior heat, rather than 'curb appeal'.

Igloos

There is probably no simpler and more efficient structure for living in severe cold than the Inuit (Eskimo) igloo. Made from blocks of snow cut from the frozen landscape, igloos incorporate a dome-shape with a small crawl-tube entryway.

.
In these old public domain drawings, you can see the relative size is small, and that each has a "window" or vent near the top.

The orientation shows all the igloos facing the same direction into the sun, perhaps to absorb heat or deal with wind. Several of them appear to have three "rooms", each slightly larger than the one preceding it. Like a geodesic dome, these structures are very resistant to both snow and wind loads.

In spite of being constructed from frozen blocks, the interiors tend to retain body heat, melting slightly into firm glassy walls. They are virtually free to build, relying on natural materials and replaceable by just the effort of building another one. The design and placement of the blocks is a learned art, however. It is NOT the same as just burrowing a cave into a snowbank, which carries the risk of collapsing on you.

Additional interior heating is not usually needed in an igloo because its natural heat-retention stores the inhabitants' body heat. However, one should not sit or lay directly on the frozen floor. Multiple layers of animal pelts or other thermal materials are needed to keep the cold at bay. Think of an igloo as a 'survival pup tent' made from ice blocks.

All Season Igloo: Earthbag

In the arid American Southwest, sun-dried adobe mud bricks were a time-tested construction material. The bricks were made from sandy mud, straw, and cements if any was available, then sun-dried until baked hard. Thick adobe walls have defied heat and cold, rain and drought, as well as earthquakes, for decades. Some adobe buildings are over a century old, proving that adobe works....in a mostly arid environment.

There is another building technique that is suitable not only in dry regions but across the country: earthbags. Picture a combination of sandbags and igloo construction, and you've got the idea. An earthbag is a textile or plastic bag, filled with dirt, sand, or gravel or a combination. Hundreds of bags can be filled and stacked in layers, with two runs of barbed wire between each layer for "mortar"-like stability. Earthbag domes are built in a circular style, like an 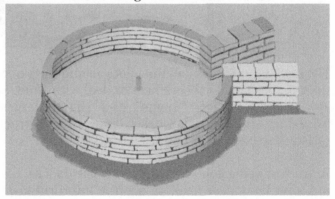 igloo, and then topped up into a bullet-shaped dome or with any type of roofing desired. A slant roof works here, too. A wire frame is attached over the exterior and interior, and the whole thing is plastered with thick stucco. When dry, it's done.

Alternatively, the dwelling could be built into a hillside. In very damp zones, extra care will be needed to assure water is diverted away from the construction and that walls resist outside pressure, including gravel around the exterior with French drains incorporated.

The construction can be made extra thick, has some excellent resistance to snow load depending on how it's built, resists high winds, and with enough stucco and perhaps water-resistant paint could stand up to heavy rains. Because of the circular construction, it will resist quakes, as well. Ballistic resistance is like any sandbag construction, too.

Best of all, it's very inexpensive to build. The plastic bags, barbed wire, and stucco will set you back less than $1500, in some cases as little as $600. You'll need to be able to  excavate a base (could be done by hand), and be conscious about how the structure is built (must be a true circle). But beyond that, your primary contribution is time and effort.

With some creativity, the whole thing could have a sod or "green roof" covering so it would disappear into the environment. Hobbits couldn't have a better spot.

Online search for "earthbag construction" will give you hundreds of listings and enough images to stimulate your creativity.

Proximity

With several households on a single property, there are social and primal benefits to siting the residences near each other. This is rather like the igloos shown previously and in the tipi settlements typical of Plains Indians. With an extended family or clan or tribal setting, ease of access to other residents is a big plus for having all the homes clustered together. Personal preference and family togetherness could contribute to siting residences so that they connect, either by being side-by-side or having covered walkways or even tunnels between them. The downside, of course, is that any aggressive force can attack from all sides and pin the clustered residents in a "fatal funnel" location, from which there is no escape. Appropriate considerations might include having several "outlying" homes, to be backup residences or decoys, or having all residences face "out" so that the surroundings can be monitored at all times.

Big Picture of "Place"

The ideal that we've explored for "place" is situated above any risk of flooding; out of direct winter wind; accessible to winter sun; has several exits, some hidden; can be heated by a wood stove; is defensible from different angles; retains heat during winter; is not obvious from roadways; surrounded by 5 acres per expected adult resident consisting of pasture, garden, hay, and woods; has access to neighbors or a small town; has fresh water and a way to retain it; and is below latitude 40°N, or above 40°S in the southern hemisphere. If there will be several residences, the lay of the land and expected directions from which danger may arise should guide placement and connections between them.

Given that, there probably are few places on the planet that fulfill all the ideals of place. However, each incremental movement toward this standard brings you closer to an environment that will be able to sustain you through cold times and even give you a secure base as an ice age swirls around.

Assuming that a southerly rural location with water, food production capacity, and defensibility is the ideal, such an ideal may simply be unobtainable – and this is not an excuse for failing to try to acquire the right spot! It just may not happen in time to be ready for the incoming Cold. Should you find yourself in a suburban or even urban setting, your priorities are:

- Community cohesiveness
- Strong defense
- Access to fresh water
- Capacity to grow food and small livestock (chickens, pigeons, rabbits; use lawn space for food production)

The book you need to prepare you for suburban or urban survival is *A Failure of Civility: How to Defend and Protect You, Your Family, Friends, Neighborhood and America During a Disaster or Crisis* by Garand and Lawson. You may be able to find copies online at Amazon, Barnes & Noble, Abe, or other sellers. It will be expensive. I cannot recommend this book highly enough, for its sensible approach to small area defense, which will be your greatest priority as the social system breaks down and becomes chaotic.

Survive the initial chaos and then your group can consider relocating to a more southerly rural site, ideally one that you all have contributed to and prepared in advance.

Acquisition

Not addressed, previously, is the very real issue of buying such a place. Taking on debt in a down economy with severe weather changes coming in, is NOT a good idea. You have to balance risks with rewards, when you consider a land purchase.

If you have several trusted colleagues – ideally, family – who are willing to share expenses, you may be able to purchase a parcel outright. Some members may just want a vacation place, others to live there year-around. As long as intentions and shared responsibilities are known *in advance and written into enforceable contracts*, you will lessen the risk for misunderstandings and hard feelings. Make sure any participant can get out of the deal easily, if they have financial or personal reversals, without damaging other participants.

Consider turning the ownership over to a Family Trust or setting up a Limited Liability Corporation (LLC) as the owning entity – the most trusted member should oversee the paperwork and legal aspects, and submit everything to participants for review and agreement before finalizing. Ideally, each participant would have a SEPARATE title to a portion of the land on which they maintain their own place – the benefit is that there are fewer squabbles over who does what when and where, since everyone has their own. The risk is that if they want out and sell to a stranger, you have a stranger in your midst. Your arrangement will depend on how you assess your family members, their stability, and their willingness to participate. Some can do this, and some just aren't suited to working together. Be realistic in your assessment.

Be creative with your arrangements. If several families are going to be paying for property, one family might live on the land with the intention of getting it ready for the others, while the rest pay off the note and move incrementally. Or perhaps land could be acquired by barter or trade, "my city house for your rural one". Look for elderly land owners who might trade property for your work, or for keeping their place going until they pass on and it becomes yours. Involve an attorney and get everything in contracts. And there are foreclosure sales announced in local newspapers with online sites, as well, that may provide outstanding property that just requires TLC. There's options, if you are willing to look for them and think outside the box.

It's a good deal easier if you are living in a wilderness and can plunk your tribe's made-on-the-spot igloos, yurts or tipis down where ever you happen to be, but in North America today there are few pieces of land that don't already belong to somebody. Our own "back-60" trackless woodland, without a speck of electric power access or passable roadways, is *privately owned*. Although most city-folk would see it as wilderness, it isn't. And if such a landowner were to find a group camping on their back-60, there would likely be some serious trouble brewing.

Keep in mind that even if a piece of land appears ownerless, it would take a genuine social collapse of Dark Ages proportions to eliminate existing legal ownership titles. Many areas have old "adverse possession" laws. Typically, you must reside on a property for a specific period of time, say 10 years, without being told by the owner to leave. At that point, you can make a claim on it. These rules are different from area to area, and likely to change or be forgotten in the face of great social calamities. Research it now, print it out, and keep copies for a just-in-case situation.

The large National Parks of wilderness woodland are not an ideal choice either, because everyone who has ever camped there will think of it when "head to the hills" becomes a survival imperative. You won't be able to bring in enough food supplies to last through a bad winter, and many of the people who head there with a bug-out-bag on their back expecting to hunt deer and live like a lone wolf will become predatory, as well. Not a good idea.

Caveat

When the late Awakening and early Zen-slap arrive, beginning about 2018-21 or so, a large number of people will realize that they need to be in a warmer climate. Some of these will be retirees who planned to move anyway to Florida or the Virgin Islands or somewhere in South America once their pension kicked in. Some of these will be people who simply cannot tolerate the past several years' weather extremes and intense winter chill. Some will be people who recognize the Cold Times that are incoming.

Now, imagine this: you are a local person living in a warmer climate comfortably carrying on your routine life. Suddenly, a bunch of foreigners start moving in...and their attitude is that they know better than you, have more money than you, and are going to make *you* live the way they want. This is the experience of *all* local peoples, from Arkansas rednecks to Appalachian hillbillies, and from Indonesian rice farmers to folks in Paraguayan villages, when foreigners start moving in.

This influx creates animosity, anger, and eventually legal and extra-legal actions to minimize the foreigner influence. In the recent past, some of these influx countries have simply nationalized the foreigner's bank accounts, that is, stole the foreigner's funds. Or foreigners become 'fair game' for grifters and conmen, with local courts favoring the locals no matter how egregious their theft.

If you don't already live in the rural area in which you'd like to reside, then *you are the foreigner.* You won't be welcomed, no matter how much cash you try to spread around. They won't be impressed by your money. That, alone, will create more local anger and animosity. If times get very desperate, you'll be a target.

For your family's sake, do not wait to relocate with the migrating hoard. And don't be the obnoxious foreigner. Be polite, listen, keep your word, join a local church or women's club or volunteer for the fire department or at the senior center, contribute to the library.

Other Weather Considerations

As I am writing this, our nearby town has had its fourth "100-year" flood in three years. It was more destructive and overflowed banks and the entry and exit bridges to town, a good 3 feet deeper than previously. Basically, bad floods are now the *new normal* here. People whose homes have been destroyed 3 times simply can't rebuild in the old location.

Flooding. California will probably lose a significant portion of farmland that lies in dam overflow zones....plus the homes there, as well. Louisiana will lose rice crops this year, from the early May floods of 2017. Flooding is the primary reason to site your residence *above* any risk of high water, but below the tops of hills where wind and lightning can be problematic.

Lightning. A cousin of flooding, lightning is killing people worldwide at an astonishing rate – and lightning is becoming more intense and erratic at the same time. The atmosphere is becoming charged in a way that is unknown to us, and lightning is the evidence of that. This may be a consequence of the planet's weakening magnetic shield, combined with the activity of incoming cosmic energies.

Whatever is causing it, our ancestors all over the world once built heavy rock structures that were partially buried underground called "dolmens". In the American northeast, early settlers called the ones they found "Indian granaries", imagining that the natives had once stored their corn in the dolmens. The Indians, however, didn't store grain there and actually said they didn't know who built them. Effectively, a dolmen is a heavy earth and stone covered shelter that would protect from severe and intense lightning – perhaps an early version of a bomb or storm shelter. The stronger grounded structure you build, the greater protection you will have from lightning, too.

There is some indication that the intensity of some lightning strikes are occurring because it isn't "true" lightning as we have known all our lives. It may actually be a previously unrecognized type of electrical plasma discharge. As such, it carries a destructive potential that is much worse than a typical lightning strike. It literally blasts whatever it hits and spreads out arcing from object to object until it has fully grounded. Some reports suggest that on different occasions entire herds of cattle and reindeer and groups of people have been killed by such plasma-like lightning.

The ancient legend of the power of Thor's hammer – a huge destructive flash of 'lightning' -- may be stories of actual plasma effects passed along within mythology. Unfortunately, these discharges don't always accompany a rainstorm. They may come from a clear sky, or behave strangely. There is one recent stunning YouTube video of a lightning flash followed by an intense blue static-y but slow moving surge of what appears as a sharp light moving across a nearby field, finally winking out and disappearing. You wouldn't want to be anywhere it was going.

We just don't know how these things will be generated or act. There may be some advance indicators, such as a tingly static charge felt on the skin, or unusual activity among birds or insects such as sudden quiet or mass movement from an area. At this time, we know so little about these discharges that we may have to resort to our own version of dolmens until we have better information and methods to avoid the effects.

Earthquakes. John Casey's research has shown that large quakes increase during solar minima. Most parts of the country are susceptible, and some areas are positively poised to undergo a deadly shaker, followed by equally deadly aftershocks for years.

The safest place to be during a quake is anywhere that something can't fall on you. Outdoors is ideal. If you are in an open area, squat or sit down so hard shocks don't knock you off your feet. If you are indoors, squat or crawl *beside* a heavy piece of furniture. After quakes, people have been found safe buried under rubble in "voids" created *beside* strong supports.

Once the quake has stopped, find family and *get outside*, away from walls and anything that may fall. Big quakes are followed, sometimes within minutes, by "aftershocks" – more quakes that are slightly smaller but still potentially deadly. Structures damaged by a first quake may fall during the second or third shocks that follow. Make sure your BOB (Bug Out Bag) is handy and easy to grab and go at all times, just for occasions like this one. More on BOBs later in the book.

Build so that your structures can tolerate movement while under a snow load, so shaking doesn't bring it down. Be aware that quakes can also trigger the kind of underground collapse that causes spontaneous sinkholes big enough to swallow your car. Avoid any new dips in the ground until they have settled and no longer move, which may take weeks to months.

Volcanos somewhere upstream from   you may send sky-darkening ash overhead...but the primary effect over time will be to deepen the cold by blocking sunlight. Ash will be good for your hay and garden soil, as long as it isn't more than an inch or so deep. Deeper ash can harden and create issues later. Avoid breathing ashy air; cover nose and mouth with a water-saturated cloth (vinegar or even urine is better to counteract the ash's alkaline lye-like effects); avoid getting ash in your eyes and if you do, *don't rub,* rinse thoroughly with clean water. Remember that the particulate matter that volcanos heft into the atmosphere can worsen the cooling by blocking sunlight *for years.* Clearly, you don't want to live within the blast zone of any potentially active volcano. They can erupt with little warning and level a city overnight.

Wind. Damaging winds are nothing new, but high wind is new in some of the areas that are currently being hit. Hurricane zones have building codes that help structures resist high winds, but most of the rest of the country doesn't – and as the jet stream undulates and dips into unfamiliar zones, excess wind is the result. While Kansas is known for its tornado hazards, Germany and New York have not been....until recently.

Expect that tornados and intense straight-line winds will also be a part of the *new normal* that the Cold Times represent. That's why your residence should be sheltered from potential sources of high wind. If you are building something new, keep hurricane-force winds in mind, and add the kinds of hurricane truss supports that will keep your roof on and walls together. It doesn't add that much additional cost to make structures extra-sturdy. Reinforced concrete block buildings have survived fierce hurricanes and cyclones in the tropics for years, and underground homes are highly resilient to wind.

Hail. Intense, damaging hail is an additional hazard, even occurring in places where it has been rare to virtually unknown. Hail the size of a dime can injure people, crops, and livestock. Larger hail stones are being reported, too, the size of golf balls, baseballs, softballs, grapefruit and larger. Clearly, such hail could easily pummel someone to death in a few minutes, strip branches from trees, and destroy your entire garden, greenhouse and solar panels.

If you are caught out of doors or in a vehicle when hail starts, try to get under a heavy structure like a bridge or rocky overhang but not a tree unless there is nothing else (trees may break and fall on you), or even crawl underneath your stopped and parked car. Don't stay in a vehicle because the glass may shatter and cause further injury.

Windows can be broken out, and roofs and ordinary siding can be severely damaged. When you're designing your residence with the Cold in mind, consider adding closeable shutters to each window. These can be made from heavy plywood, attached with hinges on the sides of windows and hooked open. Then, if hail is coming in, the screens can be pushed out and shutters closed quickly and latched from the inside. Very simple design that you can paint and add crosspieces to make it look attractive, and extremely handy if you need it. That way, you don't have to replace glass. Park vehicles under a structural overhang or garage them. Make sure livestock have a covered shed to escape into.

Heat is something we don't think of as a problem during Cold Times, but history teaches that it is. During the summer of 1708, within the Maunder Minimum, farmers died from heat stroke in their fields across France. Then just a few months later during the winter of 1708-09, another 800,000 people died from early crop-destroying cold, disease, and starvation. Although the weather will turn colder overall, there will still be extreme heat. Some of it will be unexpected and out-of-season. The "January thaw" may end up being the "January heat wave" instead. One of the important features of surviving the coming Cold Times is *adaptability*.

Critical Need: The Storm Shelter

During the transition into Cold Times, we don't merely find weather becoming cooler. Weather becomes *extremely erratic* – scalding hot one day then freezing cold the next. Gentle rain storms turn into howling gales that continue for hours, with pounding hail and near-continuous lightning. Since we have been living in an era of fair and moderate weather, we almost cannot comprehend how intense, destructive, and deadly weather can actually be. We are about to find out, though.

I mentioned the ancient dolmens a page or two back. There is no reason why we can't recreate this concept today. Many people in tornado-prone regions already have a backyard version, their storm shelter. Effectively, this is a concrete walled, vented, hole-in-the-ground that has a door which can be closed and secured from the inside.

Because everything does double-duty in a cold world, a storm shelter can also be a food-and-supply storage area. Since it is mostly buried underground, the temperature stays cooler during summer and generally remains above freezing during the winter. In this way, it can perform as a "root cellar" during pleasant weather, and still be immediately ready if you need to run for shelter during a bad storm.

Pre-fabricated concrete units that can be dug into a hillside and have dirt mounded around them are routinely available online. These typically run around $3000 installed. Sizes vary but they are small inside, really just suited for a handful of people to hunker down in for a short period of time. If you are having one installed, remember to site it *above* any possibility of flood. Keep in mind, too, that if a storm is bad enough, it can hurl debris deep enough to cover your shelter entrance. The door should open *inward* and be easily and securely blocked from the inside, so that debris won't prevent you from opening the door and digging out.

If you are having a shelter built, make the walls doubly thick, from fiber-infused concrete or fully rebar reinforced blocks. Build French drains around the exterior so that water won't infiltrate during heavy rains. Build the top so that it can support extra weight, and cover with 3 or 4 feet of earth. Include an air vent from the top, with good airflow coming in from another vent through the entry or at other low ports. It will get stifling inside during storms anyway.

A well-made storm shelter can double as a nuclear fallout shelter, as well. The surrounding concrete and earth provides shielding from fallout particulates. If you go this route, you'll need to provide air-filtration that is more robust to keep out radiated dust particles, though. The best reference for this type of shelter is Cresson Kearney's *Nuclear War Survival Skills*, available as an online document and in book format from Amazon and other sellers. It is over a half-century old, but full of very useful information for do-it-yourselfers.

Stock your storm shelter for comfort during an event. You'll need seating in the form of plastic chairs or wooden benches. Avoid metal chairs, in case the storm brings highly charged currents. We don't know how plasma discharges will act yet, and we surely do not want to be zapped inside a small space by attracting lightning with metal rod furniture. If you have enough room, make wood benches long enough that people can lay down on them in case they need to rest.

Use a sturdy, plastic, sealable, tub to store storm-supplies. Include several towels to dry off with, if you come in from the storm wet. Also inside your tub, store some bottled water, snack foods like granola bars, or MREs, battery-powered lights with the batteries out and stored in an attached baggie, a few books, a wire-bound writing tablet or two with pencils, a board game if children will be along, and a first aid kit with a day or two's worth of any routine medications. Throw in socks for several people, and a change of clothing suitable for cool weather. If you have young women in your group, include several menstrual pads as well. Seal all small items inside their own baggie if you can, because underground sites can get damp over time. You want to maintain each item so that it is safe and dry when you need it. Clean and refresh the tub once or twice a year.

If you have extra space, add a heavy plastic bag inside a 5-gallon bucket and some toilet paper to use as an emergency potty. If you're in the shelter for several hours, someone will have to relieve themselves. Include some toilet paper. Get a small quart container of RV toilet deodorizer, and store with the toilet bucket, too. A cheap plastic shower curtain and 6 feet of twine or paracord can be included in your porta-potty, to be used to set up a "privacy curtain" around the toilet. It's the little things, like visual privacy, that make incidents such as this tolerable.

Earning An Income

As long as we have access to the existing system, make use of it to help you earn income – a routine job, working online, selling on ebay.com – whatever works for you. However, the historical method for maintaining financial security over time is NOT to hold "one great job"; it is to have multiple income streams. Income streams, especially when they arise from different venues, helps stabilize your financial security over time, As one wanes, another picks up. If one is knocked out by weather or events, you still have income.

Rural living provides different opportunities for income than urban or suburban life. There's still a need for skilled independent workers that you might find in urban or suburban areas:

- Electricians
- Plumbers
- Auto repair
- Tractor repair
- Computer repair
- Carpenters
- Heavy equipment operators with their own dozers and backhoes
- Security system installation and repair
- Specialty Bakers (wedding cakes, catering)
- Shoe repair
- Gunsmiths
- Locksmiths
- Well drilling and water pump repair
- HVAC installation and repair
- Furniture movers
- Gravel and compost hauling
- Masonry builders and repair
- Accountants
- Attorneys
- Physicians and nurses
- Chiropractors
- Naturopaths
- Acupuncturists
- Beauty salons
- Retail sales
- Pharmacists
- Veterinarians
- Dance, gymnastics, and martial arts instruction

The list could cover an entire phone directory. As long as a person comes into a rural area with an entrepreneurial spirit, doesn't step on too many toes, understands that it won't be a miracle overnight success, and has a respectful attitude, any of these businesses could "go" right now. It might not be "full time" in the same way city jobs typically are, but it would be an income stream. So, the accountant who teaches martial arts and does plumbing on the side would have three income streams that would have independent customer bases and resilience against changing times.

Living on a good sized piece of property also has the potential of utilizing the land itself as a source of income. Good woodland may have trees of a size that makes them saleable to timber buyers – black walnut, oak, maple, hickory, and other hardwoods can sell for up to hundreds of dollars per tree, if they are of a specific structure (straight, tall, no bark damage, and no limbs lower than 6-8 feet). Or, with some skill and time, a small lumber mill could be developed on your land to harvest and sell cut pieces, and chopped mulch from the small pieces.

There's a market for black walnuts and pecans, too. If your land has good trees, you may be able to secure seasonal income just by picking up the nuts they produce. In my area, black walnut buyers paid around $12 per hundred pounds in 2016 for whole nuts. One person can easily make over $100 per day for a few hours of work, and a whole family working at it consistently could bring in thousands of dollars for a few weeks a year. Assuming you have many productive trees (one tree can give several hundred pounds annually). How about setting up your own nut-processing facility which can be done for less than $1000, and selling nutmeats around your area? And, of course, you can save your own nuts and enjoy delicious nutritious foods throughout the rest of the year, as well.

Pasture land that produces more hay than you need can provide hay for sale. You'll need a tractor, mower, tedder, rake, baler, and repair skills, for this. Large round bales weighing about a half-ton and comprising good grass hay typically sell for $30 or so in an average year, and more if the weather is bad. It'll cost about half of that in fuel and repair to make each bale, so you've got a $15+ profit for each bale you sell.

The livestock you raise may produce more than you use. Chickens are good at swamping a household with eggs, so selling fresh eggs for a few dollars a dozen can buy their feed and give you some pocket money, as well as all the eggs you can eat. Rabbits can be offered for sale as pets and as food. In many jurisdictions, there are restrictions on selling uninspected butchered livestock. Some folks have found that they can sell live animals, and then process the rabbit for the new owner gratis. Be alert to legal issues in your area, and don't do what will get you into trouble.

How about selling some of those extra goat kids your milking does produce? Or calves right out of the field? Or trading a 900-pound calf for something else you need? Or raising a couple dozen turkeys on grass and non-GMO grains, and offering them as Thanksgiving Specials?

When the garden overflows, the extras can be sold off your property, or at the nearby farmer's market. Herbs, medicinal plants, and early spring plant starts could be part of that income stream, too. Be alert to opportunities and changing trends.

Dog, cat, and horse boarding can provide another income stream, if you're set up to hold pets in kennels and horses in pastures and barns. You'll need insurance and a good relationship with a veterinarian, too. If you have good water, streams, or ponds, consider if raising catfish or other fish might earn some extra income; or set up a fishing area where people can catch their own, and charge a fee per fish or by weight.

Should you have sheep with clean wool, there's a market for that. Online sellers can earn $10 or more per pound of good wool. One sheep can produce 10-15 pounds, so the wool alone is worth as much as a weaned lamb. However, selling wool to local folk is more challenging since rural folk don't spin and knit or weave as they did a century ago, so right now this outlet is best if you have an online website and access. In a generation, it will probably be local again.

There's many more options, if you're inclined to develop income streams. There are potentials that most people don't even try to tap, and could provide you and yours with remarkable security in the years to come. The method is surprisingly simple: find out what people want, and then produce and sell it to them. Make it as easy and pleasant as possible for people to give you their business.

.

4 FOOD: IMMEDIATE BASICS

This basic food chapter follows the one for Place, since food is going to be as vital as where you are located. Chapter 5 deals with water acquisition, which is critical, and Chapter 6 continues the food discussion with the importance of growing your own. Place, to my thinking, is of primary importance because without a stable location, you cannot provision food, store food, or grow food – you're at the mercy of whomever hands out the bread.

History is chock-full of weather-related famines. One of the first things that happens is the migration of the starving off their land, which further pressures any place that food is still growing. During the great Finnish famines in the 1600s and 1800s, poor hungry peasants took to the highways looking for *anything* to eat. They were already making "bread" from tree bark.

Livestock disappeared, as did cats and dogs, and then children. In some areas, fully one-third of the population died. Think of that this way: count out each person you know, "1...2....3, 1...2...3," – then imagine every third person dies from starvation. *That* is what happened in Cold Times in Finland, twice, within the past 450 years. The same took place all over the planet at one time or another. The fact that these famines were related to Little Ice Age effects of poor harvests and intensely cold and snowy winters should not be forgotten.

The physical security of a warm, stable residence is improved by a generous food supply, carefully preserved and stored so that it, too, is protected from predation. Protecting your food supply, your actual physical lifeline, will be discussed in later chapters. This chapter will deal with the food basics that you need **now**, and general food storage. The next food chapter covers the principles of food growing – but obviously, this must be a general overview. The topic is too large and complex to cover in detail in a single chapter in a single book. You must acquire more information from other paper sources, and do it now. If you can only afford one food preservation book, this is it:

Putting Food By, by Hertzberg and Greene, Plume Publishing – any of the editions are excellent. Used, less than $10 plus shipping from Amazon and other online sources.

Rules of Food Storage

- Do not tell anyone outside your inner circle that you have supplies. *Anyone.*
- If a child is unable to keep this "only in the family", they must **not know** you have storage.
- Store what you eat, and eat what you store. That will mean you get to eat what you like, and it will keep your food supplies from getting stale.
- Be able to make comfort/fun foods.
- Eat something fresh every day – sprouts are an ideal easy-to-raise nutrition powerhouse. Seeds will keep about 2 years, so keep buying and using them as long as they are available. Plant the older leftovers and save seeds from the growing plants for sprouting.
- Take a multivitamin daily, as long as you have them.

Now: Long Term Food Insurance

In this early awakening stage, and carrying through into the middle Zen-slap stage, long term storage goods are your ticket to food comfort and security. These are the things you buy in bulk and in the large gallon-sized #10 cans. These are simple foods that are cooked from scratch and will provide sufficient nutrition to live on.

The point of this storage is to give you *food options* when things are coming apart at the seams in society. Having this on-hand means no last-minute trips to the market when there's a blizzard coming in, no concerns if the power goes out, and plenty to eat when the roads are too icy to drive on. These are excellent tools *now* because you can still buy them at this time, and they will keep indefinitely without much attention. Any of these goods that survive the awakening stage, can be used years later whenever extras are needed.

Ideally, your *minimum* supply is one year for each person in your group. The rationale for this is that if things go bad rapidly, you will have enough to get you through to your first harvest next year. It would be better to have TWO YEAR's supply because you might not get a full harvest that first year or may lose some during storage.

At the time of this writing, you can *easily* store a year's supply of these basics for one person underneath a queen-sized bed. If you purchase these supplies in #10 cans (see resources), you can store cases of 6 cans in closets or in any space that doesn't freeze or get over 80F degrees or so in the summer, such as an attached garage. Prices for goods in #10 cans are higher than bulk, but it is already packed and stable, so you simply stack it up.

If you buy product in 50-pound bulk bags and pack it yourself, you can put in this storage for about $600 today. Both Costco and Sam's Club carry bulk-size bags of quite a few of these items. You can spread the expense over several months, but do not delay. *The awakening is upon us.* This menu collection is NOT nutritionally complete, gets boring over time, requires cooking skill, and includes no fresh foods (sprouting seeds can fit that bill), but you won't go hungry eating this way, either. Here's your shopping list:

Per Person, One Year Supply

50#	Powdered Milk	$150
25#	Popcorn	$30
350#	250# Wheat Berries and 100# White Flour	$250
125#	Dried Beans – Pintos are probably cheapest	$100
150#	White Rice	$100
10#	Sea Salt	$10
25#	Sugar (brown, white, molasses, honey, etc)	$25
2 gallon	Olive oil or coconut oil	$45

2#	Sprouting seeds, mixed	$8

You'll also need a Corona Grain Mill, manually operated, AND a manual can opener, get 2 of each because you will wear one out; spices like chili powder, chicken and beef flavored bouillon powder, dried onions and garlic, pepper, vanilla, and cinnamon. Include active dry yeast and baking powder or baking soda. Don't forget the multivitamin and mineral supplement daily.

Why this combination of ingredients?

The list here is loosely modeled after the "original" preppers, the Latter Day Saints (LDS), often called Mormons. Way back in the 1960s or earlier, Mormon writers set up a basic food program based on these items; wheat and milk were primary to their plan. They even had a method to extract the gluten from the wheat berries to make something akin to "meatless patties" that were said to be quite tasty.

Since then, many non-Mormon prepper writers focus on these essentials – beans and rice now topping the list. These actually are excellent, filling, nutritious foods that can be prepared in dozens of ways into satisfying meals. In modern Russia, preppers stock up on buckwheat, their primary grain basic.

Wheat *berries* typically last longer than wheat *flour*, and white flour keeps longer than whole wheat flour, which can go rancid due to the naturally occurring oils that remain until it is processed to white flour. Use the flour first, then move on to the berries, or mix the ground wheat berries with flour for a lighter whole wheat bread. Many preppers prefer "hard red wheat" because it has a stronger wheaty flavor, and higher protein and gluten content, and makes a better-risen bread than "soft white wheat", which is milder flavored and better for pastries. They're both good and most people can't tell the difference.

You can grind wheat to make bread. You'll have to pass it through your Corona Mill 2 or 3 times to make it fine and powdery enough for bread. You can also boil the wheat berries like rice, and eat as a porridge similar to steel-cut oatmeal. Fresher wheat berries can also be sprouted and eaten as very nutritious "wheat grass."

There are hundreds of varieties of beans. My current favorite is mayocoba, a creamy white-colored dried bean that is related to the familiar Pinto bean. Jacobs Cattle is an heirloom white and brown splotched bean that is very mild flavored and cooks quickly. Vermont Cranberry is a tan and purplish-marked bean that bakes well. Each bean type has positives, depending on taste and your needs. If any of your stored dry beans are relatively fresh, they can also be planted to eat later when they produce green beans, or grown out to harvest, dry, and save for next year's seed.

Pintos are about the least expensive, pound for pound; lentils can be substituted and take much less time to cook, about 30 minutes total. Soak beans overnight before cooking, then bring to a boil in fresh water and simmer several hours until soft. Add dried onions and chicken broth and you have bean soup; and then leftovers can be mashed and reheated with lard or oil, and converted into "refried" beans, the familiar south-of-the-border dish. Beans can also be finely ground and used in your wheat bread to increase protein and make it heartier and denser. Fresher beans can be sprouted and the sprouts fried.

Old dried beans, five years old and older, can become so hard that they just won't plump and soften in cooking. These are the best to finely grind and use as a boiled porridge, or include in bread recipes.

The rice can be prepared as a typical boiled rice dish, or added to soups, or ground and added to breads. Using some milk, vanilla, sugar, and cinnamon, left-over rice can be boiled or baked into a very nutritious and flavorful rice pudding. Rice is filling, familiar, and easy to digest.

Popcorn is surprisingly versatile. It is popcorn, of course, and with a little of that stored oil in a heavy kettle, will pop up light, crunchy, tasty, and nutritious. Ground finely, mixed with a little flour, milk, and baking soda, it makes the very best corn bread and hush-puppies, and can be mixed with dried onions and fried as corn-cakes. Ground to medium fineness, it makes excellent boiled grits.

The powdered milk makes drinkable milk, can be added to all breads, soups, porridges, and rice pudding to increase the protein and calcium contents.

Salt is critical to good health, and should be non-iodized sea salt or the pink Himalayan salt or even the grey Celtic Sea salt. The iodized variety loses its iodine content as soon as it is opened and out-gasses. If you want iodine in your daily diet, it would be better to add Lugol's Solution 3% to your supplies, and paint 10 drops daily on your skin, than to store iodized salt. Sea Salt and Himalayan and other 'trace mineral salts' add both vital trace nutrients and flavor to foods. After you've used these alternative salts for a while, you will notice that standard white table salt really is tasteless and rather unpleasant.

The sugar/honey or other sweetener gives you a boost of energy, delicious "comfort" tastes, and a break from routine.

Other spices and herbs should be stored "to taste", so whatever items you enjoy can be on that list. You actually can raise bread with a homemade "starter" (see recipes), but it's quicker and easier to make bread if you have dry yeast or baking soda/powder.

Oils are utterly critical to your diet and your wellbeing in very cold weather. Two gallons of oil per person per year is quite a bit less than you could use in severe climates, not only for cooking but for skin care as well. Olive oil has additional nutrients, and coconut oil is one of the medium-chain fatty acids that increases your metabolism and helps with generating warmth. The more oil you have, the better off you will be. Add it to everything you eat.

What about food allergies?
Why so much carbs and so little protein?

This is a basic survival diet, not much variety, not well-rounded nutritionally, but a whole lot better than nothing. This is designed to *protect* you at low cost from death by starvation. If you have severe life-threatening food allergies to anything on this list, find an alternative you can live with and store that instead.

In my opinion, the best diet for most people is something akin to the "primal" or "paleo" approach – fats, meat, lots of vegetables, small amount of berries, few grains or beans. This is not that diet. This list is basically the complete reverse of the paleo diet, heavy on the carbs from grains and beans, and light on the fats and animal proteins, with few veggies and no fruit. These additional items will be discussed in the next food chapter.

If you are ever in a situation where the stored foods on this list are all you have to eat, it won't make one iota of difference what you "think" is the best human diet – because when you're *that* hungry, it is ALL GOOD.

What if I'm not a good cook? Or don't cook?

Learn. It's not rocket science. Doesn't matter whether you are male or female, young or old, rich or poor – why be handicapped by lack of skills? There are thousands of books, websites, YouTubes, and probably friends and relatives that would be delighted to help you get started. You can still eat your mistakes.

> The entire purpose for storing these bare-necessities long-keeping supplies is to give you an easier transition to producing your own food. Any additional things you bring in during the transition adds to the diversity, nutrition, flavor, and enjoyment.

How to Pack Your Bulk Goods

You can acquire the basics a pound at a time, buy in bulk online or at big box stores, or even go down to the nearest livestock feed store and purchase whole grains there. The feed store route will be the cheapest because the grains are not 'human grade.' The grain might have come from poor fields and was undersized, was misshapen, has weed seeds mixed in very small amounts, or otherwise does not meet the published standard for human food. That doesn't mean it is inedible or dangerous; it's okay to feed to the animals who become our food, after all.

We're talking about *whole single grains*, here – wheat, barley, oats, etc. – NOT about mixes that have any other ingredients. The grain MUST NOT BE PINK. The pink color indicates it is for planting and that it has been chemically treated to resist soil pathogens. It can sicken or kill animals or humans who eat it, so don't.

There are four things you want to avoid in storage of grains: insects, moisture, air, and rodents.

Avoiding Insects

There is no natural grain that is free of insects or insect eggs; that's the reality. For long term storage, if you buy it already sealed in #10 cans, it has either been nitrogen-treated, or sealed without air in the can. Both methods kill bugs and their eggs. If you buy your grains in a bag from any source, it's probably been previously fumigated either with chemicals or with some natural product to reduce active insect infestation. After it has set around on store shelves or in feed stores, insects will creep back in. They're pretty resilient.

One very simple method to reduce insects is to freeze your grain, and keep it hard frozen for *at least* 4 days; two weeks would be better. After freezing, let it sit at room temperature overnight before the final sealing. That will help reduce the moisture level caused by condensation, too.

Another method is to add about a half cup (a handful) of powdered food-grade diatomaceous earth to each 25 pounds of grain, and mix in well. Diatomaceous earth (DE) is a white powder, made from the finely ground shells of tiny marine creatures. It is actually mined from large deposits laid down in ancient seas thousands of years ago.

DE is effective against insects because the minute particles are razor sharp, harmless to humans, but they slice insects and their eggs and cause them to dry out and die. Because it is a mechanical insecticide, the insects cannot develop resistance. Health food stores, feed stores, and online sites offer DE for sale. *Only use food-grade DE*, not the kind for pool filters. It doesn't go bad.

A side benefit of DE in stored grain is that it adds digestible calcium to the ground grain. It's not necessary to remove it from grains before grinding, but you can remove some of it by "winnowing" the grain outdoors in a breeze (that is, dumping the grain from one container into another so the wind passes through it).

DE can be irritating if it gets in your eyes. Rinse with clean water and don't rub. Inhaling clouds of DE can be irritating to nasal passages. If you're going to be using a lot, wear a protective mask, such as the N-95 used by health care providers or the dust mask you can get at hardware stores.

By the way, insects found in your desperately needed grains *will not harm you*. It may be disgusting and repulsive to think about it, but you can grind and cook the insects along with your grain but NOT cockroaches or flies, which can carry diseases that affect humans. Grain-eating moths and tiny "thrip" type bugs are edible. You may be able to winnow or pick out insects and their eggs, if you want to go that route.

Avoiding Moisture

Moist grains either sprout, which is edible if done on purpose; or develop a fungus or mold which makes them toxic and inedible for man and beast. When you pack grains, they should be at room temperature and completely dry. Take a handful of grain and squeeze it – dry grains will fall loosely from your open hand; damp grains clump and stick together. If you dust the grain with DE, it may help reduce any residual dampness, as well. You may wish to either place your grains in a very low temperature oven for a few minutes to assure dryness, or even just blow a fan over them for a bit. Don't pack damp grain. It will mold or mildew and become potentially toxic and inedible.

Store packed grains where they won't be subject to freezes and thaws, because that degrades the quality of the product and shortens its shelf life. Use an "oxygen absorber" (more shortly) inside each pack, too.

Avoiding Air

The more free air inside a pack of stored grain, the greater the opportunity for the foods to age and become stale. Grains are actually living, even if they are stable at the moment. They do "breathe" (respire) and maintain their ability to grow while in storage. Reducing free oxygen around seeds puts them deeper into a kind of suspended animation, so they maintain their freshness longer.

Think of the tomato seeds that NASA once sent into space. Even after being in the deep freeze of space in an airless vacuum, many of the open-pollinated Rutgers variety "space tomatoes" grew just fine. A few had interesting abnormalities caused by cosmic radiation exposure, but that's another topic. After years, even in an oxygen-reduced environment, grains do eventually get less fresh and may not sprout when given the chance, but they'll taste just fine. Less free air also means a much reduced living environment for insects, too.

When grains are packed for long term storage, there are several ways to reduce free air. The previously mentioned oxygen absorber packs, about the size of a packet of sugar, are dropped into the bag with the grain – which must be the type of Mylar bag that can be completely sealed, more on that soon, too. The oxygen absorber will cause the sealed bag to draw in, as if it is creating a vacuum inside the bag. When the bag is later opened, it reinflates as free air is introduced again.

Another method to remove air is to pack grains in a heavy container, such as a plastic bucket with a sealable lid, and place dry ice on top with the lid loosely over that. Once the ice has "sublimated," that is, turned to fog and sunk to the bottom of the bucket, the lid can be sealed. The nitrogen in the dry ice drives out oxygen, and sealing the lid keeps the oxygen out. Insects cannot live in that environment, and the seeds remain as fresh as when packed. CAUTION: If lids are sealed too soon, buckets can implode and cause severe damage or injuries. This is not my preferred method, for that reason.

A mechanical method of removing air is to place grain inside a Mylar bag, almost completely seal the bag as discussed following this, and use a vacuum cleaner to suck the air out of the bag and then quickly seal it. Grains can also be packed in individual air-tight "food saver" type vacuum-pack bags, if you don't mind packing it in two or three pound sacks and fitting those into a bucket.

Avoiding Rodents

Rats and mice can get into just about any space where food is stored, either by slipping through small cracks and holes, or by getting in when doors are opened, or by chewing their way inside.

Anything in cardboard or plastic sacks are susceptible. Very hungry or large rodents can also chew through plastic trash cans and tubs to get at the contents.

Double sealing grains inside Mylar and then plastic buckets helps keep the vermin out. Apparently they can't smell it, and so don't chew into containers to get it. Keep rodent populations down by using traps and reducing their potential food sources. If there's nothing for them to eat, they'll move on to somewhere food is available. Having a couple cats around wouldn't hurt, either.

Low Cost Rodent Trap: Use a steep-sided bucket and fill about half way with water. Set a small ramp up to the top rim. Attach a small "gang plank" so that it is like a mini teeter-totter – hinged in the center so that when the rodent travels down the plank to the portion that is over the water in the bucket, the plank should tip. Rub a little peanut butter on the end of the plank. Mousie runs up the ramp, out onto the gang plank, sniffing the bait. After it passes the balance center of the plank, Mousie's weight pulls the plank down and it tips him off into the water, where he drowns. Plank then pops back up into position, awaiting Mousie II. You'll have to clean drowned rodents out of the bucket daily – add to your compost pile.

The Process of Packing Grains

Understanding the four nasties that we want to keep out of our grain stores, and recognizing that most of us don't have huge grain bins, there's a process that's been developed by the prepper community over the past decades that works at home.

For this, you will need several 4-5 gallon plastic buckets (each will hold 20-25 pounds of grains), large Mylar bags to fit inside the buckets, a wood board that will overlap the top of the bucket, a clothing iron, a lid for the bucket, your bag of DE if you plan to use it, and oxygen absorber packets. Don't open the oxygen absorber packet bag until you have loaded everything and are ready to start sealing Mylar.

- Place your buckets so you can work around them easily.
- Fit a Mylar bag inside each one with the top overlapping the lip (so it won't slip into the bucket while you are adding

grain).

- Add one or two packets of oxygen absorber to each bucket, if you're using it, and put any leftover absorbers immediately in a sealed freezer-type baggie.
- Pour grain into the Mylar inside the bucket, to within about 2" of the top.
- Add a handful of DE to each bucket, if you are using it. Mix in with your hands. Perfect distribution is not necessary.
- Heat your iron.
- Place the board across the rim of your bucket and drape the Mylar over it. Press excess air out of the bag. Try to avoid wrinkles at the edge that is to be sealed with the iron.
- Use the hot iron to seal the Mylar closed. Press the hot iron evenly across the bar so the Mylar sides overlap and stick solidly together. Let the sealed edge cool, then gently test it. If it hasn't sealed and air can escape from the bag, iron it again a little higher or lower on the bag. Repeat until you have a good seal.
- When sealed, attach the lid.
- Label the exterior bucket with contents, weight, date – use a permanent marking pen, so there's no risk of losing the label.

Buckets can be acquired from hardware stores for about $3-5 each, with lids. They should have a metal "bale" or carrying handle, too. I have also gotten free buckets from restaurants by asking for them. The ones I received had been used for holding pickles, and never did stop smelling like pickles....even after 30 years!

Lids come in two varieties: basic tap-on type; and the type known as a Gamma Lid. The original tap-on lid attaches firmly with a snap, and has to be pried off (there is a lid-removing tool like a giant bottle opener that makes this a little easier). The Gamma Lid comes in two parts: a lip that attaches directly to the bucket rim, and a screw-in inner lid that fits inside. The Gamma Lid is easier to use, and costs about $6-7 each. I have Gamma Lids on buckets that I open frequently, and regular lids on the rest.

Since they won't be in direct contact with your grain, you don't need "food safe" buckets, although it doesn't hurt to use them. Food safe buckets are marked with a symbol on the bottom, a small triangle with rounded corners with a "2" inside.

Mylar protects the grain inside the bucket, is air-resistant (but not perfectly impervious), but it punctures easily and is not strong enough to hold grain by itself. It needs the support of a bucket. You can pack grain in a food safe bucket without the Mylar. The Mylar just adds one more layer of protection to your food supply's endurance over time.

Adding Flavor and Nutrition

Once the very most basic items have been secured, then you can focus on building add-on storage to improve the taste and nourishment of meals and snacks. Remember, what we're looking at here is having enough supplies to get you through the awakening into the Zen-slap phases of the transition – this is not going to be a life-time supply of assorted foods. It will be enough to allow you and yours to make a graceful change from today's condition into tomorrow's circumstances, with a minimum level of distress and fear. If you *collapse now and avoid the rush,* as John Michael Greer has suggested, you are ahead of the game.

What should I store?

Many preparedness writers provide a list of items to store, sometimes based on average daily caloric requirements, or average number of meals served, and sometimes based on special diet elements such as vegan or gluten-free.

Personally, I've never found those lists more than marginally useful because no one else eats like my family. We have food preferences and dislikes, things that we *must* have (coffee, chocolate), and things that we likely won't eat unless we have no other choice (any Smoothie). What you store must meet you and your family's needs.

Here is a simple method to determine what to store: write down everything consumed in your household for 7 days. Write the quantities, the meals and snacks, in a table format for ease of

evaluation later like the chart on the next page.
List everything you eat, including fast foods, meals eaten out, and candy bars grabbed at the convenience store. You want a complete list:

	Breakfast	Lunch	Dinner	Snack 1	Snack 2	Daily Quantity
Day 1	2 eggs, 2 toast, 2 cup coffee w/cream & sugar	2 slices bread, 3 slices cheese, mayo, lettuce, tomato slice, 12 oz soda, 3 cookies chips	chicken thighs, 1 potato, butter, sour cream, Dinner roll, Salad, Cup green beans, 3 cookies	1 orange, snack cake, Glass milk	Piece of cake, Glass milk	5 pieces bread, 6 cookies, 1 snack cake 12 oz milk/cream, 3 oz cheese 8 oz green beans, 1 soda 2 oz chips, 1 orange Lettuce Tomato Salad dressing Coffee
Day 2	1 cup Cheerios, 2/3 cup milk, coffee w/cream & sugar Glass orange juice	2 slices bread, peanut butter, Jelly; 3 cookies, glass milk, apple	Casserole: tuna, peas, noodles, peas,mushroom soup, bread crumbs; salad, Dinner roll, slice pumpkin pie, whipped cream topping, glass of wine	Bag of chips, chocolate covered pretzels	Can of soda, chocolate peanuts & raisins	3 pieces bread,1 cup Cherrios 16 oz milk, 8 oz orange juice 6 oz tuna, 2 oz pasta, Mushroom soup, Pumpkin pie (spices, pumpkin, pie crust), lettuce, tomato, dressing, 2 oz chips, dip 4 oz chocolate peanuts and raisins Bottle wine Coffee

When you have recorded 7 full days, you will see some real patterns to what you routinely eat. For example, in the chart here, it's clear that bread is a typical part of the diet, perhaps a half-loaf in 2 days. That would be a full loaf in 4 days, so two loaves per week.

There is salad once a day and salad components used on sandwiches. That could work out to at least one head of lettuce per week. One or two tomatoes per week.

Cookies, 6 per day, is several dozen per week.

Glass or two of milk daily, plus used in coffee, is a gallon a week.

Canned or frozen vegetables like peas or green beans – perhaps 2 or three cans or a pound of frozen each week.

Fresh fruit or fruit drinks – 10 or 14 per week.

Sugar? Dip? Snack cakes? Chips? Condiments like mayonnaise, catsup, mustard? Pickles? Gum?

Notice that I was assuming that some meals are cooked or made at home (tuna casserole, egg breakfast), and there is only moderate reliance on prepared goods (such as Cheerios and snack cakes). You may use more prepared goods, or eat more meat, or eat out more often. Just write it all down.

Add it up, then add in the rest of the family's foods. *That's* why your food bill is so high – incredible how much we eat, in just a week!

Now You Have a Plan

With your list in hand, you can stock up a full month's supply merely by loading up on the routine items, except for perishables like the lettuce and tomatoes. Just multiply your existing list times 4, that is, a 4 week (one month) supply.

You can readily store a month's worth of breakfast cereal (8 or 10 boxes) and snack cakes (2 or 3 boxes), and tuna casserole fixins (10 cans tuna, 2 bags dried noodles, 8 cans mushroom soup, 4 cans peas, dried onions), in your usual cabinets. Consider replacing some of the fresh fruits and veggies you would use with canned items and tomato or vegetable juices; they can sit on the shelf indefinitely.

Fats: What's the deal?

One of the most healthful foods you can store is fat – lard, olive oil, butter, and coconut oil being the top ones. Fat is higher in calories than protein and carbohydrates, ounce for ounce, which means the same amount of space can hold almost twice as much nutrient "energy". Furthermore, during the cold, fat is super-efficient at helping your body keep you warm.

Here's one example: a friend who was stationed in Alaska years ago, said that part of their daily ration included a *cup of bacon grease*, sweetened with brown sugar. Seriously, a full cup of fat, every day. You won't have to take yours that way – just use plenty of fat or grease in your cooking. It won't cause worsening cholesterol problems or make you gain weight – look up the latest research. In the cold, fat can keep you alive.

Later, when you have livestock, save and store the fat – you can cook it down in an oven or on a stovetop, then pour off the hot liquid fat through a strainer into clean mason jars. Seal them while still hot. It will solidify as it cools. As long as the fat isn't in the open air, it won't go rancid for several years. Throw away rancid fat, or use it to grease garden tools.

If you have a stand-alone freezer, put 8 loaves of bread and several packages of rolls in there, double wrapped or vacuum-packed – they'll keep for months and thaw out nearly as tasty as fresh when you need them. To save money, you can buy the bread at "day old" bread outlets along with the snack cakes. You will end the month with a little more cash in your pocket!

When you have a month's supply, keep adding on until you have several months' worth. Your final goal is a year's supply for each member of your family.

Trial Run

Give yourself a little while, say 3 weeks, to start collecting your basics list of beans, rice, wheat, flour, milk, and to begin gathering the additional flavor and nutrition items. This should give you enough **right now** on hand, so that you could eat "normally" if you couldn't get out for some reason. Don't delay this process, though. There is no "right time", except for **right now**.

The best way to find out if you really have enough is to do a trial run. A *serious* trial run. Give yourself a full seven day test. Start on Sunday, and go through to the following Saturday. Use only the foods you have on-hand – no additional purchased snacks at the vending machine or convenience store when you get gas, no quick runs to the supermarket for a forgotten item (there will be some!), bring lunches to work or school, and so forth.

If you are hungry for something and don't have it, substitute something else or go without. Stress yourself a little, so you can experience what happens to your mood and attitude. Make two lists: the "*oops, missing*" list, and the "*wish I had this*" list. Write down any additional thoughts or ideas, too.

The trial run will be your first Big Eye Opener. If you are like most people in our society, by Saturday night, you'll be ready for a night out. Go, enjoy, and discuss your trial run experience.

Trial Run, After Action Report

Your After Action Report (AAR) is the opportunity to compare the reality of your storage with your actual needs. The list you made of "oops, missing", and the "wish I had" items provides you with a new shopping list. Fill in the "missing and wishing" items, plus get one or two extras of each and set them in your growing pantry.

Be mindful of any changes in mood or attitude that comes out of your experience. Can you keep going if you don't get something you want at the moment? Keep your AAR, perhaps with your recipes, so you can see over time how your storage improves and your ability to use it increases, as well.

For those pre-prepared foods, such as purchased cookies and snack cakes, begin thinking of ways you can replace them by cooking from your basics storage. If you have a bread machine, pull it out of the cupboard and review the recipes and ingredients there. You will be able to make a super-tasty hot loaf ($1 for ingredients or lower) for less of your hard-earned cash than buying any pre-made loaf ($2-$4 or more).

If you make all your bread at home using a bread machine and mixing the ingredients yourself for a mere 3 months, you will not be able to go back to the flabby air bread from the supermarket. That premade stuff might taste fine, but you'll notice that it leaves you feeling....strange. Homemade cookies are *always* better than store-bought, especially when you use the best ingredients such as real butter and pure vanilla. Start trying out recipes and saving those you really like, in a binder or 4x6 card box.

Incremental changes in the way you eat now will save you and your family from the shock of sudden food changes. That is a very important part of what this awakening transition period will accomplish for you.

An important note: involve family members in meal preparation – dicing vegetables, or cooking dessert, or figuring out good food combinations, or finding recipes. Children, especially, benefit from learning how to feed their loved ones.

Remember, *everyone contributes.*

Keeping Track of Stored Goods

At this point, you are probably beginning to feel like you are running out of places to store food. Continue to stack buckets and #10 cans under beds and in closets. You can also utilize your cases of canned goods by disguising them as furniture: stack boxes, cover with a pretty cloth and you've got a coffee table; add a couple pillows, and you've got a side chair or a window seat.

If you have an attached garage that doesn't get overly hot or cold, you can stack your buckets and set up shelves there and start storing. Place a curtain or doors on your storage so that inquisitive passersby can't easily see what you've got. Conspicuously mark boxes "plumbing supplies" or "Christmas Décor" or other innocuous labels so that prying eyes find them uninteresting.

If you have a spare room, or bedroom, cooled attic or water proof basement, that space can become your "pantry" for storage food. Unused bedrooms that stay at regular household temperatures are ideal and relatively easy to retrofit with basic shelves. Attics are okay if they are not subject to summer heat. Heat will destroy your storage in short order.

Basements are perfect, since they tend to maintain steady temperatures but beware of the risk of flooding, either through porous walls or because of a pipe break on upper floors or from same-level piping. Be certain your basement can drain unimpeded, even when the electricity and sump pump go out, or don't store your critical supplies there.

Records

As soon as you begin your grain and bean collection, you're faced with another reality – keeping track of what you have and where it's stored. If you've got twenty pounds of wheat flour in your freezer, that's one thing. When you have dozens of cans of various items, it starts to be a whole other problem....particularly when you need to get out one specific thing quickly. The only way to manage your supplies, is to keep written records.

My original paper records, written in pencil so changes could be erased, looked something like this:

Buy Date	Item Description	Qty	Location	Used	Comment
1/3/83	Pasta 16 oz	6#	Pantry	111	Variety pks
4/9/83	Corn, Canned 16 oz	24 cn	Basement	11111 1	Under canned beans

This was a perfectly useable system and helped me to see at a glance what I had and what I was running out of. I could write a shopping list directly off my records, rather than having to sort through cans and boxes.

Not included in my records was whatever I had in the kitchen for daily use, for example, spices and cooking herbs next to the stove, and whatever cans and boxes in the cupboards, were "unrecorded extras" for my storage. They were *bonus goods*. We could probably have eaten comfortably for a week or two on that and what was in the refrigerator.

A simple paper register, accounting book, computer spreadsheet program, or just a lined sheet of paper is enough to get your records going. Write in pencil. Get *a lot* of extra pencils and erasers.

Once you have acquired a year's worth of supplies, though, a paper record quickly becomes unwieldy. It *can* be done, but you will need a separate page for each of several hundred items, collected in alphabetical order in a binder so you can remove and add pages as you go. A paper record is MANDATORY, even if it is only a printout from your computer spreadsheet. That is because, as you know, computers go down, the grid can go down, and you will still need to know what you have.

If you are comfortable with computers, there are several good storage programs available online. Search for "food storage program", and check out several until you find something you like. Make sure you can store your data on *your computer,* not only on the provider's servers. Use a good anti-virus program while you check out any of these websites.

My experience is with the LDS-affiliated Food Storage Planner program, available as a download and in a CD format (https://www.foodstorageplanner.com/five). The program has a "standard" set up that lets you start by assessing your supplies in comparison to a time period you chose – 1 week to 1 year – by the number of people you plan to feed. You can customize the foods on your list, remove the standard ones you don't use, change quantities and food names, and decide if it is basic survival, mid-level comfort, or luxury goods. Best of all, you can print out a shopping list of needed items, and your whole pantry list as well. The system is very well thought-out and can be used with only a short learning curve.

If you store your supply information on a computer, **be sure to back it up to a dedicated flash drive and paper printouts.** When you add or use things from your storage, write it down and then update your program from your list.

Cooking Supplies

As you collect your basic food supply, it is also time to start collecting the means to cook your food and getting familiar with using each one. Recall that one of the assumptions this book is based on is that there are going to be times when the grid is down, there are no propane deliveries, natural gas is not available, and we must rely on methods that are not commonly used today.

During the awakening transition period, switching from a regular electric or gas home stove may become a necessity, at least on some occasions. People who have RVs useable for boon docking or dry-camping (away from an RV park and running off of their own power) are generally set up to cook on propane stoves. They will often use backup electric power provided by a portable generator and/or solar power – even running a microwave from time to time. So it is not a huge change from standard home meal prep, but changing cooking methods IS a change, and any change requires practice to become skilled at it.

One of the easiest transition stoves is a standard "camp stove" – either powered by a 1-pound propane canister, or by "camp fuel". Most are two-burner set ups. There are multiple manufacturers, including Camp Chef and others. They run around $65-$90. Burners can be lit  by a match, or by an intrinsic spark system. I'd suggest you get at least one camp stove, as soon as possible. Set it up and cook on it. It's a simple change. A 1-pound canister of propane will last several days, and runs about $4 each. Get 8 of them. Store canisters in an outbuilding or garage, *never* near any live flame source, such as a gas water heater.

 Another option is a butane stove. These are commonly single-burner, and use a butane canister like the type used to refill cigarette lighters. Similar types of stoves are also made by many other manufacturers including Camp Chef, Coleman, Gas One and others. They run around $35. These are used like the camp stove, but only handle one pot at a time. Their real benefit is that they are light enough to carry with you, if you have to leave in a hurry. Get extra

butane, if you go this route, and maybe a couple extra stoves for backup. Butane Canisters run around $2 each, if bought in a case of 12. With either of these stoves, you can cook a tasty meal, even if the power is out for days.

The "upscale" version of a camp stove is Camp Chef's 2-burner stove and oven set up. The improvement is the addition of a small baking oven. These run about $250, and will operate at high burn for about 5 hours on a one-pound propane canister.

If you want hot meals but want to conserve fuel, consider the "hot pot". There's lots of variations on this idea, but basically it is a heat retaining container into which you put a covered boiling pot of *something* (soup or anything that requires long slow cooking). The container is then closed, and in a few hours the *something* will be ready to eat. Fuel use is much lower than continuing to heat it for hours. The hot pot is effectively a slow-cooker, without the electricity.

One way to make a hot pot: use a large heavy cardboard box, and line the interior with aluminum foil. Next, fill it to the brim with straw and pack it down fairly tightly – that provides your heat-retaining medium. You could also use fiberglass insulation or any medium that won't melt or outgas when you put a hot pot on it (don't use Styrofoam right next to the pot for that reason).

Scoop out a bit of the insulating medium so your pot will fit down into the box. Bring your pot of goodies to a full boil, cover, and carefully settle it into the indention, then cover with the insulating medium and a bath towel or two. Check it in a couple hours – it should still be quite warm and well on the way to table ready.

Another cooking method, if you have sunny days, is the solar oven. This is, effectively, an oven-sized insulated box that has a clear glass top and reflectors that focus sunlight onto the matte-black interior behind the glass. A commercial or home-made solar oven can reach high 350°F+ degrees, and easily cook bread, soup, or meat dishes.

You'll need to make sure the glass front is pointed directly at the hot sun, and adjust the position every 30-minutes or so during the cooking time, but otherwise it's just like using a standard oven.

Commercial solar ovens run around $300. Homemade ones can be made by placing a smaller cardboard box inside a larger one, insulating the space between them with Styrofoam or layers of cardboard. Paint the interior of the small box flat-black with tempera or other non-toxic paint. Glue aluminum foil on the large box's flaps to create reflective surfaces. Place a piece of window glass over the open front – and you've got a solar oven. I made one years ago using a black plastic bag for the box interior, and it got so hot that the plastic melted!

For equipment: a fry pan or two of cast iron and stainless steel; a couple of stainless steel pots, one large for stew, one medium for everything else; a couple lidded casserole dishes or Dutch oven, porcelain over steel or cast iron; and any special equipment you like or prefer. Forget about lightweight non-stick supplies – they won't last, and you may not be able to find replacements. Consider a small pressure cooker, too – you can cook a pot roast with potatoes, carrots, onions, and spices in half an hour. Or prepare beans in about the same time. That is a huge saving in fuel. A medium sized pressure cooker/canner can also be used to purify water for drinking, too.

Finally, set in a supply of paper (not Styrofoam) plates and bowls. These can be burned on a campfire or in a fireplace after use to keep you warm. If you are in a power-down situation where you must rely on your backup food and cooking methods, you will most definitely not want to boil water to do a load of dishes several times daily.

COLD TIMES

5 WATER:
PURIFYING, COLLECTING, STORING

We've looked at storing purchased foods, setting up record- keeping systems, and methods of cooking that work when the grid and natural gas systems are unreliable. We will continue discussing food production in the chapter that comes after this one. There's a gap between the two food chapters because once you've got your basic food, you *must* immediately put in your water system. Without water, you're dead within a week. Without *clean* water, your hygiene disintegrates, and life-threatening disease sets in.

In reality, the water chapter should lead all others, including Place since a place without natural water is called "a desert". You can't live there.

So, how do you know the water currently coming from your tap is safe – that is, having a low count of dangerous bacteria, being free from damaging chemicals, and safe enough for a baby to drink?

The real answer is: *you don't*. In reality, you merely trust your community water system to take care of that for you – and, in the main, they do. Except in Flint, Michigan, or Fresno, California, where the tap water was laden with enough lead to sicken anyone who drank it, which was, of course, the entire city.

You can contact your town's water service, and request the latest analysis of the water, and I do encourage you to do that. There may be a charge for this, or it may be available at the water company's online site. The report should show the levels of various natural and manufactured chemicals – arsenic to nitrates – as well as bacteria that was found and eradicated by chlorine or other means. Of course, I would guess that Flint's routine water report forgot to include dangerous levels of lead...but other regions are hopefully more forthcoming.

There is one thing that your service's report will tell you clearly: *somebody has been taking care of the purity of your drinking water and bringing it to your tap.* It didn't just occur spontaneously. It took many people's thought, effort, time, planning, and consistency to make it happen. In most cities and towns, it has been going on for generations, literally. Prior to that, if you wanted water you had to haul it, collect it, and store it yourself.

And that's why many people take their safe water for granted. It's always been there. It always will. Until it's not. Then, having absolutely *no idea* that water in a pond, pool, stream, or river might be "different" from what comes out of the tap, they drink. After several weeks of debilitating diarrhea and maybe a stay in the hospital, they know better. Don't be that person.

The creation of modern water systems was the product of horrific outbreaks a century ago of water-borne disease – cholera, typhoid, dysentery – that killed thousands of people. At the time, city folk used public latrines that seeped sewage into the community wells. The residue percolated down into the water table and ended up at the "town pump". Public health officials found the relationship by tracing outbreaks to individual water pumps. *That's* why we have sewers and sewage collection systems in cities and towns: so we don't contaminate our own drinking water. Placement of latrines will be considered in the later Hygiene chapter.

Purifying Water

Because of the criticality of having clean drinking water, we're going to examine the purification process before we talk about getting and keeping water. Once again, we've got a way to purify water that is appropriate for the early awakening transition period, as well as lower-tech purification processes that are suitable for the Zen-slap phase and thereafter.

Least Expensive Methods

First, any water must be passed through a filter to remove particulate matter – bits of leaf, dirt, and so on – and this can be accomplished with a coffee filter, a clean kitchen towel, or even a t-shirt. Pour your water through the filter so that you have visually clean water without extra floating things in it.

The most effective and least expensive method to purify water is to simply bring the filtered water to a rolling **boil** (bubbling surface) for 10 minutes or so. That kills all bacteria and protozoa and other potentially infective nasties. *This does not remove chemicals or poisonous metals,* just the germs and bugs.

The next-most familiar and inexpensive method is **bleach**. For a gallon of water, use ¼ teaspoon (about 20 drops) of chlorine bleach. Stir well, and let sit for at least one hour. It's now ready to use. This works out to about 5 drops per quart. Use only pure chlorine beach – Clorox, Purex, Off-Brand, makes no difference, as long as it is only 5-6% calcium hypochlorite and no additional scents, detergents, or modifiers. This is NOT the "color-safe bleach", so absolutely do NOT use that type. There is "concentrated" chlorine bleach, 8.25% -- if you have that, use about 2/3s of the dose (14 drops per gallon). Your water will have a slight bleach odor, which is not harmful to you. *This kills most bacteria and protozoa, but does not remove chemicals or metals.*

Similar to bleach, **iodine tincture** can be used. You may buy "tincture of iodine" at most drug stores or Lugol's Solution 3% online. A 2 ounce dropper bottle runs about $5-$10. Use 10 drops per quart of water. Shake or stir well and let it sit for an hour. It will have an iodine flavor. **Don't use this if you are allergic to iodine or shellfish.** This kills most bacteria, although it might not kill giardia protozoa – best bet is to boil the water – *but does not remove chemicals or metals.*

You can treat water before use, or treat water when you are putting it into storage. If you have 100 gallons set back for immediate emergency use, you won't be in a panic if the electricity goes off suddenly, or you can't trust whatever comes out of your tap. Simply add the appropriate amount of bleach or iodine, and tightly cap the container. Your water will remain drinkable for a year or two. After that, use it to water your garden, and refill with and treat another batch of water.

Keep in mind that bleach in an unopened bottle will only maintain its potency about 2 years; iodine might last longer. Once the container is opened, both lose potency relatively quickly....figure a year. Clearly, treating water with these chemical approaches is a short-term method, better used in the early transition stage while you adjust to the Zen-slap that is coming. Later, if your water supply is from an unpolluted and reliable source *over which you have full control*, you will probably be able to drink that water without any difficulty, even if it is laden with local/regional bacteria. Effectively, you will have developed immunity to your water's bacteria. People new to your area, however, may develop diarrheal conditions when they sample your unpurified water.

Another method that is most efficient if done ahead of time, is to **can your water** in Ball or Mason jars. Take clean quart jars, fill with filtered visibly clean water, put on the lids and bands, and place the jars into a canner. This is "water-bath canning", as used to can jams and fruits. Cover with water 2" above the top of the jars. Bring the canner to a boil, and boil for 30 minutes. Let it cool, and remove the jars to a wooden cutting board or towel-covered surface. As they cool to room temperature, the lids will seal with a pop. Once cool, store away in a safe spot. It will remain bacteria-free indefinitely. Once again, living parasites are destroyed, but dangerous chemicals or metals may remain.

If you see white sediment settling out in your canned water, it's probably minerals from your "hard" water supply, not very good tasting but generally not harmful, either. Scoop out when you use the water, or pass through a coffee filter.

Countertop Water Filters

Moderately priced gravity water filters are among the most popular, easy to use, and effective methods of making questionable water safely drinkable. On average, these cost $200 to $300 each, and individual filter elements are about $25 to $50 each.

The Big Berkey is one of the best known; it's been around for decades and according to their advertising will remove bacteria, parasites and cysts, as well as herbicides, pesticides, solvents, radon and trihalomethanes – and reduces nitrites, nitrates, lead, mercury and, with a separate filter, fluoride. There are multiple sized Berkeys, as well. Filter elements are secured to the top container, water is added, and it passes through the filter elements and drips into the lower container. A spigot lets you get your water directly from the clean holding portion. Although they come in a pretty blue plastic form, get the stainless steel one. It will outlast you, won't break if you drop it, and still works if it's dinged or bent.

A nice feature is that you can test the effectiveness of your filters by adding red food coloring to the top (unfiltered) container. The filtered water should come out of the spigot clear, showing that the filtration is thorough. Filter elements last about 6,000 gallons. If your family filters 3 gallons of water daily for drinking and cooking, your filters should last around 2,000 days, a little over 5 years, before the filter elements need to be replaced.

Filter elements are easy to take out and put in. Each element consists of a ceramic outer layer surrounding carbon and other filtration components. Water passes slowly through the outer ceramic, then through the inner carbon combination, and out of the filter elements into the holding tank. There are two types of filters, white and black; both remove bacteria and unpleasant flavors. The black one also filters out other chemicals and metals (read their literature to see if it meets your needs). Filter elements are moderately fragile and may shatter if dropped. Get extras.

Similar gravity fed countertop systems include the Swiss-made Katadyn and Alexa Pure. Prices and filtration capacity is similar to the Berkey. These are all currently available online – just search by the names. None of these are the same as the big box store "pitcher filter," which does NOT remove bacteria; it merely removes unpleasant chemical flavors.

You can put together a lower cost homemade version of these gravity fed filter systems You still need to buy the filter elements and rubberized gaskets as well as a spigot. The homemade gravity filter consists of a 5-gallon bucket mounted atop another 5-gallon bucket. The filter elements are set into holes drilled through the bottom of the top bucket, and the spigot is set into a hole drilled in the side of the lower bucket. Water is poured into the top bucket to pass through the filter elements and collect in the bottom one.

Voila! Keep in mind that even food grade plastic will get micro scratches in it over time that can harbor bacteria, so you may need to change out your buckets from time to time. Otherwise, it's as good as any of the table-top models.

Obviously, none of these gravity filters "work" if you are putting snow into the top, unless you are in an environment where the snow will melt quickly. Even so, you'd risk shattering or damaging the filter elements if they are packed with snow or ice. Don't leave your filter system outdoors in the cold, for the same reason. Better to fill a large multi-gallon kettle with snow and ice, and place it near or on your wood heating stove. Melt the snow first – melt, NOT boil - then pass it through your water filter system.

Sand Filter

This Third World approach is ideal for any long term low cost application for improving the potable quality (drinkability) of your water. Healthy sand filters develop a "biolayer" at the top surface of the sand, that is rather like a living filter system. This is what makes the sand filter able to remove virtually all but 0.02% of the protozoa, almost 99% of the bacteria, over 80% of the *E. coli,* and many viruses and reducing diarrheal disorders by half. This design was developed for use in Third World countries to help keep their water clean.

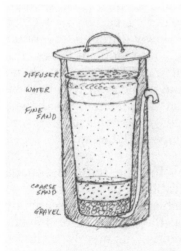

The design is straightforward. All you need is some kind of stable container such as a plastic rain barrel or a concrete "barrel" shaped holder, builder's sand, and a length of hose or plastic pipe. An on/off faucet arrangement is optional.

Here is the design in a nutshell. The top area is where water is poured in by bucket. The diffuser plate is just a flat punctured sieve, like the basket in an old coffee percolator. This is used so that the water poured into the top doesn't disturb and damage the biolayer.

Below that, a gap for the biolayer and liquids, which is at the same height as your outflow spigot. Next, fine sand, then a couple inches of coarse sand, and then at the bottom some clean gravel. The outlet hose or pipe takes the water from the very bottom, after it has filtered through all that sand. Because of water's response to atmospheric pressure, the water in your filter will start coming out of the spigot when the water you pour in fills to the same level. If you want water to keep coming out the spigot, you keep pouring water in the top. So, there will always be some water sitting in your filter, waiting for you to activate the flow by adding more water.

The filter will develop a healthy mature biolayer – growing things - over time. When your filter is fresh and new, it won't be quite as efficient at filtering bacteria and protozoa, so be sure you treat the water that you drink, by boiling or adding bleach. Keep a lid on your sand filter, and don't pipe rainwater directly into it. The sudden inflow will disturb the biolayer.

The sand filter begins to outflow almost as soon as you put water in it. Remember, this filter won't remove heavy metals or chemicals.

Key points: *use a separate bucket to fill the filter tank, and a fresh clean one to collect the output.* Otherwise, you risk contaminating your fresh water by collecting it in a dirty bucket. *Pass dirty water through a cheesecloth or t-shirt before putting it into the filter.* You may need to clean your filter annually by digging out all the sand and either sun drying it or replacing it entirely. Leave in the hot sun for a day or two, turning once or twice, then return to the filter.

Even though this is a very workable and effective filter, if you have *any* doubts about your water's bacteria level, boil it before use.

> The sand filter is an ideal long-term type of filtration system –
> *a Zen-slap and beyond solution.*
> Protect this filter from freezing.
> A greenhouse is the perfect permanent location.

Collecting Water

Water comes from only two sources: the sky and the ground, and what is in and on the ground came first from the sky. The intermittent water from the sky eventually enters the ground, so in a non-desert region, ground water is *usually* the most predictable and consistent source. It is also the more challenging source to utilize. So, we will look at rain collection first.

How much water do you need?

The current recommendation from the federal preparedness website ready.gov and the Red Cross is that you should store 1 gallon of water per day per person for emergency use. That works out to 7 gallons for one week; 30 gallons per month for one person. If there's four people in your family, that's 120 gallons for one month. Hang onto that number for a few moments.

To figure your actual water usage now, you can simply check your water bill for your monthly total. Don't be surprised if it works out to 80-100 gallons of water *per person per day,* 3000 gallons per month for one person and up to 12,000 gallons for a family of four....assuming you don't water the lawn and forget to turn the hose off for a few hours. That does include flushing toilets, taking showers, brushing teeth, washing hands, washing dishes and laundry, and filling the coffee pot. In other words, the "recommended emergency water supply" for four people for 30 days, is about the same as you *alone* use in *one day*. Stated another way, the Federal recommendation is about 100 times LESS than you actually use.

How exactly did the emergency management agencies come up with their "one gallon per person per day" figure? I've tried to track that information to its original source. Best I can determine, they just made it up. That tiny quantity of water is supposed to cover drinking, hygiene, and cooking, too. A recent study demonstrated that the actual minimum used in disaster recovery efforts is closer to 4-7 gallons per person per day, more when the inevitable post-disaster diarrhea occurs. And, in hot weather conditions, 10 gallons per person per day is not unreasonable. At 10 gallons per person per day, for a family of four, that's 40 gallons per day – 1200 gallons per month.

For now, consider that 10 gallons per person per day an absolute minimum figure – enough to drink, cook, take a "sponge bath", and maybe wash your socks or flush once.

If you have to water a garden or provide for livestock, your usage goes up considerably. One cow will drink, on average, 24 gallons of water a day. Clearly, storing that much water requires enormous holding capacity – multiple containers, ponds, or holding tanks, plus a means to clean the water so that you aren't introducing disease-causing organisms into your system.

Collecting Water in Quantity

Any upturned non porous container will collect useable water every time it rains. Using that concept, people have been placing the humble water barrel underneath any dripping water during rain storms. In fact, even in the terrible desert regions of the Middle East, ancient civilizations channeled their infrequent rainfall into water collectors to hold until they needed it.

The easiest way to quickly collect water is to set a water barrel or clean plastic trash can beneath a downspout from your home's rain gutters. Next time it rains, water flows to the gutters, into the downspout and into your barrel. *This is not clean water.* It will contain bits of roof asphalt gravel unless you have a painted metal or tile roof, bird droppings, bits of leaf or tree branches, feathers, insects, city or country road dust, and other unsavory materials. You must filter and purify this water, just as you would for any stream or river water to drink it.

A typical water barrel, the kind you can get at hardware stores, or a plastic trash can, can hold 40 to 55 gallons of water. This brings up the next issue: how much water can you collect in your barrel during a rainstorm?

Let's say you have a typical 1000 square foot roof. Assume you receive an inch of rain – a mild rain. That means that water one inch deep and 12" x 12" falls on every square foot of roof – or 144 cubic inches of rain per square foot.

A gallon is 231 cubic inches of water. So, each square foot of roof collects a little more than a half-gallon of water.

Therefore, that small roof could

potentially deliver over 500 gallons of water, in one rainfall. That would be *10 rain barrels, from one roof during one rain.* Of course, realistically not all that rain would be collected. Some bounces off, some washes out of the gutters, and some slops out of the barrel. Even so, that's enough for a family of four to run for a good week, if you're being conservative with your usage. A bigger rain, longer duration storm, larger collection area, multiple storms, or more seasonal rain could provide greater quantities of usable water.

With a larger holding tank, such as the large round white plastic ones sold at farm stores, you could potentially hold anywhere from 500 to 2000 gallons. These come in all shapes, sizes, and materials. The plastic ones generally cost about a dollar per gallon new. Squared off tanks with a metal cage  around them can be set in place on a trailer and filled for transport, if you need to. Secure it well, because moving water sloshes and tanks can overturn easily. Stainless steel tanks are more expensive, but will last just about forever. Good used "bulk milk tanks" – stainless steel - can be found for sale around farming communities and at farm auctions.

Plastic tanks must be shielded from the sun: the water will develop algae if warm and exposed to sunlight, and the plastic will degrade over time from the sun's ultraviolet rays. Plus, during hard frozen weather, the water can freeze, expand, and rupture it, even in a large metal tank.

Ideally, then, the tank is either underground or covered with a heavy insulating layer that keeps out light and stabilizes the temperature above freezing. A thick layer of cement, worked in over a metal and wire frame (ferro concrete) can also be used over the insulating layer to shield the tank from light and provide physical protection as well. If going this route, don't plan to ever move the tank again.

Tanks that are above ground are easier to access than underground ones. A simple faucet drain near the base lets gravity help feed the outgoing water into a hose, then into a bucket to bring indoors. If the holding tank is placed on a slope above your home, you can pipe the water directly into your plumbing system. All pipes should be well insulated *and* deep enough that they are below frost lines, which will be significantly deeper during the Little Ice Age ahead of us.

Many country farms still have old holding tanks, cisterns, next to their kitchens or barns. These cisterns are basically huge thousand gallon underground "thermos bottles", dug by hand, bricked up, and plastered with a thick water-resistant mortar.

Water entered from the roof through gutters and down spouts, and a drain hole near the top let excess wash out before it overflowed. A simple hand-pump brought the water right to the kitchen sink. Every couple years, the interior needed to be emptied, dried out, and re-mortared – that was the extent of the maintenance. Unfortunately, over the years too many old cisterns were turned into trash containers, or filled with gravel, or covered and forgotten when electricity and water wells became more common.

There are similar approaches still in use, with modern plastic or composite tanks buried underground. Incoming water passes through sediment filtration, then into the tank. Excess water can be released through an overflow pipe. A simple electric submersion pump is utilized to bring the water up from the tank – but a hand pump could be used just as readily. If you go with a hand pump, be sure to get REAL leathers – the gasket within the pump; plastic and rubber just don't work as well. Good ideas, like cisterns, can still be very useful and readily duplicated.

Downspout Diversion

When water pours off a roof, particularly after a dry spell, the first

rain washes off the roof – and flushes dust, leaves, bird droppings, dead bugs, whatever has accumulated over time into the collection system. It's not possible to remove all possible contaminants, which is why filtering your drinking water is essential no matter what the source, as we have already discussed. However, removing as many possible contaminants as you can makes end-filtering just that much easier, and helps your stored water stay clear.

A downspout diversion is what it sounds like: any method that permits the first gallons of water off a roof or collection system to flow away from the barrel or container, thus flushing the nasties away. After several gallons have been diverted, the system reverts to filling the container.

The simplest and least expensive method of water diversion is to move the downspout by hand away from the container – let the water flow to the ground for a few minutes – then move it back to

position. Naturally, that means walking out into the rain, with all the nuisance associated with that.

Inverted "Y" shaped diverters do the same thing simply by moving a lever so water travels out of the holding container or into it. The end result is cleaner water in storage. Remember, it still needs to be purified for human consumption. Pets and livestock can drink it as it is, though.

Accessing the Water

In the US, from about 100W longitude to the east coast, adequate rain falls to keep crops and fields going without much in the way of additional watering. From that point to the west coast, rainfall is much less reliable. Right now, farming and at-home water use is mostly handled by pumping groundwater from underground water reserves and above ground dam water impounds.

Adequate water to raise crops...now. That doesn't mean that there is *always* sufficient water. There are wet years and dry years, and sometimes crops and homes are inundated and sometimes they are dusty dry. The whole point of holding water in ponds, cisterns, tanks, and pulling it up from underground reservoirs, is to make the water available when and where you want it.

When the cold arrives in force, what happens to that previously predictable cycle? It's likely to change. If our coming Age of Ice is like the Maunder Minimum cold, it's likely that the northeast and upper central US will be markedly colder and snowier; the west coast wetter and stormier; and the deep south drier and colder. Western Europe is likely to be colder and wetter, with thick ice and deep snow. Indian monsoons may not arrive, and snow appears in unexpected places. Equatorial regions will see snow and frosts. Other currently moderate areas will become terribly dry and may experience unpredictable sudden downpours. In fact, all continents will be severely affected. Some areas, like Alaska, will be milder.

That change in seasonal behavior becomes a major factor in your water storage, one that is going to require adjustments somewhere down the line that simply cannot be predicted right now. At this time, a thousand gallon plastic tank of water can sit on the ground to supply your needs – but a decade in the future, that tank might freeze solid in October and not thaw out until April. A large full tank or series of smaller tanks in a protected basement might not freeze solid – slushy water is still usable water -- especially if heat from the house is ducted there or if your primary heater is located in the basement. Be creative.

If you run water pipes through the ground, say, from a holding tank to your home, you may have to locate them significantly deeper than the current "frost line" which is now anywhere from 4 to 6 feet deep in the US. If you place your holding tank in-ground, keep in mind the problem with deep cold. Even in the ground, hundreds of gallons of water can freeze and rupture a tank.

If you are in a region with heavy snow and ice, your water is right there. You just have to break it up and carry it indoors to warmer temperatures so that it can melt. It will take a LOT of snow to melt down to use for drinking and utility water supplies. A snow and ice filled 5 gallon bucket, for example, melts down to only a few inches of water in the bottom.

By the way, you don't necessarily need to melt snow to clean clothing. It is possible to "wash" clothing by placing it on snow and agitating it, by walking over it in clean shoes, for example – no, it doesn't come out nice and white and fluffy. The agitation loosens grime and the cold allows it to work its way out. Odors are reduced a bit, too. However, underwear and socks should be soak-washed in very hot water. Anything that is next to your skin needs to be kept clean to reduce bacterial risks during long cold winters. It will be a different world than we are accustomed to now.

Ponds and Swales

Any methods of catching and holding water for later use that are simple and reliable will be just that much more of a bonus for you. Everything that simplifies your day will be valuable. You will work harder during the cold and spend more time working because everything takes longer when you are bundled up and having to struggle through deep snow or keep your balance on ice.

A swale is, effectively, a low spot that collects and holds moisture: a swamp, ditch, or low level in a hillside contour meets the definition. In the Ozark hill country during the 1930's, Civilian Conservation Corp (CCC) workers dug – by hand – long trenches over hilly farmland to reduce erosion from gully washer rainstorms. Many of these swales directed water flow into natural or dug ponds, as well, which allowed the collection of water during spring rains for use during the summer dry spells. There's no reason the same can't be accomplished today using a tractor with a plow attachment or even with a small backhoe.

In regions with intensely dry periods, swales can be utilized as naturally moist areas for growing thirsty crops, say, fruit trees. More on this in the next chapter. Swales freeze during the cold if they have moisture in them.

Ponds are simply low collection points for water. Natural or manmade ponds also end up harboring all sorts of wildlife, many of which can contribute to your food supply. The larger and deeper a pond is, the more water and growing food it can hold. A deep pond can overwinter fish, at this time, even during regular cold whereas a shallow pond might freeze to the bottom and cause the wildlife to die off. Frogs and turtles and some fish burrow into mud at the sides and bottoms of ponds, and they can often make it through severe freezing.

Never walk on a partially frozen pond, even a shallow one. That's an invitation to drowning. Livestock need to be monitored so they don't slip onto the ice and into the pond; they won't last long in that cold water. Consider fencing livestock away from the pond itself, and setting up a small drain that leads into a watering trough or hole. That'll protect the water from disturbance by the animals, and prevent winter ice accidents.

In periods of very extreme cold, an entire pond can freeze solid, making it almost impossible to get liquid water from it. Wood fires set in a metal container atop a pond will thaw the ice around it a little for livestock to use, until the fire goes out. I have not tried one, but a Fresnel lens (basically, a large magnifying glass) might be used to melt a small part of a pond on a sunny day. Wear a dark WELDING HELMET if you do this. Don't let anyone even *look* at either a Fresnel lens in use, or even the spot it is hitting on a sunny day; it is bright enough to permanently damage vision.

Any pond fed by a natural spring is worth its weight is gold. Underground springs may help keep the pond from freezing completely, especially around the in-feed point. Because the water in a spring fed pond generally "moves" from the flow into it, the water is often less likely to develop issues related to low oxygen than a static collection pond might. If it is cold enough, even a spring fed pond can freeze solid.

If you have a pond, stock it with fish. The type doesn't matter, because all fish are edible, although some taste better than others. Catfish and carp such as goldfish are hardy in cold weather and can live in cloudy water.

During the awakening phase, consider putting in a moderate size children's swimming pool. For a couple hundred dollars, you can store over 2500 gallons of water in an above-ground 12 ft x 3 ft pool. A cup of chlorine bleach stirred in the water every 10 days or so will keep it in good condition. Cover with a dark or black cover when it starts to get cool in the fall. The dark cover will act to heat the water a little and reduce the risk of it freezing. If it does freeze, the expansion of the water may ruin the pool liner, though. After we have entered the Zen-slap stage, the kiddie pool can still be used to collect water in the warmer months off your roof. Use it to water livestock and the garden. For human drinking use, water needs to be boiled or filtered. Take it down during the fall and store it over winter.

A kiddie pool can also be used to raise frogs. Collect any tadpoles or jelly-like masses of frog eggs you find in the spring, and put into the pool. Don't use any bleach in this water. Keep the top open so that bugs get in. They feed the frogs. Toss some good garden dirt in the bottom. Float a few dry tree branches and make a pile of rocks in the center that rises above the water level, so your frogs can get some sun when they want it. Frog legs are a delicacy at this time, but can be a wholesome food at any time. It takes a lot of frog legs to make a meal, so grow lots of frogs. Empty your frog pool when weather starts to cool off in the fall, and store it for use the next year.

Water Facts

Gallon = 231 in³ (cubic inches)
= 128 fluid ounces
= 8.3 pounds
12" snow = 1" water
1000 gallons of water = 8,300 pounds

---

6 FOOD: PRODUCING YOUR OWN

Obtaining and storing your food is going to be a primary consideration during the coming ice age. The ability to grow and hold your food will be a *defining feature* of you and your family's survival. Expect to see prices going up in the next two years, along with shortages of some items. Being able to bring your own food to the table may be a literal lifesaver.

If you are a beginning gardener, you will have a very steep learning curve, and you risk losing everything because you are inexperienced and will miss something that might be obvious to a more skilled grower. That's why you'll need to have as much stored basic food supplies as possible – to allow for the inevitable mistakes. Start *right now* growing something, and keep adding on.

If you are already an experienced gardener or food producer, you are miles ahead of the pack. But you will have to unlearn and relearn food growing in cold and unstable conditions, so don't expect what you know today to always apply. That's why you need backup food supplies, too. Don't assume you'll always be able to grow as much as you have in the past – and you may even have entire years when you can't get much more than turnips. And you'll be glad you have those.

Once again, this is an enormous topic and cannot be covered in detail in one chapter. I will hit some critical aspects of growing your own food – including: choosing plants that can tolerate cold conditions, fast and long producers, saving seeds, corn and wheat as home grains, fertilizing without chemicals, dealing with insects, old tech such as fruit walls, in home and underground greenhouses, as well as ancient storage techniques. But you've still got to collect information, paper books, to help you figure things out during those situations when you can't contact outside assistance. Most importantly, you must *do* this, not just read about it. You learn by *doing*, not by *thinking*.

Here are the two "must have" books for both beginner and advanced growers:

Gardening When it Counts: Growing Food in Hard Times, by Steve Solomon. Published by Mother Earth News Wiser Series. About $21.95, less if used.

Backyard Winter Gardening: Vegetables Fresh and Simple in Any Climate Without Heat and Electricity – the Way it's Been Done for 2000 Years, by Caleb Warnock.
Published by Cedar Fort, Inc. $18.99 or less on Amazon.

Choose Plants that Tolerate Cold

There are few things more tasty than a fresh-from the garden tomato, picked and eaten within minutes, right from the vine. Tomatoes are relatively easy to grow, productive, and have multiple uses in salads, sauces, salsas, and even as a sweet jam. I adore tomatoes, and will grow them as long as I can – but tomatoes cannot tolerate cold. A single 32°F frost will wither an otherwise heathy plant and ruin green tomatoes on the vine.

During the Maunder Minimum Little Ice Age, crops growing in mid-summer were decimated by sudden and unexpected snow – costing the entire harvest. The result was famine, starvation, and death. We have history, now, as our guide. We must not only plant warm-season foods in summer – we *must* keep cold tolerant plants *in the ground all seasons.* When the cold comes in unexpectedly, you may lose your tomatoes and squash, but you'll still have plenty to eat.

Here is a list of garden plants that can tolerate some cold to intense cold:

- Chinese cabbage (Michihili)

- Heading cabbage and Broccoli (tolerant to frost but not deep cold)
- Choi
- Mizuna
- Turnips*
- Brussel Sprouts
- Kale
- Beets*
- Carrots*
- Radishes*
- Parsnips*
- Rutabaga*
- Horseradish*
- Onions (green sprouting ones)
- Garlic*
- Mustard greens
- Mangels (sugar beets)*
- Leeks
- Salsify*
- Peas, especially Tom Thumb and Lincoln
- Lima beans, Henderson Bush, grows best in cool but not freezing weather

(Items with a * grow their main crop under the soil surface.)

Ideally, a serious grower would plant these in spring, then replant a second crop in mid-to-late summer that would stand in the garden into the fall and winter. That way, there's always something growing that will survive a sudden cold spell or hail storm. You'd have some to eat and store in the summer, and still have plants you could leave in "cold storage" in the ground for the winter.

Root vegetables, including beets, rutabagas, potatoes (Irish, not sweet "yams"), radishes, carrots, and parsnips are critically important to have in your garden, even if you don't particularly enjoy eating them. All of these will survive unexpected hail and freezes that destroys the above-ground tops, and will start growing again after the storm passes. *Some* food is better than *no* food.

Additionally, plant your usual summer garden with tomatoes, sweet potatoes, corn, melons, squash, whatever you like and could potentially can or preserve for winter use. Try to find ones that mature "early", in case you don't get a full growing season. Valencia Melon (a football shaped muskmelon), and Winter King and Queen

Watermelon also have the added quality of being able to hold in storage for several months. Have "fresh" melons at Christmas!

For perennial plants, consider varieties that originated in Siberia, China, or other chilly places. Three that I can recommend from experience are the berry bush Aronia, Sand Cherries, and Manchurian Bush Apricots. Aronia is highly productive of a purple berry that is just loaded with antioxidants. Ads for this bush describe the flavor as "tart", but "sour" would be a better descriptor. This means that birds aren't all that excited about it, either, which is good news for the gardener. Plant 5 or 10 of these to assure lots of cross pollination and plenty of berries -- even if you have to sweeten the juice, you'll still have some nutritious fruit.

Sand cherry is a hardy bush plant, with two primary domestic varieties: Hansen's Bush, and Nanking Bush. They are both members of the cherry tribe, but not quite the same as the luscious sweet cherries you might find in the supermarket. Bush cherries are more like the tart sour pie cherry, but half the size. The plants are highly productive of small fruit, and begin to fruit when quite young. Plant a long row of these, because birds like them, too. These plants can come through when other domestic fruits do not.

Manchurian Bush Apricot is a type of hardy apricot that can tolerate nasty cold and come through. The fruit is virtually the same as a tree apricot, but about half the size. Makes a wonderful jam or pie. Plant a half dozen or more bushes to allow for cross pollination.

Critical Crops Not Adapted to Cold

There are two primary crops that are critical to our usual Western diets, which are unlikely to do well during Cold Times: wheat and corn. Historically, both require about 90 non-freezing days to come to harvest. A regional failure can be catastrophic if you are as dependent upon them as we are....another reason for holding back a two-year supply of these important items.

At this writing in early 2017, cold and wet weather has triggered an outbreak of wheat diseases in the Middle East and in Europe. This may, in part, be because of the mono-cropping of commercial varieties there. Or, perhaps we are entering a new situation where harvests will be hampered by wheat diseases as well as the weather.

By mid-2017, nearly half the wheat crop in Kansas was lost to the weather.

That said, your particular region may still be suitable for growing one or both of these, at least some years. Because these are so important, I'm including more information here.

More About Wheat

The typical American eats about 130 pounds of wheat and wheat products annually as bread, cake, pasta, cookies, cereal. That is down from 225 pounds in the 1880s, a change attributed to the interest in low-carb diets. Wheat also makes a decent livestock feed, with anywhere from 7 to 14 percent protein depending on variety and where it is grown. Wheat products add calories, variety, and "fill" to meals, important when food is limited.

Wheat can produce remarkable amounts of food for small planting areas – a 12'x12' plot of good garden soil sown thickly and well-managed, can give you 60 pounds of wheat harvest – that's enough for a one-pound loaf of bread every week for a year! That is a small enough space that most backyard gardens could accommodate growing wheat. Double or triple that space, and you can feed a family with bread, cake, and pasta.

Varieties and Seasonal Growth

Wheat has been bred to produce best in specific areas, and is either planted in spring for fall harvest, or fall for harvest the following late summer. The fall-planted wheat is called "winter" wheat, and can be *lightly* grazed by livestock during the late fall and early winter. It goes dormant during cold weather, and starts regrowing in the spring.

- Hard red winter wheat, used for bread flour, grows in Montana through Texas, fall planting.
- Hard red spring wheat is usually blended with soft white wheats to increase the protein level; it's good for breads. It is grown mostly in Montana, North and South Dakota, and Minnesota. Spring planted.
- Soft red winter wheat, is good for pastries, cakes, cookies and crackers. It is grown in the east and along the

Mississippi River. Winter planted.
- White wheat is used for noodles, cereals and softer less-glutinous breads. It is grown in Idaho, Washington and Oregon. Winter and sometimes spring planted.
- Durum wheat, one of the best for pasta, is grown in the colder regions of Montana and the Dakotas. Spring planted.

How Much Will it Produce?

It takes about 100 pounds of grain to plant an acre, about 1-1/2 bushels. A bushel of wheat is 60 pounds. In the 1940s, 20 bushels, 1200 pounds, per acre was good production. Today with intensive planting, fertilization, and herbicides/pesticides, 150 bushels--9000 pounds--per acre are not uncommon. Consider, if you are harvesting by hand after SHTF, that 20 bushels is great production – more than that is just gravy. Plant more than you think you'll need to allow for growing difficulties.

Starter Seeds

If you want to try wheat, buy your startup seeds at your local feed store, or ask your county extension agent to suggest a regionally-adapted variety. Keep in mind that wheat has been highly adapted for modern industrial agriculture, and will likely grow best with chemical fertilizer and may need herbicides to deal with weed issues.

As of 2015, no GMO wheat was grown commercially, but there are at least 2 GMO wheat varieties awaiting a more positive regulatory environment. Wheat has been modified by techniques of purposeful genetic mutation (not the same as GMOs), which has added genes to the original wheat plant type. I suspect these issues contribute to why so many people find themselves unable to digest it, or have health issues related to wheat-product consumption.

A source of livestock manure such as chickens, hogs, rabbits, cattle, horses, can provide "natural" fertilizer for your seeds. Just make sure it is well-composted and spread evenly to avoid burning the young plants.

If you prefer to grow heirloom wheat, look for sources NOW. They will disappear after the Zen-slap. Grow a small plot to decide if this is what you really want. Heirloom varieties tend to produce smaller harvests, but are hardier and more disease and weather resistant crops. Ancient varieties, such as einkorn, kamut, or spelt, are lower in gluten as well – meaning they won't produce the light, fluffy "air bread" to which we are accustomed – but may be tolerated better by folks who are gluten-sensitive. You can save seeds from year to year, too.

One wheat which might have some ability to survive colder weather is RED FIFE, an heirloom variety originally grown in the cooler parts of the American northeast states. I have never grown this one, so I can't provide personal experience. It's at Baker Seeds.

Sowing and Harvesting

Planting wheat by hand is fairly straightforward. A growing area is selected, and the soil is turned or broken by raking or light tilling. Weeds should be cleared out as much as possible. Then, you can "broadcast" that is, throw out, the seeds. Work toward even coverage, seeding heavily enough to get about 1 or 2 per square inch. It's not necessary to be exact.

Next, cover the seeds with a little soil – use a rake or just walk over the area to force the seeds into the ground. Birds will eat any that remain exposed. Water lightly to stabilize the soil, if possible, and then leave it alone. Water only if it gets dry. Like grass, it does the rest on its own. Winter wheat stops growing when it gets too cold, goes dormant, and starts growing again when it warms up. Spring wheat should be planted when frosts are less likely to happen. It can tolerate some light freezing once it is growing well.

It is ready to harvest when the stalks are golden brown and the seed heads are beginning to droop. You can open a handful of kernels – they should be plump, and a little chewy to firm.

Although growing wheat is easy, harvesting it is not. Lacking a wheat combine and tractor plus fuel and repair supplies, the tall grassy plants must be cut down with clippers or a scythe and stacked so that they can finish air drying. Clipping is tiring and must be done stooped over to cut at the bottom of the tall stems. Scything is a learned skill, and requires constant blade re-sharpening AND good mobility, strong back, and upper-body strength as well as a scythe, which should be purchased NOW if you plan to do this. Check Lehman's online for old-time supplies.

Stack the wheat stems, with seeds still in their pods, alternating armloads in layers so that the seed parts are toward the outside of the "stook", or gather up several armloads and run a bit of twine around the area just below the seed heads – this will form a tipi-shaped bunch. Set it on end with the seeds at the top to dry.

It can stand in the field for a few days to a week until the stems are crispy dry. Then, hope you don't have a cold wet weather phase or your harvest will mold or mildew and become inedible. If that is coming, bring it under a shed or cover to protect it. Do not eat or feed to livestock any wheat or rye that has a black "smutty" mold on it – it might be a type that can cause hallucinations and death.

Next, the wheat kernels must be "threshed" or separated from the stems and husks. For a backyard operation, the dried stems and seed heads can be laid on a tarp and beaten with plastic baseball bats – the modern equivalent of a "wheat flail" – to loosen and separate the seeds.

After several hours of flailing, the stems can be hand-separated, and the seeds and smaller plant material poured from the tarp into buckets.

Now, the seeds are "winnowed," that is, separated from the "chaff" (the plant stems and other debris) -- by pouring from one bucket into another during a windy day. The heavier seeds will fall into the lower bucket, while the lighter chaff is carried away on the breeze.

If you have flailed and winnowed the wheat well, you'll have nice clean grain ready to dry a bit, grind, and make into bread. If your effort was lackluster, you'll have hulls and stemmy material in your grain. You can grind and eat that with the kernels, but the high fiber ratio will give you poor, tough bread.

Scything, threshing and winnowing is a LOT of work, for a small amount of food. Growing and processing wheat into flour is, ideally, the work of an extended family or community. More hands make the tedious effort into lighter work.

Eating Wheat

You can eat wheat sprouted, whole, or ground. Sprouted wheat produces a green shoot, "wheat grass," and is eaten when it is about 2" tall. Grow just like any sprouted seed with daily water washing and good sunlight. Whole kernels can be treated like rice, boiled until soft and chewy, and then herbed like rice or sweetened, buttered, mixed into milk or cream, with nuts or dried fruit added like oatmeal and enjoyed.

Grinding wheat is easiest with a good-quality hand grinder. The Corona Mill, a cheap cast metal product (about $70), will grind your wheat – but you'll have to pass it through several times to get flour fine enough for bread. By far the best I have used is the Country Living Grain Mill (around $400), which takes only one or two passes to get good flour and can be set up to use a treadle or bicycle-powered pulley with some creativity. Today, with the grid humming smoothly, I use a Braun coffee grinder to finely grind one cup of wheat berries at a time. Four cups or so makes a loaf of whole wheat bread.

Home ground whole wheat produces a sturdy loaf of bread. You just plain won't get the puffy stuff that the supermarket provides. You will need to store yeast, as well, or keep a "starter" going to raise your bread. See the Recipes section for one way to make bread.

More About Corn

Corn is familiar, easy to grow, easy to harvest, and easy to store. It lends itself to fresh eating, drying, livestock feeding, quick breads and muffins, breading on other foods, and breakfast grits....not to mention backyard brewing. Prior to mechanization of farming, a typical small holding could grow 20 bushels per acre – a bushel of corn is about 50 pounds, so that's about a half-ton of corn. Given modern high production methods, tractors and harvesters, chemical fertilizer, herbicides and pesticides, and extensive genetic modification, a 150 bushel per acre crop is not uncommon. Plan on the smaller production, or less, with the arrival of Cold Times. Because corn is sensitive to cold, you may not get a crop at all.

The best thing about corn, though, is that you can plant and harvest an acre *by yourself* without anything other than a pair of hands.

Leather gloves and a "corn hook", a flat metal hook worn in the palm of the hand to help when "shucking" [removing] the husks, will make it easier, though.

Varieties

All varieties of corn can be eaten as baby cobs at 1-2" long, before the seeds form; "green" like a sweet corn right off the cob; roasted in the husks; and dried and ground or parched. Popcorn is in there, too, but has the advantage of being fairly consistent when oil-popped. All corns can be fed to livestock, on the cob or shelled off, including popcorn. So, even though there are remarkable differences between corn varieties, they're all food.

There are three broad basic types, with lots of overlap: "sweet", "field", and "pop". *Sweet* corn is generally viewed as the familiar type eaten fresh off the cob. Today, we have varieties specifically bred for that table use. *Field* corns are consumed dried and used as animal feeds. Two types of field corn, "flint" and "dent" can be separated by how the kernel dries. Dent corn has a dent in the top of each kernel, but flint does not. *Popcorn* dries rounded, so when popping it expands more uniformly than other types.

What we know as "sweet" corn is merely a lengthened stage in the development of the kernel. All corn types, including *flour* or *field* corn, goes through a sweet stage on the way to the full maturity of the kernel.

Corn that has reached "milk" stage is sweet, tasty and table ready. Most commercial varieties reach that at 60-90 days of growth. Corn that has passed milk stage is invariably starchy and chewy -- doesn't matter whether it is sold as a "sweet" corn or a "field" corn.

Modern table sweet corn varieties have been commercially developed to remain in the milk stage for LONG periods of time. That allows harvest to proceed to storage to shipping to placement in the supermarket, then to be brought home, set in the refrigerator until whatever meal, and then cooked and served. So the milk stage can last for weeks to even a month or more, if refrigerated.

That is a genetic aberration, the product of hybridization and mutations (really)! "Super" sweet hybrid varieties actually have genetic mutations that were the result of atomic tests in the 1950s and 1960s. Yes, atomic radiation created the mutants we find in the supermarkets. Historical article links are in the information resources section.

Open pollinated heirloom corn, like Stowell's Evergreen and Wade's Giant, have a short milk stage, sometimes as short as 3 days. Each ear ripens on its own schedule, so it doesn't all reach milk stage at the same time, either. You can pick an ear off of side-by-side stalks, and one is perfect, the other starchy.

Traditionally, the best table corn was picked at milk stage, shucked and raced into the kitchen, so that there was three minutes or less between field and boiling water. The boiling water "set" the sweetness, and voila! Perfect sweet corn on the table, and perfect field corn still growing outside.

You can determine milk stage, by carefully opening an ear on the stalk in the field. Press a few kernels with your thumbnail until they break. If the fluid coming from the kernel looks milky, you're there! If it is thin, it's not ready; if thick and pasty, it's past it.

Stowell's Evergreen was an unusual variety in that it would store in the milk stage a bit longer than other types. Typically, you'd pull the entire plant when the kernels were in milk, and hang it upside down until you wanted corn. When it went past milk stage, you could still use it on the table, but the kernels were stripped from the cobs and cooked with milk and sugar to produce something like what we know today as "creamed corn".

Corn can be eaten in any stage, from the tiniest unpollinated cobs as you'll find in Chinese cooking, to the fully mature hard dried kernels which can be ground into cornmeal for bread and feed. It's helpful to keep in mind that the *stuff* they sell in the supermarket is a far cry from the real food people ate a few generations ago. It's more like "sugar on the cob" from the atomic mutations, than "protein on the cob", which is what heirloom corns actually are.

Variety Selection

Selecting corns to grow should be based on your end need and your growing conditions. Since it has such broad uses, my preference is for a variety that will feed us and our livestock, plus grow quickly in what might be extreme circumstances – weather abnormalities, poor soil, high winds, sudden cold, or lack of regular rain. In a severe situation, I'll have enough to do without having to baby any tenderfoot crops.

Also, because I plan to save seeds, it will have to be open-pollinated, not a hybrid. I want corn that has a lot of genetic variability, too, so that after a few generations it isn't so inbred that "genetic depression," a loss of vigor happens...I may not be able to buy replacements.

To keep a corn strain pure, growers must separate them by a half mile, or by growing varieties so they pollinate at different times – and I don't have that much land, and maybe won't have enough time in one season for two plantings. My early thoughts were to have five or six unrelated varieties together in the field, and let them cross freely. Then select the hardiest from that and keep it going. Fortunately, someone else had the same idea a while ago and did the work for us.

Dave Christiansen wanted to grow corn in the harsh, short Montana summers, so he began looking for old types of original native corns that did well in that area. After decades, he had bred together dozens of lines of some of the last surviving examples of ancient hardy corn and developed what he called Painted Mountain. This is a multicolored corn that produces well in cold, dry conditions and short but hot Montana summers. It's also fairly high protein, around 13%, and at least one grower (Rocky Mountain Corn, see references) guarantees it to be free of GMO contamination.

Painted Mountain Alpine can be planted in chilly soil, much earlier than most other varieties. Sprouts can tolerate light frost. It's pretty wind-tolerant, and can be planted just 8 inches apart. Plants grow only 3 to 4 feet tall, and produce one or two ears per stalk, usually down low on the plant. "Table" corn is ready in about 50 days, when the kernels are filled out and before they begin to develop color. The taste is crunchy, sweet and corny. Dry corn is done in about 90 days or less, although I've had it finish in 62 days.

Cornbread made from PM is only mildly corn flavored; it would be a great corn for corn-pasta. Each ear is colorful and different, from 4 to 8 inches long. They resist corn earworm, although a few ears can get invaded. The stalks make good livestock feed after the corn has been picked, too.

Painted Mountain's big drawback in my area is that it doesn't do well in hot high moisture environments – it gets moldy. In humid, wet, warm environments, new growers could look to sources such as Southern Exposure Seed Exchange (link in references). Their ancient variety, Gourdseed Corn, is adapted to the southern US sultry environment.

Growing

Corn is a "heavy feeder", which means it needs the kind of nitrogen that manure produces. The ancient Indian method of placing a fish in each mound when planting corn, helped with that nitrogen requirement, and so will planting beans around the plants. Another option is to make a "manure tea", soaking livestock manure in water for several days and pouring the odorous results around each plant. If manure is in short supply, this is one way to stretch it. Don't get it directly on the plant itself, because it can burn the leaves. Aged compost is also an excellent source.

Corn can be planted in rows, putting one seed about 3" inches deep, 12 inches from the next plant, and then separating the rows by 18" or a bit more. Indians planted in small hills, about 10-15 seeds per hill, thinned down to the 5-7 healthiest plants. In the same hill, they planted a few *pole bean* and *winter squash* seeds. The traditional combination of "three sisters" helped the corn get nitrogen from the beans, and the squash kept the roots sheltered from summer drying – plus, the harvest would include beans and squash! In high wind areas, planting in hills helps the clumped bush-like corn stabilize individual plants, plus virtually assures pollination, which can otherwise be problematic if high winds carry the pollen away from the plot.

Weeding corn is pretty important for the best growth. Once the corn sprouts are up, weeding can be done every two weeks or so until the corn is too dense to weed through. Keeping the weeds down makes sure there is plenty of air movement in the lower parts of the plants, and helps reduce hiding places for the wild critters who also enjoy corn.

Corn is wind-pollinated, even though bees will sometimes hang around the plants when the top tassels develop. A sprig of "silks" will grow from the end of each corn cob, with each silk thread leading down to a single kernel. If you get a grasshopper invasion when the corn is in silk, you may lose the crop. Grasshoppers eat the silks, so the kernels don't get pollinated and don't develop. After the silks have turned brown, an eyedropper full of cooking or mineral oil, placed into the cob at the silk end, will discourage corn ear worms. Keep in mind that some varieties of corn have tighter husks that keep ear worms out.

Harvest and Storage

Corn can be harvested when it is dry in the field, or after it has fully matured and the husks are beginning to dry. Pull each cob off the plant and shuck it right there. If there are earworms, they won't be able to damage the corn while in storage if the critters are left in the field. The kernels should be quite dry, but still firmly attached to the cob. Put cobs into baskets or airy lattice-type bags, or store in a corncrib. A corncrib is a small roofed shed-type structure with slight gaps in the sideboards to allow air flow and drying. After the corn has dried enough that the kernels are "wiggling-loose", you can rub the kernels off and use or store them. If you have an antique corn-sheller, start turning and put ears through one by one for fast shelling. A small ear of dried corn will give you about ½ - ¾ cup of kernels.

Store shelled or dried cob corn in a dry location that is moderately cool. Mice and bugs will get it if they have access, so screens and buckets with screen lids can make a difference. Save seed from at least 500 different plants for genetic diversity, if you can, and keep enough that you can plant *at least* two years from that (5 years' worth would be better), just in case one crop gets wiped out.

Corn Supper

This is such a versatile crop, it's no wonder that corn was the primary grain in the Americas since people were here. Aside from fresh eating, the kernels can be ground using a hand-powered mill (Corona Mill is the bottom of the line, Country Living Mill near the top), or in the blender. At this time, I use an electric Braun coffee grinder and grind about a cup at a time.

Ground coarsely, it makes wonderful grits when boiled for a half hour or more. Ground medium and spiced with Lawry's Season Salt or any other combination of herbs and spices, it's a nice breading for poultry, fish, and "chicken-fried" anything, as well as homemade polenta. More finely ground corn is wonderful for corn breads. Super-fine ground corn is ideal for corn-based pastas. Finely ground corn can be used to thicken soups and stews, also. Remember, popcorn can be ground, too, with all those same potential uses.

Painted Mountain Alpine and other colored corns produce breads that are NOT yellow – the PM-A corn and Wade's Giant, give a lovely brown corn bread with almost no obvious corny flavor. I have used this corn as a base for muffins with a quarter cup of wheat flour (home ground, naturally) and all kinds of yummy extras – bananas, walnuts, cranberries, even pineapple. Most people can't tell that it is primarily corn-based.

Keep one thought in the back of your mind: pellagra. In the olden days during the First Great Depression, many cases of B-vitamin deficiency were found among poor people. The worst effects included extreme fatigue, muscle wasting, mental issues including retardation, fluid retention, and other symptoms.

The reason pellagra flourished was because poor people were limited in diet to virtually only corn and corn products – which is notoriously low in B-vitamins. Even if you have a LOT of corn, make sure you get plenty of meat proteins, eggs, especially liver which is a super-high source of B-vitamins, green vegetables, and even home brewed beer made from other grains and hops....and daily multivitamin supplements help, too. Obviously, a widely varied diet will get you what you need. Cornbread with beans and ham, with salad on the side, is a perfect vitamin and mineral-rich meal!

Native groups treated their whole corn kernels by soaking for a week or two in a solution of "lime"; this altered the corn and made the B vitamins available to human digestion. This is called "masa harina", and is currently available corn flour in supermarkets.

"Lime" is calcium hydroxide, to be sure, not the citrus juice, and not the same as agricultural lime. Lime starts out as calcium carbonate, from limestones, coral, chalk or from the shells of oysters or clams. The product is heated, burned really, until the carbon dioxide has been driven out – which leaves Calcium Oxide. Calcium Oxide is also known as "quicklime", which is highly corrosive when wet – it used to be used in cemeteries to aid the decomposition of bodies. Even the smallest amount of moisture on skin combined with Calcium Oxide can cause terrible skin burns; handle with extreme caution!

Calcium Oxide can be converted to Calcium Hydroxide by adding a small amount to water until the water heats up and evaporates. *Do not breathe the fumes.* A white powder is left behind, and that is the Calcium Hydroxide. When that powder is mixed with more water, it becomes a non-acidic highly alkaline solution.

That's the "lime" which corn is soaked in. Kernels are soaked until the husk comes loose, which can take a week or two. Then the corn is removed and rinsed to remove the lime and the husks. The lime water can be reused several times. The kernels are then sun dried, and when dry can be ground and used in any cooked product. It has a characteristic flavor that is well-known in Mexican cooking. DISCLAIMER: I have never made this and cannot give you safety pointers – this is for information only.

You can purchase the equivalent right now, called Pickling Lime, anywhere that sells home canning and preserving supplies. Buy in quantity if you plan to lime your corn.

Alternative Grains and Seeds

During the Maunder Minimum, many lives were lost to starvation when grain crops failed, principally wheat, barley, and rye. In France, the failure of the wheat crops left nearly no food, since bread was the primary food of the poor. In countries where underground crops like potatoes, parsnips, and rutabagas were significant generally because grains were already unreliable, crop losses didn't play as heavily into famines.

The most familiar alternative grains are: oats, barley, and rye, with buckwheat running a distant cousin. Rye has some ability to tolerate cold growing seasons, and it used to be a common grain crop in Scandinavia. Oats were initially grown as horse feed in the British Isles – the saying was that one could tell when they got to Scotland, because they stopped feeding oats to the horses and ate it themselves. Barley, too, has some potential as a cool weather grain. Buckwheat is still a major crop in China, and a very minor one in the U.S. Just try to find a bag of pure buckwheat at the supermarket. Organic growers consider buckwheat a good "cover crop" that gets plowed under to enrich the soil, and the flowers attract bees. Buckwheat has a harsher flavor than wheat.

Although these are familiar grains, none of them have the gluten content of wheat, so breads made from these lack the stretchy component that gives wheat breads their texture. These grains will make good quick breads (see recipes) though, and are tasty and filling meal additions.

The challenge with each of these grains is that they are a bit harder to separate the grain kernels from the papery husks, so there's more labor involved. Productivity per acre is likely to be lower than wheat, too. Furthermore, we don't know how they'll do in variable soils and hard weather. It might be worth your while to plant several "test plots" 10'x 10' each, and experiment with these grains in your region.

Some growers have turned toward ancient grains and seeds as an alternative to wheat and corn. There's some question about whether these will be commercial successes or not – the public is accustomed to eating a certain way, and it takes quite a bit of prodding to make a change if one doesn't have to. Of course, we may have to. At this writing, these are minor, niche, specialized items in modern diets.

Sunflowers

One of the most familiar is the sunflower seed. It is high in protein and oil, tasty raw or roasted, and can also be used in breads and cooking. The challenge is that it has to be shelled first. Shelling by hand is so time consuming as to be unlikely in all but the most dire situations. Shelling machines, which partially crush the shells and allow the softer seed to come lose, are available online from multiple sources. Most originate in China. Homemade shellers could conceivably be made utilizing a hand crank, rollers, and gravity feed.

The sunflower heads are ready to harvest when the back of the flower has turned yellow and the petals are browning. If you wait too long after this, birds will get the seeds or they will fall to the ground. Cut each head off leaving a stem "handle", and bring under cover to finish drying. Heads are dry when you can brush seeds loose easily.

You can feed the sunflowers to livestock, or consume them yourself as "raw" seeds. Or, soak the seeds in salty water, 1 cup salt to 1 gallon water, for 6-8 hours. Remove seeds and air dry. Roast in a warm 300°F oven for a half hour or so. Cool. Ready to eat.

After shelling, the seeds separate from the shells by dunking all in water. The shell bits float and can be readily swept off. The seeds alone can then be quickly dried, soaked in salt water and toasted – and there's a snack that's tasty and good for you. Or, merely dried and utilized later.

Livestock can eat sunflower seeds and their shells without any issues, if they are introduced to them over several days. A typical yield might be anywhere from 1200 to 1800 pounds of seed per acre. They are easy to grow on moderately fertile soil.

Quinoa and Amaranth

Quinoa (pronounced KEEN-wah) and amaranth are Central and South American grains, grown by the ancient major civilizations as a high protein food source. Both are relatively easy to grow and productive, with each plant providing around a pound or two of grain. Both quinoa and amaranth can substitute for rice and are cooked in a similar fashion. It's possible to pop quinoa in a heated skillet like popcorn, but the grains are slightly smaller than a mustard seed so they are not quite like what you'd get at a theater while watching a movie.

Quinoa is related to amaranth, and both are undemanding plants. Quinoa that can grow in temperatures ranging from 25°F to 95 °F, as long as not in overly wet ground and the freezing doesn't happen when they are flowering. Leaves are edible but bitter from saponin content, so generally are not eaten. Plants grow from about 4 to 6 feet tall, and form a large flower head on top, with smaller heads from sprouts near where leaves form. Each flowering part ripens at a slightly different time, so they need to be monitored. When the heads ripen, they need to be cut and hung to dry because they will drop their seeds if left on the plant. Once they are dry, the seed heads are threshed like wheat, winnowed to remove chaff, then dried for storage. Each seed still has a coating that can make it taste bitter from saponins, so before cooking they need to be washed and rubbed until the coating comes off. It doesn't take much effort. Then, cook like rice.

Amaranth is related to the common edible weed lamb's quarters, too, and to the invasive spiny pigweed indigenous to south central and south eastern US. Pigweed appears where ever the soil is disturbed, as when plowing a garden. It's a huge nuisance plant. The good news is that wherever pigweed grows, grain amaranth will also thrive.

Amaranth leaves are edible and tasty when young, tough when older. Different species of amaranth have different uses, including producing edible leaves and seeds, using the roots as dye, and growing for a flowering ornamental. Love Lies Bleeding is an amaranth. Like quinoa, it is undemanding and can grow on relatively poor soil. The seed varieties form a large seed head on the top, weighing up to about 2 pounds with a half million teeny seeds present. If high winds are an issue, you may have to stake the plants so they don't fall over and lose their seeds. Harvest like quinoa before the seed heads shatter. Cooking improves the flavor. Black amaranth seed has a stronger "mousie" flavor, while white seeds are milder and nuttier. It may cross with wild plants.

Both amaranth and quinoa are free of gluten. Both lend themselves to harvesting by hand and a small garden spot 4'x8' can easily produce 20 pounds, perhaps 1500 pounds per acre.

Fast and Long Producers

Plants have been developed that are, generally, of two types: those that come to harvest quickly for a "group" harvest (such as for commercial canning); and those that will stand in the garden throughout the season and produce for daily or weekly fresh consumption.

One example of fast vs. long is the two varieties of beans, bush beans versus pole beans. Bush beans grow into a small plant rapidly and then flower and produce a large harvest of pods. These can all be picked at about the same time, processed and preserved for use throughout winter. You can leave bush beans in the garden, and sometimes you'll get a second but much smaller harvest – and then the plants really decline. Typically, after the first big crop, bush bean plants are pulled and something else is planted in the row.

Pole beans, on the other hand, grow more slowly and require a tall arbor or fence to grow up and over. They flower intermittently and form pods over the entire growing season, never really giving a huge single crop. My favorite pole bean is Missouri Wonder, available from Baker Seeds (see references). This is a true old-style "string" bean, one with fibrous strings at the pod seams that need to be removed before cooking or fresh eating – the flavor is boldly beany, and the dried seeds can be used is soups, chili, or for refried beans. Best of all, the plants are tolerant of rough growing conditions. I've had "volunteer" beans for several years from pods missed during harvest, enough that I didn't have to plant my saved seeds. Japanese beetles, which decimate most other bean leaves, hardly bother these at all, which assures you get a harvest.

In a garden aimed toward storage food AND fresh eating, both bush beans and pole beans have a place. Always let some of the plants remain and go to seed – that's next year's beans.

If you like dried beans used in soups and chili, many of these are the bush-bean type. Plant these and harvest when the pods are drying on the plant. Should Cold come unseasonably, pull the entire plants, tie together in bunches, and hang them upside down in a cool garage or shed. Shell out the bean seeds when the pods and the entire plant are dry.

The same division is true in tomato plants: there are fast "determinate" and long "indeterminate" varieties. Determinate tomatoes typically grow few side sprouts, reach full size, produce the main crop of fruit, and like bush beans are then pulled and something else is planted in the row. They will continue to fruit intermittently if left in the ground, but you won't get a big second crop.

Indeterminate tomatoes, on the other hand, will form many side sprouts and keep growing as long as the conditions are suitable. When I lived in Southern California, I had a very large and bushy indeterminate cherry tomato that just kept growing and producing for three years – through all seasons. It never got below freezing, there then. It probably would have kept on indefinitely, but we needed the space for something else, so it was removed.

So, read the plant descriptions when you select seeds – get fast (bush/determinate) and long (pole/vining/indeterminate) producers of everything you really enjoy. You will have a large garden space, anyway, and the more edibles you can grow the better off you and yours will be.

A Little More About Tomatoes

When you're shopping for seeds, look for varieties that are "short season" or "early". There are tomatoes that produce small fruit as early as 7 to 9 weeks after planting, and have some tolerance to cool but not freezing weather. If your season is unusually short, you may still be able to get a harvest from one of these varieties. Plant names include *Ildi* (53 days), *Stupice* (52 days), *Oregon Spring* (60 days), and *42 Days* (42 days).

Most folks tend to grow large size tomatoes. I suppose if you like large whole or chunk tomatoes in soups or stewed or to have slicing tomatoes for sandwiches or burgers, you'd require these -- at least a few plants. Each plant can give you 5 to 7 pounds of tomatoes, on average; it takes 2-3 pounds to fill a quart jar as sauce. However, I've found that cherry tomatoes are just as good sauced and a LOT easier to prepare, plus super productive over the entire season. Instead of blanching and removing the skins from big tomatoes, I just throw handfuls of cherry tomatoes into the blender – then cook the slurry down by about a third. Then I can them in a water bath with a teaspoon of salt and vinegar per quart. The end result is a delicious pure tomato sauce that can be spiced any way we want and used for soup base, pasta sauce, chili, pizza sauce, salsa, whatever.

If you have to, you can cover tomato plants during a freeze spell – use lots of straw or hay thickly over everything, and then put a tarp or plastic cover over that and tie or weight it down so it doesn't blow during the freeze; blankets will do in a pinch. If the weather warms up within a week or so and doesn't get terribly cold below about 28°F for an extended period, your plants can survive and come back. They will look wilted and unhappy after being covered, but they'll perk right up and continue to grow as long as the weather is warm enough.

Should it look like it's going to be too cold to continue growing tomatoes, pick all your green fruit, even the tiny ones. Full size tomatoes will ripen to red if left on a countertop and checked daily for soft spots. Use those first. Use right away, or cook down for fresh sauces. You can also make green tomato salsa, or even green tomato pasta sauce – the flavor is not as rich as red tomatoes, and perhaps even has a more fruity quality. Green tomatoes can also be sliced, breaded and fried. It's all edible, however prepared. Tomato *leaves and stems*, however, are inedible and can make you sick.

Starting Seeds

If you have not already done so, it's time to buy seeds. Don't just get the "survival seed packs," because it might not be what you want, the type of plants you want, or enough of a given variety. It may not have enough cold-weather type plants, either. Instead, check out the seed displays at groceries and hardware and home improvement stores. Buy catalogs from multiple sources – just type "seeds for sale" in any search engine, and you'll get thousands of sources. Companies I have used and had good open pollinated seeds from include: Baker Seeds, Territorial Seed, Seed Saver's Exchange, Park Seed, Gurney's, Jung, Totally Tomatoes, and Burpee.

Types of seeds: OP, Hybrid, and GMOs

Look for ONLY "open pollinated" (OP) seed – by law, it must say on the seed package or plant description if a variety is *hybrid*. If it does not say "hybrid", it may be OP. Because OP is more desirable now, many sellers will identify OP plants on packages or descriptions. Open pollinated seed will breed "true", producing the same type of plant year after year, with predictable characteristics.

Many, but not all, open pollinated seeds are also "heirloom" – technically, an older type of vegetable or fruit. The word "heirloom" is often used interchangeably with "open-pollinated", although there are heirloom type plants that are actually hybrids. Some tomatoes great grandpa grew were commercial hybrids, for example. Many heirlooms have a richer flavor than more modern produce.

Heirlooms were originally developed during hardier times and often have natural strengths that are missing in modern varieties. OP heirlooms may not have some other characteristic such as long "hold" time, or tolerance to bruising that make modern varieties acceptable for shipping and sitting on supermarket shelves.

Hybrids are actually "cross bred" seeds, produced by taking plants from different family lines and crossing them together, rather like taking a collie dog and crossing it with a beagle. The resulting puppy is still get a "dog", and being a crossbred it will have improved characteristics over both parents, something known as *hybrid vigor*.

The same is true in hybrid plants. They might be stronger, have thicker stems, produce earlier or have tastier fruit than either parent. BUT, if you save seeds from your hybrid veggies, you don't know what it will produce: the seeds might be sterile, like a mule, or might produce something like one or the other parent, or might revert to an earlier ancestor. If you plant seed from commercial tomatoes, which are hybrids, the offspring are almost always a cherry-type. *Still edible*, but unpredictable.

GMOs are "genetically modified organisms." The term is usually applied to plants, but can also apply to an animal whose embryonic cells have been subject to laboratory gene-splicing technology. These are NOT the products of crossbreeding, such as occurs with hybrids; these are actually plants or animals that have had some other genes added to their cells by laboratory manipulation. Pigs, for example, have had human genes added during the embryo stage of fetal development; the resulting animals are used for studies of certain human medications. Or corn that has bacteria added to give it resistance to corn ear worms. Or grain that has had so many different genetics added for resistance to herbicides that it barely resembles what our ancestors grew.

GMOs are typically patented and some have "terminator" genes that prevent the offspring plants' seeds from growing – hence, the patent holder can charge whatever they want for the next generation's seeds; they've even brought patent lawsuits against people who unknowingly grew the seeds without a license. No long term testing on the safety of these foods in human diets has ever been done. Depending on who you talk to, animal tests indicate GMOs interfere with digestion, metabolism, fertility, and neural development – or are perfectly harmless.

There's so much biologically, historically, and morally wrong with this picture, that entire books have been written on the GMO controversy. Suffice it to say here that GMO seeds are not a viable option for sustaining oneself in the future. Please do note that GMO genetics have escaped into the wild, especially for wind-pollinated plants such as corn, so that finding seeds that are *tested* as free of GMOs is difficult – and such seeds are higher priced than untested seeds. However, if you have no other sources, eating GMO is better than starving. Just get away from it as soon as you can.

When to Start Seeds

Some plants are routinely started by planting them directly in the garden – corn, wheat, beans, potatoes, peas, and radishes for example. Others are typically started early, before spring really commences, in small pots or flats under grow lights or in greenhouses. When the little potted plants are 6 to 8 weeks old, and when the outdoor weather has warmed up enough, the "starts" are then "hardened off" by exposing to outdoor weather gradually over several days, then planted in the garden. This gives them a bit of a jump on the season. Your harvest may come in a few weeks earlier than similar seeds planted directly in the garden. This could be important if seasons are wildly out of whack.

At this awakening phase, there are multiple resources to make this a simpler process than it would be otherwise: seed starting potting mix, mini greenhouses, grow lights, and warming mats. If you want to start seeds early, by all means use this technology, but recognize that you probably won't have any of it after Zen-slap occurs. You'll have to make your own potting mix from what you have in your garden, and those small grow-pots won't be available. Your ability to use full spectrum grow-lights may be limited by power failures.

You can find a way to adapt to each of these issues, so be working toward that goal as quickly as possible.

If you have never gardened, simply acquire the "starts" at your nearby garden supply store. They will likely be hybrid (crosses from different family lines), and the seeds from hybrids may be sterile or not "breed true". This source may not be available at a reasonable cost in the future, so do not rely on it. Try to grow your own starts, too, so that you understand what is required to get plants from seed.

All seeds can be planted directly in the garden, including the ones we usually think of as early start plants. Generally, when I direct sow anything, I will put in more seeds than I need. This allows for poor germination rates, damage to tiny plants from weather or animals, and some extras just in case. Should your seeds germinate and come up thickly, when little plants have 4 leaves or so, you can dig, separate, and transplant them where you want them.

Keep in mind that when the Cold Times arrive with the full Zen-slap, we may not be able to plant outdoors and bring much of anything to harvest. This is where greenhouses come in. More on that shortly.

Volunteers

A volunteer is any plant that appears in your garden the following year from when you originally planted that thing. Typically, a volunteer is the result of a dropped or missed fruit that got turned under the soil, successfully overwintered, and then started growing again in the spring when conditions were right.

Most of my tomatoes are now volunteers. I will purposefully leave behind fruits, sometimes mashing them into the soil. Even with repeated working of the garden soil, turning it over with a tractor or tiller, adding in compost and lime, and walking over it. There will STILL be plenty of "free" volunteers in the spring. The same is true of my favorite super-hardy bean, Missouri Wonder Pole. This bean gives me enough volunteers that I haven't had to replant with fresh seeds in several years.

There are three outstanding qualities of volunteer plants that should make you alert to their value in your own garden:

1. *They are free.* When you check seed catalog prices, that one quality alone makes them worthwhile.
2. *They are hardy.* The fact that they survived through the winter without any help at all proves that.
3. *They are adapting to your conditions.* Better yet, over several years of repeated volunteering, you have developed a variety of plant that is *specifically* adapted to your region, your garden, and your way of growing things.

The primary drawback of volunteers is that, over years, your plants will have a limited gene base. They effectively have been breeding among themselves and their immediate relatives. The long term result of that is what is called *genetic depression*, the loss of *genetic variability*. Genetic variability is the valuable quality of having lots of heritable capacity to adapt to changing growing conditions. That's something we want in our plants. Genetic depression, on the other hand, represents a decrease in adaptability because the plants are drawing from a progressively more limited gene pool. It's a type of in-breeding, where relatives mate with relatives until the offspring are too deformed and sickly to reproduce.

To counteract this drawback among your volunteers, you merely need to introduce fresh plants to your garden – seeds from, say, a couple different varieties of tomato. They will grow and cross with your tomato volunteers, add genetic variability, and give you your own home grown hybrid vigor in the next generation, as well.

Saving Seeds

Part of the reason for acquiring open pollinated starter seeds is so that you can save your own seeds year after year, and have a pretty good idea what you will produce. Most common garden plants produce seeds within the edible fruits. Squash, tomatoes, beans, peas, melons and cucumbers, for example, produce obvious and easily obtained seeds. These "annual" seed producers, which take one growing season to complete their lifecycle, will produce seed during the year in which you plant them.

Other common garden plants produce seeds the year *after* you first plant them, taking two years to complete their life cycle. These include cabbage, turnips, beets, and onions. Typically, you can either leave the original plant in your garden (which might be iffy should we have intense cold), or "lift" the plant in the fall, store in cool conditions, and then replant it in the spring. These will first grow leaves, then will send up one or more seed stalks on which it will flower and produce seeds.

Seed Saving Basics

- Save seed from the healthiest plants with the most fruit.
- Let the fruit from which you hope to save seed ripen as much as possible on the vine or plant.
- If you are hoping to retain early ripening and early harvests from your plants, save seed from the first fruits that appear. Note: cucumbers will stop flowering as soon as one fruit on the plant starts getting yellow-ripe, so growing for seed may reduce your cuke harvest.
- If you want long-season characteristics in your plants, save seed from the last fruits that ripen fully.
- Remove seed from the fruit, rinse in a sieve to remove excess plant tissue OR leave seed in the plant tissue, add a little water, and let sit until it has gotten gummy and smelly, then rinse. Some seed savers believe that short period of "aging" helps trigger better germination rates later in tomatoes, cucumbers, and melons.
- Dry seeds on a plate, moving them around a little daily so they don't stick.
- When dry, place in an envelope then put inside a mason jar. Label with plant type and variety, day collected, and any characteristics you'll need to know next year (i.e., "ripens in 60 days") because you won't remember everything otherwise.
- Store your seeds in a cool place that is relatively dry. Open the jars once or twice during the winter and blow a little air into the jar before recapping – that adds a little carbon dioxide to the jar, which the seeds need to breathe. It's not necessary to freeze the seeds, but some people do.
- Save seeds from all over your garden area and from at least a dozen plants. 100 different plants for corn, for each type to maintain genetic diversity.
- Save enough seeds for *at least* two planting seasons, and keep ahead of your needs by saving some extras every year. Rotate so you are using the older seeds first.

- *Never plant all your seeds.* In a bad year, you might lose everything – you may be able to replant, and you'll still need seeds for the next year.
- Test the average germination of your seeds in the following spring. Take 10 seeds, place on a plate with a wet cloth over it. Keep the cloth moist. Within several days, some of the seeds will start to sprout. If 9 out of the 10 seeds sprout, you've got 90% germination. If 8 out of 10 sprout, it's 80% germination and so forth. That gives you can idea of how many seeds you'll need to plant in order to get a harvest. For example, if only half sprout, a 50% germination, you'll have to plant twice as much to get a "normal" crop. Put your started seeds in a little potting soil and get a jump on the garden, or plant in your greenhouse.
- Share and trade seeds with your neighbors.

Tubers and Taters

Some tuberous plants, such as potatoes (Irish Potato) and sweet potatoes (yams), are propagated not by seed, but simply by replanting the tuber itself in the spring. Potatoes grow sprouts from "eyes", the small indentions on the skin surface.

Healthy potatoes, even those in cool storage, will start to grow little stems from the eyes late in the winter – you can cut these out with a large grape-sized chunk of potato around it, let it air dry for a couple days, and then plant that. The rest of the potato is still edible, even when it is somewhat shriveled but not mushy.

For eating, cut off any parts that are green – the green shows the presence of "solanine", and that is potentially harmful to eat. Don't eat potato leaves for the same reason; they can be toxic.

There are short (65-75 days), medium (95-110 days), and long season (120-135 days) potatoes. Familiar examples are

Yukon Gold for short; Pontiac Red for medium, and Burbank Russet for long. Potatoes do well in cooler weather, and the tops will come back after being frosted. Tubers form when the soil is between 60°-70°F, and the plants stop growing above 80°F. Potatoes don't like continuously soggy soil and high humidity, either.

By the way, potatoes will sometimes "go to seed" in the garden, especially when grown near different varieties, first forming small flowers and then little seed fruit. These seed can be saved over winter and grown like tomatoes. They are a member of the same broad family as tomatoes, *Solanaceae*, which includes tobacco, eggplant, peppers, petunia, jimson weed, belladona, and mandrake. The potato seeds will produce plants later in the season – but they will likely be crosses from the varieties you originally planted, and different than you expect. But still edible.

Potatoes can be harvested before full size as "new potatoes", which are just small potatoes, sometimes a mere 6 weeks after planting. Pull back a little soil from around the base of a plant and check for the ping-pong ball size tubers. You can take one or two from each plant, then pat the soil back into place. Potatoes are full size and ready for harvest when the green leaves start turning yellow and the stems bend over, or after they have flowered. Many varieties will "hold" in the ground, often until the following spring if the ground does not freeze, developing a thicker skin as time goes by. If the ground freezes, you'll likely lose them.

Irish potatoes won't set good tubers if the soil is very fertile. Too much nitrogen will give lush green tops and no tubers. They do need phosphorus and potassium, so be sure you get wood ash from your fireplace, especially hardwood ash, worked into the garden. It's a good source of both nutrients.

Sweet potatoes will grow from small sprouts that appear over the surface of a tuber, too, and can be planted whole or cut and air dried like regular potatoes. I've never seen sweet potatoes go to seed; the tubers don't get the toxic green either. They can take 90-120 days to reach good size, and will die if frosted. I've grown plants in a 3 gallon pot in a sunroom. They'll also grow from cuttings, placed in water until they form roots. A summer greenhouse is probably a good option if the weather is very unpredictable or especially cold. Sweet potatoes prefer warm growing conditions and a long season. These may be harder to keep growing in unstable and continuously chilly weather. They grow well in any moderately fertile soil.

Put your potato and sweet potato starts in a plastic bag with a small apple – the ethylene gas released by the apple will trigger the potatoes to start sprouting.

Sprouts and Sprouting

One of the easiest and quickest ways to get mid-winter greenery is to grow seed sprouts. These seeds are still readily available and will keep for a couple years in a jar. Typical sprouts are mung beans, alfalfa, radish, broccoli, and assorted other small seeds.

Almost any small seeds can be sprouted and eaten when it is still mostly root with a pair of leaves, but not those which have toxic leaves like tomatoes and potatoes. Two or three tablespoons of sprouting seeds will produce about 2 to 3 cups of sprouts within a week. These are absolute nutrition powerhouses, too, with excellent vitamin and mineral profiles.

Rinse the sprouting seeds and then soak in fresh water for about 6 hours. Then rinse again and set in a container in a dark cupboard. The container can be a fancy sprouter set, or a ½ gallon mason jar with a screen or light towel secured over the mouth of the jar to keep out gnats. Lay the jar on its side. Rinse with clean warm water two or three times daily, pouring all the water out – enough will be retained to keep the seeds growing. When the sprouts show a couple leaves, place the jar in indirect, not full, sun to help them green up a little. Ready to eat fresh or use in stir fry or salads. If you really like sprouts, start a new batch every 3 days or so. You'll have plenty.

The seeds you buy now for sprouts obviously can grow. Plant some of the varieties you like and see what you get. Mung beans grow like any other type of bush bean, about 18 inches tall. Plant seed 1-2" apart in rows, treat as any other bean, and in 90-120 days pods with 10 or more seeds each will be dry and ready for harvest. They don't all ripen at the same time, so you may need to pull the whole plant and hang to let everything dry well.

Store the shelled seeds in a glass jar with a little diatomaceous earth to prevent insect proliferation. Rinse the DE off when you are ready to sprout. One planted seed can give you a hundred, so these are very prolific and valuable plants – BUT they don't tolerate cold or high heat or extreme wetness well, and require a long growing season. They might do better under greenhouse conditions.

Greens

Greens constitute a broad class of vegetables with leafy bases, and edible stems. Lettuce, spinach, collards, and kale are familiar examples which also grow best in cooler conditions. Greens add valuable nutrients, but are low in calories – a reason that fried greens were traditionally served with pork or other oils...to increase the fat and calories.

Most greens are relatively fast producers. For example, lettuce seeds can be planted thickly and the excess pulled to add to meals within a week or two. Chinese vegetables, such as bok choi grow fast and have multiple uses as both a cooked green, and eaten fresh.

Greens are among the most easy to grow, as well. Many do exceptionally well in greenhouses under cool conditions.

Better Harvests With Fertilizer and Compost

Good soil can be improved by the judicious use of added soil nutrients. Right now, you can have your soil tested, either by hiring someone to do it for you (check your town's University Extension office for recommendations) or buy a test kit online or at a plant nursery in your area. The test kit will show you in a general way what nutrients and minerals your garden area might be short. Do keep in mind, though, that after we are Zen'd, you probably will have to fertilize by the garden equivalent of Braille – watch your plants and let them "tell" you what they need.

Commercially, there are four primary amendments to soil: nitrogen, phosphorus, and potassium (the NPK components) and agricultural lime (calcium). NPK can be sourced in commercial chemical fertilizers, or from natural components. Nitrogen, for example, is present in manures and "blood meal," a by-product of the livestock industry, and from tilling under live or cut clover or bean plants. Virtually all agricultural leftovers including spoiled hay, leaves, seaweed, fish heads, ground bones, can be incorporated into your soil by first composting and aging, and then spreading on your garden. Good compost has all the nutrients garden plants need.

Making compost is rather like making bread or yogurt. It's a process that takes a little effort and relies on microbial action to bring it to fruition. You will need dry straw or shredded newspaper or dried leaves; grass clippings, manure, or fresh green garden waste; and some good garden soil. Don't use meat or fats in your compost pile. Pick an area *at least* 3 feet by 3 feet – bigger is better – not too close to your home; the pile will have an odor, especially after turning. Here's how to make compost:

1. Clear a spot and put a thin layer of garden soil over it.
2. Put down your straw/paper/leaf layer. This layer should be about 3 times as thick as the next manure layer.
3. Cover with a layer of grass/manure/garden waste.
4. Continue in that same pattern until you have a pile at least three feet high.
5. Sprinkle the pile to moisten but not to make it soggy. If you are likely to get a lot of rain, cover the pile with a tarp and weight it down.
6. Every couple weeks, turn the pile – use a garden fork, move the inside to the outside, and the outside to the inside. A healthy pile will be warm to steamy! There should be lots of earthworms there, too.
7. The compost is ready when it is dark and crumbly; some parts of the pile will be done sooner – leave the not-quite-ready parts as the starter for your next pile.

The Henry Doubleday company in the UK studied the use of comfrey plant leaves as a primary fertilizing method years ago – comfrey is discussed in more detail as a healing herb later in this book. The plant is very prolific in leaf growth, some growing to three feet long, and can be harvested with several cuttings in a season. Researchers found that an acre in comfrey could produce several tons of livestock fodder per acre that was high in protein (28%), and that the same leaves could be chopped and worked into soil to make an effective fertilizer. The plant is tolerant of cold, too, so has a lot of good potential during Cold Times.

Application times of fertilizers/composts vary, but in general natural amendments can be worked into the soil before planting, then "side dressed," that is, put next to plants but not directly on them, before they flower and then again as the fruit matures. Don't fertilize after mid to late summer, because it can trigger the plants to grow when they should be getting ready to go dormant for winter.

When fertilizer components are scarce, the old timey method of using what is in the outhouse, humanure, can fill the ticket. Humanure must be well aged and composted and shouldn't have much more odor than a barn does. You probably shouldn't use it on leafy vegetables like lettuce, simply because it will be touching your food directly and that's a way to pass disease. Better on fruit trees. This is also a wonderful additive when you make compost.

Another way to fertilize plants is to make "manure tea," which is exactly what it sounds like. Livestock manure is placed into a bucket, and then the bucket is filled with water. Leave it for several days until the water is smelly. Pour this on the ground around the base of plants, avoiding the leaves. It's very quick acting, and you can practically see the plants perk up. The odor can be quite strong and rather unpleasant, so don't be surprised.

One of the very best animal manures is rabbit poo pellets. They are low odor, can be put directly around plants. It won't "burn" the plant, and is high in nitrogen. Use sparingly or not at all on your potatoes, or you'll grow large tops and no tubers.

Right now is the time to acquire several 25 pound bags of commercial fertilizer at a farm/feed store. It comes in at different strengths of NPK: 6-6-6, 10-10-10, and 13-13-13. The numbers show the relative amount of each nutrient in the fertilizer. Generally, the 10-10-10 fertilizer is adequate for normal garden soil.

The price of bags of fertilizer at feed stores is much lower than compared to buying comparable amounts in smaller boxes at box stores, and it will keep in dry storage well into the coming Zen and Hang-on periods. *This is an important backup food-security item*.

Keep in mind that commercial chemical fertilizers *do not improve soil*. They only give the short term nutrition plants need to grow for a season. The way to improve garden soil long term is by routine application of compost, turning under all the garden leftovers, and growing "cover crops" such as clovers or beans that are also turned under into the soil before planting. You can use commercial fertilizers along with composts, teas, comfrey, and cover cropping, phasing out the commercial fertilizer as your soil improves over several years.

Dealing With Insects

The many possible types of garden pests that are significant to agriculture are, literally, encyclopedic. The vast majority of these pests cause "cosmetic" damage – that is, holes or tunnels in fruit or on leaves – that would make the produce unsellable in current commercial markets BUT that don't necessarily make the food inedible. Yes, finding a green caterpillar in a salad is pretty icky, but the salad is still safe to eat. So is the caterpillar, for that matter.

I'm saying this, in part, to assure you that good food doesn't have to be completely without blemish or even moderate insect damage. Prior to the 20th century, undamaged fruit was the rarity. There's a reason that old folks used their pocket knives to cut apples and peaches before eating them, and it didn't have to do with their false teeth. After you've chomped into an apple and found half a worm, that pocket knife becomes an important part of meal preparation.

There are some garden pests, though, that can decimate your crops. Japanese beetles, for instance, are notorious for buzzing in like an invading army just when fruit is ripening and consuming everything in sight. Squash bugs infest young zucchini and pumpkins, and bring diseases that kill the plant before fruit have a chance to get going. Hordes of blister beetles can strip tomato plants leafless in a day. Locust eat everything. There's lots of others.

The modern approach is to blast the bugs with poisonous pesticides. Of course, these have side effects – killing all bugs including valuable and important honeybees rather than just the ones you want to kill, runoff going into rivers and killing fish, fumes making the farmer sick – and they are all commercially manufactured. Nothing "organic" to see here, either.

Now, I am largely an "organic" grower. Keeping soil healthy, according to organic philosophy, grows healthy plants that are less attractive to bugs. We use compost and manure to fertilize the garden and tend to prefer to grow hardy plants that are, themselves, not terribly attractive to insects. Even so, if the garden is under attack, from insects or larger critters, the problem must be removed.

I've used both organic and commercial means.

A grower may be willing to accept the risks and side effects of herbicides and pesticides in exchange for getting a nice crop, but once we have been Zen-slapped, the ability to get those chemicals may decline. Especially for the small backyard grower. I would guess that in the event of shortages or prices hikes, preference will be given to large commercial farms first anyway.

Because extensive insect damage can cost your entire harvest, I would encourage you to store a *significant* supply of common pesticides, such as **Sevin** (carbaryl), a broad-spectrum killer. Acquire both powdered and liquid forms, so you can dust affected crops or just spot-spray if needed.

Also get a few hand-pumped sprayers, and set them back for use later. They don't have to be large; 1-gallon is plenty good sized when you're carrying it around; even a used household sprayer like the kind used for window cleaners will work too. Mark each sprayer with what you've used in it. Use a different sprayer for each pesticide, herbicide, and fertilizer and label them – residues left over from one herbicide spraying can still damage your plants.

Another useful commercial killer is *Bacillus Thuringensis* (BT), generally sold as **Dipel powder** in 1-pound cardboard canisters – this is actually a bacteria that causes chewing worms like tomato horn worms and cabbage worms, for example, to stop eating and die. They have to actually consume some of this powder in order for it to affect them, and the worms can still eat for a while after getting a fatal dose. Most worms can be picked off by hand, too, so BT is merely a stopgap measure if your garden is really overwhelmed.

Rotenone powder, made from a tropical plant, can be useful as well, and has broad-spectrum bug killing properties. It is very toxic and will kill lake fish, but has a short life and sunlight destroys its effects.

Thinking ahead, when the weather becomes markedly colder, there will probably be seasons when insects are reduced. The cold will kill overwintering eggs and reduce other plants the insects need in order to function. You may have some years when the garden is almost free of bug problems. On the other hand, when temperatures rise during warm spells, the insects may be out in force, overwhelming areas in which they might have previously just been a casual resident. Once you've used up your supply of Sevin and whatever other chemicals you have stored, what then?

Once again, we turn back to how things were done before commercial products entered our food chain. **Tobacco,** for example, is a potent insecticide. As few as 3 tablespoons of dried tobacco, the equivalent of four or five cigarettes, soaked in a gallon of water until it makes a light brown "backy tea", is a deadly insect spray that kills every bug it touches. The key ingredient is the nicotine. If you get this spray on your skin, wash it off with soap and water immediately. This is a spot spray product. Don't cover your entire garden with it, just the areas of high infestation.

Soap sprays have been used for at least two centuries to control some insects. Researchers believe these work by disrupting insects' cellular metabolism. Some of the most unpleasant pests, such as Japanese Beetles, are very susceptible to soaps; bees are less susceptible. The insects have to be thoroughly wet for the spray to be effective. The spray doesn't have a residual effect, so you have to treat repeatedly to catch the bugs you missed. Ideally, any plant that gets hit by the spray would be washed off within a couple hours, because soaps can damage some plants. Tomatoes can't tolerate soap sprays at all. Consider treating early or late in the day when plants have a little dew on them, as well, to help protect the plants themselves, and never use during the hot sunny parts of the day.

Commercially-manufactured soap sprays are still available right now, but you can make your own. For one gallon of spray, use about 5 tablespoons of grated hand soap flakes. Castile soap or Ivory brand, or perhaps a plain unscented homemade soap can be used. Mix and mash the flakes with a little water to make a paste. Dilute that paste with a gallon of water. That should give you about a 2% soap solution. Spray on a discrete area of plants that will be treated, and check for damage in 24-36 hours. If the plant handles it, go ahead and get your bugs.

Insects that are most easily disposed of with soap spray are soft bodied types such as aphids, scales, whiteflies, psyllids, and mealybugs; plus the aforementioned Japanese beetles and boxelder bugs. It's not so useful on larger critters such as caterpillars and beetle larva – but it's pretty harmless to beneficials including bees, lady bugs and green lacewings, too.

Don't use liquid hand soaps or dish detergents. They are too harsh on plants. In fact, if you want to kill plants in an area, go ahead and use some diluted household detergent spray on them; not all plants are susceptible, but some will dry up as if you used herbicides.

Another option is "**bacterial warfare**," something like using BT. Basically, when your garden is under insect attack, you merely collect a couple cups of the bugs – squash bugs, caterpillars, whatever is bothering your plants. Smash, or blend if you have a blender you can dedicate to this task, all the bugs in some water. Then, add about a gallon of water to the mix. Leave this sitting out for several days, until it smells awful. Strain out the bug bits, and spray the "bug tea" on the offenders. The theory is that any bacteria the original insects carried gets magnified and intensified, so that the brew becomes a source of disease to the insects involved. *Do not try this with insects that potentially carry human-affecting diseases, such as flies or cockroaches* – it could make you sick. *Don't try this with insects that excrete toxins, either, such as blister beetles* – you just spread that toxin around where it can affect you more readily.

A tried-and-true method for ridding your plantings of nasty bugs is to "**hand pick**," just what it sounds like. Take a large can, #10 size, and put about an inch of water in the bottom. Add a tablespoon or two of used oil, motor oil or cooking oil is fine, and a dash of alcohol. Don't use your good drinking stuff – cheap Ever Clear or rubbing alcohol is good enough. Carry this with you in the garden. Wear gardening gloves. Put the can beneath an infested plant, and tap on the plant so the bugs fall into the can. Or pick bugs and drop them in the can. The oil/alcohol mix stuns and suffocates the insects, and they end up in the bottom of the can. You may need a partial cover, such as foil or a cut plastic lid, if the bugs are fliers. Shake the can to get your liquids on insects as they move in the can. When you've filled the can or cleared the garden, dump the can where runoff won't end up on your plants. If you have a burn pit to dispose of unwanted trash, dump the contents there and light a fire. This is better if you have several people working on it – plenty of opportunity for light conversation while the unpleasant job is done.

The old recommendation, which I still see in places, of introducing **chickens or guineas or geese** to the garden to "eat bugs" is simply wrong-headed. Each of these will also eat your ripe strawberries, tomatoes, melons, and anything else that might be tasty, along with the insects. Turning chickens into the garden areas in the fall to scratch and cleanup bug eggs and whatever remains is probably a good idea (some people will turn in pigs for the same reason) but don't do it if you still have edibles growing.

A Word About Weeds

A weed, according to the philosopher, is any plant in a place you don't want it. In other words, it might still be something you can eat. Many common weedy plants – dandelion, lamb's quarters, wild mustard – are all perfectly edible and highly nutritious and if picked when young and tender are quite tasty.

- Pick a quart or so of yellow dandelion flowers, rinse to remove "thrip" insects, pat dry, dip in pancake or tempura batter and deep fry to a golden brown – the flavor is a little like asparagus – absolutely delicious, filled with nutrients, organic, and low cost. The young leaves make a fine spring salad addition, and the roots can be roasted, dried, and powdered to add to coffee to stretch your supply.

- Lamb's quarters are a relative of amaranth, high in protein, with a delicate almost nutty flavor. Young leaves make an outstanding salad ingredient, and older leaves can be chopped and added to soups or stews. Dry extras to add to winter meals. Make a "spinach" lasagna with lamb's quarters leaves instead – no one will be  the wiser. Or fry young leaves with a little bacon for a tasty greens side dish.

- Wild mustard is mild flavored with a gentle cabbage or mustard undercurrent. Once again, a delicious addition to a big salad; can be pan fried or used in soups or stews, and the pretty yellow flower heads make tasty garnishes.

Of course, there's lots of other weeds you don't want growing up among your garden plants – they take up space that could be used by something edible, and make the garden messy and harder to work in.

At this time, tilling with a small rotary machine is one way to keep the weeds down between the rows. You'll have to do this every couple of weeks to keep ahead of the weeds.

"Weed reducing" fibers, which come in 25' or longer rolls, can be laid out to suppress some weeds, especially when covered with gravel or mulch chips. These last about a season and are only moderately effective; grasses get through this. The fibers will interfere with tilling when you clean up the garden in the fall, and will have to be pulled up unless you have permanent paths in your garden.

Mulching heavily with cardboard, newspaper, wood chips, also works very well, plus, these will break down over time and help nourish earthworms. Mulch unfortunately also makes a comfortable residence for mice and insect pests, so keep that in mind.

And then there is hoeing weeds. This is the time-tested traditional method that works super-effectively since it kills everything it touches, and even helps suppress some insect pests. The downside is that it's not fast or fun, and it has to be done almost every time you are in the garden.

That said, get a good, lightweight hoe. An "onion hoe" like this one is my favorite for lightness, speed, and agility. Then use it to gently chop the weed stem right at the soil line. Don't slam it or bang away, just a gentle rhythmic motion around and  between your growing plants. Ten minutes of hoeing a day will keep most of the weeds under control, give you a mild workout, and help you keep track of the condition of your plants.

Warning: if you don't get ahead of the weeds in the spring, they will get ahead of you and your garden will turn into a jungle by mid-summer.

Small Orchards

Tree fruits such as apples, pears, peaches, plums, apricots, lemons, oranges, and quinces are familiar, tasty, and wonderful sources of vitamins and minerals, especially vitamin C. Many varieties of apples can be stored in a cool cellar and will be available for "fresh" eating throughout the winter. Other fruits can be preserved as jams, jellies, pie fillings, wines, and various kinds of sweet condiments.

Fruit trees generally are low-care, requiring a little trimming during the winter, fertilizer in the spring and summer, some attention to insect and disease prevention – and then you can harvest a hundred pounds or more from a mature tree. Over the course of a season, each tree probably will require less than an hour of individual attention. So, for the amount of effort, production can be outstanding.

At this time, that is.

I honestly cannot say how modern fruit trees will fare during extended cold and uneven weather. Virtually all commercial varieties have been developed during the past several generations of unusually mild, warm and stable weather. Nearly all of them are dependent on repeated seasonal spraying for insects and diseases, with a few exceptions.

At this time, heavy ice storms snap off branches; late frosts kill flower buds and destroy entire harvests overnight; hail storms in mid-summer knocks fruit down or bruises it so that it rots; early frost damages fruit just as it is ready to harvest. We must expect that these "normal" events are likely to become more severe in the next few years, with some unexpected strangeness thrown in – such as high ultra violet rays from the sun burning leaves and fruit. Just as when raising garden plants, having the ability to be agile in your adaptation to conditions may mean the difference for you and yours. It's just sensible to have a Plan B, C, D, E, and F for your

Plan A.

If you already have growing fruit trees, make sure they are well pruned so that branch structure is strong and will resist breaking in high winds or when burdened by ice or snow. Consider adding some potted mini and citrus trees to keep in a greenhouse or indoors during very poor weather years.

If you do not yet have fruit trees, here are some suggestions:

- The US has been divided into 11 growing regions, with each zone averaging 10 degrees warmer or cooler than the neighboring zones during a typical winter. This map gives an idea, but you can't really tell accurately without the USDA color depiction. Many seed catalogs and even some seed packets have this map in color, and of course it's available online. Plants will be described in catalogs something like: "grows in zones 3-8". That means the tree can live in cooler areas of the country, and that it probably actually needs some freezing weather in order to grow properly. Keep in mind that the coming mini ice age is likely to shift these zones around quite a bit.

- Fruit trees, mostly, come with a top named variety grafted onto a rootstock. Rootstocks control the size the tree will grow to. There are "mini dwarf" trees, growing about 4-6 feet tall; "dwarf" trees, about 6 or 8 feet tall; "semi-dwarf", 10-16 feet. There are also "own root" or "standard" or "non-grafted" trees that are full size, as tall as the trees will grow naturally. Full size apple trees, for example, might grow anywhere from 20 feet to 35 feet tall and live for a century. Dwarf apples, though, generally are pooped out by 12 years of age.

- Start with half your purchases as dwarf trees and half full size. The dwarf trees will bear fruit sooner, sometimes in just 2-3 years, but they are shorter-lived. After 7 or 8 years when your dwarves are aged and slowing down, your full size trees will be coming on full steam. When the dwarves stop producing or die, replace them with seedlings grown from seeds of your full size trees – that will give your descendants fruit, too.

- Select trees that are extra hardy, for example, cultivars from Michigan, Minnesota, Maine, Canada, Siberia, or northern China. Reliance Peach and Haralson Apple originated in the colder states.

- Select trees that are highly disease resistant so that you don't have to spray and treat for diseases constantly. Liberty Apple is my favorite, and Jonafree and MacFree are other ones. Read descriptions carefully.

- Be certain you have pollinators for trees that require cross-pollination. Golden Delicious is a good apple pollinator, as are most crabapples. Pollinators must flower at the same time as the trees you want pollinated, and there is some variation. Many pears, peaches, and cherries are "self-pollinating", but they will often produce better if a pollinating tree is nearby. Ask at your local Extension office, or check online for your area.

- Read about fruit tree pruning and visit a professional orchard, if you can, to see how they do it. In general, peaches, plums, and cherries should be pruned in an "open, basket" shape to allow good central air flow. Apples and pears are pruned to "central leader" shape with a primary main stem and shortened side branches. Pruned trees tend to bear heavier crops than unpruned trees, which can get overgrown and lose branches to breakage.

- Ignore 3-in-1 or 5-in-1 grafted trees, the ones with several fruit colors or varieties grafted onto one tree trunk – these are rarely worth the excessive effort to get them to fruit successfully, and are *never* highly disease resistant.

- Consider mini-dwarf trees, available on super-dwarfing EMLA-27 rootstock. These grow about 4 feet tall and can be grown in pots, but produce full size fruit. Available types include apples (Liberty is one of them), peaches, nectarines, and cherries. The benefit of these is that they can be kept in portable planters – and brought under cover if ice, hail, high winds or unseasonable cold is underway. That way, you get a crop, no matter what happens with the weather. When the weather is favorable, they are moved outdoors. If indoors, they can be hand pollinated or if outdoors will be pollinated by bees and other insects.

- Potted varieties of avocados, lemons, limes, oranges, tangerines, and kumquats can be grown in a sunny window in a home, or make excellent greenhouse plants. Yes, you can grow these from seeds saved out of commercial fruit. During warm weather, they can be moved outdoors. You'll have to pollinate with an artist's paintbrush when they flower during the winter and early spring. Very fragrant flowers, too.

By the way, the USDA's climate zone map has changed quite a bit since 1960, with zones moving southward – that is, what used to be a zone 7, now has characteristics of zone 6. That's a remarkably significant change, demonstrating that *it's getting cooler* – and it's been going on longer than most of us realize.

I've been happy with trees from Raintree Nursery (raintreenursery.com) located in Washington state and Jung Seeds. Jung carries other seeds, plants, and flowers, too. From time to time, Lowe's home store carries some nice potted citrus, and occasionally mini dwarf peach and nectarines. Watch that mini dwarf trees are marked as "fruiting." There are some, such as Bonfire Peach and Calmodin Orange, that are primarily *flowering ornamentals*.

Return of the Fruit Wall

The ancient technique of "espaliering" fruit trees always struck me as more effort than necessary. The trees were trimmed to look like the letter *"T"*

with two or more crossing bars, generally a multi-year process to complete. I mistakenly figured that people of the past just had too much time on their hands.

Little did I know that the entire process of espaliering was the intelligent outcome of trying to grow fruit trees during Little Ice Ages of the past. It utilized solar-generated warmth on stone and mortar surfaces.

In a mere century, we have almost completely forgotten what our agricultural ancestors took for granted. They simply could not plant a fruit tree in a yard and expect to get a harvest. They *had* to plant them against south-facing walls to absorb all the heat they could, and radiate that heat back to the trees during the chilly nights.

How much knowledge we have lost!

These two pictures are from old French postcards, showing the fruit-walled peach orchards bordering a small city at the end of the 1800's. The weather was already starting to warm out of the Dalton minimum – the cycle leading to the late 20th century delusion of global warming – so these walls eventually came down. Because they weren't needed any more, they were not rebuilt....and their purpose vanished.

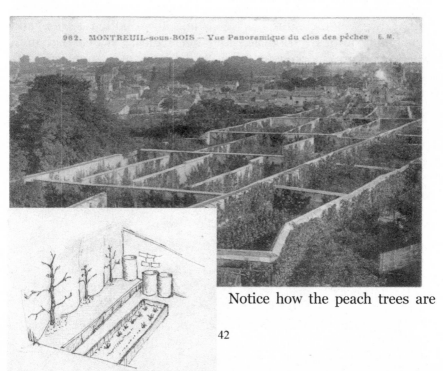

962. MONTREUIL-sous-BOIS — Vue Panoramique du clos des pêches E. M.

Notice how the peach trees are

42

trimmed and trained to hug the walls, facing south and receiving southern sunlight during the day. The surrounding wall chambers maintain a "microclimate" around each section of trees, possibly as much as 30°F warmer than the surrounding air, and retaining that warmth into the night. A light frost might not affect these trees at all, and a heavy frost would have a much less significant effect than if the trees were in the open. A little smudge pot burning through a chilly night in one of those chambers might be enough to assure a crop that would otherwise be lost.

This illustration shows an espaliered wall within a greenhouse. The fruit trees have additional benefit of the curve within the wall acting as a reflective heat sink "surrounding" the tree and focusing the heat and light a little on the leaves....a very nice use of greenhouse space and heat retention features of the masonry walls.

Small Fruit

Small fruit make a nice addition to a garden, although they take up space and only produce one large crop annually or intermittently. Even so, fresh small fruits are a joy and nutrition powerhouses. In the past, rows of fruits such as grapes or berries formed the edge or border of a garden space. They were there, but didn't fill up rows which could produce much more with potatoes or beans in them.

Grapes

There are many, many varieties of grapes, in multiple colors and with different qualities and end uses. For sheer hardiness and versatility, it's hard to beat the old favorite, seeded Concords. These are the familiar flavored grape that are used in most commercial grape jams and grape juices. It is a dark purple almost blue round grape, with a thick skin, gummy flesh, and small seeds. The plants grow in most garden soils, don't need a lot of spraying or care, and produce for decades. You can eat Concords fresh, but they're not even remotely like the seedless thin-skinned supermarket red or green fresh grapes. Even so, better to have a harvest than not.

Thompson Seedless and related types are the primary fresh green grape found in supermarkets. In my experience with these productive plants, they are sensitive to humidity and cold. This makes them a challenging choice right now, and more so in the weather that is coming in the near future. Even so, if you can get a crop, they are tasty for fresh eating, and can be canned in a light to medium syrup.

Red seedless types, such a Reliance Seedless, are a bit hardier than the green seedless types. They are more tolerant to cool weather and can stand some humidity without getting moldy. Japanese beetles will swarm the fruit just as it is ripening and even eat the leaves, so be prepared with your soap spray. The leaves are also perfectly edible for us, better when they are young, and traditionally have been used as a wrap for meat/rice mixes. This makes them a versatile doubly productive plant.

Pruning grapes for productivity means trimming back the vines in the early spring, before the buds enlarge. Grapes bear fruit off of one-year old "arms", so when pruning you need to remove older fibrous growth to allow the newer arms to fruit. Grapes can be pruned to suit any "form" – espaliered, on a simple trellis, on a "two arm" trellis (like a "T" with two crossing pieces), and so forth. Just stick to trimming out the older wood.

Farm writer Gene Logsdon suggests this way of looking at pruning:
- New fruiting growth in the spring grows from buds on the pencil-thick, smooth one-year old wood.
- Pruning should be aimed to renew the fruiting arms, growing on the main trained arms.
- Cut out last year's fruiting arms (which are now getting fibrous), leaving the young arms to grow.
- Cut back your spring one-year old wood to 2 or 3 buds (nodes) from the mainstem.

That will give you plenty of fresh, healthy fruiting growth – and still leave the plants with lots of good air circulation to reduce the risk of mildew diseases.

This will give you a tangle of dryish looking trimmed off vines. You can cut sections of these and poke them into the ground – about half of them will root and start a new vine. There is an upside down to the vines, though – make a diagonal cut on the part nearest the mainstem (the "down" side), and a flat cut 3 buds/nodes above it (the "up" side). The piece should have 3 bud nodes on it. That little stick will be 8"-12" long, about the size of a pencil, and is your new plant cutting.

Poke a deep hole with a piece of stick or cane where you want to plant the cutting, push the "down" side with the diagonal cut into the soil, leaving the top flat end and one bud above ground. Firm the soil around the cutting. If it makes it, it'll grow a few leaves and then a little stem. Just let it grow where it is, any which way. Next year, begin training to the form you want.

You can find recipes for grape jam and jelly in any book on fruit preservation. See the recipes section for a quick recipe for grape/fruit juice and an all-purpose wine recipe.

Wild Berries

Domesticated blackberries, raspberries, gooseberries, strawberries, elderberries, blueberries and cranberries, are descended from hardy wild versions that tolerate weather and seasonal extremes very well. There's even wild versions of grapes, usually called "fox grapes". These wild fruits share several characteristics: they tend to be smaller than domestic fruits, although not by much. They tend toward more seeds than domestic versions. They usually have much stronger and tastier flavor, even though they're not quite as sweet. They are all higher in phytonutrients and anti-oxidation factors than domestics.

All the wild berries are highly seasonal – if you miss the time when wild strawberries are ripening, for example, you've missed them until next year. If you don't get them, wild birds will so they don't go to waste. The same is true of all the other wild fruits. So, collect them when you can.

Wild berries are hardier and more disease resistant than any domestic variety. They don't need special sprays or extra babying to bring in a harvest. Good garden soil is like a gourmet feast to plants that have a history of growing on marginal land. These plants are likely to do as well as any plant can during the coming Cold Times. They've done pretty well in the past without any help from us.

Best of all, wild plants are free. If you own or have access to any land where these plants grow, simply dig up small plants in the spring and transplant a few to your garden. I have wild raspberries, gooseberries, elderberry, and strawberry transplants, all doing exceptionally well several years after transplanting. There are many wild blackberry stands around the farm, so getting some in the garden itself would be overkill. The whole region is thick with them.

Individually or together, these make fabulous jams, jellies, compotes, and wines. If you don't like the seediness, put the crushed fruit through a sieve after heating to soften, before processing, and that will reduce seeds. Add sweetener to the pulp to taste; they might need a little more than commercial domestic fruit.

Found Food

It would be remiss to not include the benefits of wild crafting edible foods. Every region has its own wild-growing plants, from greens to nuts to berries to mushrooms, that can provide dietary interest and the enjoyment of a day in the woods. Get a good guidebook *today* (look for: "Edible Wild Plants of [your area]"), and start looking around for what's available. Key points:

- If you cannot absolutely, for sure, positively identify the plant, don't eat it.

- Eat only plant <u>parts</u> that are edible (fruit but not leaves, or leaves but not fruit, for example),

- Eat only in the season they are edible (poke leaves in spring only),

- Eat only after the correct treatment (boil or soak until toxins are dissolved, for example).

In my area, we can harvest morel mushrooms in the spring, use them until we tire of them, and then freeze or dry extras for use later in the year. In the summer, berries of all kinds ripen. In the fall, wild hickory and black walnuts and acorns are ready for the simple effort of picking them up. Every region has its own range.

However, although there are lots of potential resources in the woods and fields everywhere that can add color and nutrients to your diet, *there is nowhere near enough to provide steady nutrition for even a small group of people.* If you plan to rely on wild crafted food as a dietary mainstay, you need to *prove to yourself* that it can be done, by doing it now – now, when the weather is tolerably good, and you aren't hungry or otherwise under duress. If your country is so rich that it can feed you just by collecting wild foods, good for you. Mine isn't, which is why we have a garden, too.

Sweetening the Meal

We are accustomed to have access to sweet and fruity tasting "stuff" that is constantly available. Humans have a natural sweet tooth that programs us to enjoy fruit in season, and to want it whenever we can get it. Effectively, our hunter-gatherer ancestors gorged on fruit during the few weeks it was available during the year, quite a treat. The rest of the time, a meal was meat, seeds, and vegetables. During the cold times, we will miss the constant access to sugary junk food. Good riddance since it's really not very good for health anyway.

Remember that canning and drying are very effective ways to store fruits for later use. Many sweet fruits, including apples and "long keeper" melons like the cantaloupe "Valencia" and the watermelon "Winter King and Queen", also store nicely in a cool cellar and can last through an entire winter in fairly decent condition, depending on the variety.

That said, even though physiologically we really don't need all that sugar, we are likely to want and enjoy sweetened goods. Store a LOT of sugar for starters. Today, we eat over 130 pounds each per year.

Keeping bees is an option, as long as no one in your group is allergic to bee stings, which could be fatal without access to immediate medications and treatments. Bee keeping is an entire book's worth on its own, requires special equipment that could set you back a good $1000, and also calls for purchase of a starter hive. Right now, bees are subject to several conditions and parasites that are hard to control; bee keepers may lose half their hives in any given year. But, having several hives can provide dozens to hundreds of pounds of delicious honey annually, as well as keeping the important pollinators around your fruit trees and garden. If this seems like a good option for you, contact your local Extension office for lists of local beekeepers and beekeeper clubs. They are often thrilled to talk about their hobby with newcomers. Also, keep in mind that we really don't know how bees will fare in the extreme cold and weather fluctuations that are ahead.

Another possibility is **tapping trees for sap** – that's the source of maple syrup – but many other types of deciduous trees can be tapped: nut trees of any type, beech, and birch for example. Trees are tapped using a metal or hollow wood tube is pounded into hole drilled in the tree bark until it reaches the inner layer beneath the bark. This is done during a 4 to 6 week period in early spring when the sap is "rising". The tap allows some of that sap to drain out the spigot and into a bucket that is hung from the tap. Buckets are collected once or several times a day, depending on how fast the sap is flowing. The sap is then boiled down and stirred constantly until it reaches a temperature of about 219°F (for maple) – then it is considered syrup. Don't let the syrup go beyond that temperature, because it can burn easily at that point.

It takes anywhere from 40 to 80 gallons of sap to produce one gallon of syrup, and that can vary from year to year, and from tree to tree. One mature sugar maple tree, 16" in diameter, can produce a quart of syrup from 40 quarts of sap yearly. So, if you like syrup, you'll need a lot of trees.

Most of the equipment needed for tapping trees can be made at home or purchased, if you're of a mind to. Taps, buckets, and boiling pans, plus a good sized fire and griddle over it, are the essential tools. Trees are tapped by drilling an upward slanting hole for the tap on the sunny side of the tree. The sap runs when it warms up into the 40s and 50°F range during the day with freezing temperatures at night. It's a lot of work, during a particularly cold and soggy time of year. But syrup is an outstandingly useful food, plus an excellent trade item in a down economy.

There are other natural sources of sugars. Sugar cane is one, and sorghum is another, but these are warmth-loving plants with long growing seasons. Odds are good that the production of these will move to equatorial regions or be available at prices that make them the province of the rich.

Extending the Season With Greenhouses

During the Dalton Minimum in the 1800s, growers in Europe extended their growing season and plant survival during unseasonable cold, by placing glass domes over individual plants – effectively, a mini-greenhouse. These "cloches", which means *bells*, were made from heavy clear glass. Plants that were started early could be covered by a cloche until the weather was warm enough for it to do without the cover. A modern version might be a plastic gallon milk jug, bottom cut off, and placed over a tender plant. Unlike a glass cloche, it would have to be attached or weighted to the ground so it won't blow away. If the weather will be very cool, each cloche could be covered with hay or a blanket, or banked with soil.

Similarly, some gardeners utilize a "cold frame", another mini greenhouse that is big enough to grow lettuce, greens, carrots or a few other cool weather items. Effectively, a cold frame is a simple rectangular box with about a 45° angle front to back, with the front edge lower and the back edge higher. The lower side faces south to catch winter sun. Over this, a simple glass window is placed and hinged along the higher back edge. Use wood screws to put this box

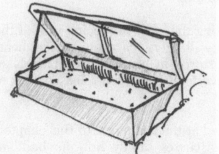

together at the edges so that it is solid and holds tightly.

The box should be set into the ground up to the bottom of the front piece so that soil acts as an insulator. You can also put a 1" layer of Styrofoam insulation along the interior walls, too. Fill the box with compost, and cover that with 4 to 6 inches of top soil up to the bottom of the front wall. The compost will keep the cold frame somewhat warm, even on very cold days. The glass lid is your greenhouse, providing light to the growing plants. On days when the sun is out and temperatures rise, the glass is raised an inch or two to allow good air flow. On cold days, the entire frame can be covered with a blanket or hay.

When the weather has warmed up, the cold frame can be removed and stored until it's needed again in the fall. This type of structure is especially nice, because it can be made from wood leftover from other projects and an old otherwise useless window. If you can, paint the interior white to reflect light onto the plants.

Like a cold frame, a large greenhouse can keep plants going through cold and even into the winter itself. The key to growing in a greenhouse during the dead of winter is *warmth*. Today, warmth can be maintained with propane or kerosene heat, or even with a well-placed wood heating stove. When we are in the Cold Times, we may not have access to extra heating sources -- except the wood stove, of course. But we can still site a greenhouse partially underground. That in-ground greenhouse tends to maintain its temperature better than any above-ground version. If compost is used thickly in the planting beds, it may generate enough heat to keep the entire area warm enough to grow whatever cool-weather crops and greens that you'd like.

Construction of an in-ground greenhouse is more complicated than building above-ground – the soil's composition affects what kind of walls you use (concrete or concrete blocks are ideal), whether you will require French drains around the structure, and how much insulation you will need. The interior walls need to be high enough to allow you to stand upright, and it must be able to collect as much sunlight as possible during the winter.

One way to store heat is by making the back sun-facing wall of the greenhouse a kind of Trombe wall. Perhaps even having heat-storing masonry or even water stored in black-colored barrels so that all incoming sunlight is converted to heat and released back to the plants during the night.

The author of the book mentioned at the beginning of this chapter, *Backyard Winter Gardening*, discusses briefly how he built an underground earth-sheltered greenhouse at his Utah home. Includes some good ideas and practical tips, from someone who has actually done it.

University of Minnesota has been exploring what they call the Deep Winter Greenhouse (DWG), an above-ground passive solar construction that makes use of a primary heat-sink and small amounts of heating and lighting.

They grow cold-weather crops such as mizuna, lettuce, cabbage, cauliflower, broccoli, kale, other Asian greens, and so forth with minimal inputs. They've completed a free online .pdf:

Cold Climate Greenhouse Resource: A Guidebook for Designing and Building a Cold Climate Greenhouse available at: http://www.extension.umn.edu/rsdp/community-and-local-food/production-resources/docs/cold-climate-greenhouse-resource.pdf

The full plans are here: https://umn.qualtrics.com/CP/File.php?F=F_78JCrtZBH8ALDgh

The book is less than 70 pages, the plans about 30 pages, and are worth printing out right now, so you have a copy on hand whenever you decide to build.

If you build planters for your greenhouse, make them double decker. On the bottom level, build boxes you can cover, fill with aged horse manure, and plant mushroom spawn from edible types. These will grow well in the moist, warm greenhouse conditions and handle the dark conditions beneath the planters, produce lots of excellent food for the table, plus high levels of carbon dioxide to help your other plants grow, too.

Calculate How Much To Plant

Having evaluated your daily use of specific foods a couple chapters ago, the next question is: *how much should we plant?* This is a surprisingly complex question, because we need to factor in **risk**, as well as the basics for fresh eating AND for storage. There was an old saying from the middle ages, advice on how to plant peas:

One for the field
One for the mouse
One for me

In other words, the people understood that there was a good chance that a portion of their harvest would be lost to natural conditions ("the field"), to hungry competitors ("the mouse"), and whatever survived that was for the people. Basically, they planted *three times* as much as they thought they needed.

In modern gardening, we have the widely shared tendency to believe that each item planted will provide the expected yield. This has worked quite nicely, as long as the weather has been agreeable and we have control over pests – and there is a perpetual backup supply available in the supermarket in case of garden misfortune.

We can't think like that anymore. We must assume that what comes out of our garden plot is what we will have to eat – and plan accordingly. Extras *always* get stored either as preserved food, or by being fed to livestock that store it "on the hoof".

Before we go on....
I want to advise you that the following numbers will stagger you. There's likely to be a moment when you grasp that the sheer amount of seed, and ground, and effort that is required to feed your group will be *impossible.* You will experience a sense of failure and defeat, even before you start. *This is temporary and a healthy stage in your understanding and growth.* You're just coming to terms with the reality that has been in front of you all your life. Just follow the plan, and learn from each problem you face. If all your ancestors could do this with only hand tools (and they did, or you wouldn't be here), then you can too.

Let's look at a couple examples that will give you the means to calculate your own needs. Garden peas, also known as English peas, are versatile when eaten as shelled peas and they can be dried to make split pea soup, too. The opened pods can be fed to livestock, put into compost, or used as the base for a delightful white sweet wine. In my garden, planting against a garden fence about an inch apart, in rough but moderately fertile soil, I grew Saber peas. I was able to harvest 10 pounds of shelled peas, plus perhaps another pound for fresh use, from 50 feet of row. That's one pound for each five feet of planted row.

Read that again: *one pound per each five feet of row.* If we eat, between 2 or 3 people in a household, a pound of peas each week at

6 to 8 ounces each once a week, we would need 52 *pounds* for a year's worth of side dishes or ingredients. At 10 pounds per 50 feet of row, we would have to increase garden space a little over five times to achieve 52 pounds. That is, we would need a row of peas 250 feet long or multiple rows that add up to 250 feet. Add another 50 feet for growing next year's seed peas, too.

Green beans are a little more productive, since the pod is consumed as well as the seeds. Planting Blue Lake Bush, I can grow a pound of green beans each two feet of row. Fifty feet of row equals 25 pounds of fresh beans – which will can up to about 20 pints (a little more than one pound of cut beans per pint). Once again, if we use a pint a week, we'd need to grow about 60 pounds. So, we'd need 120 feet of row. Add on 25% more row, about 30 feet, for seed.

Now suppose we have green beans 3 times a week; we'd need three times as much row, or 360 feet. So, between peas and beans *alone*, we'd have to have at least a 300 foot long garden, or multiple rows adding up to that much. Alternatively, in a shorter garden, we could grow half the crop early in the season and then replant to get a fall crop, weather permitting.

So, here is the calculation:

_____ amount in pounds consumed each week

X 52 =

_____ supply in pounds needed for one year

_____ amount in pounds that can be produced per foot of row
X (supply in pounds for one year) =

_____ feet of row required

+ 25% X (feet of row) for replacement seed

Now, include every other type of garden plant you'd like – tomatoes, potatoes, melons, lettuce, squash, cucumbers, celery, parsley, herbs, beets, carrots, corn, and whatever other items. It's obvious that a half-acre per person is a fairly reasonable amount to plant if your garden is your primary food source. *Assuming no crop losses to bad weather.* It wouldn't hurt to plant extra, even double the amount. Store for just-in-case you lose next year's garden. You'll still have plenty. Keep as much variety in your diet as possible. That'll make planting more challenging and require more seeds and record-keeping, but better nutrition and more interesting meals.

The highest producing garden crops, per space utilized, are tomatoes and potatoes, by the way.

Lee Wheelbarger, on Grand Solar Minimum
YouTube channel encouraged storing
5 years' worth of seeds.
He said that this will give you enough seed to
replant through several years of failed harvests, even
three successive bad years.
Many sellers offer seeds in "bulk" (several pounds) at lower
cost than buying in small packets.

A Word About Hydroponics and Aquaponics

Hydroponics is the process of raising edible plants in a controlled environment, typically a greenhouse or even a specially outfitted shipping container, under lights. The plants are started in a neutral substrate, usually "coir" made from coconut husks, and submerged in a flowing nutrient liquid. The nutrient liquid is usually formulated for specific plant varieties. Tomato nutrient is different from lettuce nutrient, for example. The nutrient solution is circulated past the plants at a rate that promotes fast, steady growth. You've probably already purchased hydroponic tomatoes and lettuce at larger supermarkets.

Aquaponics is similar to hydroponics, except that instead of using a chemical nutrient solution, the plants are fed by water from fish tanks. Fish may eat a pellet feed, leftover greens, and whatever bugs can be lured to their tank. The water in the fish tank is circulated past the roots of the growing plants, which utilize nutrients from the fish waste, and clean the water enough that it can be reintroduced to the fish tanks. In this way, two crops, plants and fish, can be gained from similar amounts of space.

These are marvelous systems that work very efficiently right now. There are some significant issues, however, that limit both hydro- and aquaponics going into the Zen-slap and Hang-on eras. First of these issues is that the plants, either in a greenhouse or shipping container arrangement, must have light and warmth. That means having electricity. If the power goes down for any length of time, plants and fish will be lost for lack of light and warmth.

Also, the nutrient solutions are produced in factories today. There's no guarantee they'll still be available later at reasonable prices, and if they are, larger commercial operations will have first dibs. Even though aquaponics has little need for nutrient solution, you'd still have to acquire "fry" – baby fish – from some source to restock your tanks. Most home operations are not set up with the right environment for raising hatchlings.

Finally, pumps to circulate fluids are both electrically operated *and* they wear out and break down. That means having backup power as well as replacement pump parts or replacement pumps.

The ability to grow food in a temperature and light controlled environment may become an important way of producing food on a commercial scale, as we enter into Cold Times. Setting up a system that overcomes loss of grid power, importation of nutrient chemicals, and access to small fry – as well as replacement seeds, since you'll harvest everything before it seeds out – makes this system very challenging and costly on a small scale.

Better than focusing on a single source, consider growing food in as many different venues as you can – an indoor sunroom, a greenhouse, outdoors in fields, in gardens, and in a small hydro- or aquaponics set up. That way, if you lose one or two venues, you'll still be able to have a harvest.

Keeping the Harvest

Once you have gathered your harvest, you have an important decision to make about how you will store it through the cold winter months. At this time, the most common and familiar method is **freezing** (keeping in a deep freezer in vacuum packs or other packaging). Almost all foods with which we are familiar can be frozen for long-term use. The costs include packaging and packing equipment (such as a Food Saver vacuum-packer), a large deep freezer, and electricity to run it.

Second to that is "**canning**", which is actually done in glass jars with single-use or repeated-use type lids – this is the canning that I discuss through the food chapters. It can be done with a "water bath" large canning pot, or with a big heavy multi-quart pressure canner. Most common fruits, vegetables and meats can be successfully canned, although some are better frozen (broccoli and cauliflower, for example).

In addition to canning jars and lids (about $12 per dozen), you'll need the canning pots (boiler runs about $60; the All American Pressure Canner is the top of the line at about $250), jar lifters, funnels, and additions (sugar or honey for the fruit, salt for the veggies and meats), fresh water, steady heat source that is either propane or electric but NOT glass-topped stoves (they will crack).

Ball and Kerr lids are sold as "single use", although some people do reuse them with the risk of a sealing failure. Tattler lids are fully reusable, but cost quite a bit more than the other types of lids – the initial investment is recouped as you continue to use them through the years. Ball and Kerr are available at supermarkets and department stores. The only place I've seen Tattler is online.

A third increasingly common method is **dehydrating or drying** foods. This is a method that can be done with an electric dehydrator or in an oven set on pilot or the lowest temperature. Fruits, veggies, spices, and meats (cooked and as jerky) can be dehydrated. The best home dehydrator I've found is the Excalibur at $250 or so. It is much easier to use and gives a better result than the round ones sold at department stores. Before use, you may need to "rehydrate" the food, placing it in warm water for a period of time to let it fluff and puff a bit. Dehydrated foods can be stored for long-term in mason-type jars, out of direct sunlight. If you have a Food Saver or other similar device, you may be able to vacuum-pack in your mason jars for really good quality long term storage.

Fermenting is another method we are familiar with. Cheese, sauerkraut, and wine are examples of food preservation by fermentation. Preparing foods by fermenting is a fine art and requires time and practice. You'll need jars, vats, additives like yeast or starter cultures, and a clean, cool, environment to store in such as a basement or fruit cellar.

Pickling and brining are old traditional methods, utilizing vinegar or salt to achieve storage of some firm vegetables, and some varieties of ocean fish. Pickling can be done in a "quick" form, and in a longer process that involves an initial brining followed by a vinegar treatment. Quick pickling uses canning jars, but brining is usually done in a larger plastic or heavy ceramic vessel that can be tightly covered to keep out gnats. Brined foods may be left in their jug in a cool covered area, like a cool storage, for months. Startup costs are small and include the brining vessel, canning jars, vinegar and flavoring ingredients such as mixed pickling spices.

Smoking can be done on a large outdoor dedicated building or small portable smoker scale. It's generally used for meats of all kinds, and can result in meat that is fairly dry and can be stored for months, or in meats that are moist and must be frozen but taste delightful and smoky. Dry smoked meats must be soaked to rehydrate and remove some salt from them before use. Like fermenting, this is an art and takes time to get good at. Some meats require soaking or injection of flavorings or spices that help with the preservation. You'll need the smoking chamber, and firewood coals - apple, hickory, maple, mesquite are all good.

Cold storage is similar to keeping fruits and vegetables in a refrigerator. It used to be that people had a special "fruit cellar" – a simple basement, sometimes just a dug pit basement under the house where firm fruits and vegetables of all kinds were stored for winter use. Something as simple as a large plastic barrel set in the ground with the lip well above any risk of water infiltration, filled with your foods, and covered with dirt and hay to retain the cold and, hopefully, prevent freezing. Different foods have their own requirements. Carrots, for example, do best if stored in slightly damp clean sand, whereas tomatoes store for a while if wrapped in newspaper and placed side-by-side. The cold space needs good air circulation, but must be protected from freezing. Freezing will ruin many of your stored goods. Try not to store apples with other foods; apples release ethylene gas, which stimulates "ripening" in many other types of foods.

Freeze Drying is a relatively new method of food preservation. It preserves the quality, flavor, color, and nutrition of multiple types of foods for decades, if stored in cool, dry, dark conditions. Most long term canned storage food is either dehydrated or freeze dried. There's varieties of freeze dried meats that look precisely like fresh steak, chops, or codfish, but they're rock hard and room temperature. There's even freeze dried ice cream bars, that look just like they came out of the freezer, except they're not cold.

Freeze dried foods are a little more costly than dehydrated. Like dehydrated foods, they need to be rehydrated before cooking; meats are cooked after rehydrating, just as if they were raw. Color and flavor retention are very good.

Freeze drying is much more expensive to use as a method of home-preserving. The freeze drying machine costs around $3000. Then, you'll need air-tight vacuum sealable jars to store your supplies in. The machine requires electricity to run, and interruption of the freezing or drying cycle means the loss of the food that is being treated.

If you're able to freeze dry your current garden's produce, that might be a viable option for generating a large supply of long term storage. However, the ability to use a freeze drier after Zen-slap is questionable unless you have a consistent supply of electricity. Remember that we are focusing on methods that can be carried on even without most modern amenities.

Niceties

It's extremely difficult to run a rural home without good tools. Hoes, shovels, rakes, pruners, axes, picks, pry bars, and weed trimmers all come in manual versions. New ones are generally pretty poorly made, so look for "antiques" that are in good condition or that you can replace handles on. Country auctions are good places to find these, often just for a few dollars each.

Keeping the garden free of weeds requires either a lot of diligence and many hands, or a tiller of some kind. Modern gas-powered trimmers and tillers are a real work-saver, but you'll need more than the machine itself. Cord, motor oil, gasoline, replacement parts, and know-how are the basic add-on items you'll have to keep in storage.

A small lawnmower, the basic old-timey push type, will cut a maintained lawn just as good as a gas-powered one, and will keep running as long as you do. For larger areas, a garden tractor/mower combination does the job easier, with the need for belts, replacement parts, oil and gasoline storage. Alternatively, "lawns" can become pasture for small livestock; sheep are particularly good at keeping a lawn short and attractive and eating flowers, fruit trees, and shrubs, if they're not protected.

Finally, the major expense: a tractor with bucket and tiller. If you're doing serious farm work, you can't function without it unless you are Amish and have big horses and willing neighbors. Old tractors require constant repairs, but cost less upfront and generally don't have the kind of electronics onboard that could fail during a CME or EMP event. Plenty of spare parts, plus a couple hundred gallons of diesel – and a good repair manual for your make and model – and you'll have years of service.

Horse-drawn equipment can fit the needs well, but this isn't something a person can do as easily as hopping on a tractor. Horses must be maintained, which calls for food, medications, fences, corrals, and pasture, as well as the harnesses appropriate to the equipment.

Once again, "many hands make lighter work." Everyone contributes and the job, whatever it is, gets done faster.

7 FOOD: SMALL SCALE LIVESTOCK

Meat and animal fat are critical to survival in cold climates. The Inuit lived primarily on fats, fish, and mammal meat, and were strong healthy people until the introduction of modern diets. The ability to produce your own meats may be one of the most valuable skills you will have in the times to come. Livestock not only provide meat and fat, but also milk, eggs, valuable skins, fibers such as wool, down and feathers, bones for soups, and manure for the garden.

If you have never raised livestock, you must start small with the intention of growing your flock or herd. Routine animal care really requires "the eye of the farmer" to see early health problems, whether the animals are getting enough to eat or not, when they need trace minerals or other supplements, and so on. You won't learn any of that from a book – only by doing and observing.

Here's an early and serious word of warning: *The animals you raise are not pets. They are food. Do not give them "names," except maybe "Fried" or "Hamburger". They will live pleasant happy lives, and then they will die quickly and efficiently and feed you and your family. Hens that don't lay, goats that don't milk, calves that limp, old friendly sheep, and doe-eyed cows are all meat. This is the nature of the real world.*

For those of us raised in cities who have formed bonds with animals like dogs and cats at some point in our lives, this is a psychologically difficult transition. Baby goats are unbelievably cute and fun and inquisitive. Even so, you MUST remind yourself that they exist for only one reason: to eat. No normal person enjoys butchering day, but that's how those animals become meals. You can console yourself that the animals had a good life and didn't suffer at the end, and that makes it a little easier. This is one of the features of the post-warmth world that we all have to face and deal with.

Best Starter Animals

The two easiest animals to raise in a small setting are chickens and rabbits. Chickens can produce both eggs and meat; rabbits produce a nice mild white meat and a soft furry skin that is excellent for retaining heat. They don't take much space, and are fairly tolerant of cold weather. Both can live on homegrown grains and grasses and garden waste. Comfrey can feed them both, another plus for comfrey. Rabbit manure doesn't have much odor, comes as pellets, and can go right into the garden. Chicken manure is good compost starter.

I've written several books on raising small stock over the years under my previous name, Anita Evangelista. One is out of print: *Backyard Meat Production: How To Grow All The Meat You Need In Your Own Backyard* (1997); the other one is available on Kindle for $4.99: *Your Meat, Egg, and Milk Garden: How to Raise Small Livestock in Your Own Backyard*

Chickens

For the cold times ahead, chickens will need an insulated shed for housing, one that will shed snow as well as possible sin you don't want them crushed by a collapsing shelter. An "A" framed structure is suitable. The edges should have a poultry wire mesh buried around the immediate perimeter so that predators like skunks and raccoons can't dig in. They *will* try, because inside the chicken house is a smorgasbord for hungry animals. Make your defenses stronger than you think you'll need.

The shed will need mesh-screened windows that can be closed and covered by shutters so that they keep in warmth in winter, and be opened in summer and for fresh air and light. Try to have at least one glass insulated window that you can use for daylight year around. Ideally, the shed floor itself is dirt. A wood-floored shed has the benefit of repelling predators if it is solid, but needs to be thoroughly cleaned out twice a year; dirt floor doesn't need cleaning as often or at all, plus gives the chickens access to dirt to eat. They need it.

Inside the shed, a thick flooring of hay a foot or more thick to start the winter, with more added through the season. All that bedding helps keep the birds warm and clean and busy. They will spend a lot of their time scratching the flooring around and breaking it up. A feeder may be used or their grain and greens can just be strewn around the floor. They will find it. If you feed grain, try to get a feeder that hangs above the floor to reduce easy access for the resident mice. The chickens will also need a waterer.

Inside, you'll need one 12"x12"x12" nesting box for each 3 birds so that their eggs will be easy to find. Make it from cast-off lumber, plywood, or even old buckets laid on their sides. Put some hay or wood chips inside for them to make into a little nest. Hens will appreciate a ladder-like set of perches away from the nest boxes, because hens like to sleep above the floor.

That's what they'll need for the cold months. For the warm months, they will additionally need some outside space they can go into safely, which means a heavy wire-surrounded yard. They'll return to their home when twilight approaches. I prefer to have "free range" chickens, letting the birds go where ever they want and collect their own food. But, during the coming Mini Ice Age, their freedom will convert them into a meal for hawks, coyote, neighbor dogs, owls, and anything else that can grab them. Getting replacements may be problematic and costly.

Getting Started

During the Awakening stage, the easiest way to start with chicks is to buy "day old" birds. You can find these in the spring at farm and feed stores, typically costing about $3-4 each. Our local farm store ran out after a week in February 2017, which makes me think people are already awakening and trying to get ahead of the curve. There's also sites online that sell chicks, including Murray McMurray and Estes Hatchery.

If the chicks are fluffy and have no true feathers, you'll need to keep them warm until they have feathered out. You can invest in a "brooder box", which is a metal-sided cage with a small heater in it, about $150. You just set the temperature, load the feeder and waterer, and put in the chicks. Alternatively, you can use a heat lamp and set it over a low cage lined with cardboard to keep the warmth in. Make sure the lamp can't fall into the box because it can start a fire. The old granny method of keeping chicks warm was to place them in a covered box beneath the warm wood cook stove, one with legs, and that method works, too. The flooring will need to have some loose clean sand and/or garden dirt scattered around, because the chicks will need grit in order to digest their feed.

Use a small outdoor thermometer in the brooder; start the temperature at about 97°F, lowering it gradually over the next two or three weeks to outdoor temperatures. You can tell if the chicks are too cold: they'll pile together and make loud cheeping sounds. The chicks are too warm if they scatter away from the heat lamp and hang around the edges of the box. Raise or lower the heat accordingly.

Once the chicks have feathered out, they can be moved to a warm shed with a grassy run area outdoors. Make sure it is fully protected against predators including snakes, because the chicks are at their most vulnerable right now. Put in a heat lamp that cannot be easily dislodged and drop on them or into the bedding due to fire risk. Use the heat lamp at night or any time the temperatures get down below 60°F. By the time the chickens are 4 months old, they should be able to tolerate all but the coldest temperatures, particularly if they have an insulated area to get into.

What Breeds?

This is a surprisingly important question. The chickens you start with will form the foundation of the flock you may have for decades. In the coming Cold Times, you may not be able to acquire replacements as easily as today. Furthermore, the tools to raise them may be unavailable as well including chick starter grains, heat lamps, and continuous electricity.

Given that, I'm going to discuss what I believe is a good option. If you've raised chickens before, you may have a different approach. To my mind, the ideal chicken is one that can lay a good quantity of eggs, that has a meaty build, and that is willing and able to set eggs and hatch more chicks. You'll also need one rooster for every 10 hens.

Typical breeds which fit that description are the Barred Rock, Buff Orpington, Cochins, and old style Rhode Island Red (not the Production Red, which doesn't set). There's also minor breeds, such as the Turken AKA Naked Neck, and the Arucana or Amerucana version. These are called large-bodied or dual purpose chickens, since they both lay eggs and produce meat.

Some breeds have feathers on their lower legs and feet, and some have "clean" featherless legs. There may be some real benefits during cold weather to birds with feathered legs. However, in muddy circumstances, or if the birds get into the snow, those feathers may gum up or freeze and cause further problems. I have opted for "clean" leg varieties.

The ability and willingness to "set" or hatch eggs has almost been bred out of chickens today. If you want assured setting ability to breed into your line, consider keeping a few Bantam hens. They are superior setters. They are also much smaller birds, but will interbreed with bigger roosters and hopefully produce larger offspring that are able to set eggs, too. A hen that is willing to set eggs is called "broody". She will stop laying eggs and want to stay setting on eggs most of the time, and protect them by pecking at anything that bothers her, including you.

It takes 21 days for the eggs to hatch. The hen will watch over the chicks and keep them warm until they can make it on their own. That's a lot easier than trying to hatch eggs yourself. You may need to keep hens with chicks away from the other birds because chicks look like food to some of them.

The reason for keeping crossbred chickens has to do with the genetic depression that occurs in purebred livestock, especially when you are breeding from a very small starting population. The reason we have "breeds" is because people have selected for certain traits and characteristics such as egg laying ability and color and feathering. What we call a "breed" is actually a closely related *family*. That's why they all look the same.

The only real benefit to a purebred anything is that the offspring will be relatively predictable. Not *perfectly* predictable, but in a general way. We can predict that a purebred bloodhound dog, for example, is going to have a great sense of smell and enjoy sniffing and tracking scents – much more so than, say, a purebred Chihuahua which has been bred to predictably sit on the owner's lap and be cuddly.

Predictability in livestock is important when an agriculture corporation needs to make every animal into a dollar sign and get all the return possible from them; they can't afford the cost of raising a chicken that doesn't lay at a high rate for its short life. So egg producers "sacrifice" the large body for lots of eggs. Commercial layers can produce 300-320 or more eggs yearly, but the hens are small at 3 to 4 pounds and nervous.

In a home setting, that predictability is handy but not vital. I am suggesting you start with dual-purpose birds because we can predict that they will grow slowly, develop a large meaty body, and produce more eggs than an average family can use – over 200 eggs per hen per year for several years. If you have 12 hens, that's 2400 eggs a year, over 200 dozen, four dozen per week. That's plenty to eat fresh, pickle and can, make rich cakes and cookies using extra eggs, hatch out an annual replacement and meat supply, and still have some to sell or give away.

Your second generation crossbreds and beyond will still be predictable large meaty birds since all their ancestors were, and still lay plenty of eggs like their ancestors, but other features will vary – color, feather type, ability to set eggs, and so forth. Disease resistance should be pretty good, since you have increased genetic variability by cross breeding. Your third and fourth generations should be even more cross bred. They will be even healthier in the long run if you are able to trade a few hens or a rooster with a neighbor who has another breed entirely. That will prevent in-breeding depression in your little flock.

All "pitiful" chickens should be removed and eaten or destroyed. These will be the limpers, the ones that become pets because they need extra attention, the ones that are scrawny or sickly. The pitiful ones will pluck your heartstrings and be the hardest to get rid of, but if you keep them, you'll be breeding weakness into your flock. Remove any birds that don't do well or that appear sickly. Cull them out of your gene pool and into your stew pot.

When your chicks hatch in subsequent generations, about half will be female and half will be male. Figure that most of the males will go onto the menu when they are about 5 months old, just as they begin to crow. You can eat them earlier, of course, but they will be smaller. Remove any hens that don't lay or cause trouble, and pressure can or convert to broth. Remember to use the scaly part of the legs and feet, minus toenails, in the broth for the best healing properties! Replace 3 year old roosters with the fastest growing, healthiest, biggest, feistiest young ones from your new batch.

Basically, you will trade "predictability" for "adaptability." In Cold Times, *adaptability* is a critical survival trait.

Feed

Chickens will eat anything. They can survive and thrive hunting up their own bugs, worms, your garden, roadkill, leftovers from the kitchen, weed seeds, and anything that wiggles. They will eat other chickens, too – no moral high ground for this livestock. However, during Cold Times, you'll have to bring the food to them.

166

Prepared chicken feed is available at feed stores in 50 pound sacks, costing about $8-$9 each right now. Prices are going up. You can buy chicken feed in pellet, crumbles, or whole grain form; it's all fine. Stock up on 50 pound bags and store the bags where they cannot be attacked by rodents, because they will find it if they can. A chicken will go through about 6 ounces of feed daily, so for 15 chickens it's a total of about 5 to 6 pounds a day, about a gallon.

The more you can produce or provide on your own, the less of the commercial feed that you have to buy. That includes garden leftovers, things that are past ripe, and whatever the family doesn't eat. Corn, sunflower seeds, and comfrey are among the easiest garden items you can grow, and they are all superior chicken feeds.

For one year, feeding 15 chickens entirely from your supplies, you'll need about 1800 pounds of grain, 30 fifty pound bags. You can buy that TODAY for less than $300. If you supplement that with lots of greens, melon skins, and last-night's pasta, you could stretch it much longer than a year. If you make cheese at home, the whey left over from cheese making can also feed the chickens, and it is a top level high quality protein easily digested food for them. They love it.

Chickens also need calcium in their diet. It's how they form the shells on their eggs. If they don't have enough, they will utilize calcium from their bones, causing weak and easily-broken bones. Egg shells become thin and easily cracked if the hens are deficient. The absolute best natural source for this calcium is the chitin shell on insects. Chickens thrive on their natural foods.

However, if your hens are locked up, they can't get enough insects to keep them in balance. The commercial source for this calcium is an "oyster shell" supplement. It is actual shells from marine creatures, ground into small size. A 25 pound bag costs about $10 and will last 15 chickens for 6 months to a year of "free choice" access.

After Zen-slap, save all the shells from your eggs, wash thoroughly, dry in a warm oven to help kill bacteria or leave out in bright sun for several days, and crush or grind to a crumbly powder. Don't leave the shells looking like eggs though; no point in giving the chickens ideas. Set it out in a container so the chickens can get at it when they want some. Ideally, you'd also save all bones from cooking, boil them down as for soup, then take the bones out, dry in an oven, and crush or grind them up as well. Get two or three bags of oyster shell calcium right now, and store with your grains.

Chicks to Chickens

The day you buy chicks during the Awakening or early Zen-slap stage, buy 50-100 pounds of "chick starter", un-medicated if you can find it. This is a combination of grains that is finely ground and tasty to chicks. As I write this, those two to three bags of grains should set you back less than $35. Consider a $6 brick of pine shavings, too, for the bottom of your brooder, but don't use that until your chicks are at least a week old because if used earlier it confuses them and is hard on their feet. Pine shavings will help reduce the nasty odor from the brooder. You will need two quart-jar waterers for each 25 chicks, and two small tray-style feeders, about $25 total.

I suggest you get 25-50 chicks to start with. That will seem like a lot. Make sure that you have split that between at least THREE different breeds. More breeds are better.

When you buy chicks, it's a bit of a learned skill to be able to tell the boys from the girls. The simplest approach is to buy "straight run",

which means, 'just as they came from the incubator.' It works out to about half male and half female. In around 16 weeks, the males will be obviously male, with larger combs and tail feathers; they tend to stand more "upright" than females, too. By 6 months, your young roosters will be crowing. Almost all of the males will be destined for your freezer.

The remainder of your starter chicks will be hens. If all your chicks have survived (don't expect it), you should have about 12-25 young hens. They are called "pullets" until they start laying. Hens will lay whether there is a rooster in the henhouse or not. In order to get fertile eggs, there must be a healthy rooster among them.

At 6 months of age, you'll be deciding the breeding of your future chickens. Examine your roosters closely. You will want to save two to three of them. Choose the largest. Pick the birds up, feel how meaty they are, weigh them. Ideally, choose ones of different breeds than the majority of your hens. In other words, you will be producing *crossbred* chickens from now on. This will increase the genetic variability off the offspring. They may look entirely different than either parent and show some hybrid vigor by being healthier or having other positive qualities than the parents.

The roosters that don't make the cut can be given away, sold (they don't bring much), or put in your freezer. I suggest the last option, so that you have some practice with the process. Butchering is discussed after the Recipes section later in the book.

Hens start laying at about 6 months of age. The first eggs are usually small, and some won't have a hard shell, just a leathery sack like turtle eggs. After several weeks, most of the eggs will be medium to large size, and the girls should be using the nest boxes regularly. Each hen will lay one egg daily, on average. You will be swamped with eggs. Look up lots of new recipes, because you'll need them.

The hens should continue to lay fairly consistently for about a year to 18 months of age. Then they go into "molt" – a 6 week period when they shed their feathers and grow a new set. They look pretty ratty during this phase, so don't be surprised. They don't lay when they are molting, either, so it's a good time to use your stored eggs.

Dual-purpose hens will start laying again after molting, and will lay larger eggs, some will be jumbo. On average, they will also lay fewer eggs, but probably not so much that you would notice. If you keep the hens another year, they'll molt again in 12-18 months, stop laying, grow new feathers, and then start laying again. A three year old hen is an aged bird. By 5 or 6, they are getting old. Old hens make good broth, soup, or stew. I did have a Rhode Island Red that lived for almost 11 years, and was still laying eggs occasionally until she keeled over in the barnyard.

Hens also slow down their egg laying during the winter if they are very cold, don't have enough fresh water to make eggs with, and if the daylight drops below 8 hours a day. Many chicken raisers use artificial lights in their hen houses to keep the birds in light for about 12 hours a day. That'll keep the eggs coming during the winter.

One way to do this is to get 4 or 5 inexpensive solar "yard lights." Set them in the sun during the day, and move into the henhouse at night. They'll get enough light to help them continue to lay. Solar yard lights will last well into the Zen-slap stage, especially if you're only using them during the winter and put them in a safe place during lighter months. After that, in the Hang-on phase, unless you have access to technology or electricity, your hens are likely to be off the job during the winter months.

Keeping Eggs

When you have productive hens, you will be awash in eggs in the spring and summer. In spite of the hysteria in the food industry, you can leave unwashed fresh eggs sitting in a basket on your countertop for weeks without any problems. At this writing, I've got about 150 eggs in baskets on mine. I've also got 7 dozen eggs in cartons in my refrigerator – these are 4 to 5 months old. And about 10 dozen frozen in the freezer. And another 10 dozen or so pickled with jalapenos and other flavoring ingredients. That's after giving away dozens and dozens anytime someone comes to visit. Several procedures for keeping eggs, and a pickling recipe, are included in the Recipes section.

By the way, eggs keep better if you don't wash them. The hens leave a permeable coating on each egg called "bloom" that provides a protective barrier against bacteria. If your eggs have dirt or manure on them, just brush it off. If you must wash eggs, use those first.

Rabbits

Rabbits are among the easiest animals there are to raise. They are quiet, clean, calm most of the time, friendly, easy to care for, efficient reproducers, and can do well in small spaces. Rabbits are very tolerant of cold

weather, even having hair on the soles of their feet, which is a real plus in the times to come. They're also similar to regular pet animals, so transitioning from "taking care of pets" to "taking care of rabbits" is an easy step. That also makes butchering day a hard one for many people. Again, I caution you not to name your food, especially not cuddly cute ones.

Housing

Commercial rabbitries keep one female (doe) rabbit per 30"x30" cage raised off the ground. A feeder passes alfalfa based feed pellets through one side of the wire, and a waterer – either a drip-bottle on the wall of the cage, or a heavy dish – completes the setup. I

generally include a piece of untreated pine 2"x4" or piece of wood off an apple tree in the cage for the bunny to chew on. They'll chew everything else otherwise. Add a small "landing pad", about 8"x8" made from plywood so the bunny can rest its feet off the wire.

Bottom of the cage is ½"x½" wire, large enough to allow the manure pellets to fall through. Sides of the cage are 1"x2" squares. Could be smaller openings, but not much larger. If making cages, wire over all wood supports to prevent chewing. Generally, the cages are set about 3 feet off the ground on supports or sawhorses, for our convenience. It's just easier to get at a cage that's at waist level.

I've also made double-decker stacked cages, which takes up less ground space than the same number of individual cages, with the lower cage about 24" off the ground, and the higher cages set above that. I used untreated 2"x4" and plywood, with a simple plywood and metal roof over the top of each level so that waste drains out the back and is easy to gather for the garden. I've seen many variants on these designs, and it almost doesn't matter as long as the animals get good air circulation and some room to move around. Rabbits are very forgiving on space requirements.

You can also house rabbits in a group pen, basically at least 8'x8', give or take, with 5 or 6 does and one buck (male). Only one male, or there will be some vicious fighting going on.

Now, this kind of housing is perfect for the weather we've had in the past, but potentially problematic going into extremely cold weather. First, the housing is uninsulated and really rather flimsy. Light wire will not hold up to predator attacks very well, and the 2x4 construction won't support heavy snow loads. A group pen has the benefit of allowing the rabbits to huddle for warmth, but it is similarly light weight and unable to withstand heavy snows, high winds, and drenching rain.

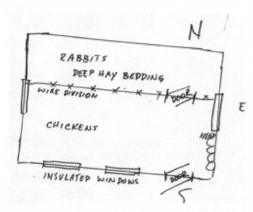

Rethinking livestock housing is part of getting ready for these changes that are coming. At this time, our chickens, rabbits, and goats live in their own separate housing, sheds, and barns. There may be a time when the small animals share a corner of a larger greenhouse, in part to keep them warm, and in part for them to help warm the greenhouse with their body heat and manure.

There were periods in history, where livestock lived in earth sheltered partially underground barns, with the human housing above. The animal's body heat rose and helped moderate the people's zone, and it was easy to get to the barn even during terrible weather.

Thinking ahead, grab a napkin or envelope, and sketch some ideal designs. Suppose a single structure housed rabbits and chickens – a long rectangular shed, perhaps an A-frame style, built strongly with

2"x6" wall studs and rafters, insulated, with the rabbits in a large open pen on the north side and chickens in their own area on the south. Insulated windows allow in light throughout the winter giving the animals the exposure to sunlight that they need. The rabbits' bedding is so thick and deep, 2 or 3 feet, that it insulates against the cold northern temperatures, while giving the bunnies plenty of room to dig burrows into the hay and have babies in comfort. Because it's cooler on the north side, the rabbits can tolerate a little chill, and have the means to stay warm in the hay. The chicken side has thick bedding, as well, but the hens keep moving it around, keeping busy. The rabbits and chickens don't mingle well. Hens will annoy and peck the rabbits and steal their food, but this way they can share the heat and have some interesting interactions by watching each other through the wire during the long cold winter.

Alternatively, bring the animals into the greenhouse in cages. Place them so they do not get direct sunlight, say, under a table on which plants are growing. They need light but direct hot sunlight can kill them. The animals' manure and body heat help warm the greenhouse but won't substitute for good insulation or backup heat, and their actions keep the air moving around.

Breeds

Any rabbit can reproduce, but if you want the best feed-to-meat conversion, the commercial meat rabbits are best: New Zealand Whites or Reds, or Californians. By eight weeks of age, a bunny of these breeds will top 5 pounds and be ready for the table. The New Zealand Whites are actually albinos, with pink eyes, and have the advantage of being almost indistinguishable from each other. That makes butchering a little easier than if you can tell them apart.

Feeding, Breeding

Modern commercial rabbit feed comes as a firm mostly-alfalfa pellet that is convenient and meets the animals' basic needs. They still like to have some hay to chew and carry around, and occasional greens, root vegetables, and firm fruits. A high protein (18%) pellet diet generally is sufficient for a doe to produce a litter every two months, 6 times a year, and raise out the babies to butcher size. However, that's pushing the animals quite hard. You can feed less and breed less often – say, every three months – and still have plenty of meat.

Does can be bred for the first time at about 6 months of age. The doe is carried to the buck's cage for servicing. If she's receptive, the breeding will take place in a couple minutes. The buck will mount, fall off to one side, and may make a squealing sound; don't be alarmed. Remove the doe immediately. If left with the buck, they will fight. She can be put back with the buck in a few hours to make sure she conceives. If she won't accept the first breeding, take her out after 5 minutes and try again later that day. If a doe refuses to be bred consistently, she should be consigned to the stew pot and replaced. Rabbits in a pen will take care of this without assistance.

One female can have a litter of 6-10 "kits". They are born 30-32 days after breeding. The doe will need a nest box with hay or other filler placed into her cage about 3 days before expected due date, "kindling." Earlier than that and she'll use it as a toilet. The doe will pull hair from her chest, move hay around into the box, and line it with her hair. Babies will be born without assistance. The doe will leave the box, and only return to feed the babies a few times a day. Don't check the babies until they are at least 36 hours old, otherwise the mother may reject them. Remove any dead or squashed kits from the box. A kit may fall out of the nest onto the wire or get dragged out while nursing. The doe won't put it back like a cat or dog would do with their babies, so you can gently replace it in the nest if it's still alive.

In a group pen, the doe will dig a hole into the hay, pull hair to make a nest, and have the babies there. Don't bother the nest at all. If you don't remove the buck rabbit to his own suite, he'll rebreed the females right away and there will be more babies in a month.

At 10-14 days, the kits will be exploring outside the nest. They will still nurse on the doe from time to time, and eat the doe's feed. By four weeks, the bunnies can be moved to a separate cage and grown there to full butcher size (4-5 pounds at about 8 weeks of age). The doe can rest for a month and then be rebred. With an average litter of 8 bunnies, each reaching 5 pounds at processing, that's 40 pounds live weight, about 25 pounds of edible meat. If you have three does, that's 75 pounds of meat every three months about 300 pounds a year. Butchering will be discussed near the end of the book.

Milk Goats

Between rabbits and chickens, you'll have plenty of meat and eggs. Add some milk goats into the mix, and you'll have milk, cheese, ice cream, plus additional meat, as well. A milk goat can give you, conservatively, a half-gallon of fresh white gold every day for about 10 months of the year. If you have two milkers and breed them about 2 months apart, you'll have a good gallon of milk *every day* all year. Even if you have a big milk drinking family, that's still a LOT of milk. That's why you'll end up with cheese, too. Cheese is one way to store and save extra milk for later use.

Goats are inquisitive, fun, adventurous, troublesome, and enjoyable livestock. Like bunnies, *they are food*. It's easy to forget, so a reminder about names: "The spotted one", "Ground meat", "Sausage" are good choices.

Goats can live comfortably in a large pen or with access to fields and forest land. Their preferred food is "browse", leaves, twigs, and some grass. They tend to take a bite and then go to something else; that's normal. Multiflora rose, usually a pest plant, can be eradicated by a herd of goats. The grains and seeds you raise for your own use – corn, amaranth, sunflowers – all make excellent goat feed. Goats will also enjoy soft pumpkins that have been hit by frost, especially in the winter, and will eat them seeds and all.

Selecting a Milk Goat

Hopefully, before you acquire your first goat, you have had some

experience with chickens and rabbits. If things in the world are falling apart rapidly around you, there may be some benefit to just buying any goats you can get. That is, even if they are rough quality, *some* goats are better than *no* goats.

Ideally, you will set up a holding pen/shed and small pasture area for your milker before she arrives. The space will need to be expandable or have access to pasture because your milk goat will have kids before long, and they will need room, as well. Additionally, if you do not live within walking distance of someone who owns a buck goat, you'll need one of those, too.

The best way to start with a goat is to buy one that is already "in milk" and is accustomed to being milked. If she comes with at least one kid, that's even better. Basically, you're looking for an animal that has been trained already, that has proven she can have a kid successfully, and that is proving that she has no condition that might ruin her ability to milk.

Keep in mind that if you are buying somebody's already-milking goat, you will NOT be getting their best milker or top producer. The Nubian doe and kid shown at the start of this section were being sold by the breeder because "the doe doesn't produce as well as I'd like" and because "she had a buck kid – I wanted a doeling." That worked out perfect for us, because we wanted a buck from milking lines and we didn't need a huge amount of milk from one animal (we were getting two other unrelated does around the same time).

The doe gave us a quart of milk two times a day, a half-gallon of milk daily – which worked out to ice cream and cheese, with whey for the chickens. Everybody was happy. In terms of productivity, this one goat would be sufficient to meet our needs at this time....but having only one animal and being dependent on it, means if that animal is sick or unable to produce or dies, you're out of luck.

> Two is one. One is none...

You can acquire goats from a breeder who has animals that are generally more predictable and more expensive; from a hobbyist who has friendly pets; from a livestock auction (challenging); or by placing an ad that says something like: *will take your unwanted goats for homesteading.* Answer all inquiries!

Auction goats may or may not be good deals. Generally, you'll be paying "meat" prices because you really don't know if you are getting healthy animals or not. Hobbyist goats have usually been handled a lot and are very people-friendly, or they have just been on the "back 40" and are fairly wild "scrub goats". Free goats are a coin toss – sometimes great, sometimes worth exactly what you paid.

Aim toward the healthiest animals you can find. If you can't tell a good-quality animal, bring a friend who knows or have a nice long conversation with the seller or other auction buyers.

My preference, usually, is to go to the goat-breeder's farm and look at the rest of their animals. Healthy animals tend to produce healthy offspring. Some breeders will sell pedigreed kids without pedigree paperwork at reduced price. If you are looking for a particular breed and aren't terribly concerned about the joys of registering animals, that might be an option.

The biggest problem with pricier goats from breeders is that, even with a great pedigree, you're going to get pampered babies (whether they are adult or not) – and that means higher time, energy, and medication requirements for you in the future. You might get great milk production, but there's a price for that.

It's rather like buying a new Porsche versus buying a dinged 4-wheel drive pickup. The Porsche is fabulous and drives like a charm *on good roads*. On rough backcountry gravel roads with washouts and ruts, the Porsche will fail you. That old tough pickup will just keep going. It's not a "nice ride", but it will get you around. Same idea with purebred versus scrub goats.

Qualities to look for: well-balanced udder that is without hot spots, significant lumps, or more than two teats; clean, easy gait, with hooves that are not overgrown "pixie toes"; no sniffles, cough, drooling, rashes, repetitive behaviors; head shaking, staggering, or anything else that looks odd. Horns are a nuisance, but might be a plus for some self-defense; many who raise goats have the horns "disbudded" from kids when the horns are nubbins at about 2-3 weeks of age. You can't remove the horns from adults because they are actually grown out of the skull bones – you risk cracking the animal's skull if you cut them like cattle horns, and sawing off horns can bleed the animal to death. Different coat colors can indicate ancestry, and might give a little indication of milking potential (or not).

Goats of both sexes can breed at about 6 months of age. Some owners will prevent does from breeding until they are older, believing that the doe will have an easier time with labor and birth if they are a bit bigger when they deliver. The gestation period is about 5 months, so a goat bred in November will likely deliver kids in March.

Does come "into season" for about 3 days, and if not bred she'll cycle again in about 3 weeks. When she's in season, the doe makes more noise and "flags" or waves her tail, and there may be a little puffiness or discharge from her vulva. These signs can be fairly subtle. The doe can be brought to the buck for service when she is showing signs, or left with the buck to take care of at the appropriate time. The actual breeding takes about 30 seconds. One or two breedings is sufficient for healthy animals to assure pregnancy.

Breeds

There are many breeds of dairy goats, and a few of meat goats. Dairy goats are finer boned and don't develop the heavy muscling of meat types.

Meat goats, up until a couple decades ago, were called "Spanish" goats. There were believed to have been brought to the New World during the age of exploration on Spanish sailing vessels as food for the crew. When ships landed, goats were put on land to fatten up and took off into the wild country. Their descendants still roam unpopulated areas, and have been gathered into herds in Mexico and Caribbean Islands. From there, they made it to the US. These are typically mid-sized goats that appear sturdy, of any color whatsoever, and usually have horns.

A more recent import is the Boer goat from South Africa, usually white with a brown or black head coloring. These are large, heavily muscled, and do well on grassy pasture. Their temperament is calm, and they don't climb fences as readily as dairy goats do. Females produce about a quart of milk twice daily for four or five months, then taper off.

Of the mini-goats, Nigerian Dwarves are the milkers, giving perhaps a quart of milk daily. Pygmy goats are much chunkier and are usually kept as pets; they will produce milk but are not known for quantity. Both of these are good for small spaces, but are perhaps more ornamental than useful.

Dairy breeds are numerous and each one has devoted supporters. Nubians are the ones with long, floppy ears. They are the most vocal of the breeds, and come in many different and sometimes flamboyant colors. They originated in the Middle East and tolerate humid and dry conditions, but may be challenged by continuous cold. A good Nubian should be able to produce around a gallon of milk a day, but I have never seen one who gave that much. Their milk is usually higher butterfat and slightly sweet when on good pasture or hay. Nubians are sometimes crossed with Boers to produce a larger sized meat kid. When crossed with other dairy breeds, they produce offspring with "airplane" ears that are partially upright and stick out to the sides, and tend to improve the butterfat of the next generation's milk.

The Saanen is a solid white dairy breed that originated in the Swiss Alps, perhaps having some extra cold tolerance. They are the Holstein of the goat world, producing large quantities of moderate to lower butterfat milk. A gallon daily would be average for these goats and more is pretty typical.

La Manchas are the "earless" goats. They have a mutation that causes them to have truncated tiny ears. Their hearing is normal. When crossed with other breeds, the offspring may have partial, whole, or tiny ears. They are built a bit heavier than typical milk breeds.

Alpines are similar to the Saanen, but black with brown markings on face and legs. They are also generally a little smaller than Saanens, but good producers.

Kinder goats are a breed developed from crosses of dairy goats with miniature goats (Pygmy and Nigerian). Over the last several decades, they've been standardized, that is, bred among other Kinders to develop a consistent type. They are good milkers, friendly without being cloying like the Nubians can be, and fairly hardy.

I'm skipping over many other breeds here, including Angoras which grow a long hair coat but are not noted for their milk or meat, and others that are quite nice simply because they are somewhat less common than the ones I've mentioned. Having an unusual or rare breed tends to be pricey and unnecessary if all you are seeking is milk and meat. Bragging rights don't count at the dinner table.

Kids and Milk

Goats, like cattle and other mammals, produce milk to feed their offspring. In order to get milk from a goat, a "doe" or "nanny", she must first be bred by a male goat, called a "buck" or a "billy". Gestation is about 5 months, and goats are seasonal breeders, that is, they tend to breed during certain seasons. Most dairy goats breed in the fall; colder weather seems to trigger mating. "Meat" breed goats such as the Boer often breed spring and fall. You may get two crops of baby "kids" from them.

Buck goats generate a rather unpleasant musky odor, worse in the breeding season, which the does appear to enjoy. If the buck hangs around milking does, the bucky-odor will permeate the milk. For that reason, many goat breeders keep their buck(s) in a pen or field separate from the does. If dividing fences aren't sturdy, the buck will find a way in with the girls.

Does may have, on average, 1 to 3 kids at a time. Sometimes they will reject a small one, or one may not be able to compete for one of the does' two teats and ends up stunted or dead. Occasionally, you'll have to either bottle feed an extra kid, or farm it out to another willing doe. Option 2 is easier on you, but it takes a while for a doe to accept another animal's kid. Some people will squirt milk from the adoptive doe on the foster kid to impart the doe's scent to it.

Even with only one kid, most goat mothers will be nursed from both sides of her udder. We collect colostrum, the first milk, on day one or two after a kid is born, and freeze it. Colostrum is vital to populating the young goat's gut with high levels of nutrients and microbial life that it needs to stay healthy and digest food. Kids that don't get any colostrum will be unhealthy or may outright die. They must receive it within 12 hours of birth; their gut is "open" to the colostrum bioflora only for a period of time, and after that it is much less helpful for them.

Goat colostrum can be given to newborns of virtually any mammal species, including humans, to help get them going, as well. Although saving some by freezing it works now, if there is no electricity and it's not freezing outdoors, we won't be able to save frozen colostrum. We will likely make an effort to dry some on clean plates, the dried chunks to be rehydrated in clean water if needed. I don't know how well that will work in the long run. Better than nothing, though. Heat-canning colostrum will destroy the bioflora.

You may need to pen the mother and kid together for a few days to protect the kid from being bumped by other goats, or you may simply be able to leave doe and kid to their regular routines. She will nurse it multiple times daily.

Check the doe's udder at least once a day. If you find "hot" or "hard" spots, she'll need to be hand-milked until that improves. That's typically a sign of "mastitis", or an inflammation in the udder. Use warm moist packs to the udder, and gently massage all around. A single 325mg aspirin tablet crushed in some sweet feed might help bring down some of the heat and tenderness, or you can bring willow leaf and chipped inner willow bark for the goat to nibble. Willow contains salicylic acid, the primary pain relieving ingredient in aspirin. Chopped garlic might help, but it will strongly flavor the milk. If you have antibiotics, an injection of DuraPen (penicillin) based on the goat's weight will usually resolve it in a day or two. Don't use the milk when a goat has mastitis – it may be off-color and appear to have streaky strings in it -- but it's okay for the kid or other animals like chickens or dogs to drink.

Castration

At about 5-10 days of age, you can wether the male kids, assuming the kid is healthy and testicles have descended into the scrotum. The unpleasant business of castrating the males has two benefits: it prevents unwanted breeding and harassing of young does; and it reduces to zero the musky flavor that will permeate the meat otherwise.

A brief castration tutorial is

available online as I write; check the references section. This is a job for 2 to 3 people – holding the animal is sometimes a challenge.

The easiest way is to have one person sit down and upend the goat in their lap, holding the animal's rear legs up so that the scrotum is exposed. Use an "elastrator", which is a hand held device (about $25) that opens a heavy rubber band enough that the second person can slip it over the animal's scrotum, and press against its belly. Feel to be sure both testicles are present and that the goat's tiny nipples aren't getting pinched, then push the rubber band off the device's pegs, and remove the device leaving the band in place. It will hurt, and the little guy may roll or lay down uncomfortably. Immediately let him go to his mother. He will nurse and quickly forget. The area will go numb, since both nerve and blood supply are pinched off. After a few weeks, the scrotum will dry up and fall off.

Another common method is the use of a Burdizzo, effectively a large clamp that crushes blood vessels and the spermatic cord at the same time, but is too dull edged to cut through the animal's skin. A certain amount of arm strength is critical to doing this right, as you have to close the Burdizzo and squeeze it tightly. For small livestock, place the clamp between the scrotum and body, close slightly and feel to be sure both testicles are down below the clamp. Then close the clamp and hold. Small animals don't require an intense squeeze. Like the elastrator, there is no bleeding – although this is also a painful procedure and the kid will struggle and cry out. Release to his mother for reassurance. The scrotum will shrink over several weeks but remain present.

A third method of castration is simple, but probably has greater risk of infection. In this, after securing the kid, you feel for the testicles and push them up away from the bottom of the scrotum. Using a sharp pocket knife or scissors, cut the bottom third of the scrotum off and discard. Now, push one of the testicles out the cut, and using the dull part of your pocket knife SCRAPE but DO NOT CUT the spermatic cord and blood vessels until it breaks. You want to scrape because it reduces bleeding over cutting. When one side is done, discard the testicle and do the same on the other. If any bit of cord hangs below the end of the cut scrotum, pull it down and scrape higher up to shorten it. Let the kid go to his mother, then pen up on clean hay or straw for a day. Check several times to make sure there is no excessive bleeding. Drainage from the goat's open scrotum actually can be somewhat protective, as it will keep flushing bacteria out for a while.

Ideally, with each of these methods, you'd also give the animal a tetanus vaccination – the third method, especially, since he's going to have an open, draining wound that will be exposed to bacteria. Tetanus is caused by a naturally-occurring bacteria that lives in the soil; if it gets into a wound (puncture wounds are the worst) it can cause the muscular rigidity of tetanus, It is which is terribly painful and fatal. If an animal comes down with tetanus, it must be put down. Wear gloves and remove it to be burned immediately after killing it – don't expose your dogs or cats to the risk of gnawing on the carcass.

Castrating adult animals can be done best using the Burdizzo squeezing one side above the scrotum at a time. Restrain the animal securely, such as in a milkstand. Place the clamp, and feel for the "cord" or cords (spermatic cord and blood vessel – the testicle will be down and out of the way). Then squeeze and hold. Standing animals will kick, go a little weak in the knees, and bawl. Then, do the same on the other side above the scrotum.

There may be some swelling in the scrotum for days to a couple weeks. Blood trapped in the scrotum and inflammation from the castration process is responsible. Alternatively, you can use the knife method. The adult animals must be strongly restrained because they will struggle and kick. Castrated adult males will be off their feed for a day or two afterwards, and may continue to have breeding behaviors for several weeks after until their system clears out the testosterone. Then, they behave more like females, are calmer, less prone to fighting, and will gain fat. The musky flavor will be out of the meat in a few months.

Milking

After a week or two, when mother and kid have bonded and she is milking well, you can separate them for 12 hours daily. At this writing, people who raise goats strictly for milk will often "bottle feed" kids after they are 3 or 4 days old, saving the does' milk for themselves. Purchased dry bottle-fed formula is adequate for raising goats, although it will increase your costs somewhat over not buying formula. Don't try to use calf-formula, though, as it will weaken and eventually kill the baby goats (the fat particles are too large for the goat to absorb). Little goats do better on fresh mother's milk, and there's no additional cost for that. We may not always be able to get commercial dry goat formula, either.

The reason for separating doe and kid for 12 hours daily is to allow you to milk the goat out and get half of her production for your own use. The other 12-hours' worth goes to the kid; this will be plenty, and helps encourage the kid to eat vegetation or hay during his time away from mommy.

The first two or three times they are separated, both will be upset and may bawl piteously. Stick to your guns. They will adjust, once they get into the rhythm of the change.

When the kid is around 8 weeks old, you can permanently separate them if you like and wean the kid. At that point you will need to milk the doe twice daily, approximately every 12 hours, until she completes her lactation (milking) cycle, roughly 10 months.

Since we have several milking does, our plan is to separate does and kids for 12 hours daily. We milk all the does at the same time in the morning, then turn them out with their kids. This give us plenty of milk. In the evening, the girls are penned up with fresh hay away from the babies. By morning, they are ready to be milked again and then back with the kids.

In this way, we only milk once a day, and the kids get to bond with their mothers and have extra milk feeding until they are naturally weaned. If we need to be away from the farm for a couple days, we simply turn them all in together. We don't have to worry about finding someone to handle the milking chores.

How to Milk a Goat

Unless you are very flexible and can stay in a squatting position for a period of time, you'll need a stand for your goats to be milked upon.

Any flat surface, about a foot or 16" off the ground will do – you can put a ramp up to it, or simply let the goat hop up (they have no problem doing that).

You'll need a way to restrain the goat – a large eye-hook screwed into a nearby wall with a leash on it to attach to the goat's collar is adequate – but a stanchion-type arrangement is a bit more effective because it will keep the goat from moving around too much.

The stanchion in the photo was made from 2x4s and other wood leftover from various projects. The flat part of the stand was an old drafting board almost a half-inch thick. To the right is a box-feeder midway up the stanchion outside the headgate. To the left is a ramp that isn't very visible from the photo's angle.

If you start with a milk-trained goat, she will know to walk or hop up onto the stanchion at milking time. Place her feed in the box-feeder, and she'll stick her head right through the stanchion head gate (more 2x4's on a pivot or hinge), and they are closed and secured around her neck. She will munch happily while you are milking her and wait for you if she's done with her grain before you're done with milking. Turn her loose when milking is finished.

If you are milking more than one goat, always milk them in the same order. Goats, like people, are creatures of habit, and they will learn the order after a few milkings so you won't be mobbed. Keep the ones who are in line away from the stanchion, perhaps behind a gate, or they will all try to hop up at the same time.

Stanchion head gate, open on left, closed on right. The metal pin holds the bar in place so the goat doesn't pull her head out. The one moving bar on the right pivots on a bolt secured in the base, which acts as a hinge.

If you need to train a goat, put a collar on the animal when they are young. Train them first to "lead", which is the same as leash training a dog. Use a can with some grain in it to encourage the goat to follow the lead. Let the goat follow the grain with nudges from the leash. Put the grain in the stanchion feed box, and let the goat hop up and find it (she'll know it's there). Let her eat a little, then add a little more grain and *gently* close the head gate. As long as she has food, she is likely to be willing to be handled a little. Pet her, rub her udder, pick up her feet, pull on the teats. The idea is to get her used to being handled, and that it is a pleasant procedure.

Feed for a goat while milking can be grains or a mix of grains and greens or fruit. A commercial "all grain", while low protein, usually has molasses added which goats love. At this writing, complete goat pelleted feed is typically used. It doesn't add any unwanted flavors to the milk, and is easy to measure. Feed one pound of grain for every 4 pints of milk the goat is giving. That's a rough calculation but fits for most goats; you may need to add or subtract a little to keep her in good shape.

The milking process takes a little while to learn to do, but isn't hard. Brush or rub all around the udder to get loose hair and dirt off -- you'll have cleaner milk. Some goat owners actually will wash the udder with mild soapy water or udder cleaning solution, and dry with a cloth (I never have). Place your milking bucket or can under the goat's udder. Ideally your milk bucket is stainless steel, but whatever it is should be clean, have no rust, and have no sharp edges.

Sit down on the edge of the milking stand, your right shoulder next to the goat's right shoulder, facing the opposite direction as the goat (reverse if your milk stand is reversed). This allows you to put a little pressure with your shoulder against the goat and gives her a sense of security. Grasp a teat between your thumb and the edge, not tip, of your index finger, and compress. That causes the milk in the teat to be trapped within the teat.

Now, squeeze with your middle, ring, and pinky finger in order – pushing the milk down to the opening in the bottom of the teat. A stream of milk will pour out. Repeat until you can't get any more, then do the same on the other teat. From time to time, bump upward against the udder just like the kids do. It helps stimulate milk "let down" reflex and keeps the flow going. Go back and forth between the teats, as milk will build up again a little.

If the goat has been nursed on, the milk will flow right away. If the kid has only nursed on one side or didn't nurse, there may be a "plug" in the teat (normal), and it will take some squeezing to get it out.

When you milk, do NOT stretch the teats downward. That is unnecessary and tends to break down the tissues and even the udder itself.

Milk each goat into one bucket individually, then pour that into a holding bucket that can be tightly covered to keep out flies and barn dust – if there's an incident with one goat, you won't lose all your milk. Some goats develop a bad habit of lifting a back leg, and may put a foot into the milk container. That ruins the milk (feed to dogs or chickens). Be alert so that you can snatch the can out of the way, and prevent loss of the milk, then go back and milk some more. Pushing the can firmly against the legs can help reduce this, or even restraining the offending leg to the stanchion with a leash might help. Remember to release the leg *before* you release the neck, otherwise the goat might try to jump away and injure herself.

Handling Milk

Once your goat or goats are milked out, bring your collected milk indoors right away. You'll need to pass it through a filter -- a clean, boiled, dry t-shirt or muslin, or special goat or cow milk filters are fine -- to remove any particulate material, and then into a clean jar. Immediately cool the milk in the jar, either by refrigerating, putting the jar into a bucket of snow, or into cold water. Cooling the milk slows the growth of bacteria and will prolong the time you can keep it good. You can pasteurize the milk if you wish by heating it to near boiling for a minute or two. The milk around the very edge of the container will form tiny bubbles. Then cool as above. Cleanliness is very important to have good milk.

Healthy raw milk will keep in good condition for several days to two weeks. Cooler milk will keep longer. If it's cold and frozen outside, store the milk in a covered snow-filled box outdoors in shade, the best freezer there is. If the milk starts to firm up and separate, smells tangy and good, it's still fine to eat – ever hear of "curds and whey"? That's what is happening.

Use the curds in place of cottage cheese, which is what it is. Feed the whey to chickens, pigs, or pets, or use it in cooking or drink it. It is the same whey that is the basis of high protein health drinks, except better because it contains all the natural enzymes and microflora. It should smell tangy and appetizing. If it smells musty or rotten, that's a different story.

Pasteurization destroys those beneficial bacteria, so instead of converting to curds and whey, pasteurized milk just goes off; that milk should be disposed of. Frozen milk may separate or get chunky when it is thawed, but it is not fermented; makes great pudding, sauces, and used in cooking.

Wash all milk utensils first in cold water, then in hot or boiling water. If you have dish soap, use it with the hot water stage. Rinse in hot water. Use the cold wash first to release the milk fat from your container. Otherwise, using hot water first will "set" a fatty residue on your container that is hard to remove and may contaminate your next milkings.

Should you have more milk than you can use, make cheese. "Fresh" cheese methods are in the recipes section. You can also pressure can milk for later use, also in the recipes.

Housing

Goats do not like to be rained or snowed upon. They will need some kind of shelter that gives them relief from rain, snow, and sun. With very cold weather, there should be deep bedding of hay or straw, and holes in the shed should be closed or patched to prevent drafts. Insulation will help, but make sure the goats cannot get to it. Cover with wood planks or plywood, as they will chew insulation and could die from eating it. Access to stalls in a horse barn or a separate portion of your chicken house will work fine, keeping in mind that most goats are escape artists and will break through flimsy barriers.

They will also need access to a pasture, field, or woodland to get exercise and additional food. In winter, they will still need pasture *and* hay. Good fences give you control over where your animals go, and where they can't go (such as your garden). Make permanent fields, even if you start with a small area because you'll be using it for years. Should you have limited funds, get cattle panels, 16 feet long, and set up a portable corral using metal t-posts to hold up the panels. Then you can move your corral to fresh ground when the plants have been eaten down.

With more funds and time, you can acquire "sheep and goat fence", a heavier type of wire with 4"x4" openings. Installed around a field, it will keep most goats inside and most predators out. People can't climb it easily, and getting under it means finding a low spot and scooching through with some effort. In our area, sheep and goat fence runs about $250 for 330 feet, plus add t-posts every 8 to 10 feet, which are about $5 each. There is a cost involved in good fencing. If your goats have horns, be cautious of "field fence" that they can get tangled in. They poke their heads through the 6"x6" holes, and can't pull out as their horns get caught. Count the goats when you check daily, and if one is missing, check your fence line.

Without cash or options to buy fence materials, consider natural materials and "found" materials (recycled, repurposed). In the past, farmers chopped down small 4"-5" diameter cedar trees, stripped off branches, and pounded the resulting post into the ground with a sledge hammer. People were much hardier in the old days. A fence might require hundreds of posts, so that is quite a job to collect posts. Barbed wire was then strung post to post, 4 to 5 wires high. Less expensive, still, is collecting shipping pallets, often as simple as asking for pallets at businesses where you see them stacked. Each pallet may differ in size, but on average they are 36" wide. One hundred pallets, stood on edge and wired together, would fence about 300 feet of fence line.

For long-term fences, rock walls made from stones collected right in the field can be stacked 4 feet high. It's physically demanding work, no doubt about that, but the rock fence will outlast the builder.

Finally, fence lines can be created over time using existing plants and with judicious new plantings. Each region has its favorite fence trees. In my area, "hedge apple", also known as bois d'arc used to be planted and interlaced as they grew where the farmer wanted a fence. The woven young branches get bigger and stronger with time, and the prickles on the tree become large and sharp. Very few large animals even try to get through a hedge apple fence.

Predators

Goats are high on the menu for predators – coyotes, bobcats, and the neighbor's dog are among the worst. In fact, the neighbor's dog or your own is likely to be the hardest on any given farmer's goats and sheep.

Many commercial goat breeders keep livestock guardian dogs among their flocks – these big dogs are literally raised among the goats and seem to consider the livestock their 'pack'. If any livestock are threatened, the guardian dog goes on the defensive. They are often large enough to fight off coyotes and other predators. Common breeds are Anatolians and Great Pyrenees, and crosses of these can work well, too. We have crossbred guardians, and they are Great Pyrenees/Bloodhound X Collie – easy going very large dogs that keep coyotes, raccoons, possums, armadillos, bobcats, skunks, and other predators away. The dogs have the run of the farm. They have to, in order to patrol and repel threats to their herd.

In this area, many livestock owners will also run a donkey or two with cattle or small livestock. Donkeys have a reputation for driving off coyotes and the neighbor's dog, as well. If a livestock guardian dog or donkey saves a single goat or lamb from being killed by a predator, that guardian probably paid for a year's worth of its own feed.

During every downturn of the past livestock have been poached from farmers' land. The human predator is the hardest one to control. The only option we can think of is to pen the animals up at night, and keep them in an area where they can be easily observed during the day. If times get very difficult, frontier justice may again be instituted for "rustlers."

Goat Meat: Chevon

Goat is a favorite food worldwide. It's only in the US that we've forgotten what a nutritious, tasty meat that goats produce. It can be used in any way you'd use beef: soups, stews, ground, or as mini-steaks and roasts.

Young castrated male goats, at about 40 pounds, are the most tender and delicious, excellent roasted whole on a BBQ spit. You can eat adult goats, but you'll have to cook at lower temperatures and longer to keep the meat tender, but they make outstanding lean ground meat and sausage.

You'll get approximately half of the animal's "live weight" in meat, so a 100-pound goat will give 50 pounds of meat, more or less. You can also save livers and kidneys to eat, if you like organ meats, and bones for use in soups, stews, and broths. Goat meat from dairy animals tends to be lean, so use slow cooking methods, or pressure cook it.

Extra meat can be canned, dried, or smoked for later use; a few recipes are included in that section. Instructions on butchering are later in the book.

And/Or Sheep

Sheep are so much like goats in their feed and housing requirements that you can keep them alongside each other. They won't crossbreed because they are different species, which probably had common ancestors millennia ago. The primary differences are that sheep have heavy wool that must be sheared off annually; and sheep are more group-oriented and less independent than goats. Sheep can also provide a rich milk, meat (as lambs), fine skins for clothing and mittens, and wool for warm sweaters and blankets.

If you hope to use sheep wool, some breeds are better suited and have finer, easier to spin wool – Ramboullet, Targhee, Finn, Merino, and crosses of these large white-faced white-wooled breeds – are top of the line. "Heirloom" breeds such as Cheviot and the black-and-white spotted Jacob generally have very good spinning wool as well. Other heirlooms such as the Leicester Long Wool have long coats and a coarser wool, easy to spin, but better suited to outerwear than something that contacts your skin. One of the most common large "meat" breeds of sheep, the Suffolk, has short coarse wool. It can be spun, but hard to work with and rough on your skin.

There's also varieties and crosses of "hair" sheep – the Katadin and Barbados are typical – that develop a short dense coat in the winter that sheds in the spring. Finally, the ancient Shetland breed, a small sheep, has a "double" coat, dense soft wool undercoat and a coarse hair outer coat.

Shearing

If you only have a few sheep, you can trim the wool using a good pair of scissors. Have the animal secured standing in a stanchion, and trim from the neck back to the rear. Be extremely careful that you leave about a half inch of wool on the animal, otherwise it could sunburn or simply get too cold if the weather turns harsh. Leaving some wool also helps prevent scissor-cuts on the sheep's skin. Very easy to do, as their skin is tender. Keep a scissor-sharpener on hand, and use it often. Figure on taking an hour per sheep.

With multiple head that need to be shorn, you can use the traditional sheep shears. Some garden stores still carry them as grass trimmers. Plan to sharpen them many times during shearing. If you have electricity, an electric shear – a bigger version of the kind of trimmer used on dogs and in barber shops – is the quickest method. You can still cut a sheep badly with electric shears, so take your time. Try to pull the underlying skin fairly taut so there is less likelihood of a cut. Top sheep shearers can complete an entire sheep in a minute or less, holding the sheep on its bottom using the shearer's knees, and moving it enough so that it can be shorn from different angles. It's quite an art.

The goal is to trim the sheep clean of the entire fleece, including the matted and dirty wool on its legs, back end, and face. The dirty wool can be added to your compost pile or used as mulch on the garden. If you've trimmed the sheep from the neck back to the tail, the fleece will "roll back", almost intact. If not, that's okay. When you're done, gather all the clean wool up, and package it for storage in a large paper sack or cardboard box.

The fleece will be greasy with lanolin, very good for your skin, and may have grass and other bits in it. Fleeces do not have to be washed before spinning, but some spinners prefer to do so. If you do, use NO agitation whatsoever or the fleece may "felt" or mat down too thickly to use. Use cold water and a gentle soap, like shampoo or even Dawn brand dish soap, to reduce the lanolin content. Rinse by carefully lifting the fleece and placing in cold clear water. Air dry on a screen or other porous flat surface. If you spin the fleece without washing, you'll need to wash it after it is spun – that helps to set the fibers and relax the wool.

Spinning Wool

Spinning wool takes a short period of time and some determination to do – and you can spend a small fortune of $500-$800 buying a really nice spinning wheel with all the bells and whistles. There's a learning curve and these are fun to use.

You may be able to find used or antique ones at lower cost on eBay or Craig's List. You'll need extra spindles, so watch for ones that fit your wheel whenever they come up for sale.

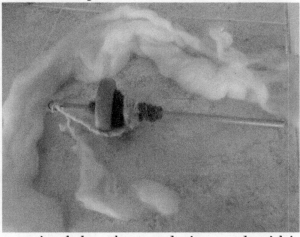

You can also spin very nice wool using a dowel with a round wood weight on one end, that you can put together for $6 or for free if you have stuff laying around.

Tie a string onto the section below the round piece, and twirl it around the dowel above the round piece. Sit down and lay the dowel with the round beside your left thigh (reverse if left handed), with the long end of the dowel toward your right side. Attach a piece of "carded" or "picked" or "combed" (basically: fluffed) wool to the string, and start rolling the dowel away down your thigh. The wool will cling and twist. Now stand and hold the growing yarn and give the hanging dowel a spin. Feed the fluffed wool onto the twisted part, spinning the dowel as needed, then repeating. When your growing piece of yarn gets too long to handle easily, wrap it onto the dowel below the wood round.

When the wrapped area gets so big it interferes with spinning the dowel, break the yarn and unroll it from the dowel over your arm. Use your elbow and crook of your thumb as the form. Your first yarn will be chunky and rough-looking – but it is STILL yarn, and can be knit into one-of-a-kind warm hats and scarves. With practice, your yarn will be as smooth as you want it to be.

When all the yarn is on your arm, carefully slip it off as a hoop of multiple strands. Tie it in a few places to keep it organized. When you have made several of these "hanks", fill TWO sinks or buckets with lukewarm water. Put a little bit of shampoo or Dawn dish soap into one of them. Put a tablespoon or so of apple cider vinegar into the other one for rinse water. The acid restores the wool's natural resiliency.

Drop the hanks into the soapy water and swirl GENTLY. Some people say to just let them sink of their own weight. After the wool has soaked for a few minutes, lift each hank out and squeeze, NOT WRING the excess water out, then drop into the vinegar water to rinse. Wash and rinse water need to be at nearly the same temperature so not to "shock" the wool and risk felting it. After a gentle rinse, take each out, squeeze, and hang to drip dry. When dry, start knitting!

Other Livestock

Hogs and cattle are larger animals and generally require sturdier fencing, have higher feed or pasture requirements, and much stronger, more expensive equipment to move the animals around. There is a large financial investment involved before you get your first cow or piglet. Both are capable of injuring or killing you or your kids. Don't attempt these until you have some experience raising smaller stock, and then, spend some time around the big animals before you acquire any. Ask among others you know, about what to look for and what to avoid.

Some homesteaders start with Pot-bellied pigs or Guinea Hogs, which are smaller, gentler, and more easily handled than the big commercial hogs. They taste the same as the big pigs, and perform the same functions on the farm by eating leftovers, excess whey, and cleaning up the garden in the fall, but require less space, feed, and equipment.

Not to be too graphic about it, but horses and donkeys have been considered food in historical times, as well. Jenny-milk, from the female donkey, makes good food, too. During the Venezuelan financial crash of 2016, reports filtered out about desperate folk breaking into the main zoo and "harvesting" zoo animals, including a prize stallion horse. Humans get much less particular about what we eat when we are hungry. If you opt for equines for transportation, get mares (females) so you can breed them if needed. Look for ones with *gentle, friendly* personalities, not fancy coat colors.

Hunting

It seems like quite a few part-time preppers imagine that they will head to the hills and live off the fat of the land, hunting and fishing the apocalypse away. Even those hard backwoods campers who can manage a weekend, week, or even a month out in the woods, come in with supplies, build visible fires, and sleep, all done during a time of relative peace and prosperity, when other campers aren't scared and hungry, when the weather is predictable and warm. Hint: those people will die early.

During Cold Times, game will disappear within the first year, if not earlier – just as it did during the Depression of the 1930s. Either everyone in the area will try to take as many deer, squirrel and turkey (opossum, ground hog, wild geese, wild hog, and raccoon will be next on the menu) as they can – hunger does that to a person – or the animals will become more adept at hiding. A few years ago, a hunting buddy and I strolled up to within 3 feet of a huge white-tailed buck, hiding in underbrush. If it hadn't jumped up and run, we would have walked right past it without seeing it. That's how good they are at hiding in normal times. The woodland survivors of the hunting pressure in the Cold will be even more cagey.

If you plan to hunt, you need to start practicing at the first opportunity. You won't suddenly know what you need to know just because you're hungry. *This is a learned skill.* You won't learn it by reading about it, only by doing it.

At this writing, you'll need a hunting license. Should things get really bad, that may be one more social amenity that goes the way of the dodo.

Here's some tips for the Cold Times:
- Set up feeders or minerals to attract game. It is not sportsman-like, but it will put food on the table.

- If there aren't many other hunters, try to leave the female animals to rebreed next year. If there are lots of other hunters, someone will take them.
- Use quiet weaponry
  - Bows (recurved, longbows, crossbows, compound bows); get at least 5 extra strings and *hundreds* of arrows, dozens of hunting arrow heads at a minimum. You don't want to have to learn how to make arrows or chip arrowheads from rocks, so get more than you think you'll need.
  - Slingshots for small animal hunting, with extra elastic tubing and *thousands* of ball bearings.
  - Air guns – good ones are high power, make a crisp soft popping sound, and cost $300-$400. If you plan to use CO_2 powered ones, get a hundred canisters plus thousands of pellets. Pump air guns may last longer and are definitely cheaper at less than $100, but they are accurate only for shorter distances. Pellets will eventually run out, too. Use on small animals and birds.
  - Snares – ideal for rabbits and other small animals. A snare is just a noose made from wire or other strong material that will tighten down when pulled and not reverse and open. The end opposite the snare itself must be tightly secured to a solid object, such as a tree or fence post. Place these so that animals must walk through them along a narrow path or at a hole in a fence, ideally putting their heads through and then getting snared. Keep in mind that snares are non-specific, and will catch and choke anything that gets in them, including pets and skunks. Snares can be reused indefinitely.
- If you must use rifles, plan your shots so that you get a kill with a single shot. Do not shoot twice from the same place. That will give away your position to any unpleasant people that may be around.
- During the ammunition squeeze shortage 2014-15, one round was consistently available even when shelves were otherwise bare – the .270. Two-seventies are excellent hunting rounds with good penetration and sufficient power to bring down deer; the rifles and rounds are fairly inexpensive, too. It's not a glamor caliber, and it's not a high-tech rifle, but it does the job. You can hunt with almost

any caliber or style of long gun (your AR-15, too) if you are an accurate shooter and can place your bullet in a vital organ.

8 KEEPING WARM

There are three principal ways to maintain warmth: warm yourself, warm objects, and warm the space around you.

This illustration shows the typical rural wear from about 1890 in Russia where it has historically been very cold. The outfit is made from sheepskin with the wool turned to the inside. It reaches down to the knees, with an outer jacket to the hips, belted at the waist. The hat is fur lined, and so are the boots and leggings. The mittens are thick and bulky, probably removed if the person had to use his hands. Instead of a scarf, the collar is turned up around his neck, another way of retaining warmth.

Today's artic nomads, the ones who follow reindeer herds, still dress the same way. That tells us something important: this

method of dressing against the cold *works*.

This is serious "self-warming", proven over centuries, highly effective, and *still* the absolute best way to keep warm – wear wool. Wool and many other natural animal fibers, retain body heat even when wet; animals live in the weather, after all. Other natural fibers that are super warm include alpaca, camel, musk ox, bear, elk, and canid – that is, coyote, dog, fox, and wolf. If you look at old photos of arctic explorers, the fur around their hoods was typically coyote or dog. Big fluffy dogs shed out copious amounts of undercoat in the spring, which can be spun and knitted into super warm scarves and mittens. The only downside of dog hair is that when it gets wet, it has a doggy odor, no matter how it is treated.

Rabbit is generally fairly warm, but it doesn't retain warmth when wet. Rabbit skins are thin, and tear easily. So, when it is used, it needs a lining to support it. It does make a comfortable, light vest that can be worn under an outer coat, or trim on collars and wrists.

Most people who live in cold regions have a good understanding of how to keep warm. Skiers have special lightweight clothing that is pretty good, as long as the wearer is active. Here's some basics that should form the foundation of keeping yourself warm:

- Avoid cotton, except for underwear and as *summer* clothes. Cotton wicks moisture and heat AWAY from the wearer. This means, cotton will let you get cold, no matter how many layers you wear. People who teach wilderness survival put it this way: *cotton kills*. The only time to use cotton clothing during winter is panties, boxers, briefs, and bras. *Never socks*. Read labels.

- Layers work. Start with underwear and wool-based socks. Consider OmniWool or SmartWool brands. Put on thermals. Polypropylene or nylon is better than cotton (which is useless), wool blend is better than both. Silk is a good next-to-the-skin material when it is heavy weight silk, but you still need wool over it because damp silk loses heat. Hunting stores like Bass Pro and sporting goods stores such as Dick's or Academy carry good brands; they are fairly pricy but worth it because they can last for decades.

- Over that, a wool-based shirt and pants (***not** jeans or sweat* *pants or flannel, which are cotton).* Over that, a thick jacket that is water resistant but breathable, *not canvas or corduroy* which are cotton. Boiled wool makes a strong, water resistant, warm, and relatively lightweight jacket material. You can't beat a *genuine* "shearling" (that is, sheep skin with the wool on the inside) jacket for warmth and wind resistance. Ideally, your jacket should cover your thighs down to your knees – just like in the old illustration.

- For your feet, over your wool socks, wear *boots* that are lined with wool or that can have a wool foot bed insert (check the UGGs wool inserts), and are waterproof. An outstanding brand are Muck Boots with neoprene tops. They are not really designed for extreme cold weather, but with extra wool socks and wool foot bed inserts, they perform as good as more expensive hiking and hunting boots.

- Always wear a hat outdoors, wool naturally. Knitted acrylic caps are suitable, but there is nothing warmer than wool, especially thick and heavy wool caps. You'll lose more heat from the top of your head in cold weather than anywhere else on your body. If you need a brim to provide shade, wear a ball cap *over* your knitted cap. It'll look funny, but you'll be warm, and that's what counts. Or consider an old-fashioned style wool-felt fedora-type hat. In extreme cold, wear a baklava – a knitted hat that folds down to your neck leaving holes for eyes and mouth. In worst-case cold, there are few warmer hats than a rabbit-fur lined "mad bomber" hat with the side flaps down over your ears and the flaps tied under your chin. You need to keep your ears warm, too. Frost bite will cause you to lose part of your ears, otherwise.

- For your hands, fully lined gloves especially if they are leather. Unlined leather alone is too cold and provides no warmth at all. Knitted mittens are great, too. Old wool sweaters can be cut and sewed into excellent, attractive mittens with a little ingenuity. Indoors, wear "half gloves," knitted like mittens but without fingers, to keep your palms toasty but allow you to use your fingers comfortably. Knitting directions for "half mittens" are available in many books and online.

- Wrists and ankles – major blood vessels run through here,

and these are sites of heat loss. That's why sweaters and socks have knitted cuffs right at those locations, providing flexibility while keeping warmth on them. When wool socks are worn out, cut the cuffs off and hem them, then wear them on your wrists or over your ankles. These are good locations to wear a "bracelet" or "anklet" made of rabbit fur, too.

- For your neck, wear scarves or neck warmers. Scarves should be long enough to go around your neck twice, be tucked into your jacket, and be able to pull a portion up over your nose and mouth to protect your breathing during very cold weather. Wool is the only thing that works for this, since the outside of the scarf will form ice from condensation as you are breathing. The wool will prevent cold air passing through, even when it is wet with icy condensation. Neck warmers cover from your chin to upper chest, and can be tucked into a shirt or jacket. Ideally, a neck warmer could be pulled up over mouth and nose, as well. A turtleneck sweater can work here, if it's wool, of course.

So far, mostly everything we've discussed has been wool. Some people think they are allergic to wool. Odds are good that most of them are not. They're actually reacting to the chemicals used in dying the wool, not the wool itself. Most modern wools no longer use the harsh chemicals that were common in the past. If wool still bothers you, wear silk undergarments to keep the wool off your skin.

Good wool clothing is ridiculously expensive when it's new. Let me encourage you to visit thrift stores soon and check out both men's and women's sweaters. Read labels; avoid anything except 100% wool. Buy all you can find. You can always cut them up for gloves, vests, and making different warm items from them.

The best wool garments are made from Merino wool, a fiber from the very fine yarn produced by Merino breed sheep. Sweaters made from Merino can be worn right next to even the most sensitive skin, it's that soft. Cashmere goat wool is even softer, and even though it is usually a thin garment, it can be used as underwear. Cashmere is made from exceptionally fine goat undercoat, is very expensive new, and moderately expensive at thrift stores, too.

While you are at the thrift stores, look for wool jackets. Pea coats are usually all wool or high percentage wool. Don't ignore men's long dress coats, either. My son found a beautiful extra-large men's knee-length camel hair coat for $3, and gave it to me. I'm turning it into two vests, mittens, shoe liners, slippers, a hood, and assorted other small projects. Camel hair is as warm and durable as wool. Real camel hair fabric runs anywhere from $30 to $70 *per yard* at this writing, so that was a real deal. Consider any wool blankets you can find, as well. It's pure wool fabric that can be repurposed in dozens of ways, including as filling for quilts. There are similar deals at a thrift store near you today.

For the long term, the most consistent way of acquiring wool is to raise wool-breeds of sheep. Raise them, shear them, eat the lambs and save their wooly skins to make into clothing (see a hide-tanning guide in the Recipes section). Spinning wool isn't hard, but there is a learning curve – children often learn this very fast and enjoy the process of developing the skill. Once it's spun, it can be knit or crocheted into warm and long-lasting garments.

Care of Wool Clothing

Almost all wool clothing carries a tag that directs you to dry clean it. That's not likely to be possible during the Cold Times that are coming. Most wool garments that are not worn right on the skin can be "dry cleaned" by rubbing them in fresh crisp-dry snow – that helps take out odors and grime. Finer garments may be washed in COLD water with a small amount of shampoo. Don't agitate, just swish the clothes around and let it soak for a time. Rinse in COLD water to which you have added a small amount of apple cider vinegar or white vinegar, and don't agitate. Squeeze NOT WRING the water out, and "dry flat", pulling the garment into shape *gently*. Don't use any heat to dry the wool, and don't put it into a drier unless you actually want the garment to shrink to doll size.

When you put your wool wear away for the summer months (if you're not wearing them year-around), try to put the wool into brown paper bags or "kraft wrap", brown paper that comes on a roll – the paper's cellulose helps keep wool moths out. Save the paper from year to year. Place the folded, wrapped garments into plastic tubs or a cedar chest (better), and top with a piece of cedar wood, drier sheets such as Bounce brand, cedar chips or even some moth balls. Moth balls are cheap at this writing, and you can store them almost forever in a mason jar. One or two in a tub of wrapped sweaters will keep moths out. The price is that the clothing will smell like moth balls when you take them out in the fall. You'll get used to the smell, because lots of people's clothing will smell like moth balls.

Should wool moths get into your clothes, they chew small holes. These can be repaired by patching or sewing the holes closed. On wool knits, if you are handy, you can reknit the sites. A few little patched holes won't affect the warmth or wear-ability of your wool.

Other Than Wool...

Although wool products are your best bet for long-term survival of your group, in the current situation you can still acquire (or may already have) other types of cold weather gear. **Ski clothing** is great for moving around outdoors and being active, because it is designed to be worn while exercising. It's not so good if you have to do any kind of labor, such as hauling wood, checking on livestock, or hunting, because it's not designed to stand up to rugged conditions; it'll tear too easily when moving through thick underbrush or crawling across jagged rocks. Prepare to patch these items as soon as you return indoors – that will keep the garments functional longer.

Many country folk today swear by their **Carharts**, a tough and hardy brand of lined canvas outerwear including jackets and overalls. If you must work outdoors in cold weather, these have a good reputation. In my experience, this type of clothing is too stiff and heavy and binding to allow me to work easily in cold outdoor weather, and if they get wet I get very cold through my clothes underneath them. Many people do wear regular clothes under their Carharts, and it would certainly be possible to wear wool-based thermals beneath these, too.

If you live in a cold environment and have clothing that works for you, stick with it – perhaps adding a few additional sweaters, hats, and thermal underwear. Just remember to avoid cotton garments for winter use. Cotton is fine for the heat of summer, so don't get rid of t-shirts and jeans. You'll still need that, too.

Cold Clothing Etiquette

When you go indoors after being outside, stand by the door and remove hat, scarf, gloves and jacket. Snow and wetness doesn't get tracked around the house if the outerwear is left by the door. Hang these on a rack or on wall-mounted hooks. Even if it is chilly indoors, it is colder outside. Your shirt and thermals should keep you warm enough if there isn't much air movement inside to cool you off.

Aside from the housekeeping effects, the reason for removing the outdoor items is that you will need extra warmth from your hat, scarf, gloves, and jacket when you go back outside. Being inside in lighter clothing allows you to physiologically adjust to indoor temperatures. If, instead, you leave your warm things on while you are indoors, you will actually experience greater cold when you go back outdoors.

Use a low chair or rail to sit upon while you remove boots, also near the entry door. Leave them by the door, too, or carry to your heater to help them dry out. If your socks are damp, take them off, dry your feet, and put on a fresh pair – dry feet stay warm and healthy. Store a small basket of dry socks by the boot-changing seat, too.

Ideally outdoor clothing removal is taking place in a foyer or mudroom arrangement, so you aren't tempted to track snow and dirt into the living area. Indoor slippers by the door encourages you to get into those when the boots come off.

Tips on Keeping Warm Indoors

Furniture should be placed to catch warmth from heaters (more on this shortly). Wear a wool cardigan indoors, and perhaps a light hat to keep warmth around your head. Think: sleep cap, just as people used during the last Little Ice Age. This is the place to wear something like "Polar Fleece", a brand of polyester fleece. Take your "indoor vest/sweater" off when you go outside and change into your "outdoor" clothes.

Don't go around the house in socks – your feet will get too cold. Fleece lined slippers, or wool lined ones like UGGs or similar brands, will help keep your feet from getting too chilled on cold floors. Keep your wool socks on inside your slippers. Heavy carpets and subfloor insulation keeps you warmer, too.

When you sit down, use a lap robe to cover your legs and keep warmth around you. A lap robe is typically the size of a large bath towel or beach towel, and made from fleece or other warm fabrics – there's no reason you couldn't recycle sweaters into a lap robe, or make some up like a down or polyester fluff-filled small quilt.

During the Dalton Minimum little ice age, when indoor temperatures were generally barely above freezing, people kept warm by "bundling" – cuddling under a blanket together. There's no reason a family couldn't bundle while playing a board game, or reading books, or even watching a movie if those are still available. Pets can be included, with a dog or cat or two cuddled up as well. Everyone benefits from the group warmth.

Keeping Warm in Bed

When you make up your bed, place a wool blanket – even a cheap rough one, such as an army surplus one – beneath your bottom sheet right on the mattress. This is warmer than mattress pads, and will prevent excess cool air from reaching you as you sleep. An alternative to this would be a *genuine* down (goose or duck) "feather bed" mattress cover, with the sheet over it. This is probably one of the most comfortable, warm, and relaxing elements in a bed.

Sheets, ideally, are good quality flannel. The warmest and most durable non-pilling flannel is made in Germany and will run $100 per set, but it will last decades with good care. Flannel is brushed or fluffed cotton, but using cotton in this situation makes sleeping more comfortable as excess heat and moisture is wicked away from your skin.

Above you in bed, one sheet with a *genuine* down comforter over that, and a light wool blanket on top. This will not be excessively heavy, but it provides an astonishing amount of non-sweaty warmth that breathes and allows you to turn and shift in bed without struggling. No matter what size bed you have, get a king-size comforter. The excess that hangs over the sides traps heat next to you, reduces drafts, and helps keep you warm.

Polyester fiberfill in "down-substitute" comforters is a poor replacement for real goose or duck down. Use it if that is all you have, but you'll need more wool to keep warmth in. Note: all down comforters will lose feathers over time. That's just the way they are. The feathers are light and waft into corners and under the bed; relatively easy to find and clean up.

During the Dalton Minimum Little Ice Age, most upper-crust people had 4-poster beds, not just because they looked good, but because they could hang heavy curtains around the bed on those 4 corner posts. The curtains blocked excess cold air movement, so that when the room cooled down during the night, warm air continued to stay around the bed itself. And don't forget the bed-cap to keep your head warm.

Finally, sleep wear: thin silk or cotton, or nothing at all. Surprisingly, wearing heavy clothing to bed (such as a sweatshirt and hoodie, and sweatpants) will leave you significantly colder and more uncomfortable than wearing nothing at all. The clothing binds your movements and traps heat on your skin, causing sweating and subsequent cooling. Have a thick, fluffy robe and slippers next to the bed, in case you have to get up quickly during the night.

Warm Things

Keeping yourself warm, as we've seen in the preceding section, means retaining the body heat you already produce. The second way of maintaining comfortable warmth is by warming a *thing*, and letting that radiate heat to you.

Most people are familiar with "rice bag" therapy. That's basically a pound or so of rice sewed into a cloth square bag, or put into a clean sock that's tied shut, and then heated for a minute or two in a microwave. The microwave treatment heats the rice, which generates heat, and the fabric sack allows it to be placed comfortably on achy joints or cold hands. Simple, comfortable, and inexpensive.

It's possible to do the same thing without a microwave. Merely place the rice bag on a wire rack in a standard oven and let it heat at a low temperature (say, 250°F) for about 10 minutes or so. Watch it, so you don't end up with a roasted rice bag. Alternatively, the same rice bag could be placed in a cast iron covered pan, such as a Dutch Oven, and heated over a wood stove until it's warm enough to use. Only use dry heat with a rice bag. Any moisture will start to cook the rice.

In the Victorian past, soapstone, a particular type of soft colorful rock, was quite popular. Soapstone absorbs heat readily and will give it off for lengthy periods of time, sometimes for hours, depending on the size and thickness of the stone. Heated on a wood stove, a piece of soapstone could be placed on a footstool and covered with a flannel cloth to provide warmth to chilly toes.

Lacking soapstone, poor folks used bricks or smooth rocks heated until warm *on top* of a wood stove (never in direct contact with coals or flame because the rocks can explode). Then the rock or brick was wrapped in flannel, and placed under the covers at the foot of the bed, a cozy inexpensive way to warm it up before climbing in. In the same way, a warmed block could be placed beside someone in a chair or couch or used as a footrest.

In the previous section, we talked about placing your furniture around your heater to collect heat. Think back to a style of chair known as a "wing back." These are stuffed chairs with sides that jut out a little at about head level, looking a little like side wings. Many people don't realize that those "wings" are a remnant of the end of the last Little Ice Age. The wings help trap heat close into the person sitting in the chair. Pull that wingback right in front of the fireplace, and they become quite warm and cozy, even if there are drafts in the room.

The wingback's Little Ice Age ancestor is actually a more heat-retentive overstuffed chair called a hooded chair or a Porter's chair. Historically, these were made from wood, and then later in upholstered forms as they are today. You can imagine snipping off the top hood, and ending up with a typical wingback. Indeed, that's what a wingback is actually: a hoodless chair made for a warmer world.

In a cooling world, just place that Porter's chair facing a warm wood heating stove, and it will trap heat within the curved sides and hood effectively creating a warm micro-climate inside the curvature. When you climb into it, it's already warm, and keeps that toasty comfort all around you. Throw on a lap robe, wool cap, put your feet on a warmed soapstone block, and enjoy a cup of hot herbal tea while you read a good book – now, that's living!

Consider how to make or acquire hooded seats for more than one person, such as loveseats and couches. You can purchase these for a couple thousand dollars, which is all right if you have that kind of money. Some modern pubs and restaurants actually have semi-private seating that is suggestive of heat-retaining furniture, such as high-backed circular booths. You can duplicate that design with a little creativity and time, or even acquire them from restaurant sales and auctions. There will be quite a few of these in the near future.

The Rocket Stove

One inexpensive method to heat "things" rather than space, is what has become known as a Rocket Stove. These are usually small, homemade, and have a "chimney" that is diverted though a flue that passes through a masonry or cob bench or ledge. The diversion area heats up and becomes a warm seating or resting zone in itself. In the Orient, including Japan and Korea, similar small stoves had their chimney ducted through a slab or large bench that was used for seating and as a sleeping platform.

This outstanding little book pictured on the next page, still available, is one of the first ones to explore the concept in detail – and today there are many YouTube videos and other books devoted to the idea. Rocket stoves can be made on the fly with rocks, bricks, mud, a handful of concrete masonry blocks, or even a couple of #10 cans and fine sand.

The idea is to make a small burn chamber with a taller chimney that draws air past the small burning material and increases the heat output. Because of the way it draws the air through the system, you can actually leave burning sticks part way out of the chamber and feed them in overtime as the end burns off.

The woman on the *Rocket Mass Heaters* cover is sitting on a cob-type "couch" built around the flue for the heat, which was fired in the barrel to the right. Along with providing heat, the barrel stove can be used as a cooking platform, as well.

The real benefit of Rocket Stoves, aside from the ease and homemade quality of constructing one, is that they can operate on smaller pieces of "biomass" – that is, twigs, burnable small branches, and even dry grass and leaves. That means that they are very economical to operate, and can provide warmth even when larger pieces of wood aren't available or haven't yet been cut.

Rocket stoves are a distant relative of the larger masonry stove, but they share the feature of fuel economy. Rocket stoves have been developed in Third World countries where fuel was in short supply or very expensive.

Masonry stoves were the product of chilly Norsemen, who didn't have chainsaws; every stick of wood had to count. Modern wood heating and cook stoves, as well as fireplaces, are terribly inefficient by comparison, requiring armloads of wood to heat through the night.

Heating Space

American freestanding cast iron stoves and stone fireplaces are the end product of our nation's pioneer beginnings. Wood was abundant, cheap, and so available people merely had to gather it. There was no need to conserve wood or create heating systems that were economical in fuel use.

The early settlers who came over from crowded Northern European countries left places where wood was expensive and scarce, or had to be hauled long distances. Consequently, the American bounty of firewood led to inefficiencies that would have been unthinkable in the European homelands. The centuries long culturally-transmitted memory of America at that time is the jolly crackling flame in the stove or fireplace – something that was the province of the rich and nearly nonexistent in the lives of the poor in the Old Country.

In the short run, during the Awakening and early Zen-slap periods, there are two basic options in heating stoves: wood based heat, and propane based heat. I am excluding natural gas heat, because although it is similar to propane, it is dependent upon long, functioning, city-wide nat-gas pumping and piping systems. Electric heat requires a functioning grid, and we cannot reasonably make the assumption the grid will be continuously available during extreme cold. We are trying to move away from dependence on strangers and large, fragile systems, so anything fired by electricity and natural gas must be off our list.

Heating With Propane

Many people are familiar with propane bar-b-que grills. In those, propane – a gas that is a by-product of gasoline production – is stored in a 20 pound container and used to fire up the grill. In a similar way, propane can be stored in huge cylindrical tanks of 250 gallons, 500 gallons, 1000 gallons, and larger. This propane can be used with propane-specific ventless room heaters, to operate cooking stoves, water heaters, and even for propane-powered lights.

Propane is a bit different from natural gas, burning at different air-gas mixes than natural gas. Consequently, the propane-burning device has a differently-sized intake orifice than natural gas, so the equipment is not interchangeable without also changing the orifice.

The benefit of propane is that it can be stored, indefinitely, in the large cylinder tanks which can be above or below ground. The propane gas feeds by pressure within the tank, so no electrical power is needed to make it work. Most varieties of propane cook stoves do require electrical connections to power timers and electronic burner ignitions. You can still find completely non-electric propane stoves if you look around online. Non-electric propane stoves may use a small battery pack to power ignition to light burners; batteries should last a year. Without batteries, you light burners with a match instead, so if batteries are dead you can still cook.

Ventless propane heaters comes in many sizes and styles. Fancy and pricy ones are designed to look like fireplaces with nice mantel pieces around them. Moderately priced (around $300) plain heaters can be hung on a wall with propane plumbed to them. It will heat the central area of a home without any more effort than setting the onboard dial to the level of heat desired.

A well-insulated home can be heated to a comfortable level with moderate propane usage. Our leaky old farmhouse, for example, used less than 500 gallons in two heaters over winter. At about 70 cents per gallon at the time, we heated for an entire winter for less than $400. In June 2017, propane was $1.19/gallon delivered in the Midwest.

Setting up a propane system requires the holding tank, piping (some must be underground and some goes through your home), the propane heater(s), AND propane. A new 1000 gallon tank runs about $1000 – supports are extra. Piping is several hundred dollars. Backhoe work could run another couple hundred. Testing for seals is usually done by whomever installed the pipes, but your area may have requirements for specialists to certify that. Ask about legal requirements at your nearby propane company.

Filling tanks in summer is generally quite a bit less expensive than during the winter, perhaps ½ the cost or even less. Propane trucks will come to your location and fill your tanks on whatever schedule you need – once a year, or once a month. You pay on delivery.

Consider a propane heater as a backup to primary wood heat. That way, you're mostly using a replaceable product (wood) but have a workable propane heater to fall back on. Or, if it is tremendously cold and the wood heater doesn't keep the house warm, you turn on the propane to assist and bring up the temperature. The propane can also be left on at a low level, say, enough to keep the house at 45°F-55°F if you have to be away for a while. That way, water pipes won't freeze.

A thousand gallons, used frugally for cooking and occasional heating would readily last 2 or 3 years, or even 5 years if you're very careful. Two thousand gallons might well last a decade with just occasional use. Even used very cautiously, eventually propane runs out. If you're able to get more, that would be wonderful – but don't place any bets on it just yet. Propane will get you through the initial difficult Zen-slap years, though, so you have a chance to adjust to the rhythms and labors associated with wood heat.

Heating With Wood

For the Zen-slap and Hang-on periods, a solid wood heating stove with a flat surface on which pots and pans can be placed for cooking, is still the most sensible alternative. It might take an armload of wood to keep the house warm during a freezing night, but if you have woodland and chainsaws or handsaws, you've got it made. The next generation or two, during the Hang-on phase, might be able to continue to use that old stove or changes may need to be made to make the stove more efficient. The idea is that there will be time to perform those changes. Your people have got to make it to that point first.

Wood Stoves

Farm writer Gene Logsdon stated that there is one important quality you need to seek out in a wood stove: mass. Basically, the heavier the stove is, the better. The greater the mass, the longer the stove will hold heat. The greater the mass, the longer it will take to warm the stove up, too – but once it's warm, it will keep generating heat, even after the fire has gone out.

Typically, a stove is heavy because it is made from cast iron, and that is why it can hold heat so successfully. However, some manufacturers are building new wood heating stoves with the option of a soapstone exterior, another successful approach to holding and slowly releasing stored heat.

Wood stoves, in general, are more efficient heaters than using a fireplace. Fireplaces pull in room air at a high rate, tend to burn fast, and lose a good deal of heat up the chimney. Stoves, on the other hand, that close up tightly have "dampers" that allow you to adjust the air intake and the chimney outflow, thereby controlling the rate at which the fire burns. Control that, and you can make a fire hot and fast by opening up the dampers, or make it slow and long-lasting by closing down the dampers. You never close the chimney damper all the way because that will prevent smoke from leaving the stove.

Stoves come in all shapes and sizes. Low cost homemade stoves constructed from metal barrels are just as good at heating a home as a fancy chrome and porcelain model. A typical modern stove, new, will run around $1200-$4000, not including chimney pipes. Old, functional stoves, refurbished, might be half as much. Unrefurbished old stoves can be found for a couple hundred dollars. Even an ugly old stove can heat a house.

Wood Stove Cooking

Most wood heating stoves have a flat top surface that can be used as a hot zone to cook on using your existing pots and pans. Many winter-time soups have slow cooked all day on a wood heating stove, ready for you when you return from the cold outdoors. A hot wood heater can also be used for quick cooking meats or boiling water, too, depending where on the top you place your pan. There will be hotter and cooler zones on your stove top.

A wood-fired cook stove is also a great way to heat a room while preparing meals. Old, restored wood cook stoves typically run from $800 up to $1800. If you're handy and find a run-down stove without cracks in the metal and an intact firebox (the spot that holds the wood or coal), these can be restored to perfect function without too much effort. I have seen these old reliables sell for a couple hundred dollars at country auctions. Prettier ones usually sell higher.

If you have outstanding insulation, say, in an underground home, a wood cook stove might be a good option for cooking *and* heating. They have a large top cooking surface, a baking oven, and sometimes a warming shelf above the stovetop. Most cook stoves require a somewhat smaller piece of wood than wood heaters do – which either means you have to cut and chop wood into smaller pieces, or you can use more fallen small branches to keep it going.

Additionally, most cook stoves need to have their burning wood replenished much more frequently than a wood heater, roughly every 40 minutes, so they are best if there is someone in the house to keep an eye on it. This works if that someone is cooking an extensive meal, making jam, or canning pickles at the time. In a larger home, the wood cook stove is unlikely to be able to keep up with generating enough heat, especially if it's very cold outside, but makes nice additional backup heat.

Hot Water on a Wood Stove

Typically, a household would have a kettle of water on the stove to humidify the air and provide a quick hot cup of tea as needed. More creative individuals have attached metal side containers to their stoves, having metal spigots to act as hot water reservoirs. These humidify and provide enough water to wash dishes, take a sponge bath, or hand wash a small bucket of laundry as well. Five gallons of water beside the stove also banks the heat a bit, and keeps the temperatures that reach the room from swinging wildly between highs and lows. You just have to remember to refill any water removed from it right away, or else you risk warping and damaging the reservoir metals.

Wood Stove Mistakes

If you are looking for a stove, do not get one that *requires* an electric fan to operate. If the power goes off, your stove will become much less efficient and negate a large part of its off-grid value. That means that the fashion of building a stove and water heater in a separate building, and piping the heat to the house underground, while a great idea in good times, is a bad idea if the grid is down. In this book, we assume the grid is down pretty much all the time. We are preparing you for the worst and hoping for the best.

For the same reason, do NOT get a pellet stove. Pellet stoves use manufactured wood pellets, about the size of a small vitamin capsule, to fuel the stove. Pellets come in bags, are dumped into a hopper at the top of the stove, and feed into the fire at whatever rate you set. You have to buy the bagged pellets, and it takes a room full of bags to get you through a cold winter. You can't make pellets at home; they arrive at your stove via semi-truck through your retail store. Alternatively, you can power some pellet stoves with dried corn kernels. That's not good for multiple reasons, including burning up your food. The controls for the rate of pellet feed are electric, too. So, pellet stoves have two strikes against them: you can't make your own fuel, and you need electricity to run the stove. Failing to place your wood heater on a suitable fireproof surface, such as stonework – or put a fire resistant shield on the nearest wall – is one of the best ways to burn your house down. Wood heating and cooking stoves just aren't the same as conventional heaters.

Emptying the ash from a stove is something of an art form: you want the stove interior to have sufficient room for good airflow, but enough ash to retain heat and maintain coals overnight. Each stove is different, so you have to learn your stove's "personality" and ash level that works best. It's a mistake to remove *all* the ash, and a mistake to let it build up thickly; trial-and-error is your friend.

Ash should be scooped with a metal shovel made for wood stoves into a *metal* pan. Even if you let it sit for a day or two, it can still have live coals in it, so don't dump it where it might start a fire. Ash is outstanding on the garden, especially where you plan to grow potatoes or other root crops next year. Just dump it and work it in well in the spring. Ash dumped on snow or ice will help it melt because of the increased absorption of solar energy by the dark color. Additionally, hardwood ash is the primary ingredient in making *lye* for soap, so save some ash in dry metal buckets with closeable lids if you plan to make soap.

Fire Woods

Today, wood is widely available and comes in two broad types: hardwoods and softwoods. Hardwood is from trees that grow slowly, lose their leaves in the fall, and develop dense wood. Hardwoods include oak, cherry, alder, walnut, teak, hickory, and mahogany. Finer grades of these woods are typically used for furniture. Softwoods generally are evergreen, have needles, and grow quickly, including pine, fir, juniper, spruce and redwood. These are used in construction.

Both types of wood burn, obviously. Whatever wood is available in your area is the wood you'll use in a wood stove. However, hardwoods burn more slowly and release heat over time. Softwoods burn fast and hot, releasing heat quickly and then dying down to short-lived coals. Softwoods also generate more creosote than hardwoods. The best wood for a wood stove are the hardwoods that have been cut and aged for a year or a bit longer – then the wood is low in moisture, solid, and creates a long-lasting fire. If you live in a pine forest, just plan on cleaning your fireplace and chimney several times during the cold season.

Buying and Cutting Firewood

Right now, you can still buy cut, split firewood. Different regions identify a specific amount as a "rik" or a "cord". In my region, a rik is as much cut wood as can be loaded in the back of a standard pickup, level with the top of the bed – a stack approximately 16" wide, 4 feet high and 8 feet long. Other regions call that a cord. Because there is so much variation, rather than buying a certain number of riks or cords, you may have to eyeball the quantity. Depending on your area, a rik might run anywhere from $40 to $120.

It's hard to estimate how much firewood any given home will require during a 'typical' winter. Factors such as the size of the home, insulation, type and efficiency of stove, how warm the home is kept, and quality of firewood all play a role. When weather gets

colder and winter lasts longer, the 'typical' amount then becomes insufficient – and maybe double or triple the ordinary would be required to be comfortable.

To give you a ballpark figure, we have a thousand-square foot, well-insulated home. In an ordinary winter, 4 rik will keep the place comfortable, using about a rik a month. Previously, when living in an old, uninsulated 1400 square foot 2-story farmhouse, it took a good 10 rik to keep it comfortable, and that was using one wood heater and one wood cookstove.

Ideally, you'd have at least two years of wood cut and stacked at the start of the winter. That way, if the cold dragged on or you weren't able to cut wood the next year, you'd have enough wood to get you through. Given that we're heading to very cold times, it would be sensible to have 3 to 4 years' worth of wood set back and ready to go. Old timers in New England built woodsheds, a simple covered area, to keep wood dry and easily accessed when everything was covered by deep snow; a very sensible idea.

If you have plenty of woodland, you can just cut your firewood and leave it stacked out in the timber, as long as you can remember where it is when everything is covered in snow and ice...and don't mind going out "to the back 40" to bring it up when you need it.

Cutting firewood is a chore, no way around that. Today, using a chainsaw, one person can cut a month's worth of heating firewood from downed trees and branches in a afternoon. A week's worth of concentrated cutting and stacking can provide a winter's worth of wood *provided* said person can work at it steadily. Most people today can't work that hard and consistently at what is, effectively, a mindless physically-demanding task. Plus, that kind of labor is best done when the weather is cool and the woodlands aren't overgrown, so it's not a summer job.

And that all assumes you've got two good-quality chainsaws -- two, because one is going to poop out on you at some point in the middle of the work and require a trip back to the workshop to get it fixed or sharpened. If you don't have a set of good chainsaws, or don't have gas to power it, you need a sharp wood axe PLUS a heavy-duty two-man saw, PLUS a wood maul for splitting the bigger pieces. And at least two people, although four people would be better, faster, and would reduce the labor load.

Now, think about this for a few minutes and put yourself there. Can you chainsaw for hours at a stretch? Can you lift and stack hundreds of pounds of wood? Can you repair a chainsaw or sharpen the blades? Do you have multiple gallons of non-ethanol gasoline set back already, plus chainsaw oil? Replacement parts? Can you wield an axe without bouncing it off the wood and cutting your leg? Do you know how to stand up a large piece of wood so that it splits easily (hint: upside down)? Can you swing a maul so that it hits where you want it to? How will you transport your cut and split wood from the woodlands up to your house, especially if there's been a serious downturn and gasoline is hard to come by?

As strenuous as that may sound, I can assure you that you not only *can* but *will* if you have to. People already do that today. I've done it myself using an axe and maul, and hauling it with a Shetland pony pulling a homemade pony-cart. When the going gets rough, you will be able to do it too.

If you think it through now, and begin the process of learning how to do it efficiently, you'll save yourself a great deal of distress later. It's just going to be an entirely different lifestyle – more physically demanding. Think of it as a "free gym workout" with a bonus pile of firewood at the end. It can even be enjoyable watching your pile of firewood grow.

Now's a good time to start building that firewood store. The more wood you put ahead, the less work you'll have to do later when you have other things to concentrate on.

Creosote

Creosote is a black flaky or tarry substance left on the inside of your stove and its chimney, as a by-product of burning fuel. It's perfectly natural, although it is also potentially dangerous if heavy build-ups are not removed, that is, by cleaning your chimney.

More resinous woods, such as pine, generate more creosote when burned than do hardwoods. Burning woods at lower temperatures creates more creosote than burning at higher temperatures.

The risk of extensive creosote buildup is that it can catch fire within the chimney itself. This causes an enormous. spectacular, very noisy flame to shoot out the top of your chimney – rather like a Roman candle firework. The flame quickly burns up the creosote, BUT it also can crack the inside flue of a masonry chimney, soften and bend metal chimneys, and set your roof and interior walls ablaze. Clearly, this is not something you'd like to have happen. Should you hear a great, roaring fire suddenly in your chimney, shut down all the dampers to cut off air to the fire. DO NOT PUT

WATER ON YOUR STOVE OR CHIMNEY DURING A FLUE FIRE, as that will create a potentially deadly burst of steam or crack the metal. Leave the house and watch from outside.

The best way to avoid a flue fire is to keep your chimney clean of excessive creosote. That means cleaning the chimney *at least three times a year*, once in summer, once in the middle of winter, and once at the end. Summer cleaning should take place if you're using your stove at that time. Clearly, if you're cleaning your chimney during the mid-winter, you'll have to pick a relatively warm day and let the fire go out and the stove cool off completely beforehand. Use backup heating to prevent the house from cooling too much.

Cleaning a chimney means taking the stove pipe down, and passing a chimney brush or wire brush through it to scrape the creosote. The black residue is messy and will be airborne easily, so do this outdoors. If you don't have a chimney brush, fill an unwanted pillowcase with gravel or dirt, and rub that through the stove pipe until it is clean of creosote. Get up on the roof, tie the pillowcase to a rope, and pull it up and down the chimney on all sides. The process shouldn't take more than a few minutes.

Starting Your Fire

It used to be that every kid knew how to kindle a fire. Camping and being outdoors was a part of ordinary living. Today, however, even adults have little experience with the simple art of making fire. Remember the scene in Tom Hanks' movie *Castaway*, where he struggles with a drill and bow to get even a little flame going? And his joy at having a bonfire?

Starting fires in stoves or fireplaces for the first time is a similar experience, especially if you have to really work at it. Here's how I do it:

1. Make sure chimney is clear (no bird's nest in it, for example), and that there isn't excessive ash in the stove

already. Open the chimney damper all the way (vertical).

2. Take a couple sheets of newspaper or anything similarly flammable, give it a few twists, and lay it in the bottom of your stove on top of the grate. Put the same under the grate.

3. On top of the paper on the grate, place light, dry kindling about 2 or 3 inches deep, crisscrossing all the little sticks and chips so that there's pretty good airflow around them.

4. On top of the kindling, lay 5 or 6 small pieces of split wood, crisscrossing all.

5. Now, take a piece of newspaper, feed bag, or similar, crumple and twist it, and light one end. Hold that inside the stove near where the stovepipe exits, so that it draws smoke up the chimney. This is basically priming the chimney to draw smoke upward by heating it a little.

6. Once you can see the stove is "drawing" good, light the paper *under* the grate. The draw will pull the heat and flames up through the kindling and set the whole thing ablaze.

7. Leave the stove front open until the fire is "merry".

8. Put in larger pieces of wood, crossing them several ways to allow continued airflow.

9. Close stove front, and adjust air intake(s) and the damper so that the fire is burning, but burning slowly – you'll be able to hear the sound change as you adjust everything. It burns more slowly with the vents turned down but not closed completely, and the damper closed about halfway. *Never close the chimney damper down completely if the vents are open.* That will fill your house with smoke. If you get a roaring chimney fire, close all vents first, then close the damper.

10. Check the fire in an hour or so, or if you start to feel a chill. Add wood as needed to keep it going continuously. At night, "bank" the fire by turning vents down low and damper about ¼ open. It will burn down to coals by morning.

11. The next morning, open the damper, open the vents. Open the stove front. If you still have coals, just reload small wood over that as you did initially. If the coals are cool, start over. You may have to scoop out some ash to get it going.

CAVEAT: Everyone starts fires differently, so experiment. Find an approach that works for you. Don't even bother trying to light it with damp leaves or tinder, because all you'll get is smoke. If you're keeping your fire going, you may be able to use but a single match for the entire season. That's the high challenge for good fire maintenance. Store lots of matches! As a backup, keep a large magnifying glass and some very dry tinder. Light the tinder by using the magnifying glass to focus sunlight onto it, then bring the burning tinder to the stove.

Firestarters

As tempting as it may be to start a reluctant fire with a wee bit of diesel fuel or gasoline or barbeque lighter, **DON'T**. That's one of the best ways to burn down your house and turn yourself into a living torch.

There are materials that burn well and allow enough time for your tinder to catch, which you can make readily today. For example, you can make an excellent Firestarter with Vaseline and genuine cotton balls, smearing the Vaseline over the balls – when you want a fire, place the Firestarter on your tinder, and light the ball.

You can do the same with some dryer lint in melted wax – place a cotton-ball size hunk of dryer lint in a dry ice cube tray section, and cover it with melted wax, either fresh wax or saved old candle wax. When hardened, store it in a baggie and use one or two on your kindling.

If you make up lots of these now, you won't have to make them later when wax, Vaseline, genuine cotton balls, or dryer lint are hard to find.

Awakening Stage Temporary Heat

It is wise to keep several forms of backup heat, for any just-in-case situation that may arise. I'm calling these "Awakening Stage" heat, because once the Zen-slap sets in, it may be difficult or impossible to get these supplies.

One of these is a kerosene heater, effectively, a portable stand-alone smaller stove that runs off of kerosene. These cost around $200 or less, are lightweight when empty, and can run all night on a single kerosene fill of a few gallons. The heat generated is warming and moderately clean. You'll need to leave a window at each end of the house partially open a crack so that you get air movement through the house. The challenge with these is that you then have to store lots and lots of kerosene, another cost.

If you have a barbeque grill propane tank, you can use that to feed into a propane heater but DO NOT use your BBQ grill as a heat source or for cooking when it is not HIGHLY ventilated. You will die from carbon monoxide poisoning, without even knowing it's happening. Instead, the "Big Buddy" type is a ventless heater that is usually used for camping. For the same cost, you can buy a small wall-mountable ventless standard heater that will run for several days to a week on a portable jug of propane. These are probably safer than the camping heaters, because they are designed for use in a home.

If you have a non-electric propane cookstove, your oven makes a fine heater as well. Although manufacturers say not to use these for heating, it's unlikely to kill you. Proof is that there aren't a spate of "Thanksgiving deaths" related to cooking the turkey all night or running the cookstove all day.

These are all temporary heat sources, because eventually the manufactured fuel runs out. Once again, that wood stove and heater will last as long as there are trees, so it's a better resource for the long run.

Keeping Heat Where You Want It

Modern houses are made to be well insulated and air tight – hopefully not so tight that you'd run out of breathable air if doors and windows are all closed! Closing off portions of your home, such as bedrooms, is a good way to localize heat.

During cold winters in the old, leaky farmhouse, we would crank up the woodstove and close off doors to the rest of the house – that kept heat in the room we were in. We'd sleep in sleeping bags next to the stove, plenty warm. The rest of the house could get below freezing, and we'd still be toasty. At the time, we didn't have water pipes to worry about. *Don't close off rooms where water pipes are located*, such as bathrooms and kitchens. We've also set up heavy curtains in doorways to control heat flow. Curtained rooms can be opened just before use, letting warm air back in.

The novel, *Stacey's Quest* by AK Steele available on Amazon Kindle, is set during a social collapse in a snowy winter. In one scene,

Stacey goes to a neighbor's home. Inside the house, she finds a camping tent with the neighbor family dead inside. They had set up a propane camp heater, and were all asphyxiated. Pretty graphic, but a strong reminder of *what not to do* in a cold situation.

Keep heat around you, but remember that all flame utilizes the same oxygen you breathe. Give it its own air, by cracking open a couple windows on opposite ends of the house. It will be chilly, but you'll survive. That's what counts.

9 POWER AND LIGHT

One of the important features of the modern age is so commonplace and so foundational to everything we do, that it is virtually invisible. Because grid power is so ubiquitous, most of us can scarcely imagine a world without it. That is, until the power goes down, and we stumble in the dark turning on switches that don't work, and continuing to be surprised when we open the refrigerator and the light doesn't come on. All of our entire lifetime of experience tells us that the power outage is temporary, and we merely need to wait it out until 'they' get it fixed.

A lifetime of experience is profoundly hard behavior to change, much harder than choosing to break a habit like smoking or eating too many carbs. Two years after we went off grid and largely non-electric, I was still absent-mindedly flipping dead light switches. Forty years of training doesn't just go away. When power is interrupted, a normal part of our lives is lost, our control is lost, our ability to perform competently in the world we have built is shattered. Some people will *literally* not know how to function.

As we move deeper into the Grand Solar Minimum, the risk of long-term grid-down incidents increases. Storms, snow, and floods become more severe; electronics-destroying power surges and brownouts increase; and the risk for a systemic failure grows. As national economies contract, the funds for repairing failing facilities dry up, so repairs aren't made. Electrical power is a fragile foundation on which to plan a future.

Unfortunately, because universal power is so involved with our lives, planning a non-electric future becomes extremely hard to envision. If you can't imagine it, you can't plan for it. The only way to imagine it is to experience it, so you have a non-electric challenge ahead of you. You *must* practice with these supplies before you need them. This is particularly true if you have children; they can adapt, too, but need to feel like the non-electric life is just one more version of "normal".

Solar, The Pros and Cons

One of the first options many people consider is to go "off grid" with solar applications. Solar has some real benefits. It can be portable or stationary; it can provide consistent power that is "free" after the initial expense; it will continue to function when the main grid has gone down; and it returns control over your energy needs to *you*.

However, the downsides of solar are very real, too. The first is that it is *very costly* to try to duplicate grid power with solar, if you keep using electricity as most people do right now. Retrofitting an ordinary house can easily run into $30,000-$70,000, if you don't change out appliances for propane-powered or low electric-draw stoves, refrigerators, driers, and water heaters. Buying those is an additional thousands of dollars of initial expense.

Another downside is that solar is 100% dependent on the sun....and we already know that the Total Solar Irradiance (TSI) output is dropping and will get lower during the Cold Times ahead. That WILL affect the efficiency of your solar panels and power collection – which means that you will need about double the collection panels that you would have needed a decade ago, in order to get the same power output. That also ups the initial expense. EMPs and CMEs have the potential to impair panel circuitry, as well.

Solar panels have a life-span, a decade more or less. They can be damaged by hail, can get cloudy and suffer decreased efficiency, and need to be cleaned once or twice a year. Unless your panels are very securely attached, they can be lifted by high winds and lost during storms, too. So you'll need to buy more panels than you think you need to replace ones that are damaged, worn out, or lost.

Yet another issue is that you need to store your solar collected power in batteries. Even if you buy the top of the line, batteries have a life-span of about a decade. That means, even with the top level equipment, you're going to be unable to store power efficiently for longer than a decade, unless you store "sleeping" batteries (uncharged) as replacements, another expense.

A critical piece of your system is the charge controller, an electronic device that manages the input from your panels into the batteries. Because your systems cannot work without a functional charge controller, you'll need *at least* two. One of them is for backup. More expense.

Another downside is that you have to learn how solar works, and how to maintain your equipment. This is about as challenging as learning how to rewire your house, or replace hardware components in your computer, so it's not impossible to learn. However, if you don't have an inclination to do that type of electrical work, you won't develop the interest just because you bought a solar panel. Don't make your future dependent on a technology that you have little interest in maintaining.

That said, there's no reason why a home or community couldn't install smaller solar applications – say, a single battery with a small solar panel to charge it – and run a few lower power items off it. A few LED lights, a laptop or two, a small DVD player, an ebook reader, a backup battery charger, a cell phone or even a field phone could be charged off this kind of system. With two batteries and two panels, you could run a still-air (Styrofoam) incubator and hatch chicks, too, or expand your other charging operations.

Right now, there are many solar operations offering a wide assortment of solar panels, set ups (arrays), batteries, and charge controllers. Each operation has its own view of the best way to do things and the best equipment for the job. Watch some YouTubes and get familiar with the basics before you leap.

For now, if you have a limited amount of funds, aim toward a small solar system. Check and compare online prices and systems. Don't go for the cheapest or the most expensive; go mid-price. On the low end, Northern and Harbor Freight both have carried complete "portable" systems, with four 15-watt panels (a total of 60 watts), charge controller and wiring – you supply the marine deep-cycle battery or car battery. A marine deep cycle battery or golf cart battery is generally more expensive than a car battery, but can tolerate being discharged more "deeply" before it needs to be recharged than can car batteries.

Variations on Solar: Generator Plan

The concept of solar power has been so glamorized in the past couple decades that it's easy to lose sight of what solar is all about:

acquiring and storing useable electrical power. Solar panels are merely the way we "grab" potential electricity and transform it into a form that can be readily "stored" in batteries. Basically, solar panels are just one way to acquire and store electricity in batteries. Any system that can "save" electricity for use later is points ahead during trying times – so, consider this:

1000 watt gasoline generator → battery charger → battery

Grid → battery charger → battery

Driving your car to work → battery charger → battery

Tractor → PTO generator →battery charger → battery

Solar accomplishes the *exact same end point* – charging batteries.

So, one plan might be to store treated[1] non-ethanol[2] gasoline. Use that to power a $400 generator, which is hooked to a battery charger, which charges deep cycle batteries, one at a time if you have to. While the generator is running[3], depending on your available power[4], you could also do a load of laundry, pump enough water to fill a holding tank, charge cellphones and tablets and laptops[5]. The energy you store in batteries can then be used for lights and small appliances (blenders, for example) and laptop DVDs[6].

1. Treat gasoline with Stabil or Pri-G, which keeps it in good condition for long periods of time. Also, store gasoline where it is away from flammables and your residence and relatively cool, such as in a tank that is heavily shaded by trees.
2. Use ONLY non-ethanol gasoline in small engines, such as generators, mowers, and trimmers. Ethanol gasoline ("corn gas") is widely recognized as damaging to small engine carburetors and gaskets. Corn gas doesn't keep in storage, either, no matter how you treat it.
3. Generators must never be run in a confined space, such as a garage or closed shed or near a sleeping area. There's the risk of killing yourself with a carbon monoxide overdose. Keep in mind that the sound of a generator when the grid is down is like a lighthouse beacon on a dark night. It will

draw in lots of people you might not want around. Muffle and suppress the sound as much as possible. If you run an exhaust hose outside a shed and another air intake vent, you can operate the generator inside a closed and sound-insulated shed. Don't leave the generator where it can be stolen; lock it down tight.

4. Depending on your finances, get a generator that will give you at least 3000 watts of power, if you want to pump water or carry on several operations at one time. A 5000 watt one is even better. But you can certainly charge batteries with a small 1000 watt generator – just not run a microwave or washing machine or freezer off it. Make sure it's got an automatic low-oil shutoff – and check the oil level *every time* you fire it up.

5. All electronics such as laptops, tablets, and cell phones should be separated from energy sources by at least one surge protector. This is especially the case when you are charging off of a generator – power is just not consistent, and the little surges that are typical of generator power can damage your electronics otherwise.

6. Batteries are "direct current" (DC) whereas most household appliances and electronics are "alternating current" (AC). That means that you'll need a device called an "inverter" between your DC batteries and your AC appliances. The inverter changes (inverts) DC to AC.

Less expensive, still, to start storing power, is to use grid power while it is still up. Buy an automotive battery charger ($100 or so), hook to your deep cycle batteries, plug it in, and start charging. You can charge them one at a time, or charge in series if you have several hooked together. In order to use the power, you'll have to have an outlet connected to the battery – a car-style DC "cigarette lighter" type is inexpensive and relatively simple to clip to the battery (with a fuse between them, of course). Then, if you wish to power AC equipment, you'll also need a small car-style "inverter" that will plug into the DC outlet and make regular AC power accessible.

Probably the cheapest start-up method is to use your existing car or truck as the charger and battery. Just acquire an inverter that will plug into your car's "cigarette lighter" outlet, and use the AC outlets on that to charge several small items and rechargeable AA, AAA, C and D batteries, while you are doing your daily driving. You can also charge with your vehicle sitting in the driveway idling, but that's not an efficient use of gasoline.

If you use the generator to charge your batteries, you'll be more than halfway toward a solar setup, too. Additional items you'll need at that point to go solar will be: solar panels, a charge controller (a small box with electronics that regulate the power flow into the batteries) which goes between your input and the batteries, and a method to extract power from the batteries (an AC inverter/outlet).

Variations on Solar: Gasoline Engines

Before there was solar, there was gasoline. Have you ever seen a gasoline engine power a washing machine? Chain saw? Lawn mower? Power washer? Chipper-shredder? Wood splitter? A boat outboard motor? You get the drift – there are multiple ways to utilize non-electric and off-grid tools to make your life easier.

Farmers store gasoline in 200-300 gallon tanks set up on stands so that they can gravity feed through standard gas hose arrangements into their vehicles – so, it's certainly possible to acquire and store gasoline in a rural setting. Be sure to check local and regional regulations before launching on this plan. If you can't get it delivered, you can bring it back to your place in 5-gallon plastic gas cans, several at a time, until your tank is filled. *Only store non-ethanol, and be sure to add Stabil or Pri-G to keep your gas in good condition.*

If you use gasoline-powered equipment consistently, plan to store motor oil (including 2-stroke), belts, hoses, filters, gaskets, spark plugs, chains, and anything else you might need to make repairs on your things. Don't assume there will always be access to critical parts – so get them in advance.

Practical Alternative Power

The big difference between utilizing the grid to run your equipment and using battery or diesel/gas power for the same operation is one you'll need to keep in the back of your mind: the grid is "limitless" but batteries and fuels are not. You can't just plug something into a battery or gasoline generator and expect it to keep running indefinitely, as you can with grid power. Eventually, the battery or fuel runs down and won't run your equipment. And, if you run your batteries down that far, it takes longer to recharge *and* you'll shorten your battery's life span.

Battery powered lights in your home will give better stable light if you use LEDs or low-draw CFL bulbs, rather than the higher-electricity drawing incandescent bulbs. You can light a family room with a string of mini LEDs, too – nice, indirect lighting that gives a pleasant glow. Use individual task-lights when doing close work, such as knitting or reading to minimize power draw. Small fans run nicely on battery power, too.

Wind-powered water pumping and energy generation are an effective non-solar option – these systems work well at generating power as long as the wind is blowing at a minimum speed (7 mph to 15 mph, for some systems). Old farms used wind power to pump water up from shallow wells for livestock at remote locations, and today's Amish families often draw their water the same way.

Like solar, wind is pricey to set up. It's dependent on consistent steady winds that don't reach too high a speed (high winds can destroy the towers and blades). Ice and snow can impede or stop blade rotation, so power isn't generated. You'll also need a battery bank and charge controller, as with solar. Personally, I am leery of wind power, simply because we seem to see wind patterns changing and storms intensifying – the risk of losing a primary power source to a tornado or hurricane is real. Australia's national wind power plants lost generating capacity as wind flows changed in 2017, too, causing customers to lose power during brown and black outs. However, for pumping water from a shallow source, it might be an ideal application.

Hydro power – that is, turning a power generating turbine (motor) using the flow of water – is the basis of many modern power plants, especially those at the foot of dams. It can be scaled down to mini or micro levels for a small farm, home, or community use as long as you have a continuous steady water flow. This appears to be one of the favored systems offered to Third World countries that have rich water supplies. The continuous water flow could be from a year-round stream, from water "impoundment" (a dam or holding tank) that allows you to release water at a steady rate, or even a system of pipes and holding tanks off of a stream that gives you the same type of control.

Clearly, you'd also need a battery backup system to store energy you don't immediately use, plus extensive power-carrying lines to bring the electricity from the river or generation point to your home. You'd need about 5-10 kilowatts from your system to run your house the way it is right now – less if you cut back on electricity-powered devices. A micro hydro system typically runs about 1/3 the cost of a similar solar system, and generates power 24/7 as long as the water is running.

A mini or micro hydroelectric system is a little harder to source than solar approaches, although Amazon does have a mini-hydro that can generate enough power to run a cell phone or tablet, priced less than $35. An entire system, ready to set up, might run from $3000 to $8000, surprisingly little compared to other alt-power approaches. If you avoid digital monitoring and stick with something analog, your risk from EMP/CME is also reduced.

Risks to this system include flooding, and components do wear out with use. If your water flow freezes or is buried in snow, it will stop generating power, which is why battery backup is important. You can also get electric shocks from the power lines, just like with grid power.

Off Grid Living: How To Build Wind Turbine, Solar Panels And Micro Hydroelectric Generator To Power Up Your House, by Anderson, Swarz, and Thompson (available on Amazon) – gives a good general overview of each approach.
*
https://www.brownellmicrohydro.com/
Brownell Micro Hydro carries systems and has lots of info on set ups, as well as a blog with helpful discussions.

Lighting Without Electricity

For all the millennia of human history, except for the blink of an eye which was the last 120 years, there was no electric grid, no widespread electrical power, no batteries, no street lights, and no flashlights. There were no cars, no buses, no power saws, no motor boats, no motor cycles. No radio, television, internet, copy machines, cell phones, GPS, landlines, or security cameras. No computers, no ATMs, no hand-held calculators, no digital cameras, no electric typewriters.

Yet, each of those powered "things" took the place of something else that was powered by human beings: calculators replaced pencil and paper addition and subtraction; motorized transportation replaced horse and buggy; internet, radio, and television replaced newspapers and handwritten letters; cell phones replaced having a conversation in person.

All that fancy technology merely replaced a simpler, less-expensive, original way of doing things. Although it would be quite a change for most people, it's still possible to return to those original ways, and become more familiar with our actual human behaviors and roots, unfettered by expensive toy intermediaries.

Light

One of the most important things for long term comfort is light. Clear, bright, unwavering light is actually pretty hard to come by in a non-electric setting. The modern method of determining "light output" of bulbs and LEDs, is based on the *lumen*, basically, the equivalent of one candle a foot away with the light falling on a 12"x12" square. So, a lightbulb that gives 20 lumens would be the same has having 20 candles burning a foot away from you, illuminating an open book.

Incandescent Bulbs WATTS	Typical Light Output LUMENS
40	450
60	800
75	1,100
100	1,600

Notice in this chart that a low-wattage 40-watt light bulb, the type used in many refrigerators, gives about the equivalent of 450 candles. That's a lot of light, packed into a small bulb – or, said another way, it takes a huge number of candles to give even a modicum of good light.

Candles are familiar, easy to operate if you have matches or lighters, but give pretty poor light. Candle flames flicker in the slightest breeze. It takes 3 to 5 large candles to give half-way decent light to read by, and a few more to do needlepoint or tie fishing flies.

Solar yard lights are pretty good indoor home lights and work in grid-down or brown out situations, as well. Typically, these are small LED lamps on a short pole, something that could be set up to light a walkway or indicate a door. Each yard light has a small solar panel, a couple inches square, which provides enough power to charge onboard AA or AAA batteries. Prices typically start low at just a few dollars each for small lights. For better indoor lighting, get the multi-lamp ones, about $45 each. Place in a sunny spot during the day. At night, bring them indoors near where you need light. They can also be carried from room to room as needed. They don't get hot when lit, and a couple of them provides decent light to read or do small work. The higher priced ones can be turned off when you're done with them; lower priced ones stay on until the batteries have discharged for the night.

LEDs are becoming more common, and give a good clear electric-powered light that can replace the standard incandescent or florescent bulb. The benefit of LEDs over standard lights is that they use less energy. A 13 watt LED can give as much light as a 75 watt standard bulb. If you have even a small solar system, you may be able to charge a battery enough to run LEDs in individual lamps, or even a couple of LED string lights. For up-close small work, such as reading, an LED clip-on battery-powered light may be all you need – you can find these at bookstores.

Oil or kerosene lamps and lanterns are those familiar old-style homestead lights. They are easy to use but do require access to lamp oil (not the same as cooking or motor oil) or kerosene in order to function. Most oil lamps have a wick, a flat woven cotton cord that draws the fuel up to the chimney area. These are simple to use, will burn a cup or two of fuel in 8 hours. However, the light they give is low power and flickers. It takes, easily, 4 lamps in a room to provide comfortable enough light to carry on family life, and at least two lamps to read by. Each lamp is roughly equivalent to a single large candle. These generally cost less than $10 each. The burning lamp oil or kerosene is incompletely combusted, so there is an odor with these lamps.

An improved oil lamp is made by the Aladdin company. The design incorporates a wick that draws the fuel up to a lacy "mantle" that surrounds the small flame. The mantle heats up and glows, throwing off lots of heat and a clear, strong, unwavering light, equivalent to about a 40 watt incandescent bulb. The light is very bright and hard to look at directly, so you'll need a shade with this one, as well. Aladdins are the Cadillac of oil lamps, and they are priced like it too. Prices start at about $100 and go up from there. There are some very beautiful Aladdins, with intricate glass bases and decorated shades. For the long run, you'd find the all-metal lamp and a cloth shade perfectly suitable. Less chance of breakage, too. Aladdins burn hot and clean, so there is very little fuel odor with these. Just don't put them where something flammable is within 3 feet above the chimney. One Aladdin will burn 1-1/2 to 2 cups of fuel in 8 hours.

For all oil type lamps, you'll need multiple extra glass chimneys, and extra wicks; Aladdins will also need lots of extra mantles. They are lacy and fragile, and after a few uses they fall apart easily if touched even very lightly. Remember, kerosene and lamp oil (liquid paraffin) are products of the oil and gas industry. If that shuts down, so does your source for light.

Store a LOT of extra lamp fuel. If you burn a single lamp and use, say, 12 oz (1 -1/2 cups) of fuel a night, then in a week you will have burned about 2-1/2 quarts of fuel. That's over half a gallon in one week. In two weeks, you've burned over a gallon, which is about 3 gallons a month. At that rate, you'd need 36 gallons of fuel a year to keep ONE LAMP burning each night. Two lamps would require 72 gallons; four lamps would use 144 gallons. There was a reason our rural ancestors went to bed and got up with the sun. Running lamps for hours gets expensive after a while.

Propane Lamps operate in a similar manner to the Aladdin. They have one or two mantles that generate the light. Coleman and other camping suppliers make one- or two-burner lamps that can run off of a 1-pound propane canister, or even a BBQ-size tank if you have extra attachments. These are efficient and give good light, cost around $70 or so. Obviously, they'll use up your propane stores and when you run out of gas, they will be useless.

Fat Lamps have been used for thousands of years. It's just some oil or animal fat with a wick stuck in it. Each lamp gives the equivalent of a single candle, and it will be smoky and smell like burning fat. This is a "if you have no other options" type of light.

Light Discipline

The concept of light discipline arises from the simple knowledge that if the grid is down, most people won't have light. If you do, you're going to stand out *for miles*, attracting unexpected and probably unwanted visitors. Light discipline means controlling the visible light in your area. Use thick "blackout curtains" to prevent light showing through your windows, and turn out lights before opening doors. Don't shine flashlights any more often than you need to, or use red or green-tinted ones.

Test blackout curtains before you need them: turn all the lights on in your place, pull the curtains closed, and go outside. Look your house over from all angles, and make notes on where you see light coming through. Repair those spots. Every now and then, do it again, until your place is completely dark from every possible direction.

Alternative Power Sources

This is a very brief overview, enough info that you can pursue any area that might interest you. You've probably heard or seen a bicycle-powered battery charger – it's a small car alternator, turned by pulleys attached to a stationary bicycle wheel. When someone pedals the bike, it turns the alternator and generates enough current to charge a battery or power a small light. Simple and elegant in design, and relatively inexpensive to make.

Suppose you had that alternator and battery, but didn't want to pedal a stationary bike all day – how else could you turn a wheel to the pulley? In the 19th century, people operated mechanical devices like lathes and small grain mills by putting a horse or dog on a sloped treadmill. As the animal walked "uphill", the treadmill turned, turning a wheel attached to a pulley, that turned a gear, that turned the device. Might as well be turning an alternator, and charging a battery, all while giving the pet some good exercise.

If you've been out around horse stables, you may have seen "horse walkers" – an upright circular clothes-line like contraption, that is used to exercise horses. The animal's halter is attached to a pole, and as the horse walks in a circle around the device, it turns the pole. Using a series of gears, that action could be translated into another source of power to turn an alternator.

This is the same basis as hydropower generated by turning water wheels, by the way. During the 19th century, criminals and the poor in England were sentenced to *the treadmill,* a giant human-powered wheel that was turned as they "climbed stairs" for a daily 8-hour shift. The treadmill turned a mill stone, and was utilized to grind grains.

Today's treadmill can still be applied to generate power – and improve one's health at the same time. It just takes a little ingenuity and, perhaps, necessity.

10 HEALTH AND HYGIENE

When the Cold arrives, it won't be announced on the legacy news. There won't be any headlines screaming, "THE ICE AGE IS HERE". Even so, it will be undeniable and people's mindsets will change but not without some harrowing times first.

Today, a person might hop in their car and drive 300 miles without even a glance at their tires. They know that if they get a flat, or have a breakdown, they'll just make a cell phone call and get a tow truck or other service to come fix the problem.

After the Cold Times are well underway, it will only be the terminally dim who travel outside their area without a survival kit that includes wool blankets, several days of food and water, extra clothing and boots, and a shovel to dig out of snow. That's a profound change in the way the average person thinks and plans.

Planning, especially advanced planning, will make the difference between life and death.

There are few places that "thinking ahead" will be more important than in how you and yours tend to hygiene and health, both mental and physical. Advanced planning can save your people from disease, broken bones, and worse. Making these kinds of connections (linear projections, actually) is a learned art. Registered nurses are exceptionally good at this kind of thinking, so if you have a nurse in your group, count yourself lucky and enlist that nurse to help pave the way.

Watch a ball, tossed through the air. Because of your life experience in a world with gravity, you can immediately project just about where that ball will come to ground. You see the arc and do a near-instantaneous calculation: given that the ball is going *that way*, at *that speed*, then it will end up *there*, assuming nothing changes that trajectory such as wind or something that gets in the way. That's a linear projection.

In the same way, much of what we understand about the way disease occurs is based on a linear projection. For example, if a person shows certain symptoms, say a high fever, and has joint and muscle pain and fatigue, maybe a cough, we can pretty well say that this situation will likely last about 14 days. We project those symptoms forward in time and recognize that we are looking at influenza. The natural course of that disease, by linear projection, leads to recovery in 7-14 days. We know we can decrease the severity of the effects by encouraging the person to keep warm, rest, and drink plenty of liquids, allowing the body to recover more readily – and then they should start feeling better in a few days. That is the *natural course* of influenza. It follows like a ball tossed through the air comes to ground in a predictable arc.

Suppose the person comes to their influenza symptoms terribly undernourished, perhaps even near starvation. That new piece of information changes the linear projection. There is a predictable arc to the outcome here, too. The malnutrition changes the trajectory of the disease. The positive outcome, recovery within 14 days, is no longer assured.

Human behavior, too, has predictable arcs for all manner of linear projections. History, like gravity, is one of our great teachers. Despite our deep-seated conviction that "it will be different this time," it won't be.

When the sun's output changes, it affects mankind on a psychological and neurological level. In effect, a lot of people go bonkers. It isn't just the unstable weather, or food shortages, or financial instability, or propaganda that sets it off. It is *literally* abnormal solar energies short-circuiting some people's capacity for rational thought. Not all people, but enough people. Enough that an unaffected person will notice that it seems like folks are more touchy, aggressive, illogical, irritable, sad, and easily provoked. Compare the electromagnetic changes in the environment to someone nearby banging on a loud bell constantly – after a while, a person exposed to that just feels on edge.

The "on edge feeling" will manifest in different people in different ways. Intelligence, education, and income won't make a bit of difference. It's a biochemical and electromagnetic effect. Other people may feel energized by the changes: upbeat, focused, and directed. Hopefully, those people will aim their drives in a positive direction. It has happened in the past, EVERY TIME the sun's output decreases. Poor decisions are made at the top. Empires fail. Nations fall. Forewarned is forearmed, because it is part of the Big Picture of the Cold Times.

Psychology of Living in a Different World

Psychologically, even those who are minimally affected by the changing solar output will experience a sense of rootlessness, anxiety, failure, and depression. *This is normal* at the end of empire cycles. Many familiar things will disappear from your life – say, for example, your favorite popular music. Music itself will change and become local and regional. People won't stop making music. But if you prefer one vocalist, or a big band sound, or grand classical opera, there's a chance you won't have much access to that. Or it might be loss of the routine of a daily job and regular paycheck. It might be the loss of a familiar and favorite food or that morning coffee.

The loss of that familiar *something* might not hit you until an incident or sound or smell triggers a memory. Then, the loss will come crashing down on you. It may really knock you for a loop, bring you to tears, rekindle melancholic recollections, bring back faces of people who have vanished. This is a common reaction among people who have survived a great tragedy. It's normal to experience this. Just pause whatever you are doing, remember those things, and the memory will move along and lose steam. It can't hurt you. You're in a different place, and making new memories now.

If you experience these effects, solider on. The loss and the sudden impact of it is not your fault. There wasn't anything you could have done to prevent it. Nothing. Your job now is to preserve and protect and promote your people – that's all.

Children are particularly sensitive to emotional or behavioral changes in their parents and siblings, and changes in their environment. This can make them moody or withdrawn. That's normal, too. It's a method of dealing with the adjustments. Not fun, but a normal response to traumatic experiences. Fortunately, kids are very resilient. Their world is already somewhat chaotic, since they don't comprehend even the ordinary ups and downs.

Parental strength and consistency can go a long way toward creating stability in children's lives. What you react to calmly, children will respond to calmly. If you panic or have an emotional episode, so will your kids. Tell them the truth, and don't shield them from reality ("Daddy lost his job, so we're going to have to cut back our spending;" "We're going to turn our rabbits into dinner, and we'd like your help"). Involving children in daily tasks balances them and makes them feel useful and skilled. Hoeing the garden, feeding and watering livestock, helping around the house with daily chores – that's what makes a child's world feel safe and routine.

Children do not need to be shielded from ordinary reality. More often than not, adults who "shield" children are really trying to protect themselves. Discuss birth, death, and dying in a plain facts-of-life way....because it is.

Educating Children

Part of the process of moving from this era into the future is finding a way to educate our children in the concepts that are important to navigating both reality and our culture. Children absorb the essentials of family life and cultural norms nearly spontaneously, and require no direct verbal instruction ("teaching") to internalize these basics – in the same way toddlers learn to walk and talk. In fact, children learn so quickly and so intently, that it's virtually impossible to stop them from gathering data and making sense out of them.

Children's innate curiosity drives them to understand whatever they have contact with, particularly those things their parents and other significant adults are interested in. One of the easiest ways a parent can trigger a child's lifelong love of learning is to read. The child who sees a parent reading will seek to understand and imitate the parent's focus. When you read to your child – and it doesn't have to be boring "children's books" – the child learns the same information you are learning. When a child sits in your lap and follows along as you read aloud, the child begins to mentally form the rules of the written word. Girls learn this more quickly and at a younger age than boys, but both assimilate the basics. Alphabet songs program the knowledge of letters, and a-e-i-o-u jingles teach writing rules.

With daily reading over time, often less than a year, a child can read efficiently enough to begin choosing his own books. Then you cannot derail the child's ability to learn. It really is as simple as that. Once a child can read, they are able to be self-teachers, and will select from topics that interest them. Over the years, their interests will grow, with one subject leading to the next until they have a broad base of useable knowledge.

I know this to be true, in part, because that is how my own children were raised. Once they could read, there was no stopping them. A trip to the library was like finding buried treasure. After reading a book, they shared the information with the rest of us – thus, learning to summarize and speak extemporaneously – plus giving the rest of us interesting information. Both are accomplished, literate adults who continued into college studies; one has a master's degree and the other is an independent filmmaker. Both still follow their interests and are widely read and well-informed *and* socially competent. A kid doesn't have to be locked in a classroom with other kids the same age for 12 years to learn how to socially interact.

You don't have to "teach" children in the way the current compulsory school system has trained us to believe. Merely provide the resources and get out of their way. Children read to understand concepts and develop new ideas, and also learn efficiently by *doing*: planting seeds, sautéing mushrooms, using a compass, building a barn. Innate curiosity and an inborn love of learning will carry them forward.

What? No hours a day at a desk? No bells for the end of classes? No homework? That's right. All of these are artifacts of the industrialization of education, effectively training youngsters to be compliant factory workers. The future doesn't need obedient servants to the machine. It needs independent thinkers who are already 'outside the box'.

241

The ancient classical form of education had three primary levels, the basic *grammar,* the middle level *logic,* and the higher level *rhetoric.* **Grammar school** is just like it sounds – learning the very most foundational ideas – say, the addition tables (2+2=4) – usually by *rote.* "Rote" means memorization, no more, no less. Addition tables lead to multiplication tables; the alphabet; "I" before "e" except after "c"; the difference between *their, there,* and *they're*; how an apostrophe is used; spelling; critical dates in history - 1099, 1492, 1776. This is the age to memorize poetry, Bible verses, the Bill of Rights, Morse Code, another language or two, and anything else, because the child's growing brain is uniquely set up to absorb by pure memorization.

All the memorization of grammar can be done while milking a goat or repairing a roof or taking a long drive into town. It doesn't have to be done in a classroom. Sitting back leaning against an old apple tree is as fine a location for learning as any other. Recite the poem or verse or other material together as a family. Better yet, sing it. Set it to music and the child will remember it word-for-word into his old age.

The **logic (dialectic) level** is the point, usually around age 10-13, when the child takes all those memorized bits and finds that they actually apply to the physical world, interactions with others, and conceptualization of his or her way in life. That moment when a conversation brings up a memorized quote, or the laborious arithmetic tables suddenly makes sense while handling money. *That's* when the brain takes a great leap. Now the foundation of *grammar* becomes a structure that *logic* can build upon.

From roughly age 14 onward, as grammar and logic intertwine, the **rhetoric phase** of learning is entered. We today think of the term "rhetoric" as referring to overly wordy largely meaningless statements (it is, sadly, what rhetoric has become). However, the significance of *rhetoric* in classical education is the 'acquisition of the ability to speak coherently and persuasively' – and, by implication, to think rationally based on the foundation of essential knowledge.

That is the point where the allusion to some shared grammar becomes shorthand for a larger issue. A reference to "The Lady of the Lake" (the mythical mystical woman who arose from a lake to give Camelot's Arthur a sword that came with a heavy price) can be utilized as shorthand for "receiving a providential gift with strings attached". Or when conveying the idea of a confusing situation, saying simply "Who's on first?" – a reference to mid-20th century comedians Abbott and Costello's routine about baseball player's befuddling nick-names.

With classical education, learning actually does become a lifelong joy, continually building on a strong foundation throughout the years.

During the logic phase, the child who has a strong grammar foundation becomes ready to contribute to the community, even as he learns a practical skill. In the ancient world, youngsters were apprenticed to an expert in some field. As the child grew and observed the expert at work, the youngster acquired the skills of the profession....and, with that, an income for life. Generally, the child became not only a student but a worker. First, doing the basic cleanup and preparation for the expert, and later doing the expert's work. Their labor paid for their education. The expert often became a surrogate parent and then a lifelong friend and mentor to the child.

There's no reason why we cannot advance the apprenticeship model of education into the Cold Times. Children learn first at their parent's knee, then in the family, and then out into their community. Their knowledge comes from memorization of key facts, learning to apply those facts to the real world, and then acquiring a useful skill. In this way, children are no longer an expensive burden to their parents, lingering as dependents in their parent's homes well into their own third decade, as they do now.

Times are changing. The way children learn is the same as it has always been, but the way we impart knowledge, and what we impart, will be different by necessity. Think about it now, so it's not a surprise when it happens.

Caring for the Elderly

One of the primary tenets of this book is that "everyone contributes". This is important because daily life is going to be much more challenging in the Cold Times, and the Day of the Non-Contributor is rapidly passing into history.

Old folks who have worked and been useful their entire lives continue to desire usefulness, even in small ways. Grandma can string and snap beans, fold washed clothing, or even just set the table for supper. These are the little domestic chores that color and texture our lives. "Thank you," is often a sufficient return for such contributions. Grandpa might change a light fixture, or set up a trust account, or hunt a deer from a blind, continuing the skills he already knows. Don't discount the value of a lifetime of experience.

Elderly, as well as others, who are dependent on medication are going to die if things get bad enough. There's no nice way to say that. Once they cannot get their medication, their days are numbered. They know this fact. Many old people will already have reconciled this reality, and are as prepared as someone can be. Allow them their dignity, and grant them the pleasures of their last days. Don't critique their choices on what they put into their body (food, drink, or smoke, all small joys), and celebrate their life with memories.

Many modern elderly had no children or live distant from them. That means, they are dependent and alone. You may need one member of your group to be assigned to the task of monitoring and visiting the elderly, keeping them motivated to stay and contribute to the group, and preparing the community for the elder's passing. Odds are good that many elderly who enter the Cold Times will not survive the first years of the Zen-slap phase, so the caregiver assignment transitions into another type of work over time.

Preventing Disease Transmission

Clearly, this one book cannot cover all possible situations or conditions (there are entire libraries devoted to this topic), but I will suggest some commonsense time-tested options. There are two primary methods of controlling disease. The first is to prevent it from occurring – by treating injuries right away and keeping immunity strong by a healthy diet and moderate exercise – and by avoiding contact with disease sources. We'll look at these here.

The first step is to *take care of any known health issues NOW.* If you have nagging issues with your teeth, get them fixed as soon as possible – you don't need to be faced with an abscess or bad tooth when things are falling apart around you. If you're hooked on soda or junk food, stop – drink carbonated water and eat fresh whole fruit and nuts instead of processed junk. Make it a personal rule that if it went through a factory, it won't be in your mouth – apples, oranges, melons, carrots, mixed nuts of all kinds, even freshly homemade popcorn are all great replacements. Your body will thank you.

The second step is to improve you physical health right now. You know if you are not fit enough to handle a challenging life. Be honest with yourself. A fitness goal that is achievable in a few months or less is to be able to walk four miles in two hours, that is, 30 minutes per mile. Many "normal" people can't even cover a single mile in 30 minutes, which is an ordinary walking pace. That's sad and says a lot about the condition of our people. Start where you are now, walk every-other-day (NOT daily – you have to allow your body recovery time) and work up to the full distance and speed.

Once you can cover 4 miles in 2 hours, speed up a little and aim to complete 5 miles in 2 hours. Make this an every-other-day hike, during which you can check out your property and make sure fences and livestock are well. That way, the exercise serves two purposes. Don't be surprised if you lose weight and sleep better, too.

If you don't already do so, start taking a good quality natural multivitamin supplement each day. You may also do well with mineral supplements including magnesium, calcium, selenium, potassium, zinc, and iodine. Do your homework on these supplements and be willing to spend the extra money to boost your health and that of your family.

Hygiene, that is, keeping a sanitary (NOT sterile) environment is the foundation of all the social health improvements over the last century. The great epidemics of cholera and typhoid fever were controlled largely by keeping human wastes out of the drinking water supply – simple and obvious in retrospect. Influenza and measles were slowed by having people stay home and away from crowds. Malaria was controlled by killing mosquitos that transmitted the disease. The very same measures still work today.

Clean Water and Outhouses

The methods for keeping your drinking water free of infectious agents was covered in the chapter on water – boil and/or filter your water, and draw it from an uncontaminated source. Unless you have a means to TEST your water, you won't know if it is contaminated, so boil or filter drinking, cooking, dish-washing, and tooth-brushing water routinely (that is, any water that will go into your mouth).

Control of human wastes is not terribly complex, but it is not one of the most pleasant pastimes, either. The principles are straightforward: place your septic, outhouse, or latrine *at least* 100 feet from wellheads and rivers or streams, situated so there will be no drainage into your water supply.

Ideally, wastes should feed into a septic system with a drainage field. The septic system consists of a waste holding settling tank that has been "started" with beneficial bacteria and yeasts (such as a product called Rid-X) which digest the waste material and allow relatively 'clean' fluids to feed out into the drain field. Most regions, right now, enforce permit programs on new septic systems, so if you are installing a septic tank you'll need to investigate your area's requirements and unnecessarily large permit costs. You'll also need a backhoe or many strong backs and shovels to dig the tank hole and field.

The alternative, a historically proven method, is the pit toilet AKA outhouse, pit house, cesspit, and back house. There are several reasons for preferring an outhouse over a septic system. The primary one is that an outhouse requires no water for flushing. In Cold Times, and "hard times," there's lots of other things a person could do than haul 7 gallons of water into the house every time you need to flush the toilet into the septic system. With several people in the home, repeated flushing – even if there's a well-fed water system – is an enormous use of precious water, just to swish away wastes.

An outhouse is, effectively, a five foot deep by approximately 3 foot square hole, over which a small covered closet-sized (about 4'x4' x 8 feet tall) space has been built. The interior seat should be a tightly closed box with a 10"-12" hole in the top. Place a tight toilet seat on top for all the comforts of home. The doorway should also close tightly. A high set screened window can provide ventilation and light. Tight closings and screens help keep out insect pests. The building itself needs to set very close to the ground, perhaps on an unmortared concrete block or stone base, to keep out rats, mice, and other animals.

Inside the outhouse, you'll need a bucket of ashes, hay, lime, wood chips, leaves, or other organic material, and a cup. After using the outhouse, toss a cup or two of this over the waste. That helps eliminate odors and reduce insects. Also, store toilet paper or whatever substitute you have chosen and handwashing supplies (bottled water and soap) in the outhouse in covered containers. Handwashing should be done into the pit itself, with a small quantity of free-flowing water, NOT into a sink or basin which can become contaminated with bacteria. Wet hands, turn off water, soap up for 20 seconds, rinse hands *and* soap with a small amount of water. Dry hands on a small towel which goes into a basket to be washed. Try not to share or reuse towels until they have been boiled/washed to prevent spreading any residual fecal bacteria.

Set your outhouse above any possibility of infiltration from heavy rainwater or flooding, and berm it so runoff goes around it, because it will overflow if it is swamped. When the outhouse pit looks like it is getting full, dig a new pit and move the house. Cover the old pit with soil from the new hole. In a year, plant a fruit tree where the old pit was. It'll grow like crazy.

One consideration to keep in mind with an outhouse is that you do have to go *out* to use it. If a blizzard is blowing, people still need to relieve themselves. What then? Well, you can tie a guideline from the home door out to the outhouse, so people can feel their way out during the terrible cold, hopefully not freeze while in the outhouse, and then feel their way back along the guideline. A better approach is to keep a couple covered 5 gallon buckets in the bathroom, that can be used during those events and then hauled to the outhouse when the weather has lightened. Use a cup or two of ash, hay, wood chips, sawdust, or other organic material over the fresh waste and put the cover on the bucket between uses.

Personal Hygiene

Many people have the belief that they must shower daily to maintain good hygiene. If you're not doing heavy, sweaty, hot, and filthy work, daily bathing is simply unnecessary. Clean dry underclothing *is* a necessity, as we'll see shortly, but healthy skin bacteria THRIVE on normally clean skin. A person doing average work, indoor work, anything that doesn't makes them excessively sweaty, rarely will require full-body bathing more than once a week. Daily bathing in urban chlorinated water actually strips away healthy bacteria, and leaves our skin vulnerable to invaders.

Our great grand-parents maintained the "Saturday Night Bath" whether-you-needed-it-or-not custom. In a bath room – a small room set aside specifically for the bath – water was heated and placed in a low tub, not big enough to sit in, but large enough to stand in. A large cup or small pot was used to pour water over oneself while standing unclothed in the tub. Then the person used a wash cloth and bar soap to soap up, wash and lather hair. Finally, the cup or pot was used to rinse off using the water in the tub. After drying off, more hot water was added to the tub and the next person hopped in – yes, into "used" water. As horrifying as that sounds to we modern germophobes, there's no record of anyone getting sick or dying from bathing is pre-used water.

When it is more difficult to bring dozens of gallons of water into one's home – today's typical leisurely shower can cost 25 gallons of heated water – methods for staying clean and getting clean become quite a bit more challenging.

For basic hygiene, a daily soap and rinse of face, armpits, and groin hits all the "hot spots" and makes you feel and smell clean. Rinse the wash cloth thoroughly and hang outdoors in sunlight to dry, or over a hot stove. Ladies having their menstrual period will require more frequent washing, but this can be done with only a small amount of water. Remember handwashing as discussed previously, and use a small brush to scrub around fingernails daily. Store extra nail brushes or recycle old cleaned toothbrushes!

When deodorants run low (and it's a good idea to stock up three or four per person), a quick pat down with baking soda in the armpits will control odors as good as any commercial product. The fancy version of this deodorant powder is half-and-half baking soda and corn starch, with the addition of a few drops of your favorite essential oil or even vanilla flavoring.

Washing Clothes

Along with keeping oneself clean, maintaining reasonably clean clothing helps prevent skin rashes and irritation that can come from dirty, gritty, grimy fabrics. If you have laundry detergent, use it sparingly on the assumption that you may not be able to get more at a reasonable price. Most modern fabrics are designed to be washed in commercial detergents but you can use homemade soap, as well. Heavy cotton fabrics, such as jeans, can be briefly boiled to really clean them out. Man-made fabrics such as nylon and polyester simply take some agitation since they tend not to hold stains. Wools and other animal fibers require cold water and NO agitation, just a mild soap.

Assign specific clothing to specific tasks. For example, a set of old clothes for painting or working in the garden, ones that you don't mind getting dirty and staying permanently stained. Not many of today's household cooks still use an apron, but that will help protect clothing from oily splashes and foods that discolor clothing. It's a lot simpler to clean an apron than to wash a set of clothing. Similarly, a set of clothes designated specifically for the arrival of visitors or going to town allows you to have a clean outfit ready on a moment's notice.

Clothing can be soaked in a large dark-colored trash can that has been set in full sun for several hours. The sun will warm the water. Add soap or detergent, and use a stick or plumbing plunger to agitate the clothes for about 10 minutes. Pull items out one by one, wring or gently twist, then place in a second tub to rinse. Swish in the rinse water, pull out, wring or twist, and hang up to dry.

Clothes pins make hanging wearables on a line easy, but if you don't have them, then hang clothes over a fence (not metal as it may leave a rust stain), over bushes, or indoors over a shower curtain rod or even on lines strung inside the house. Sunlight UV rays are very helpful for killing bacteria, and a bit of wind outside will dry clothes quickly. In cold or wet weather, you'll have to dry washed goods indoors where there is warm airflow. A few hours of clothes hung in the living room is a small price to pay for clean duds.

The most critical clothing to keep clean is underwear – pants, bras, long johns and socks. These are the items closest to your skin, most likely to soak up excess skin moisture, and get stinky and crusty fastest. You'll need at least 3 sets of everything. Most of us already have more than that in a drawer, which is probably half forgotten. Ideally, you'd wash underwear after two or three wearings, more often if you get really sweaty. It's not necessary to change every day, and it's hard on underwear fabrics if you do wash them daily. If you're changing every second day, you'll need 4 pairs of everything (4 pants/panties, 4 bras, 4 pairs of socks, 4 sets of long johns). That way, you'll have enough to last and won't have to do laundry more than once a week. As with everything else, don't let yourself get down to the last set of underwear before you do laundry.

Skin Care

Cold weather is particularly hard on most people's skin. The very best protection for skin is natural oils – lard, olive oil, coconut oil and even butter are some of the finest. These can be consumed and rubbed directly into the skin. Coconut oil is particularly nice on the face because it is light and quickly absorbed. Clearly, should weather get extra cold, coconut oil will be hard to come by and probably quite costly, so use what you have. Exposed skin needs to be treated before going outdoors, and again in the evening. Everyone's skin. Cracked skin on the hands are a sign of dehydration AND dry skin, so drink more water and lather on the oils. During the warm weather – and there *will* be hot days during the coming years – skin still needs to be protected. Once again, a layer of good quality edible natural oil is the best.

In my opinion, there is NO NEED for sunscreen; these prevent the body from absorbing solar rays that generate the critical vitamin D_3. There is, in fact, an epidemic of low vitamin D_3 among Westerners who spend too much time indoors and who slather up whenever they go outside. Low levels of this important vitamin can contribute to bone loss, depression, depressed immunity, fatigue, some types of cancer, and a host of other unpleasant symptoms. Children raised without sufficient vitamin D can develop rickets, a condition of severe bone weakness that results in the obvious sign of bowed legs.

On a sunny day, 10 minutes of exposing your arms and face to the sun between 10 a.m. and 2 p.m. will give you a full daily dose of vitamin D_3, about 10,000 units. On an overcast day, you may need to expose more skin surface to achieve a good dose or stay out longer. It's comfortable to work in a greenhouse in the winter in short-sleeves and pants, and helps you get sufficient sun exposure. Some cases of SADD (Seasonal Affective Depressive Disorder) may be worsened by lack of sufficient vitamin D.

Keep in mind that there are some indications that ultraviolet solar radiation, the type of sun ray that causes the skin to tan or burn, will increase during the Cold Times. There are two types of solar radiation that we need to be aware of: ultraviolet type A (UVA) and ultraviolet type B (UVB). UVA is the solar radiation responsible for tanning and sun burns, and is low in Vitamin D3-forming properties. It is fairly consistent throughout the daylight hours, without peaks or troughs.

UVB, however, is less-responsible for tanning and burning, but is critically important in Vitamin D3 formation. UVB is at its daily high between about 10:00 in the morning, and 2:00 in the afternoon. That's when you need to expose your skin to the sun – not all at once, but a little bit more surface for longer times each day.

That means that even though our bodies *must have* daily sun exposure to keep healthy, too much exposure during the wrong times of the day could result in rapid burns without the benefit of building Vitamin D3. *Always* wear a large-brimmed hat that shades your face, ears, and neck, whether it is sunny or cloudy, during the early and late parts of the day. Avoid excessive exposure of arms, back, and legs as well.

Sun exposure during the critical Vitamin D3 forming hours between 10 a.m. and 2 p.m. may still risk a burn because UVA continues at the same level, so build up to longer exposures slowly, perhaps 10 minutes at a time. That way, you'll be getting the important Vitamins in your system, as well.

Sun screens, by the way, effectively reduce the UVB our bodies receive, but don't reduce the UVA very well at all – so sunscreen actually may be detrimental to health.
Sunburns need to be treated quickly by cooling the area with chilly water. If you have Silvadene (silver sulfadiazine) crème, apply some to the burned area. Should the skin blister, the condition becomes more serious and should be treated with a cooling poultice of herbs such as comfrey or cucumber. Don't puncture blisters.

If the spots become infected, treat like any skin infection with antibiotics or antibiotic herbs added to the diet (for example, garlic and elderberry), and gentle washing with clean or antibiotic soap.

Eye Care

Ice and snow reflect sunlight intensely, so do not assume cold weather means the sun won't be too bright. Ancient Inuit, the Eskimo people, even wore a type of sunglasses – basically, a wrap-around sunglass-shaped eye covering carved from drift wood that had a thin open line carved through the horizontal midline.

They could see out, but the intense eye-damaging sunlight coming off the snow and ice was largely blocked. Acquire several sets of ski goggles right now to protect vision when there is snow or ice glare present. Standard sunglasses aren't sufficient. Excessive exposure to UV rays can result in cataract formation in the eyes and eventual blindness.

Sunburned eyes get reddened and feel gritty and dry. Don't rub them. Lay down and keep the eyes closed. Cool packs of eyebright herb may help relieve the discomfort. Eyes heal quickly and should recover in a few days.

Skin Critters

Fleas and lice are the bane of humankind from as far back as anyone knows. There is a specific species of lice that only lives on people, and it requires contact with another person's body, clothing, bedding, or hair in order to move from one to another. Fleas actually spend most of their time off the host, hiding in bedding, clothing, flooring, furniture, and on pets, livestock, and wild animals.

The sign of lice are tiny white eggs attached to hair shafts (head lice), or scurrying ones in other body hair (also known as body lice or "crabs"). Head lice can be smothered with thick oil applied to hair and left on for several hours, then washed out. The "nits" (eggs) will need to be picked out individually – time consuming and seldom very effective.

In the modern era, there are over-the-counter pesticides that can be applied ("Rid" is well known), but these may be harder to come by in the Cold Times. Best alternative treatment is to shave off all body hair including on the head, coat the person with a thin layer for lard for 30 minutes (oils smother the parasites), and then wash everything off thoroughly. All clothing and bedding then needs to be washed in super-hot water, line dried in sunlight, and packed away for at least a month before the next use. Check regularly-used furniture, too, and remove any that show lice or nits to the outdoors for a month. A covered shed, barn, or place in full sunlight is ideal.

Fleas are a bit more challenging. Most fleas today are resistant to pesticides. That's why companies have to keep inventing new flea remedies. People typically pick up fleas from their pets, so keeping the flea population down on Fido and Fluffy helps prevent their migration to us, as well. Treat all pets *now* and keep the fleas under control. Dust all pet bedding with insecticides specific to fleas. Dogs and cats should have their own beds, not sleep with their people unless it is horrifically cold indoors, the proverbial "three dog night". Change the animal's bedding once a week, leaving the bedding in sunlight or in the snow to kill fleas and eggs.

If you are infested with fleas, the remedy is similar to removing lice from the environment. Wash all clothing and bedding in very hot water, dry in full sun. Remove furniture outdoors for a month or so. Scrub floors, particularly floors with indentions or cracks, and flush with Lysol or soapy water. If you've got it, use a few "flea bombs" (stock up!), and vacuum floors and furniture paying special attention to crevasses.

The traditional herbal remedy for fleas is to "strew" pennyroyal herb in bedding and where ever pets lay down. Pennyroyal is a member of the mint family, and tends to repel but not kill fleas. Use pennyroyal cautiously because it has been implicated in causing deadly miscarriages in pregnant women who drank tea made from it.

Modern pet owners aren't fond of it, but both Fido and Fluffy really should have their own outdoor homes, and not be permitted into the human dwelling. The risk of infesting yourself with fleas is one of the primary reasons for this.

Quarantine

Quarantine is the act of isolating any person or group of people who have a contagious disease in order to reduce the spread of the disease to the healthy. When I was a child, any kid with chicken pox, strep throat, scarlet fever, measles, mumps, whooping cough, or rubella was placed in at-home quarantine. A representative of the health department was notified by physician or school officials that the child was sick, and showed up to put what was effectively a KEEP OUT sign on the family's front door. Sometimes, the adults had to stay home, too, until the health department took down the sign, typically about two weeks after it went up.

Quarantine wasn't fun, but it did help alert healthy folk that there was a health risk in entering that residence. It probably also slowed the spread of the disease, especially since every sick kid had to stay away from the modern petri dish known as public school. Now, with antibiotics, we have all but forgotten about how effective quarantine could be with some diseases.

Ideally, you will have a separate building, or at least a separate room, that can be used as a formal quarantine. A caregiver, preferably someone who has had the disease, recovered from it, and now has immunity, will stay with the sick, providing oversight and nursing care. Food and water should be brought to the door and set down, to be picked up after the person delivering has left. A bucket can be used for a toilet should you not have active plumbing.

Clothing, bedding, anything contaminated with body fluids, cloth tissues and so forth, should be put into a plastic bag or piled together. If the illness is mild, the materials can be thoroughly washed and sun dried. If the illness is severe and causes some deaths, all the contaminated supplies should be burned. The person stays in quarantine until all symptoms of fever, rash, or whatever, have been gone for 72 full hours.

If only a few people in your group are sick, quarantine might be helpful for slowing or stopping the spread of the disease. If a good percentage are sick, quarantine is not likely to be as helpful. You may consider quarantining outsiders for 10 days before letting them into your group. If they're sick, it should show before the quarantine time is up. That'll help prevent disease from getting a foothold in your group.

Conventional Medical Supplies

There is no perfect list of medical supplies for the coming Cold Times. Each household should have their own supplies that fits their individual needs (prescriptions and vitamin supplements, for example), and the group itself would benefit from a central medical supply for "in case" situations.

There is something of a minor controversy on the types of medical equipment that a group should store. One side states that supplies should be suitable for the skill level of the providers – nurses should have nursing supplies, paramedics have emergency paramedic supplies, and so forth. The other side of the argument states that having a well-supplied on-site urgent care suite, with as much medicine and technology as can be afforded, is the ideal. That way, even if the group doesn't have top level physicians, nurse practitioners, paramedics, or other health care professionals, they have the equipment should one appear.

Gathering medical supplies is often dependent on two elements: cost, and access. Some items are simply excessively expensive, even though they would be nice to have, and some items are "prescription only" so you can't get it without first talking a physician or nurse practitioner into writing a scrip for it. In some areas, it's still possible to get livestock antibiotics, in pill or injectable form at feed stores, but even those may run short during any kind of calamity.

Here's a short list to get you started making your own version:

- 3 months of routine prescriptions, ideally 12 months' worth
- Over-the-counter pain relievers:

- o Ibuprofen
- o Aspirin
- o acetaminophen
- Band-aids
- Gauze
- Medical tape
- Tubes antibiotic gel
- Anti-itch (Cortaid or other similar remedy) cream, spray, lotion
- Anti-diarrheal (Immodium)
- Antacid and anti-gas
  - o Pepto-Bismol
  - o Tums
  - o Gaviscon, etc
- Ben-Gay, Icy Hot, or Tiger Balm or other rub on pain reliever
- Benadryl (Diphenhydramine) liquid (faster acting than capsules or tablets)
- Multivitamins
- Vitamin C 500-1000 mg tablets
- Vitamin D_3 4000-10,000 IU capsules
- Ankle and wrist braces
- Blood pressure cuff (non-electric, manual version)
- Stethoscope
- Otoscope (for checking ears)
- 10 or more pounds of Epsom Salts (more is better)
- "Salt Replacer" with potassium – store several pounds
- Standard thermometer (non digital, non battery)

Medical professionals will want additional supplies and medications.
- Sutures of various sizes
- "needle drivers" (vet supplies will work)
- Hemostats and tissue forceps
- Gauze – sterile and non-sterile
- Syringes, 3-6 cc, with 21 gauge 3" needles
- Antibiotics (see following)
- Specialist supplies
  - o Casting material for setting broken bones
  - o Scopes for examining the interior of the eye
  - o IV fluids including sterile saline and dextrose
  - o IV sets, needles
  - o Nebulizer and albuterol

- o Vaginal speculum, metal, medium size
- Injectable lidocaine/Marcaine
- Injectable epinephrine
- Injectable propofol, versed, and anti-nausea medications for light sedation
- Injectable meperidine, morphine, toradol
- Injectable antibiotics such as cefriaxone
- Injectable tetanus toxoid and antitoxin (refrigerated)
- Injectable insulin, Humalog, Levimir
- Injectable steroids such as Kenalog or dexamethasone
- Oxygen tank, filled
- Oxygen tubing, masks, nasal cannula
- Sterile and non-sterile nitrile or latex gloves
- Pressure cooker for autoclaving metal tools
- Multiple stainless shears, hemostats, probes, and forceps.

Antibiotics

In the world of preparedness, there is a general sense that if things go bad, antibiotics will be in short supply or gone entirely. Given the difficulty in producing mass quantities of healing drugs, and given the problems *currently* associated with shortages and deliveries, there's a lot of merit to that assessment. Just as in any other preparedness issue, the obvious course is to acquire supplies *now* that could be used in the event of a need *then*.

The problem is that antibiotics aren't like stored toilet paper or freeze dried veggies. Each antibiotic has a limited range of effectiveness in different body systems and against differing bacteria. There's no "one size fits all" medication. And, there's no "one size fits all" sick person, either. He or she may be allergic to the appropriate antibiotic, so a secondary choice has to be used instead.

Keeping that in mind, the following is a basic guide to the most critical oral antibiotics (pills or capsules) currently on the market. In most cases this is focused on generics, simply because they are affordable. What follows is a discussion of the general classes of antibiotics and their primary uses. After that, we'll get down to specific cases. Finally, we'll close with a list of recommended antibiotics to keep on hand.

About Antibiotics

All medications are risky. Anyone can have an allergic reaction, or face dangerous side effects – even when taking an antibiotic they've used in the past without problems. Although I've used good sources for the following medical material, it is provided for *informational purposes only*. You can find the same info in any medical or nursing textbook.

Antibiotics are primarily "bactericidal." They kill germs during the phase when they are dividing. A few antibiotics (Tetracycline, for example) are "bacteriostatic." They stop the germs from reproducing, without actually killing them, so the germ population ages and shrinks until the person's immune system can wipe them out. Bactericidal antibiotics may be ineffective if given with bacteriostatic ones, because the germs stop reproducing so they can't be killed during cell division. Antibiotics do not work against viruses, such as Chicken Pox or Influenza, although taking an antibiotic may help prevent "bacterial sequelae" (bacteria-caused secondary infection) following a viral infection.

Antibiotics can interfere with the effectiveness of some other medications, especially oral birth control agents, making them less effective. They also can make some medications *more* effective, such as the blood thinner Coumadin/warfarin, leading to risk of bleeding or other nasty side effects. Some antibiotics appear to interfere with heart rhythms in susceptible people. One class has been associated with tendon ruptures. To repeat: all medications are risky. We balance the risk of taking the antibiotic against the risk of not taking it.

Most antibiotics can give the person a mild case of diarrhea. This occurs because the antibiotic kills not only disease-causing bacteria, but kills off the beneficial bacteria we have in our guts, as well. Mild diarrhea can be controlled with daily yogurt or probiotic use, or an anti-diarrhea med such as Imodium. Severe, watery, bad smelling, bloody, or hard-to-control diarrhea that starts after you begin taking an antibiotic means you *must stop taking* that antibiotic.

Worst case antibiotic-related diarrhea can be caused by a particularly unpleasant bug called *Clostridium Difficile* (known as *C. Diff* among medical professionals) leading to a condition called *pseudomembranous colitis*, which can be life threatening. If this occurs, you must decide if the severity of the illness that called for the antibiotic is worth the risk of damaging the person's intestinal tract and possibly killing him or her that way. Stopping the antibiotic is often the most prudent course. *Always take probiotics, and fermented foods (yogurt, sauerkraut, etc), daily whenever using antibiotics.*

Allergies to antibiotics can be mild, appearing just as an itchy skin rash, or severe, such as difficulty breathing. Occasionally, a person's mild rash allergy to an antibiotic they *must* have can be treated with Benadryl (diphenhydramine) – but more severe allergies indicate that the particular antibiotic should not be used at all. If a person is allergic to one antibiotic within a class, they should be considered allergic to that entire class -- so someone allergic to peni*cillin* should not take amoxi*cillin* either, both in the "cillin" class.

Some women may develop a yeast infection after taking antibiotics. This is an overgrowth of *candida albicans* fungus in the vaginal area, and is characterized by a white chunky vaginal discharge that causes genital skin redness and an itching, or burning or irritated feeling. This isn't contagious, but it can be uncomfortable. Diflucan 150mg, one time, is the pre-fan treatment of choice, although most yeast infections will go away if the person reduces sugars and starches in their diet and increases yogurt consumption. Douching with 20/80 white vinegar/clean water will sometimes resolve the problem.

Antibiotic Classes

There are eight basic classes of antibiotics appropriate for preparedness uses. There's a few others that are intravenous only, or have such terrible side effects that their blood levels must be checked – we won't consider those. Each class has uses that are distinctive, but overlapping with other classes. Ideally, you would have a general Big Picture of each class and its areas of treatment in your mind, when you begin to consider which one to use. Here are the classes, names, and uses on the following pages. Additional comments on each item are numbered on the right hand side and explained on the Notes pages.

CLASS	NAMES	ALL USES	SPECIFIC FOR	ALTERNATE FOR	DOSE	NOTES
Cillins	Penicillin, PCN, Pen-VK, Amoxicillin, Amoxil, Ampicillin, Augmentin (amoxil x clavulanate)	Ear/nose/ throat infections, skin infections, some respiratory infections, bladder infections	Ear infections; strep throat, sinus infections, skin sores from abrasions (not boils), some pneumonia (Augmentin)	Cephalosporins Cipro or Levaquin for severe sinus infection	**Adult:** 500 mg three to four times daily for 10 days. **Children** less than 100 lbs: 40-70 mg per kg of weight per day x 10 days	(1)
Cephalo-sporins	Keflex , Cedax, Omnicef Cefdinir, Ceftin, Cefadroxil, Cefaclor, Cefpodoxime	Ear/nose/ throat infections, skin infections, respiratory infections	Dental abscess, strep throat, cellulitis (skin infection), sinus infections, bronchitis	Cillins	**Adult:** 500 mg three to four times daily for 10 days. **Children** less than 100 lbs:7 mg per kg of weight every 12 hours x 10 days	(2)

| Sulfas | Bactrim DS (Double Strenth), Bactrim, Septra, Sulfamethoxazone /trimethoprim | Bladder infections, sinus infections, traveller's diarrhea, chronic bronchitis, some ear infections | Children's infections, women bladder infections, MRSA skin sores and boils, folliculitis (sores at the base of hairs) | Clindamycin MRSA sores for | Adult: 1 DS tab or 2 (3) regular tabs (total 800/160mg) twice daily for 7-10 days Children: calculate dose based on the sulfamethoxazole component – 40 mg per kg of body weight divided into 2 doses x 10 days |

Macrolide	Azithromycin, Z-Pack, Zithro, Biaxin, Erythromycin, Clarithromycin, Clindamycin Eye drops: Moxeza, Opthalmic, Vigamox	Ear/nose/throat infections, "atypical" or walking pneumonia, COPD, bronchitis.	Chlamydia, 1 gram one time. Atypical pneumonia, sinus infections, choice for strep throat, repeated ear infections. Eye infections, as prepared drops. Clindamycin is choice for MRSA if sulfa allergy or ineffective, and for dental abscesses.	Cillins, Cephalosporins 3rd	(4) Zithro: **Adult:** 250 mg, 2 tablets day one, then 1 tablet x 4 days OR 500 mg daily for 3 days. Refill and repeat. **Children:** 10 mg per kg daily, with double dose the first day, for 5 days total. *Biaxin, Clarithromycin:* **Adult:** 500 mg twice daily for 10 days. **Children:** 7.5 mg per kilogram twice daily for 10 days. *Clindamycin:* **Adult:** 150 to 300 mg three or four times daily x 10 days. *Eye drops:* 1 to 3 drops in affected eye for 7 days. Stop if irritation increases.

| Cyclines | Tetracycline, Doxycycline, Minocin, Monodox, | ANTHRAX, LYME'S, skin sores, bronchitis, COPD-related pneumonias | ANTHRAX, LYME'S Amoxil for Lyme's in children under age 8. | **Adults:** 100 mg twice daily for 10 days. In Lyme's, same dose for 21 to 30 days. In Anthrax, same dose for 60 days. **Children:** older than 8, and over 100 pounds, treat as adult. Older than 8 and less than 100 pounds, use at rate of 2 mg per 1 pound of weight daily total, divided into two daily doses. | (5) |

| Fluroquinalones | Ciprofloxacin, Cipro, Levaquin, Moxifloxacin, Ofloxacin, Avelox | Upper respiratory, bone and joint, prostate infection, bladder or bowel infections (Cipro only), sinusitis, pneumonias, bronchitis, nephritis (kidney infection), ANTHRAX | ANTHRAX - Cipro preferred but all in class are effective. Cipro for bladder and kidney infections (others do not enter urine as readily). Levaquin for prostate infections. Levaquin more effective against most pneumonias but may use others in class. | Sulfas for bladder infections, Augmentin for sinus infections, Doxycycline for pneumonia | Cipro: **Adults:** 500 mg twice daily for 10 days, or in Anthrax same dose for 60 days. **Children:** (not recommended, see notes) 10-20 mg per kg, max 750 mg, twice daily for 10 days, or up to 60 days in Anthrax. *Oflox, Avelox, Moxiflox:* **Adults:** 400 mg daily. *Levaquin:* **Adults:** 500 mg to 750 mg daily for 10 days. In prostatitis, may continue for 21-28 days. 6) |

Azoles	Nitroimidazoles, metronidazol, flagyl, diflucan	Anerobic infections (internal organs), intraabdominalor skin, gynecological, septicemia, joints.	Diverticulitis (with Cipro), women's bacterial vaginitis, trichomoniasis. Diflucan is specific for vaginal yeast infection.	Azoles are specific for fungal and yeast infections	**Adults:** *Flagyl or Metronidazole:* 500 mg two or three times daily for 10 days. May also be used intravaginally as a cream for 7 days at bedtime. *Diflucan:* 150 mg once daily for one to three days (7)
Nitrofurantoin	Macrobid, Macrodantin, Furdantin	Bladder infections, urinary tract infections	Bladder and urinary tract infections, especially if chronic and must take daily.	Bactrim for UTI, Cipro for severe UTI	**Adults:** 100 mg twice daily for 20 days. **Children:** NOT RECOMMENDED, but > 1 month old may take total 5-7 mg per kg daily in 4 divided doses. (8)

NOTES

1) Children who have been treated repeatedly for ear infections or strep throat will do better with Cephalosporin or Azithromycin. Okay to use in pregnant or infants who are not allergic.

2) If a person is allergic to cillins, there is a small risk of cross-sensitivity to cephalosporin. Monitor for allergic reactions!

3) Not for infants less than 2 months old. Avoid in late pregnancy.

4) Increasing bacterial resistance to Zithro, may require refill and longer dosing. If the person is not improving after 3 to 4 days, consider switching to another antibiotic class. Clindamycin should be saved for last resort as it has more severe side effects and has a history of leading to *C. Diff*. Macrolides can cause Q-T prolongation (changes in heart's ability to beat) and cause heart attacks (rare).

5) Not recommended for children 8 and under due to possibility of staining of permanent teeth. However, in a *lifesaving* situation, dental staining should be considered of lesser priority than restoring health. Skin becomes very sensitive to sunlight and person can sunburn severely. Medicines in this class can become toxic over time. Avoid using if there are color or odor changes in the meds, or if exposed to moist or humid conditions.

6) Rare side effect of tendon rupture - discontinue use if pains in heels or shoulders or elsewhere occur. Should not be used in those under 18 years old or over 60 years old, as risk of tendon rupture increases. In lifesaving circumstances, risk of tendon rupture may be outweighed by survival possibilities. Fluoroquinolones can cause Q-T prolongation (changes in heart's ability to beat) and cause heart attacks (rare).

7) Not recommended for children or the first trimester of pregnancy. Azoles are specific for fungal and yeast infections

8) Some women who experience bladder infections following sexual intercourse benefit by taking this routinely, 100 mg daily. Do not use in late pregnancy.

How to Calculate Doses

If you notice in the dosing calculations, adults are provided a routine dose (say, 500 mg twice daily). This dosing is actually based on the "average" adult weight of 150 lbs. For most people, even heavier people, this is still a suitable dose. For children or adults who weigh less than 100 pounds, however, the dose is lower and is based on weight. Typically, and unfortunately, the weight is stated in kg or kilograms.

Step one: change weight from pounds to kilograms using this formula...
 Weight in pounds divided by 2.2 equals kilogram weight
  Example: 100 pound person divided by 2.2 equals 45.45 kilograms
   Written like this: 100 lb / 2.2 kg/lb = 45 kg

Step two: multiply weight in kilograms times the dosage
  Example: Dose is 7 mg (milligram) per kg (kilogram)
   Child weighs 82 pounds.
    First, 82 lb / 2.2 kg/lb = 37 kg
    Then 37 (kg)x 7 (mg/kg) =259 mg of medication
    Round the dose to 260 or even 275 mg.

Step three: Divide the dose as indicated, if needed.
  Example: Dose is 10 mg per kg, in two divided doses daily
   Child weighs 67 pounds
    First 67/2.2 = 30.45 kg
    Then 30.45 x 10 = 304.5 mg (round to 300)
    Then divide by 2: 300 mg/2 = 150 mg
     So this child receives 150 mg once in the morning and once in the evening, for the length of the treatment course.

Storing Antibiotics

Store all antibiotics in a cool, dry place out of sunlight or fluorescent light. It is not necessary to freeze these meds, and freezing may cause unexpected changes in the product, especially if there are variations in temperature as occurs in freezers that are opened often.

Antibiotics in pill or tablet form are surprisingly stable over time. Recent government studies indicated that Cipro, for example, retained its bacteria killing ability 10 years past its expiration date! Medications in capsules are a little less stable. Penicillin in capsules will tend to become less potent, so you may need to increase the dose somewhat several years after expiration.

One class of medication that is problematic, though, are the tetracyclines. They may become toxic over time. Tetracycline is a fine yellow powder. If an opened capsule shows color changes of any kind, or if the powder is clumpy or granular, discard that medication completely. Better not to use it than risk damaging your internal organs by using it.

Group Supply

Given a limited amount of space and money, plus the recognition that we may never need these medications, this quantity can be stored in several shoeboxes and covers the majority of common needs:

- Penicillin VK, 500 mg, 200 capsules. This is roughly 5 full treatment courses of 40 tablets (4 daily for 10 days).
- Amoxicillin, 500 mg, 500 capsules. 30 capsules is one treatment course (3 daily for 10 days), so this is about 16 courses.
- Cephalexin (Keflex) 500 mg, 500 capsules. At 30 capsules over 10 days, this is 16 courses.
- Cipro 500 mg, 1000+ tablets. Dosed at 20 tablets per treatment course, this is 50+ treatments.
- Levaquin 500 mg, 200 tablets. At 1 tablet daily for 10 days, this is 20 courses. Reserve Levaquin for more severe upper respiratory disorders, such as pneumonia.
- Bactrim DS 800-160mg, 200 tablets. 2 tablets daily for 7 days for bladder infections, provides 14 courses.
- Metronidazole 500 mg, 100 tablets. Dosing at 2 tablets daily for 7 days, this provides about 7 treatments
- Zithromycin 250 mg (as a Z-Pack of 6 tablets). Ten Z-Packs, providing 10 courses.
- Clindamycin 300 mg, 200 tablets. At 3 tablets daily for 10 days, this provides about 6 courses.

In total, this is about 140 treatments for various ailments, which works out to roughly 10 treatments per person in a group of 14 individuals. Assuming that most of us are fairly healthy, and hoping that infections are caught and treated before they require antibiotics, there would probably be several year's-worth of medications in this supply, enough to get through the initial difficult stages of the Cold Times. This assumes you are not treating or giving prophylactic treatment for anthrax, and only treating a possible Lyme's disease once or twice.

There are some new studies that indicate the full 10-day course is not necessary. The take-home point of one study was that a person should take antibiotics 'until they feel better', then hold off taking any more unless they relapse. If you follow this route, your group's medications will probably last longer, since people often feel better after only two or three days of antibiotics.

For children who do not or cannot take pills, you can crush tablets or open capsules and provide reduced doses based on their body weights. Crushed pills may be mixed into fruit, applesauce, chocolate syrup, flavored drinks, popsicles, peanut butter, or whatever it takes to get it down.

Sources for Antibiotics

If you are not a medical professional able to write prescriptions, it will be significantly more difficult to lay in a supply of these antibiotics or any other medications, for that matter. Non-prescription sources include: fish medicines from aquarium supply sources online or stores (FishMox is amoxicillin, for example), and the injectable medicines for livestock available at feed stores (penicillin and tetracycline, mostly). I cannot recommend these, as I have not personally used them. However, if I had nothing else, I would definitely stock these.

Antibiotics from overseas sources are a bit more problematic. I have seen an amoxicillin from an overseas online source used. It caused an itchy allergy reaction. Previously, the individual had not reacted to amoxil. Since then, they have taken domestic amoxil WITHOUT getting a rash. So, I suspect there was *something else* in that overseas medication that they reacted to. This has put me off of overseas sources, but others may be willing to take the risk.

If you are related to or have a friend who is a physician, nurse practitioner, dentist, or physician's assistant, you may ask them to consider writing you a prescription for "just in case". Many health care providers are open to the idea of keeping some antibiotics on hand. If you are seen routinely and given an antibiotic prescription, ask to have a refill or two. Some providers are okay with that, but some are not - so use some sensible discretion here.

There are online domestic sources for antibiotics, as well. Two of these are shopmedvetsupply.com and HenrySchein.com – you will need a state medical license to order prescription medicines. They also carry other non-prescription medical supplies and equipment – shopmedvetsupply is very reasonably priced. This is a legitimate source for medications of all types; livestock meds are labeled for animal use only. Prices vary depending on their supplies.

Nothing here should be construed as suggesting you break the law.

Alternative Antibiotic and Antiviral Remedies

If you are simply unable to acquire pharmaceuticals and no health care provider can be found, but you must treat an infection, there are multiple herbal and alternative approaches. I'll give some common ones following, but here's a couple outstanding books that should be on your shelf:

Herbal Antibiotics:
Natural Alternatives for Treating Drug Resistant Bacteria
and

Herbal Antivirals:
Natural Remedies for Emerging and Resistant Viruses
both by Stephen Harrod Buhner
published by Storey Publishing

Three common "natural" remedies that are helpful and may act as effective antibacterials and antivirals are garlic, elderberry, and table sugar or honey.

Garlic

This is the go-to herb for any kind of infection; it has a centuries-long track record as a natural antibiotic. The most effective garlic is a fresh whole clove, recently dug from the garden and peeled and rinsed in clean water. Older garlic will do, but fresh is always best so keep some in your garden at all times – it may overwinter underground unless the ground freezes.

Garlic can be applied to the skin as a poultice. It can be taken by mouth as fresh chopped cloves, as a cooked or fried food, or crushed and made into a tea. Be cautious in applying garlic directly to the skin, especially sensitive skin or on children, because it is capable of causing blisters and caustic burns.

Garlic Poultice: Mince or grate several cloves of garlic, mixing with a little lard, cultured butter, coconut oil, or virgin olive oil. Place on a clean, thin, cotton cloth (such as a cut strip of cotton bed sheeting or clean t-shirt), lay over the affected area with cloth protecting the skin from the garlic, and cover all with clean gauze or cotton to keep it in place.

- For children with an ear infection, first oil the feet with lard, butter, coconut or olive oil, place the thin cotton cloth on the *bottom* of the feet, put garlic in oil on that, and cover with clean white cotton socks. Leave on overnight or as child sleeps. The child will awaken with "garlic breath," demonstrating that the herb has been absorbed in the entire body. Don't put garlic into the ear in any form.
- For open wounds, mash the garlic and oil into a paste, and place into the wound then cover with a clean cloth dressing. Replace the dressing if there is excess drainage. Monitor and replace daily. Stop if getting worse. Also take garlic by mouth.

Garlic Tea: As nasty as it might sound to make a tea from garlic, it's actually quite tasty and soothing. Take one or two cloves and crush in a mug. Add hot water and steep for a few minutes until the liquid is still warm but cool enough to drink. Remove the garlic. Add to this a tablespoon of honey and lemon to taste. Can also add fruit juice if desired. Stir and sip. May be rewarmed. Okay to drink often.

Garlic by Mouth: The secret to making the best use of garlic as a remedy is to take it internally as well as externally. Cloves may be peeled and chopped to "pill size", and swallowed as-is. Cloves may be peeled and gently fried whole in butter until lightly browned, or even deep fried. The flavor mellows and it's easy to consume an entire bulb or two without realizing it. Whole bulbs can be oven baked, by cutting off the top fourth or so, and setting the bulb into a baking dish with a little water in the bottom. Bake until the cloves are soft, 20 to 30 minutes. Squeeze the clove onto fresh bread and spread around, add butter and a sprinkle of basil, and eat.

Elderberry

This ancient herb is effective against bacteria and viruses, and has the benefit of tasting good enough that children will drink it as a tea or syrup.

Harvest wild-grown or garden elderberries and dry the berries, or purchase dried berries, for later use as a tea. Add 1 tablespoon (more or less to taste) to a cup of boiling water, letting it steep for at least 5 minutes. Strain tea into a cup, dispose of berries. Flavor tea to taste with a little honey, lemon, or other fruit juice. Drink while still very warm. Make take 3-6 cups daily.

To make syrup, boil 2 cups of elderberries in 3 cups of water for about 10 minutes in a covered pot. Let cool to very warm. Drain through a sieve into another pot, pressing the berries to extract as much juice as possible. Dispose of berries (chickens like them). Flavor the juice with a cup of honey and squeeze of lemon juice. Add ¼ cup of vodka, Everclear, or Brandy to help preserve this. Store in a cool place or refrigerate. Take 2 to 4 tablespoons (adult) or 1-2 tablespoons (child) every 3 hours at first sign of illness and throughout the duration.

Alternatively, you can take two cups of fresh berries, boil in clean water that just barely covers them for a minute or two, then put berries and water into a quart mason jar. Add a cup of sugar or ½ cup honey per quart, then fill the jar with vodka, Everclear, or brandy (cheap is okay, as long as it is at least 40% alcohol on the label). Shake daily for 2 weeks and it is ready to use. Strain before using. May be served hot or cold, a half cup twice daily.

Elderberries also make an outstanding summer wine that mellows with age, while retaining its healing properties. See the wine recipes.

Sugar

Sugar is another remedy that has a long history treating wounds and still works like a charm. It is believed that the sugar affects bacteria it contacts by interfering with their cellular fluid balance, causing the bacteria to die. It may also act as a tissue "irritant" that stimulates new cells to form. This is used as a simple paste (a little clean water plus sugar as needed to make a thick paste). This can be placed into a wound or on a sore, covered, and replaced daily until the wound is healed. I have seen deep bedsores close and heal with this simple basic treatment.

For those who have little background in healthcare, there are two excellent books you MUST have in your paper library – you can find them online for free as .pdfs; be sure to print them out:

Where There Is No Doctor by Werner, Thurman and Maxwell
Where There Is No Dentist by Dickson

For health care professionals who need a refresher on general and emergent practice, consider this outstandingly useful work:

Improvised Medicine: Providing Care in Extreme Environments by Kenneth V. Iserson
McGraw-Hill, 2011. About $70 and worth every penny.

Alternative Herbal Supplies: 10 Must-Haves

Herbal remedies are true health care treatments that cost next-to-nothing if you are willing to grow them or can find them growing wild. There are, literally, thousands of plants that have been successfully used to treat disease, infection, and pain. Medicine didn't begin with the pharmaceutical industry or the establishment of medical schools; folk remedies were passed on from generation to generation *because they work*.

Keep in mind that herbal remedies aren't "one pill fixes all" –

there's a great deal of art to utilizing plants for healing. The ill person's own physiology can help or slow the herb's ability to treat a condition, as well. So "the eye of the healer" is very critical to the process.

Don't expect an overnight cure from any herbal approach. Results are typically slower than using pharmaceuticals, but with many fewer negative pharmaceutical side effects.

Garlic

We've already discussed using garlic as an antibiotic replacement, so I won't repeat that here. Garlic also has been used to lower blood pressure and reduce blood clotting (that is, it slows platelet aggregation or "thins the blood"). Plus, you can't make a good pasta sauce without it. If there was a single herb that I absolutely would never want to be without, it's garlic.

Uses: skin infection, coughs, flu, colds, diarrhea, upper respiratory infections of all kinds, high blood pressure, bruising and excess blood clotting.

Forms: tincture, whole fresh, chopped/minced, baked/fried, poultice, paste, tea.

Comfrey

This is another fabulous and underutilized plant. Not only is it one of the best medicinals, it also is a rapidly growing outstanding livestock feed which can be fed green, and dry as a hay-replacer, PLUS it can be easily harvested and used as a green mulch around trees and other plants.

Symphytum Officinalis is an ancient plant with a long history of being used on bruises and broken bones. The long, spiny green leaves are tropical-looking. The drooping small purple flowers attract bumblebees and other pollinators. There are few pests that bother this plant, and it **tolerates cool growing weather and moist soil conditions**; it originated in Russia.

The Henry Doubleday center in England did studies some years ago, and found that plants could be harvested two or three times during a growing season (cut leaves and stems straight across about 5 inches above ground level), and it would continue to grow until hard frost puts it to sleep. Using this technique, *tons* of dried comfrey, to be used as hay, could be harvested from each acre. That's critical if grass hay and grain harvests are compromised by bad weather. Livestock really love comfrey, too – chickens, sheep, goats, horses, rabbits, cattle, hogs – it's a favorite of all, and high in protein, too. It also spreads like a weed.

Comfrey grows on a large, knobby root, with multiple side sprouts. In the spring, new sprouts can be separated with a bit of root attached, and planted where ever you want another stand. Also, side-roots can be cut off and planted separately.

The large root, stems, and leaves are high is "mucilage", a thick and somewhat slimy juice. *This* contains the high-power bruise repair and bone-knitting agent, *allantoin,* which triggers healthy cells to grow. You can pick a leaf right off the plant, and squeeze the juice onto a new bruise, sore, skin injury, psoriasis, boil, or whatever, and immediately notice the pain subside.

If you accidentally hammer your thumbnail, apply comfrey (fresh, as a tincture, or a salve) right away for *immediate* pain relief and bruise repair. You might not even bruise at all, it's that amazing. I even used comfrey salve on a dislocated finger, after putting it back into place, to reduce swelling and pain.

You can grow this plant from seeds and from root cuttings. Online, strictlymedicinals.com, an herb company, has different varieties and other excellent resources.

Uses: skin sores, bruises, broken bones, psoriasis, livestock feed, hay, mulch, topical pain relief, damaged aged skin.

Forms: fresh, tincture, salve, topical tea, paste of leaves.

Elderberry

I previously mentioned this roadside plant for the outstanding antibiotic and antiviral properties it has. The berries, produced in mid to late summer, are small and dark purple, and form a plate-sized "umbrel", or umbrella-shaped group.

There isn't any other plant that looks quite like it, so it's easy to spot, usually growing in clumps at the edges of fields or roads. Historically, the stems of these plants were used as splints to set broken bones back in place by splitting the stems and putting the cut sides next to the skin. It was said to help the bones heal.

There are domesticated and wild varieties – prefer the wild ones if they grow in your area, because they are hardier and have better healing profiles. Two well-known domestic varieties are York and Adams – you must have both to ensure pollination.

Uses: antibiotic and antiviral, upper respiratory illness, fevers, headaches.

Form: tea, tincture, syrup, wine.

Tulsi (Holy Basil)

Tulsi is a member of the basil family and a relative of mint. Like the familiar culinary basils, the small leaves have a pleasant fragrance. Cultivation of tulsi is just like other basils. It doesn't do well in the cold, but grows into a small bushy mound during the summer, sends up flower shoots, makes seeds and then dies back. Like culinary basils, pinching off the growing ends of the stems will cause the plant to grow more thickly.

The medicinal uses of this outstanding plant are dual, aside from its delightful flavor. Before the plants flower, leaves and juice are a natural antiseptic. This is due to the presence of relatively high levels of *eugenol*. Plants harvested before flowering can be preserved in a tincture to be used as a wound and skin injury cleaning agent, or dried for a tea that can be used for washing sores or as a mouthwash or gargle.

After flowering, the plants increase their level of *rosemarinic acid,* which is a calming anti-anxiety remedy – this can be made into a pleasantly flavored tea that will settle children and adults down after a trying day – and help both to get rest.

Richo Cech of strictlymedicinals.com reported a study that examined different varieties of tulsi for their relative levels of eugenol (antiseptic) and rosemarinic acid (anti-anxiety). He found that Vana Tulsi had the highest levels of antiseptic eugenol, and Amrita Tulsi had the greatest anti-anxiety rosemarinic acid even though all varieties have some levels of both.

Krishna Tulsi came close to the top performers in both eugenol and rosemarinic acid – so if there's only one tulsi in your garden, Krishna would be a good choice.

Uses: antiseptic before flowering, skin and mouth sores; calming anti-anxiety after flowering, as a tea or chewed leaves.

Forms: tincture, tea, paste.

Yarrow
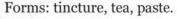

This hardy wild plant has many domesticated forms that are used for color in the flower garden. The wild version, with plain white flowers, stands for a long time - several to many weeks - beside roadways and in untrimmed fields. The feathery foliage and strong medicinal aroma make it easy to identify.

Achillea Millefolium, like some of these herbs here, has a long history as a medicinal. The primary use I've made of it is as a fever-reducer, which works remarkably fast. A teaspoon of dried flowers, made into a tea (sweetener and lemon help), will bring down a fever within half an hour and induce sweating. That makes this something you can use if you don't have acetaminophen, aspirin, or ibuprofen. The only challenge with yarrow is that it does have a very strong and not necessarily wonderful flavor. "Taste bad, work good."

Uses: fever reduction, brings on sweating

Form: tea from dried flower heads

Mullein

Verbascum thapsus is a truly remarkable plant, with a history as a medicinal that dates back at least 2,000 years. It's a biennial, so it takes two years to go from seed to flower. The leaves are covered with a downy hairy surface that makes them feel soft and fluffy. The tall flower spike, up to 6 feet tall, appears in its second year, and has tiny yellow flowers on the upper portion. They grow in poor soil, overgrazed fields, disturbed soil, beside roads, and just about everywhere in the world.

Mullein is often known by its alternate name, *cowboy toilet paper* – and it is really an ideal, natural, soft, and gentle wipe. Wipe in the same direction that the downy hairs grow to avoid stickery leftovers. The plant has a mucilaginous fluid within the leaves and root that have multiple applications that have stood the test of time.

Uses:

- Calming coughs from bronchitis, pneumonia, lung and throat irritations of all kinds, when taken as a tea or gargle. Put through a coffee filter or cheese cloth to remove the tiny hairs before drinking.
- The dried leaves have also been smoked in a pipe to treat lung ailments.
- Hemorrhoids could be treated with poultices from the leaves.
- Sores, irritations, and skin infections can be treated with a poultice made from the roots.
- The flowers have bactericidal (germ-killing) properties. Soak a cup of flowers in a cup of olive oil for a month, shaking daily, then strain off the oil and dispose of the flowers – use as drops for earaches, to treat rashes, and boils, and carefully worked into the skin if frostbite occurs. May also be used on hemorrhoids.
- Finally, if that wasn't enough, the flower stalks can be dipped in animal fat or wax, and used as a torch.

Forms: tea, dried, poultice, smoked, decoction in oil, ear drops, toilet paper.

Valerian Root

This attractive garden plant, with its feathery leaves and sweetly fragrant small white to pink flowers is another ancient remedy. *Valeriana officinalis* has a long history of being used as an oil decoction or taken as a powder to restore sleep to insomniacs, to relieve anxiety, and to reduce migraine headaches. One ingredient in the root is also the basis of a pharmaceutical anticonvulsant medicine valproic acid – and valerian has been used to treat convulsions, too. Don't make a tea from it, though, as hot water can drive off some of the volatile healing constituents of the root. The leaves aren't potent for most uses.

Valerian root has a strong odor, quite the opposite of the sweet flowers. Some people compare it to the odor of gym socks; others say that it is heavy but sweet. The odor is said to attract rats, and historically valerian was used in rat traps as bait.

One of its best uses is as a sedative and sleep inducing agent. This will be especially helpful during trying times. Valerian shouldn't be used on a daily basis, though. It's for occasional use only. Pregnant women should not use this medication -- use chamomile instead for its gently calming properties.

Uses: sedative, anti-anxiety, sleep, pain relief, convulsions, migraines.

Form: tincture, decoction in oil, powder, in a poultice or as the green leaves bent and bruised and laid over the head or any injured area for pain relief.

Cannabis

Despite the modern hysteria surrounding this ancient herbal remedy, marijuana has a 6,000 year history as a medicinal treatment for multiple conditions. Many states now allow sales of medical marijuana by prescription, and some have deregulated growing the plant for personal use. The laws are constantly changing, so you'll need to check your local regulatory environment online for the current information.

There are two primary strains of this plant, *indica* and *sativa*, although most wild varieties have become crossbred and carry qualities of both. Sativas have narrow leaves, a somewhat fruity odor, and when used produce a sense of creative energy. They originated in warm climates, grow well outdoors, and take three to four months to reach full height and flowering. Excess recreational use can lead to anxiety.

Indicas, on the other hand, have a broader more rounded leaf, a "skunky" odor, and when used produce relaxation and sedation. They originated in harsher mountainous climates, grow as smaller bushier plants than indicas, and flower in about half the time. Excess recreational use can lead to depression.

When utilizing cannabis for recreation, it is most often the flower bud that is used. Bud is somewhat sticky and collects into "nugs" or clumps. Dried, the bud can be taken internally within baked goods (the proverbial brownie), as a tea or tincture, or smoked. The plant material must be heated to at least 350°F or extracted with 40% or higher alcohol, to release its tetrahydrocannabinol (THC). THC has qualities in controlling epilepsy, reducing pain, stimulating appetite, relieving glaucoma, and producing the feeling of being high. In other words, it has neuroactive potential.

More current studies have found that the green leaf itself -- generally not of much value to those who use the plant for recreation since it is low in THC – may have remarkable healing and pain relieving properties. Green leaf, juiced or eaten raw, has potent levels of cannabidiol (CBD) which is the active agent that appears to prevent inflammation, reduce the risk for Alzheimer's, inhibits rheumatoid arthritis, inflammatory bowel disease, multiple sclerosis, diabetes, and reduces symptoms of Parkinson's disease. It is neuroprotective, and may even shrink cancerous tumors.

While there is little pharmaceutical research on such a potentially valuable medication, reports from individuals who have used cannabis to resolve their own medical problems are appearing more and more consistently online and occasionally in the main stream media.

For the Zen-slap and beyond, cannabis is shaping up as a valuable resource for pain control, sharpening the mind, fighting dementia, relaxation, and maybe even eliminating tumors and other cancers. The challenge today is finding a good source for seeds, growing it under the coming potentially harsh conditions, and avoiding problems with law enforcement in jurisdictions that don't yet allow private individuals to grow or use it medicinally.

Uses: pain relief, controlling epilepsy, reducing dementia, appetite stimulation, relieving glaucoma, treating tumors and other cancers, relaxation and sedation, recreational highs.

Forms: smoked, baked, tincture, or tea of dried bud; paste, or fresh consumption of leaves. CBD healing oil can be extracted from whole plants using the technique at:

http://www.growweedeasy.com/cannabis-extract-hash-oil

resulting in a CBD rich oil that in rice-sized bits can be taken orally or used as a healing and pain-reducing rub.

White Willow Bark

Willow trees are lacy or feathery plants that grow as a clump or as a standard tree form. All members of the *Salix* willow family contain the active *salicylic acid* that is capable of reducing inflammation, pain, and fever. It was the first natural medicine that was commercially synthesized and sold: aspirin.

White willow, a variety that is often found near rivers, streams, and ponds, has the highest amount of the medicinal component among willows. It generally grows in more of a tree form, rather than as a bush. The portion of bark that has the potent medicinal agent is underneath the crusty outer bark, and right next to the inner tree – it has a very slight pinkish color to it. Some people experience the same medicinal effect by chewing the green twigs.

It's possible to harvest bark from a single tree or from many. The bark dries readily, better under low heat in a dehydrator, Harvesting the bark requires a sharp knife and a small prying bar or screwdriver.

Select a tree that is healthy and has a fairly large area of bark. The area you will cut can be as small as 1" wide by 4" long, or even up to 10" long. Make it a narrow up-and-down cut. Don't cut a wide strip that goes around the tree. That's called "girdling a tree", and it kills it by preventing the tree's transport of sap from roots to leaves.

Make your initial outline slices, and then press and cut deeper. The pinkish inner bark may be 1/3" to ½" or maybe deeper on a big tree. Pry back a little of your piece, and look at it. When you reach the right level, the cambium layer, the outer bark hunk will separate from the inner tree a little easier. Pry the section out. It's okay if you get it in pieces.

To use this, cut off one or two hunks about the size of your thumb and chop it into small bits. Bring two cups of water to a boil, let it cool a little, and drop your bark into it. Let it set until cool, strain out the bark; then it's ready. Start with a half cup, sweetened a little and with a squeeze of lemon. You should notice pain relief and fever reduction within an hour. Take another half cup in four hours or so, if needed, and may continue until it is all consumed. If you don't use it all, it will keep for a few days if stored at near-freezing temperatures.

You can also gently dehydrate or air dry the bark, too. The useful medicinal qualities are preserved for later.

Collecting Wild Herbs

Make sure you know *EXACTLY* the plant you are collecting, and be sure to collect it in the right season and form (leaf vs fruit vs root). *NEVER* take all the plants in one area. Leave some to reseed and provide plants for future years. Native American tradition requires practitioners to leave a "gift" to the remaining plants, usually some tobacco. It's a good idea to leave something for the remaining plants for two reasons: (1) it trains you to respect the natural supply; and (2) gifting a sprinkle of compost or dried manure helps feed the remaining plants.

Basic Care

Having a physician, dentist, veterinarian, nurse practitioner, physician assistant, registered nurse, paramedic, EMT, military medic, or someone skilled in first aid will be a huge asset to your group. For the long run, a naturopath, chiropractor, acupuncturist, Ayurveda, Chinese medicine, or a herbalist would be your best bet. That's because these alternative types of healing practice utilize much fewer manufactured pharmaceuticals than the first group, pharmaceuticals which may be in short supply, extremely expensive, or non-existent. Ultimately, anyone who is a healer by nature will learn to use whatever supplies you have on hand and become pretty skilled utilizing natural medicines.

Acquire first aid training for as many people in your group as possible. The more who are knowledgeable, the better chance you have of catching some incident before it gets worse.

Boost immunity by daily sun exposure between 10 a.m. and 2 p.m. to build Vitamin D_3, especially during the winter. Make sure you have sources of Vitamin C during the winter months. Pine needle tea, made from fresh pine needles, is an excellent vitamin C source. So are rose hips, the round red seed pods of wild and domestic *rugosa* roses, as is a tea made from blackberry or raspberry leaves. Grow and eat microgreens from extra radish, mustard, turnip, and bean seeds.

Use the healing power of hot or cold water soaks, especially when a handful of Epsom Salts have been added. Skin infections, muscle aches, sprained ankles, bruises, and overused joints all improve with soaking in Epsom Salts water. Use hot water soaks for infections and muscle tension; cold soaks for new bruises, sprains, and strains. If you treat a sprained ankle with cool packs, elevation, and immobilization for the first 24 hours after it happens, it will heal significantly faster than if you try to "walk it off." Store Epsom Salts today!

Tinctures

Tinctures are extractions of the healing properties of herbs in an alcohol base. These are very simple to make and work nearly as effectively as fresh herb, allowing you to store your herbs in a very small space in an immediately accessible form.

A basic recipe that works adequately for most herbs (some do extract better in heat or in oils) is to take about a cup of dried, chopped herb, or two cups of fresh chopped herb. Add to that twice as much drinking alcohol of 40% proof *or higher*. Everclear, vodka, rum, brandy, or other alcohols are suitable. Let it soak for at least two weeks – four weeks is better -- shaking the container daily. Strain out the herbs and dispose, storing the tincture alcohol in tight small containers, ideally with droppers. Use 10 drops, more or less (1/8 tsp) in liquid to drink or as a rub on, depending on the herb involved.

Decoction

A decoction is an herbal remedy that consists of a hard, woody, or brittle herb (roots and bark) that has been ground and put into boiling water, then gently boiled until the water has been reduced by half. The end result is an herbal concentration. Use about 1 ounce of pulverized herb to one quart of water, boiling that down to about 2 cups of liquid. Strain out the herb, and store the decoction in tight, closed jars, ideally in cool and dark conditions. You may add a tablespoon or so of 40% or higher alcohol such as vodka or brandy to help preserve the contents. Use ½ tsp orally or as a rub.

Infusion

This is the most familiar form of herbal remedy, effectively a tea. It's generally used with soft herbs, fresh leaves, flowers, and citrus peels, and herbs that are very volatile and could lose their subtle properties under other methods. Simply boil water, and add a tablespoon, more or less, of herb to the water. Let steep for 5 to 10 minutes until it has cooled to drinking temperature. Strain and flavor with sweetener and lemon if desired.

Salve

This is the form I prefer when utilizing the wonderful qualities of comfrey – simply because it can be used at any time, even during the winter when fresh comfrey is in hibernation. Check the recipe section for the method I use.

A Word About Essential Oils

I'm a big fan of essential oils, and make several home remedies with different combination of ingredients, including tea tree oil, camphor, menthol, peppermint, bergamot, sweet orange, oregano, eucalyptus, cassia, rosemary and others. If I had the means to produce my own essential oils from various plants, I would be one happy camper.

But, I can't make essential oils at home. It requires distillation equipment, solvents, and presses I don't have, as well as copious plant materials that don't grow in my area. Should we all find ourselves in circumstances that limit us to what we can produce at home, essential oils will be far down on the list.

Consequently, I am storing extras of the oils I like and use routinely, but I am also not making them an important part of my medicine chest. If you have the means to make your own, it's definitely worth the effort to produce them. They will be valuable home care materials after the Zen-slap.

Four Conditions and Their Treatments

Of the hundreds or thousands of potential conditions that healers may see during the Zen-slap and Hang On phases, including the resurgence of many forgotten diseases such as cholera or smallpox, we will deal with only four here, These are the most likely to be seen early on under "austere" Cold Times onset conditions, and the ones we can readily care for within our groups.

Acquire medical books now, but be prepared to substitute alternative remedies for pharmaceuticals.

Diarrhea

Every major disaster is followed by a remarkable increase in diarrhea among survivors. It is consistent and predictable, so expect to see this recurring among your group. Diarrhea is the onset of watery feces, sometimes accompanied by lower abdominal cramping. Occasionally, some blood streaks will be seen in the feces, along with chunks of stringy or mucous tissues.

Usually diarrhea is "self-limiting", that is, it resolves on its own if the person rests, drinks plenty of fluids, and takes light meals or soups. However, the distress associated with Zen-slap, along with decreased immunity resulting from stress and shortages, can make a "simple" diarrhea into a big problem.

Worse still, is diarrhea caused by eating tainted food or drinking water that is contaminated – problems that also accompany disasters.

The first step is to identify the probable cause and type of the diarrhea. This can often be determined by either asking the person to describe the appearance and odor of their feces, or by examining the waste yourself. If it is mostly clear fluid with liquid feces and a few pieces of feces, treat conservatively. Conservative treatment is designed to replace lost fluids, repopulate the gut with good intestinal bacteria, and slowly add foods back to the diet.

A solution made with 2 tablespoons white sugar, 1/2 tsp potassium "salt replacer", ½ tsp salt, and a pinch of baking soda fully dissolved in quart of water will replace critical electrolytes. A half cup of solution can be sipped by teaspoons over the course of 30 minutes. A small amount of fruit juice may be added, if the flavor is too unpleasant. This is similar to drinks like Gator Ade and Power Ade in its action. If you have some of that powdered, you can reconstitute it and use it instead.

You can use the formula for children over age 2, but reduce the sugar by about a third. Better to NOT use commercial Gator Ade or Power Ade in children – too high in some elements for little kids and can make diarrhea worse. Pedialyte is much preferred, if you have it. Pedialyte also is okay in infants with diarrhea, along with breastmilk.

Next, feed yogurt, clean raw milk, kefir, cottage cheese or buttermilk. These contain probiotic that will help replace the gut bacteria. Colostrum from newly freshened dairy animals is also a suitable source. So is the juice from homemade sauerkraut, which is loaded with nutrients, enzymes, and biologicals.

Finally, a drink or slurry made from "rice water," water in which rice has been soaked for several hours; or a solution of oatmeal water made the same way. This will sooth the bowels and slow the diarrhea. Homemade, salty chicken soup made from bones, cleaned chicken "paws", vegetables and lots of garlic can be fed until the diarrhea has stopped. See recipes section. Then resume normal foods as desired and tolerated.

If the stool shows significant mucous, blood staining or is frankly bloody, and if the person is very weak, pale, sickly, drawn up, or unable to stand on his own, the case is much more serious. This may be seen in people who are horribly run down, or even with cholera or other contagious diarrheal diseases, so the wastes should be treated as potentially infectious and kept in a separate area so they don't contaminate your water supply. Wastes should be disposed of by thoroughly burning.

Conventional medical treatment would include fluid and electrolyte replacement by IV, along with oral or IV antibiotics (usually Cipro), followed by commercial probiotics, anti-diarrheal medications, and slow refeeding.

The great problem with this severe type of diarrhea is two-fold: the loss of beneficial bowel bacteria, and damage to the lining of the intestines. This causes bleeding, dehydration, and increasing weakness. Lacking IVs, it's difficult to restore fluid balance since most fluids given orally are simply swept through the person's system, taking additional fluids out of him at the same time. Remarkably, mucous membranes, such as the lining of the mouth, vagina, and colon, become more permeable – and may be a route by which fluids can be brought back onboard.

First, give teaspoonfuls of the rehydration solution. The person should hold this in his mouth, beside the cheeks. Some of it will absorb, and the rest will move down his throat. Give a teaspoon every 5 minutes, and do not rush this, until a full cup has been consumed. Stop for 10 minutes if vomiting occurs, then resume.

If the person cannot swallow or is not alert enough to follow directions, infuse about a cup full of warmed rehydration solution (at body temperature) into the person's vagina and/or rectum. Place the person on their right side, with hips elevated so that the fluids won't run out; it will eventually, so have something waterproof and extra towels under their hips. Repeat until you notice a change in their demeanor, either coming to consciousness or getting worse. If improving, you can start giving fluid by mouth, a teaspoonful at a time. Keep in mind that a person who is this bad off who can't get emergency medical care probably won't survive, so understand that using your limited supplies may not be helpful anyway.

Once the person is beginning to retain the rehydration solution, start adding probiotics. For a very irritated bowel, colostrum would be better than milk products, and water-based kefir would be tolerated better than milk proteins. If you have no other options, use what you have. There's some new research that using a small amount of "healthy" stool from another person, and putting that high into the sick person's rectum, may help restore good bacteria – no studies on if this might help in desperate situations, though.

Refeeding should be carried on slowly, backing off for an hour or two if diarrhea resumes or vomiting occurs. Continue the probiotic sources, varying them, several times daily. Chicken soup as noted previously, along with rice or oatmeal water, are the next steps. The soup contains good levels of vital proteins, vitamins, minerals, and electrolytes, which are severely depleted in this type of diarrhea.

Recovery for a severely weakened person may take a month or longer, and he may have relapses. During relapses, go back to the rehydration solution, probiotics, chicken soup and rice/oatmeal water until symptoms improve. Good nursing care can make the difference.

Hypothermia and Frost Bite

Cold injuries are going to be an issue everyone needs to understand and deal with on a near-daily basis during the winter.

Hypothermia occurs when a person's core body temperature drops below the usual levels. Someone who is stuck outdoors during a cold spell, who sits down to rest, can quickly become too cold to carry on and can become hypothermic. The person may be pale, drowsy, shivering or may have stopped shivering, and in worse cases may feel a paradoxical sense of heat and may try to remove clothing.

The goal with someone who has become intensely cold is two-fold: avoid having them move around or be moved in a jerky or abrupt manner; and rewarming. Too much movement and sudden movements can send a chilled heart into "fibrillation," which is fluttering instead of regular pumping contractions. In a serious situation out in the field or without cardiac emergency care, this can be fatal. *No sudden movements.*

Rewarming can be started outdoors and continued once the person is inside. Remove all wet clothing, even outside, and put on DRY wool-based clothes or blankets. Wet clothing robs the body of heat, although wool tends to retain heat even when wet. Put hot water bottles or warm packs in the armpits, belly, and groin. Be careful that these aren't so hot they will burn the skin. Replace often to keep the warmth up. Lacking heat sources, lay the person on his *right* side, remove clothing, and have two other people spoon up to him, front and back, skin-to-skin. Cover all three with wool blankets. Warmers may need to be replaced, if they get chilled themselves. Body warmth is one of the best ways to rewarm the hypothermic person.

If the person is conscious, he can sip heated but not hot chicken soup, coffee, or cocoa. Don't give alcohol beverages. They increase body cooling by opening pores. If shivering stopped, it may return as the person gradually rewarms.

Once the person has become warm enough to be conscious and retain heat, let him sit near a warm stove with feet elevated. It may take a day or two to fully return to feeling normal – allow them to recover before returning to outdoor activities.

Frostbite can occur with or without hypothermia. Frostbite is when a portion of the skin and underlying tissues becomes frozen or near-frozen. The area is generally pale white or even black, cold to the touch, firm, and numb. If it is fingers or toes, they may not be able to move them.

The goal is to rewarm the area *and keep it warm*. It's worse to rewarm and refreeze the area, than to let it remain cool for a short time until you can fully rewarm it. Frostbitten fingers and toes will hurt intensely as they are rewarming. As sensation returns, even lukewarm temperatures feel like flames.

Place the frostbitten area into body-temperature or slightly warmer water. Do not rub the area at all. Keep changing the water to maintain a warm level. You may also place the area against bare warm skin on the belly or armpits. If the person can tolerate it, aspirin or acetaminophen or willow bark tea may be given to help relieve pain. The area is sufficiently rewarmed when it is pink, able to move freely, and feels warm to the touch. There may be some mild to moderate swelling afterwards, which is normal but may be uncomfortable.

If the area was blackened, consider this similar to a severe burn. Once it is rewarmed, it will need to be treated as such. Monitor the site for infection. It will hurt.

After a day or two, you may have to carefully remove blackened tissue that has been cold-killed, since it may interfere with healing.

Use a scalpel or very sharp pair of scissors. If you have to do this, the blackened area won't have sensation, but the tissue around it will. Trim as close to healthy, bleeding skin as the person can stand. You can also treat this area with a sugar paste, as discussed earlier. Make sure the person is eating garlic daily, and use a comfrey poultice to help stimulate new tissue growth.

Starvation and Refeeding

During the past Little Ice Ages, starvation was the great killer of populations. Harvests failed, and the food simply ran out. It is hard to even imagine people being that desperate in this age of unprecedented wealth and plentiful foods – rather like trying to imagine a world without the electric grid.

During WWII, physician Ancel Keys realized that when the war was over, there would be many in Europe who were malnourished and literally starving. His research, involving wartime conscientious objectors who were starved until they lost 25% of their weight, is considered one of the most comprehensive studies of starvation and refeeding. More current research has been focused on psychiatric patients with eating disorders, who are treated in hospital settings.

What this gathering of information tells us, is that the process of starvation not only affects a person's weight, it affects his ability to think reasonably and act appropriately for his own wellbeing. In other words, you simply cannot give a starving person all the food he wants – he will quickly eat enough to overwhelm his weakened organs, and die. His physiology must be *slowly* reintroduced to food.

The most current studies state that a person who has had negligible food for two weeks, should start with no more than about 500 calories per day for several days, increasing a few hundred calories per day over the next week or two.

Ideally, the refeeding would be done with strong clinical observation, such as metabolic and bloodwork studies. Lacking that, the key points are:

- Monitor heart rhythm; it can become irregular and that

can be fatal. *Go slow.*
- Probiotics: yogurt, kefir, juice from sauerkraut by the spoonful. This stimulates and protects the bowels.
- Plenty of fluids. Soup is a good choice for refeeding. Sips of rehydration solution for the potassium and salts.
- Include vitamins B complex 3 times daily, thiamine 200-300 mg daily, and a multivitamin and mineral supplement. Good sources for the B and thiamine are cooked green leafy vegetables, such as spinach and kale, and also liver. Soup is a good way to get these nutrients into the digestive tract.
- Additional supplements of potassium, phosphate, and magnesium are important, as well. Potatoes and meat have the first two; green leafy vegetables contain magnesium.

Outside of a clinical setting, then, a rich broth made from meat, bones, and plentiful vegetables of all kinds can be given twice daily, with additional unsweetened fluids such as herbal teas, as desired. Increase that each day that the person is able to tolerate, adding solids foods such as crackers or soft fruit, so that within two to three weeks he is eating as are others in your group. Continue the probiotics, and watch for either constipation or diarrhea. The person will be very tired and may take several weeks to months to recover sufficiently to participate fully in daily routines. Encourage walking, covering more distance as strength returns.

Concussion

Injuries are common in rural settings, and falls lead the list. Falls can lead to concussion. Concussion is, basically, a hard bump on the noggin (BOTN) accompanied by aftereffects in order of severity: a swelling and tenderness at the site, headache, vomiting, blurred vision, memory loss, personality changes, mental and/or emotional or psychological disorders.

Effectively, when concussed, the person's brain is bounced inside their skull, causing it to become "bruised." Brain cells die, and the tissues swell, which causes other issues over time. The goal of treating all BOTNs is to minimize brain cell loss and swelling, and then let the body do what it does to repair the damage.

The majority of BOTNs are mild, with little to no aftereffects beyond a sore spot and little headache – treatable with a cool comfrey poultice and bit of willow bark tea.

Mild to moderate concussions, on the other hand, require more aggressive treatment plans. In a situation like the Cold Times where outside medical care is likely to be unavailable, it can become more challenging.

First, anyone who bangs their head hard enough to have a bad headache and vomiting, should immediately begin *fasting*, or a *strict keto diet*.

Fasting is the act of eating nothing, but continuing to drink water or other liquids (coffee and tea, unsweetened, are permitted). A strict fast will induce the body to begin utilizing one's own fat, which triggers ketone metabolism – the beneficial form of ketosis. Hunger is transitory and easily resolved by drinking more water, and usually isn't noticed much after the 3rd day of a standard fast.

A **strict keto diet** is eating to stimulate ketone production. In effect, it is a diet focused primarily on beneficial fats including animal fats and oils including olive and coconut. For short term purposes in treating concussion, a keto diet might consist of green vegetables (broccoli, cabbage, lettuce, mustard, turnip tops, etc) cooked in bacon grease along with bacon. Coffee or tea are permitted, served hot, with a teaspoon of butter and coconut oil in it. All green vegetables are acceptable, and fatty meats are ideal -- and eat all the fat. Avoid fruits, starchy foods (bread, pasta, potatoes, corn, etc), although a half cup daily of blueberries, blackberries, or raspberries can be eaten for variety. One writer called the keto diet "Atkins on steroids", a reference to the low-carbohydrate, moderate protein diet promoted for weight loss. Hunger is almost absent, but for the first 3 to 5 days, there may be intense cravings for sweets, bread, or other carbohydrates.

The rationale for this is a series of new research that has shown that ketosis induced by fasting or a keto diet confers "neuroprotection" by reduced oxidative stress where the bump occurred. This actually increases action on the cellular level within minute cell elements called mitochondria, and helps protect mental function. It's accomplished by increasing beneficial ketones within the body, which occurs within 24 hours of the start of the fast.

For Zen-slap treatment, the person could initiate ketosis by immediately starting a 24-hour fast on water, coffee, and unsweetened tea alone. The next day, begin a *strict keto diet* for at least a week – longer if symptoms persist – with bed rest or reduced activity. Use a cool comfrey poultice to the head, and may sip willow bark tea. The keto diet also promotes weight loss while preserving muscle tissue, so don't be surprised to see the pounds come off. There may be a "fruity" or "acetone" odor to the person's breath at the start. This will disappear within a week or two. Remember to drink lots of water.

The use of fasting and ketosis to control concussion symptoms appears to be very successful in the young, and only mildly helpful in older adults. Adults will do better if they fast, then eat a keto diet for 5 days, fast for two, then keto for 5 days – repeating that as needed over weeks to months. However, everyone benefits to some degree, so this can be the "go to" plan for all BOTNs.

11 SAFETY AND SECURITY

There are multiple types of risks to safety and security that any group faces, day-to-day type challenges and long-term ones. Some people who newly discover the preparedness concept focus on acquiring and storing firearms, making preparedness an excuse for their gun-buying hobby. We will briefly discuss firearms in this chapter, but there is a vast sea between owning lots of guns and promoting safety in your group.

For example, do you know the primary cause of premature death among so-called primitive people now living on earth? Is it tribal warfare? Infection? Food poisoning? Childbirth? Being killed by predatory animals? Wildfire? Epidemic disease?

No, it's *falls from trees*. Of all the possible things that could happen in a wild setting, simple *accidents* are the greatest danger to health. The same is true in our culture – not falls from trees so much, but accidents cause more deaths than any other single reason. Right now, motor vehicle accidents alone kill 40,000 men, women, and children in the US *each year*, and maim another 200,000 innocent victims. Statistically, getting into a car carries a greater risk of death or injury than does being blown up by terrorists, catching Ebola, going down in a commuter jet crash, or being caught in an earthquake and tsunami. Yet, somehow we fear all those exotic causes of death, while blithely hopping into our killing machines without a second thought.

In the same way, when we think about the possible risks to safety and security in the Cold Times ahead, we may imagine running gun battles or perilous escapes from marauders as our major risks. Now, these kinds of things *may* happen – just as terrorist bombs, jet crashes, epidemics, and earthquake tsunamis claim lives every year. Even so, the greater risks to your group are likely to be the mundane ones – falls from *ladders*, accidental cuts and subsequent infections, a trash fire that gets out of control.

Fire Safety a Priority

Uncontrolled fire is a risk everyone faces in modern society. It's the main reason people buy home insurance, in case the place goes up in flames. Fire is a tool we use in cooking, and is a tool we will most likely depend upon for warming once we are into the Zen-slap phase. For some of us, fire of one sort or other will be our primary light source, too.

Fire within the home is a potential problem, but fire that comes from somewhere outside is also a risk. There is no woodland, prairie, or community that doesn't face some potential fire problems – either a campfire that gets out of control on a windy day, or from a neighbor whose lit candle burns down and sets their house and the rest of the neighborhood ablaze. Fire risks appear to be increasing in areas that previously were considered low fire risk, as many ranchers in the Midwest and homeowners in California found in 2017. We all face this right now, but most of us don't pay sufficient attention to the risk.

Another potential fire risk will arise from EMP (electromagnetic pulse) or CME (coronal mass ejection), an important aftereffect that is rarely discussed. There are indications that during grand solar minimums with changes in earth's magnetic field, CMEs from the sun increase in potential intensity of damage. Effectively, earth's protective shield is down and even routine CMEs can generate damaging electromagnetic effects. The EMP of concern is one caused by one or several high altitude nuclear explosions – no fallout, but the EMP damages unhardened technological infrastructure.

The EMP/CME risk to the grid and related infrastructure is, of course, a significant concern, and that is what usually captures our attention in novels like Forstchen's *One Second After*. However, both EMP and CME propagate across long chargeable lines, such as power lines. During the Carrington CME event of 1859, telegraph lines burst into flame, burning down telegraph stations and shocking telegraph operators. We live in an environment that is laced and threaded with a super spider web of power lines now. If the intense energy of a CME or EMP propagates down all those lines....well, it will end up somewhere. Every electrical appliance plugged into the grid will be instantly fried. Some of those will burn, too. Imagine something catching fire in, say, every third house in your neighborhood – or several things in every house. No fire department would be able to contain the fires. There would be no way to stop the conflagration that ensued. It would burn until all the fuel was exhausted.

There is no time in history when humanity has faced a risk like this. Never. We simply cannot know what might occur.

But, we know fire. Boy Scouts and campers of old know that anywhere you build a fire, you make absolutely certain that it is out before you move on – dowsing the fire with water, stirring it, and dowsing again. In the same way, fires within the home must be fully controlled within fireplaces with live fire extinguishers beside anything with flames. Right now, standard commercial extinguishers start at about $20 each, some of the cheapest insurance you can find. After Zen-slap, a small bucket of sand will work as well. Tossed onto an errant flame, the sand will shut off oxygen and the fire will die.

In the power chapter, I suggested *metal* Aladdin lamps because they're durable, but a dropped metal lamp's fuel chamber doesn't break like a glass one does, either. In the place chapter, I encouraged building from stone and concrete, because it doesn't burn. *Always* put out candles before you leave a room where they are burning. Clear shrubbery and burnables (firewood, too) at least fifty feet away from homes, or replace it with low-burn water holding plants such as cactus or "ice plant". The rules of simple fire management won't change after Zen-slap. They will just become more critical for long-term survival. There's no place for "casual" fire management.

For the long term, plan to have a backup location that is fire safe, in case wildfire ravages your area. Stone and concrete "dolmens", discussed elsewhere, may have helped our ancestors survive conflagration risks as well as intense lightning storms. Mankind has resorted to caves during difficult times in the past; they may be awaiting our use at some time in the future, too. A fire intense enough to create a regional "firestorm" may also deprive the entire area of breathable oxygen. Options include storing a tank or two of oxygen (you'll need either a scuba card or a physician's order), or a smoke hood with filter like the Safe Escape Smoke Hood. The Safe Escape version provides about 30 minutes of filtered air, inside a sealed hood with a clear visor. At this writing, two hoods can be acquired for around $100. They must be replaced in five years, as the filters lose capacity.

Establishing and Maintaining Social Order

Maintaining a cohesive group is a challenge in good times, and may be even more challenging during chaotic ones. It takes a special ability to organize, motivate, and carry out all the duties and responsibilities of a group's leadership. It is a rare person who can handle it all.

The American Declaration of Independence states clearly that those in authority rule expressly by "the consent of the governed." That is, leaders aren't in their position because they are better, smarter, or more entitled than anyone else. They are "the government" because the people they govern *agree* that they should run the show. If the governed, the "little people," can show that the government is failing to carry out its duties or is overstepping its authority, they have the moral, lawful, and just responsibility to depose the old government and create a new one.

When your group forms, it is incumbent upon them to determine the type of governance under which they will live. Don't assume that this will just sort itself out, because that kind of failure-to-plan often results in the strongest (most violent? Most psychopathic? Most charming?) person rising to the top.

Group Organization Plan

Every group organizes itself, whether it is done with a purposeful plan or by trial and error over time. Having a plan will make it that much easier for your group to function right out of the gate. My guess is that most groups will form around one or several adults who are concerned about the coming issues, and who are proactive in preparedness. They will be looked to for future guidance, a heavy responsibility.

Consider the organization of an existing highly functional stratified group, for a basic guide. The Raconteur Report has a very valuable brief 5-part tutorial that gives a great outline for organization and skills, online – another one to print out and store on paper:

> http://raconteurreport.blogspot.com/2016/02/military-organization-for-dummies-pt-1.html

Rule Making

Modern society has policing and adjudicating systems, however faulty, in place. In a family, a respected figure usually is the final arbiter of decisions, typically an older trusted man. In a small community, decisions are often reached by group consent – town halls, voice votes, meetings to present and discuss plans, etc.

Roberts Rules of Order is a well-known and widely accepted method to hold and organize meetings with a balanced structure – called "Parliamentary Procedure." Get a copy of the handbook as soon as possible (you can find it online), and having several paper copies on hand will be a real boon when you need it. There's even a simplified "cheat sheet" version available online for about $3 – acquire several so they can be passed around at meetings.

Most people have a passing familiarity with Robert's Rules, since it is the standard method by which most Boards, committees, and associations conduct business. Parliamentary Procedure allows each person to have a say on any given issue, by following a set of guidelines that theoretically everyone knows.

In order to make Parliamentary Procedure effective, a leadership assemblage must have the accepted and visible standing or authority to actually expect the consensus of the community. Westerners achieve this by *the consent of the governed,* the agreement by all involved that certain official duties can be carried out by specific persons who have been formally granted authority by the group by majority *vote.*

This status begins as a group draws up a Charter or Statement of Bylaws. Effectively, this Charter or set of Bylaws is similar to what a corporation or social group draws up at its founding. These are the reasons the group exists and the simple protocols for:

- who will be in charge (Chairman? President? Facilitator? Board?),
- the description of duties and *limits of their authority,*
- the additional officers (Vice-Chairman, Secretary, Treasurer, Historian, Officer-at-Arms are common offices)
- term limits and compensation, if any, should be indicated
- method of installing new officers (by group vote? Appointment?)
- method of removing officers who exceed authority or fail to perform to standard
- obligations of group membership
- times when official meetings are held, and how announcement of meeting date and time will be made
- method for handling grievances (should they be submitted on paper or verbally? Decided by the entire Board, or one or two members, or by committee? By group vote?)
- a means for amending the founding document, and how it will be accepted (vote of the group? Vote of the Board?)

Group meetings can be handled utilizing the meeting format of Robert's Rules, effectively:

- Meeting called to order by ranking officer or appointee.
- Minutes of the last meeting are read and motion made by one member and seconded by another member to accept the minutes.
  - o If accepted, continue to next step
  - o If rejected, discuss on how to correct the minutes, make amendments to the minutes, make a motion to accept amended minutes, second the motion, and vote. If accepted, continue to next step. If rejected, repeat this step.
- Read treasurer's report. Similar motion, second, and vote to accept as with the minutes.
- Committee reports. Discuss. Motion/second/vote.
- Complete any other old business.
- Move on to any new business
- Other discussion as warranted. Assign work, appoint new committees if needed.

- Any other business
- Close meeting by motion/second/vote.

Robert's Rules is a *procedural* guideline, not a statement of mission, rights and responsibilities, or moral code. What I've noted here is a simplified guide – the actual Rules have procedures for handling contention, challenging another speaker, and so forth.

Most of the original legal code of Western Civilization derived from the Biblical Ten Commandments – that it is socially condemned to kill people or steal things, for example. The rights of the individual in Western Civilization were established in law a thousand years ago with the Magna Carta and enshrined in the 10 articles of the Bill of Rights – freedom of speech, religion, the duty to protect oneself utilizing lethal force if needed, privacy of oneself and one's papers and possessions, and so forth. These are in-born rights of each human being, not "given" or "granted" by government. The Bill of Rights merely pointed out that these natural rights existed before government, and will exist after all governments are dissolved.

There isn't much point in reinventing the wheel in our little groups, so these kinds of documents can provide a useful foundation for future development. However, keep in mind that an egalitarian group may still find itself dealing with other groups who are more feudal in their thinking and behavior (with a strong-arm person leading who makes all decisions for the group and dishes out harsh penalties to those who disobey). It's prudent to remember that without a universally-accepted Rule of Law, there isn't any universal law –and act accordingly.

Trouble Makers

This is a hard category. These are the people who will not contribute, no matter what justification or rationalization they provide. Some are constitutionally unable to cooperate in a group; some are so self-involved they don't consider others; some are innately destructive, malingerers, pot-stirrers, agitators, addictive personalities, disloyal, blamers. Some are mentally ill, some are born criminals, some are parasites. Some are quite charming, golden-tongued, fun to be around but always seem to generate problems. Some are our spouses, sisters or brothers, parents, or even children.

Takers and breakers will weaken and potentially destroy your community, but you already know this. You cannot turn these people out, because they will go to another group with your *inside* information, such as how much food you have stored and where, and barter that information for acceptance. Ideally, these people are kept separated from each other and marginalized, since they tend to congregate and magnify their negative influence. No important information should be imparted to them whatsoever. If they have been given important information at some point, every effort should be made to convince them that something else is the reality – that is, confuse them about the facts.

Ugly situation, but it will arise. Obviously, in any human gathering, there are people who are contributors and people who are problems, but in functional communities the safety and security of all is paramount. Even the "ordinary" quarrelsome and negative folk realize that, and will do the best they can in their awkward way. The biggest problem is when takers and breakers place their desires above the needs of the group, and imperil the group as a result.

In today's society, the usual approach to troublemakers is to call the local authorities – police, sheriff, security, and so forth. Hopefully, then the troublemaker goes into the legal system, is appropriately fined or confined, and sees the error of their ways. Repeat offenders may return to their home base to re-offend, be re-incarcerated several times, and either reform, become a permanent jailhouse resident, or have an unfortunate accident.

In the coming times, the judicial system may continue to operate, at least in form if not function. Should troublemakers and breakers continue their unsavory activities in spite of repeated lawful attempts to make them stop, it is possible that the local populace will have to handle the situation another way. There needs to be a lawful and moral means to confine, "jail", minor offenders, and permanently remove serious offenders. The time to think about these grim issues is now.

Those who make critical decisions of this type must be able to justify their decisions and actions with great clarity and wisdom, and should actually keep strict and accurate paper records of each step in the process should their decisions come under scrutiny later. It is best to consider options long before any such situation arises.

Setting Up Security

If you have military-level fit young men, *with appropriate training and actual fighting experience*, you may be able to set up patrols to explore the area around your group's base should things devolve into a true SHTF scenario. Most families, groups, preppers, and retreats *DO NOT*. This can't be finessed or sweet-talked: your group will likely NOT be able to field exploratory patrols of any kind, no matter how fancy or expensive your tactical equipment. These are not skills you can just pick up or learn on-the-job, online, or by reading about it.

Your best plan for survival long term is to establish a strong defensive position, and keep your people safe within it. Your group's land has an established boundary along the property lines. You will only be able to hold that land as long as you can protect and secure the property lines.

Your security team will have routine duties of guarding the property from unwanted interlopers. This will be especially important for the first year or two of the Zen-slap phase, when other people are desperate and potentially dangerous.

That means developing a clear understanding of your vulnerabilities and strengths, both in the property and in your human assets as well. There's no "one way" to do this, since your terrain, groups skills, equipment, and *willingness* is different than any other group's qualities.

If you have experienced military combat members in your group, they may be able to contribute valuable ideas and skills to the planning and execution phases, as well.

There are multiple ways to set up and maintain a security team, and multiple sensible books on the skills a team will need, including military manuals. Here's a good basic free one from the US Army:

> **Warrior Skills, Level 1**
> http://www.milsci.ucsb.edu/sites/secure.lsit.ucsb.edu.mili.d7/files/s
> itefiles/resources/STP%2021-1-
> SMCT,%20Warrior%20Skills,%20Level%201.pdf

I'm going to cover some general principles and basics here, which will assist your planning. Keep in mind that any security team must train continuously (*you fight as you train*), repeatedly explore possible ways that the group could be under threat, and find ways to respond quickly and efficiently when the unexpected happens.

Define Duties

Security is a broad field. There are many different aspects to keeping a place safe and maintaining security in a community. Think about the systems we have in place in the modern world: police officers, firemen, ambulances, emergency medical services, tow trucks, emergency linemen, crypto security for computer systems, security monitoring via camera systems, even call-anytime plumbers. As long as we have these services, we can utilize them to the fullest means possible.

During Zen-slap, there is likely to be a break in some or all of them. We've seen that happen time and again as it did during Hurricane Katrina. From the Awakening onward, though, the idea that we cannot *depend* on any security beyond that which we create ourselves must be hammered into our consciousness. While there is Law we have to work within it, but if the Rule of Law breaks down, we still need to have a security system that works for each of us.

In our groups, we will develop a clear understanding of what our security team will do, how they will carry it out, and when it is time to call the entire group or outside services for assistance. Write this down and maintain it as part of your group's Standard Operating Procedures (SOPs). Develop this alongside your By-Laws or Governing Mission paperwork, and store together.

Points to include:
- Define "security": defensive, group oriented, when actions can be escalated if needed, primarily the province of a

trained team but ultimately the entire group's responsibility.

- Security team: how many persons, ages, basic skills required, temperament (i.e., stable and able to respond situationally), training routines.
- Compensation to security team members: will this be a primary duty of a sub-group? Or a requirement of all group members? What will they receive in return for service (extra food, currency, time off other duties, choice of tools/weapons, housing, etc.)?
- Specific duties: monitor entrances, monitor fence lines, alert for weather/fire/intrusion, maintain security cameras, electric fencing, deter or detain or stop dangerous intruders, and so forth.
- Group leaders, qualifications, skills, teaching duties.
- Backup plans for sickness, injury, times when increased numbers of personnel are needed.

Mapping and Visualizing

Acquire maps of your land, surrounding property, and the region out to about 25 miles. Get topographic maps, those that show terrain; and overhead "satellite" type maps that show trees, houses, roads, rivers, ponds, and hills. Acquire multiple copies. You can print these out from Google Earth, and paste together enough to give you a large view of your area.

Mark one of the maps with neighbor's names and details (for example: *Joe (machinist) & wife Phyllis (teacher), children Rex (9) and Bob (7), possible guests including 4 male, 5 female adults*). Indicate whether someone has been helpful to you (+++), cool but not hostile (++), or outright hostile (+). You'll want to know which neighbors might be potential trading partners and which ones won't.

Mark places where there are good fences, and where gates go through. Go off your land and inspect it as if you wanted to get in – look for weak spots, open areas, easy entrances and mark these areas in red. Look for spots on neighboring lands – high areas, trees, hillsides – from which your property could be watched. Have two or three other people do the same thing, and compare notes. Mark these spots on your maps.

If you are able to get a drone with a camera or GoPro type of product into the air – lofting up with a big kite on a long line will do in a pinch – use this to explore your property terrain in places that are too difficult to traverse on foot: cliffs, gullies, rivers. Get a *really good* look at your land. Mark anything interesting or unusual on your map.

Next, map and mark important outlying sites on your maps – civil structures (town hall, police, sheriff, county seat and offices); religious buildings; medical centers; food centers and distribution; banks; bridges, rivers, canals, harbors; airports; livestock holding or auction sites; rail lines and stations; power plants and utilities; high-tension power lines; and other facilities unique to your area.

Now, go through and draw three large divisions in your land, representing an outer ring near the boundaries, a middle ring, and an inner ring right around the dwellings. Later, when you set up your defensive perimeters, you'll form strong outer boundaries – but if someone gets through that, you will still have two strong inner defensive rings before they can get into your residence(s). The final defensive ring around the house(s) should be the first one you really fortify. Work out from there to the edges of your property.

With the ring system of property defense – an outer ring at the perimeter, and inner ring around residences and living areas, and a middle ring somewhere between the two. Each ring layer needs static as well as active defense. The outer ring acts as the first alert, letting you know that someone or something has entered the property. The middle ring alarm will tell you how quickly the intruder is proceeding into the property, as well as which direction they are going (direct to the center ring? Or catty-corner just crossing the land?). The innermost ring is the one that sets off the highest level of alert, with all hands on deck.

Finally, divide the three rings into "sectors" and name them. Don't name them things like "front gate" or "west pasture" or "cattle barn" – use something that won't be clear to someone listening in on a private chat or radio communication, such as "Sector A", "Region 23", or "Blue Zone".

Store your maps in the most secure portion of your property which is also readily accessible – something like a Command Post (CP), which might be the middle of your kitchen table. You don't want outsiders to get copies, but you'll want to be able to look at a map when communicating with someone at an Observation Post (OP).

Observation Posts

Using your maps, consider the best places to put observation posts (OPs) – sites which give you a ground level or elevated (tree, building, hillside) view of the terrain, passing roadways, weak spots in your boundaries. Try to find locations from which you can see more than one direction, near the top of a rise but not silhouette-able along a ridgeline, and within "shootin' distance" of the observed site.

These OPs should be concealable in outcroppings or shrubs, and covered among sandbags that provide ballistic defense for observers within. If you have artists in your group, they can help design camouflage that mimics the surroundings. Then your OP blends so well that it becomes invisible to viewers. When observers go into each OP, remember to use different entry paths so that there isn't any outward sign of trails or use.

Communications

One of the foundations of a successful security plan is the ability to communicate among team members in the field and with the main center. Any usual activity noticed at an OP can be communicated to the CP and even the entire camp if needed. Handheld walkie-talkie type radios are the go-to tool for this. Most have a dozen or more channels, so a team can have several conversations going at one time. These are relatively inexpensive and available online and in Wal-Mart and camping stores. Each *person* in your group should have two radios at minimum, plus dozens of batteries set aside for each radio. Some radios come with an earbud (only use one so you can hear other sounds too) so that noise can be kept under control.

Set one channel aside for emergency communications to the whole group, a fire or severe weather alert, for instance. The head of each household would then leave one of their radios constantly on, set on the emergency channel, so that everyone can be notified of an emergency at one time. Batteries may need to be changed daily or every other day on that radio. Solar rechargeable batteries are extra handy here.

A second channel would be designated for OP communications, using site codes ("Blue Zone") to represent which area is being discussed. Other channels could be designated for specific types of conversations, such as when people go out hunting. Radios shouldn't be used for routine personal or idle conversations. That's not their purpose and defeats security of your group.
Any radio, especially these walkie-talkie types, are *absolutely insecure*. Everything said over the radio can be overheard by outsiders with their own radios, including the ones who are scoping out your group with nefarious purposes in mind. Always keep in mind that outsiders can listen in, no matter what is being discussed.

People who have cell phones should NEVER carry them, keep them on vibrate, and DO NOT CALL OUT. They are to receive emergency calls from relatives ONLY. The risk of letting outsiders know about your set up is too great, otherwise. Yes, smart phones can be tracked and monitored from outside your location.

Consider utilizing the knowledge that others may be listening to plant tantalizing false information from time to time, in order to lure outsiders into showing their cards. Think through all possible ramifications before doing this. It may not go the way you'd like.

If there has been an intrusion into one area of your property that resulted in radio conversation, *immediately change the name of each area*. For example, "Blue Zone" becomes "Sector 9." Intruders may be probing your defenses and code names, looking for clues to your defenses. Don't help them out.

Several members of your group ideally would also be skilled in use of amateur radio (**HAM radio**) and have appropriate equipment. At this time, there is an FCC requirement for licensing of HAMs; the test is not difficult, mostly memory work, and can be taken with a minimum of cost.

HAMs can often contact the outside world, get information on conditions elsewhere, ask for or offer assistance, and keep your group up-to-date on current events if the internet or other news media is down. Real proficiency would include the ability to tap-out and receive Morse Code at a good rate. HAM radio is also *absolutely insecure,* so there should be restraint on naming your location and no information whatsoever on your supplies, personnel, or security should go over the airwaves.

During a grid down CME or EMP incident, or if power is just unavailable in your area due to severe weather, you may need alternative or backup communication methods. You'll need to develop a **signaling** system – blinking lights, ringing bells, whistles, car horns, or even trumpet blasts can all work. Work out a code, too, such as "three clangs of the bell means intruder" or "six flashes of headlights signifies a health emergency." Write your code down and make copies available in critical locations. If something knocks down your radios suddenly, your groups needs to immediately be able to go to backup signals. Practice!

There are systems that can be set up over limited areas that make use of wifi, especially ***directional wifi*** utilizing special antennas. This is a small industry, with devoted followers, constantly updating with new techniques. Your best way to find out the latest is to do an internet search using the terms "directional wifi" or "third-world wifi". Using this presumes functioning grid or battery power, plus computers, in order to utilize the technology. Directional wifi is *moderately secure.* Intruders can still see the transmitters and receivers, and by positioning equipment on the line between them and using their own receivers, intruders can "listen in" to what is being transmitted....obviously, at the risk of being seen themselves.

If computers are functioning and you need to relay information to someone that is too detailed to talk about, or if you wish to have a "newsletter" type info sharing, consider **flash drives or even mini or micro SD cards**. Reports of local news, copies of books, or requests for medical help, or trades/barter, music, videos, photos, and whatever can be loaded onto a drive. When you visit a neighbor, drop it off. They can download the info, then pass the drive along up the road. Soon the whole area will be communicating. This presumes there is power for computers, neighbors have and can use computers, and that people are willing to use this method as a bulletin board. This, too, is *absolutely insecure.*

Don't ignore the old "low tech" methods of communication, either. The ancient **landline phone systems** were simple battery-operated contraptions. A ringer was triggered by turning a gear, rather like the modern wind-up emergency radios, which sent a pulse along a buried or elevated electrical line to a receiver-phone. The same basic idea was behind the WWII "field phones".

If you have several locations within your property that you want to connect "by phone", consider hunting down army surplus field phones on ebay.com. Virtually all the old WWII field phones are interchangeable; some have schematics right on the phones. Basically, each phone is powered by a pair of D batteries, and connected to one other phone by a powerline, or connected to an actual human-activated switchboard that acts as the router to any number of other phones attached to the same switchboard. The field phone system is elegant in its simplicity, and because its components were manufactured for use in war zones, it's hardy and built for ease of use. Don't use it during lightning storms because a direct strike can send a pulse of deadly electricity into the handsets.

There are multiple online tutorials and plans for putting in a field phone system, plus many youtube.com videos with step by step instructions. Field phones are *more secure* than flash drives, wifi or radio transmissions. Potential hackers would have to find, dig up, cut, and attach listening devices to the actual electric line or in the handsets.

Static Defense

If your land is larger than a city lot, you simply do not have enough time, energy, or manpower to monitor all the potential entry points 24 hours a day. That's the reason for lockable gates at potential drive-through entries. Gates act as a stationary or static defense against unwanted intruders. Gates aren't perfect – people can climb over them, pull them down, or ram them with a tractor – but they do provide a level of visual deterrence. Anyone found on your property must have come through at least one barrier.

Same thing with locks on our doors. People can smash a window and gain entry to the house, or even kick in a door. But all those things take *effort*. The type of person who gets involved in smash-

and-grab generally prefers an easy target. So a locked gate or door provides an excuse for those people to just move along to a place that's got easier entrance.

A fence, even a simple barbed wire one, keeps in cattle and provides deterrence to intruders – most of the time, anyway. Cattle still escape, and people still trespass.

"Most of the time" works fine in typical times and ordinary years. In the coming Cold Times, more people will have a sense of desperation and justification. Cold, hunger, not having enough money, or any other excuse will make it seem all right to them to encroach on other's property or food.

But not if it's *your* property or food. Not if it's the food that your children or family needs to get through the winter, or the supplies that you set back by sacrificing when times were good. You have a moral, legal, and historical right to your property and supplies, and no obligation whatsoever to allow anyone else to take it from you. You can share all you want, but that's a different story.

So, static defense of your property must be considered along with other security and safety issues. When you created your property maps, there were probably areas that had existing static defenses: rough terrain, cliffs, fast rivers, swamps, or other natural barriers to entry. That's static defense in those locations. Cutting down and dropping trees across potential entry points is another form of defense.

Standard fences that have been enhanced with additional barriers to entry can also be exceptional static defense. Rolls of barbed wire woven into an existing fence makes it that much more difficult for intruders to get through. Concertina wire, the kind with sharp razor-like edges, is even better defensively but some jurisdictions don't permit its use right now.

In the middle ages, peasants made fences by weaving woody plants together, forming "living hedges". If someone was willing to wait a few years to get a tall fence, planting and then weaving something like "hedge apple" (AKA bois d'arc, Osage orange) or thorny locust together, they'd have a nearly impenetrable hedge that was full of spikes and snakes. The only way through would be with a tank, or a flame thrower. Once a year, you'd have to go through and mow all the sprouts that were trying to expand into your fields. It's a small price for a sturdy living barrier.

Other commonplace static defenses include trip wires set to jiggle rocks in tin cans, for example, or trigger a flashbulb alert, or ring a loud bell – you get the idea. There's a risk of having this triggered if livestock, wild animals, or pets pass over it, too.

An electric fence is another form of static defense that can operate on solar power. Anyone who touches it gets a shock, which is quite a surprising deterrent. Electric fences can be easily defeated, though, by grounding them out: a tree limb touching the ground and thrown over an electric fence will impede the flow of juice to it, and probably drain the solar battery pretty quickly. Grid-powered electric fences may throw a fuse and quit working when grounded. Ideally, if you have an electric line as part of your static defense, you would rig up a light or bell to go off if the fence is interrupted. That would signal you that something was breeching your defense.

Some people suggest booby traps as a form of static defense, such as boards with nails in them with points turned up, a dug trench with pointed sticks in it, spikey farm equipment left lying in tall grass, etc. For right now, *don't*.

The first problem with having an array of booby traps as static deterrence is that everyone on your place must know where they are and be able to avoid them during all seasons including tall grass, rain, and snow. That really means you'll have to pull a screaming kid off a nail board at some time or other.

The second problem is that they are illegal in most jurisdictions. You can be sued into the poor house if some trespasser crawls under a fence and onto your punji sticks.

The third problem is that booby traps aren't terribly effective. Unless you can dig a 10 foot alligator moat around your entire property, an alert intruder can find a way around most other traps.

Your OPs will be part of your static defense. Each OP provides the means for your security team to monitor sections of the perimeter. If any intrusion is noted, communication with the CP alerts the entire group.

Dogs

This may seem like an odd spot to put in information about dogs. We most often think of dogs as family pets whose primary job is to keep us company. We tend to treat dogs as if they are our children. That assumption about these useful animals is about to change.

There is credible evidence that humankind's first use of the dog wasn't in hunting, as many anthropologists would like us to believe. The first use was actually as an intruder alarm. Virtually all dogs will bark at strange noises or people, giving "alarm". Packs of feral and wild dogs do the same. It's a means of alerting their pack that something unusual is going on. That brings the pack to attention, and threats can be dealt with.

Some dogs are better at this than others. Most small lap dogs are so high strung that a wind-rattled window can trigger a volley of alarm barking. Many large breed dogs, originally bred as estate guards, have now been overbred for docility so they rarely alarm bark. That huge mastiff or Rottweiler or Great Dane or St. Bernard may look imposing, but at their hearts they often are big, fluffy teddy bears. We have bred these once lion-hearted giants into frightened, dependent children.

As we progress into the Cold Times, we have to honestly assess the value of dogs on our property. A dog that does not work for its living in some fashion, is a mouth that requires food...that is, food which may be expensive or hard to come by as the weather reels and changes. Try not to look into Fido's big, soft, loving brown eyes while you think about this. It's easy to be led astray by emotion.

A good resource is to read about "working dogs" – breeds and crossbreeds that have been developed to carry out specific tasks to aid their owners' livelihoods. I'm referring here to herding dogs, such as Border Collies or Blue Heelers, who run dozens of miles daily to drive sheep or cattle so the owner doesn't have to. And to livestock guardian dogs, such as Great Pyrenees or Anatolians, who live out in the elements with sheep or goats or cattle and protect them from predators both human and animal.

A good working dog can replace a human hired hand. The dog

works for nothing more than kibble and a little pat on the head now and then. The dog doesn't complain about having to work in bad weather, doesn't care how you're dressed, doesn't go to town and get drunk or tear up expensive equipment like the hired hand might.

A good dog is a valuable asset. A dog that doesn't pull its own weight and then some, is not. Here's how a dog that is a valuable asset pulls its own weight:

- The dog has a job, and does it consistently. Most working dogs learn "their job" early and have it utterly down pat by the time they are 2 years old.
    o We had one collie whose self-assigned job was to patrol the edge of the property, a round he made several times daily until he had cut a path into the field. He continued that job until he was too old to make the rounds any more, day and night, in all weather.
- Sometimes you can assign a job to a dog by raising it among the livestock you want it to guard. Sometimes the dog picks its own job by figuring out what needs to be done.
    o We have a crossbred Great Pyrenees x Bloodhound, whose leg was injured as a pup and she was not expected to live, so we let her take it easy as she healed. She limped over hill and dale, and found that she could sit atop ridges and keep a close eye on cattle in the valleys below. That became her lifetime job. She will sit out in the pastures, watching and guarding, for days at a stretch returning home only for a meal and encouragement – then back out she goes.
    o Another dog, a collie-shepherd cross, self-assigned "watching the house" as his job. He stayed between the house and barns, kept down the squirrel and armadillo population (and fed himself at the same time), and let us know if something unusual was going on.
- A good dog can be trained to perform a task it might not otherwise choose to do – bring water to someone working the field, for example, or learning to search for someone who is lost. But, the dog won't do it for love of helping out someone in need. The dog will do it because he gets

something *else* that he wants as a reward afterwards – a treat, chasing a Frisbee, tugging on a rope, attention and loving.   Remember that dogs are not volunteers or humanitarians; they are "paid" workers. You have to find out what "pay" the dog is willing to work for.

- The dog is hardwired to protect his home and his people. He is alert, barks, and looks for backup from his people or other resident dogs when strangers arrive or predatory animals invade. A normal dog doesn't carry out *unprovoked* vicious attacks – badly trained, psychotic, or mentally ill dogs might. An otherwise stable and balanced dog that attacks *has been* provoked.
- Dogs that have the run of your property will *learn your boundaries*. They might not be precise to the fence line, but they are generally pretty close to it.   They aren't inclined to wander off and get lost. If they do, generally they don't come back.
- A good dog learns his limits. You and your people are the dominant species, and dogs actually need the boundaries and behavior control that your dominance provides. Young livestock guardian dogs might rough up their livestock charges when the dogs are pups – but stern discipline from you, the dog's alpha owner, teaches that kind of behavior isn't tolerated. The dog gets *one chance* to make a mistake. If you discipline the dog (seriously, because you *mean it*), and it does the same thing again, the dog is *gone*. No excuses.

You can trust a good dog to be a reliable dog. Never, never, ever put *all* your trust into a dog. Always, in the back of your mind, you must remember that all dogs are self-interested *predators*. They are programmed to chase and kill smaller animals and eat them – and they enjoy the chase and kill. They have sharp, biting, and flesh-tearing teeth, with strong molars to crunch through bone. They will eat herd animals' manure like candy, and roll all over dead carcasses until they stink of dead-thing. A dog is not a person. Dogs have many qualities that endear them to us, but they are not us. We are the pack leaders, and the dog is the pack.

Dogs are not static defense in the way a fence is, but a dog that understands your property boundaries will alert if trespassers come onto your land – therefore, becoming part of your security infrastructure. With their keen hearing and sense of smell, they can perceive the presence of intruders before we do. The dog may stiffen up, sniff the air, the hair on its back may raise, and it may growl or whine to let you know something's amiss. Pay attention to that, and remove yourself from harm's way.

Whenever someone in your group goes out to check locations in the outer rings of your property, they should take a dog along. Many rural residents have stories about the dog that barked and distracted an attacking pig or bull long enough for the person to get away, or the dog that got between the person and a venomous snake. Children benefit by having a dog, and there are thousands of stories of children rescued or protected by their dogs. That's how dogs protect their pack and their pack leaders.

In the coming Cold Times, don't spay or neuter dogs. At some point, you'll want to replace your old dogs with puppies. There may not be any decent ones left since hunger has taken many pets in past cold ages. Female dogs come "in season" and can be impregnated for about 2 weeks, once or twice a year. The signs are unmistakable.

If you don't want pups, put the female into a tight pen during that time. When she is in season, your male dogs will fight among each other; when she's done, they'll be friends again. The rest of the time, she's got her job. If she has puppies, she'll have them under a car or in a hay-filled barn if it's cold outside, and she'll raise them without a speck of help from anyone else until they are 4-6 weeks old. Then, they'll need some extra food. Some will probably die. Let that happen. Pups that live will be strong and hardy, what you need for the Cold Times ahead.

In hard times, dogs eat whatever they get – soup, oatmeal, moldy bread, leftovers, dead chickens, wild animals they have hunted, bad eggs, guts and leavings from livestock that was butchered. They'll do better on this varied diet, loaded with natural nutrients and important vitamins, than they ever did on GMO-corn-based kibble. If you can, make sure each dog gets a rabies vaccination every two years. If there aren't vaccinations available, be prepared to destroy any dog or cat with strange symptoms, such as staggering, unable to drink or eat, or personality changes, so you don't risk your family's health. That's another reason you need more than one dog.

If you currently have a dog, keep it until extenuating circumstances force another decision on you. If you only have one, get another one – NOT neutered or spayed. Look for "free puppies" signs. These will be crossbred, which is exactly what you want. Buy some dewormer and a "puppy shot" at the nearby feed store, and treat the dog. Get or make an insulated outside house, bowl of water, and something to eat. Dog lives outside.

Don't get a purebred anything. You will have no need for registration papers, and papers don't make a good dog. Purebred dogs, like purebred chickens, come from limited gene pools, and you sure don't want to end up with the products of intense inbreeding when you need smart, healthy animals. Look for dogs with herding or guardian ancestry.

"Drop offs" are dogs and other pets that someone has dumped out on a lonely country road. During downturns in the economy, backcountry farms are inundated with dogs of every breed, crossbreds, and everything else. The same will happen during the Zen-slap. I've had purebred Bassett Hounds, Rhodesian Ridgebacks, Australian Shepherds, and an assortment of mixes "show up" starving and desperate. One of the best dogs we've had – who saved elderly Granny's life by finding her in the woods in the middle of the night – was a well-trained pit bull, not a breed we usually think of as a rescue dog! Hard to believe someone could just abandon such a nice dog out in the wilds to its fate.

Most drop off dogs die of hunger, being shot by farmers, or being killed by coyotes, by the way. So if you know someone who's thinking of doing that with their dog, advise them to do the right thing and just take the dog to be euthanized at the vet. It would be kinder to the dog.

Finally, if things really go bad, be aware that someone may try to capture your free running dogs to turn them into meals. Or, worse yet, you may be at a point of desperation so great that the dog ends up on the menu. Do what you must with no regrets. If it helps, remember that the dog is a carnivorous predator, and it would eat us if it had to without a moment's hesitation.

Controlling Entries and Boundaries

Each entryway has a single, visible sentry behind a locked gate on the perimeter of the property's outer ring. The sentry's job is to either allow entry or to prevent it. The sentry waits in a protected warmable structure, the "guard shack", which might be a stalled vehicle or something similar. Somewhere nearby, that sentry is visible to one or two others who are hidden and ready to take defensive action at a distance. A method of discrete signals, perhaps raising a hand, or taking off a hat, indicates to the watchers that the sentry is under threat, and immediate action is needed.

The sentry may be in radio contact with the command center, or may be empowered to make his own decisions on who gets in and who doesn't. The group may be looking for people with specific skills (medical, construction, electrician, etc), or may simply have no additional food or space; the group may be willing to let in relatives of those inside (the sentry should have a list of 'acceptable' names). These are all factors in the sentry's decisions.

Potential entries are told to remove jackets, lift shirts, turn around, demonstrating that they are not carrying concealed. Any visible arms should be placed on the ground and retrieved by the sentry, for return later. All new entries should spend a couple weeks in quarantine before exposing the main group. Exceptions can be made for emergency messages or other situations, of course.

If the entryways have previously been "tried" by outsiders, barricades and funnels may be necessary. Old vehicles, downed trees, or other obstacles can be utilized.

Sentry posts need off-property monitors, as well, to let the sentry know when there is movement on the road. That means OPs need communications or visual signaling such as semaphore or blinks of a light, that can be received by the sentry day or night.

Boundaries and gates need to be watched even more carefully at night, since intruders often seek the cover of darkness. If you or your group are able, night vision (NV) and/or infrared (IR) goggles or monoculars will give you the ability to "see in the dark".

Better yet, if you can outfit your OPs with NV or IR, their ability to give advance warning and manage potential intrusions at night increases dramatically. The high price of the equipment would be worthwhile, if it prevented potentially damaging intrusions.

These battery operated devices are expensive at a couple thousand dollars and up, but would be worth their weight in gold during any serious downturn situation. Store them with the batteries out, and use only for brief periods of time rather than continuously. Some of these have a small light or illumination that is visible at a distance; shield or otherwise cover this, turn it off if possible. That light gives away your position to distant viewers. There's no indications if NV or IR equipment could survive an EMP; a Faraday cage wouldn't hurt.

If you still have power and wifi, you can send a drone with camera aloft to monitor your boundaries from a distance. These are becoming increasingly inexpensive with good ones for $200 or so. If you have the funds, spend extra to get one with a longer flight time and NV or IR capabilities. It can help you find lost livestock and live game, as well, without having to hike through the woods.

Sentries and gate guards will have the responsibility to turn away travelers and beggars, for lack of a better word. In any kind of downturn, this is the hardest and most wrenching job particularly if the individuals in question are young, or children, or defenseless-appearing women. These pitiful cases, if allowed entry, can be your undoing. They may be "spies" sent by other groups to identify your assets and weaknesses, or they may merely be desperate folk who have lost everything. You can't tell by looking, so you must assume the worst. If there is a refugee center in a nearby town, send them there. As hard as it may be, don't offer food. That will signal that you *have* food, and make your group a target.

Weapons

Every person over the age of 10 in your group should be skilled enough to shoot accurately and on target at a distance of 50 feet, load and unload, and handle a firearm safely, at the very minimum. It wasn't that many years ago that rural kids carried their trusty .22 to school for lunchtime target practice, and in the hopes of bagging a rabbit or squirrel on the way home to help with supper. In a very worst case situation, your group's ability to muster overwhelming firepower may make the difference between having a future and not having one. Start training this week, and continue once a week until you have the skills down – then train continuously once a month after that. People quickly unlearn this skill, so it has to be practiced to maintain it.

We can thank "the Father of Prepping", Ragnar Benson, for publicizing the idea that there are three types of firearms that a prepper needs: a shotgun, a handgun, and a rifle. Each of these weapons has uses for which it is ideal; there is no firearm that meets all the uses by itself.
Shotguns are for "home defense" and for hunting large animals if you use slug shot. They are good defensive weapons, because under duress your aim can waver – but a shotgun's blast widens out as it leaves the barrel and puts pellets into a relatively large area. Shotguns using slug ammunition put a single powerful slug in nearby targets with ease.

Handguns are for close-by defense, and have the ability to be concealed easily. In a desperate situation, the handgun in your coat pocket can be fired right through the fabric, negating the need to pull the weapon out before shooting. The old saw about *a handgun is only good for fighting your way back to your rifle* is true enough in battlefield conditions, but we certainly hope we never have to get *there*.

Rifles are "to reach out and touch someone" at a distance. Ideally, if your group utilizes rifles efficiently, you won't need to worry about using handguns or shotguns. Rifles are also the go-to tool for hunting large and small animals.

Caliber represents the relative "size" of a round of ammunition. The size is a designation generally based on millimeters. Therefore, a .22 round is smaller than a .38 round, which in turn is smaller than a .44 round.

What I'm not going to tell you here is what type of shotgun, handgun or rifle to get, simply because there is so much variance between users. A small woman with tiny hands won't be able to control a big Smith and Wesson .357 revolver very well, for example, although these rounds pack a wallop and can stop threats quickly. She'd be better off with a smaller caliber, such as

Walther .22 or lighter Sig Sauer semi-auto 9 mm – because a small well-controlled round does more damage than a large heavy round that misses the target. The 9 mm is a common mid-range caliber that lends itself to many applications and many skill levels.

Semi-automatic handguns generally called "pistols", and manual handguns called "revolvers", may shoot the same caliber of ammo but some shot is made for semi-auto specifically. You must read the ammo box to be sure. Pistols have the advantage of being able to shoot more rounds than a revolver – over a dozen or more in some cases. Most revolvers must be reloaded after 5 or 6 rounds. Revolvers, however, have the advantage of being simple and mostly trouble-free, whereas pistols may jam at inopportune moments.

Common shotgun choices are .410, 12-gauge and 20-gauge, with the 12-gauge being a more powerful shot than the other two. Four-ten ammo is fairly lightweight and is generally used for bird hunting with "bird shot" (basically, bb's), but "slug-shot" (a single bullet) can be efficient against larger animals as well. Shotguns come with either a single barrel or double barrels, and manual reload or semi-auto. There are few things more chilling to intruders than the *chuk-chuk* sound of a pump shotgun being readied to fire.

Rifle type and caliber are among the most contentious areas of discussion among preppers – AK? AR? Moisin? .22? 30.06? Suffice it to say that each type of rifle has positives and negatives. Moisin-Nagant, for example, has a strong positive of putting 7.64 x.54 bullets on target hundreds of yards away using simple peep-sights, with practice – but equally strong negative of being heavy and unwieldy to carry. Being older, it has a plus of being a relatively inexpensive firearm to buy, but a negative that the ammo is harder to find than more common rifles.

In the same way, AR-15's have the advantage of good accuracy and high capacity magazines – but have the drawback of being finicky and sensitive to environmental changes or grittiness. AK-47's, on the other hand, can tolerate poor care and harsh environments and just keep going, but their accuracy leaves a lot to be desired.

Selecting Firearms

Your best bet in weaponry is to explore different types – that is, actually go out and shoot them, at shooting ranges that will lend to you, for example, or with friends who have what you think you might like. You won't know what fits you and works best for you, until you try it out. If you buy a firearm that you decide you don't really like, sell it and buy another – you do not want to stake your life on equipment that doesn't work for you.

Firearms that are all tricked out with the latest hot gadgetry typically indicate an owner with more money than skill. Serious shooters need a sighted-in accurate weapon with a good peep-sight or scope....everything else is nice but unnecessary.
If you have no experience with firearms, go to a shooting range and ask for guidance. The range may offer classes, live individual instruction, or have contacts with people who do. Don't be shy – you won't be the first newbie they've seen, and gun-folk *love* talking about their firearms.

Each firearm you own needs a *minimum* of 1000 rounds of ammo. Three thousand rounds each would be better, and allows you some for routine practice. Remember, there may come a time when finding new ammo may be very hard. Explore ammo reloading to reduce costs a little.

Given all that, for group use, it would be exceptionally handy if all members had the same type and caliber of firearms – say, for example, Ruger 9 mm semi-auto handguns, Colt AR-15 rifles, and Browning 12-gauge shotguns (I'm not suggesting these brands or calibers, just using them for example). If everyone in your group had the same firearms, it is easy for someone in a threatening situation to grab a colleague's weapon and handle it competently – because it is exactly the same as what they have themselves trained with and became familiar with. Plus ammo can be readily found, since everyone in the group will have the same kinds. Those are real tactical advantages. Even so, any firearms are better than no firearms. Just try to avoid exotic makes and calibers.

Ideally, your group would also have two or three people who are interested in and good at repairing weaponry. These "armorers" are the folk who keep your firearms in good condition and can fix problems as they come up. Check local gunsmiths for information on learning the trade – offer to help them out in exchange for instruction; ask about local schools or online programs. Lacking armorers, your group should keep extra firearms on hand for the day when someone's breaks. Be sure to keep cleaning kits and supplies, as well.

Alternative Weapons

Alternatively, hunting bows and crossbows, as well as longbows, are handy, quiet, and deadly accurate tools. They are typically used at moderate distances (say, 50 yards), and the "ammo" can be reused multiple times. The main drawback is that you can only fire one arrow at a time, and it takes several seconds to reload. Plus, they do require significant practice time to get good at shooting accurately. These are nice to have as backup armaments to regular firearms – just buy lots of extra strings, arrow shafts, and hunting arrow heads. If things have devolved so much that you hesitate to hunt for fear of disclosing your location, there isn't anything better than a good silent crossbow for bringing home the game.

Everyone in your group should have at least one good utility knife, such as a pocket knife and a larger hunting-type knife for hacking and chopping. My preferred brand are Mora Knives, made in Finland – they are produced from carbon steel and take a sharp edge easily, plus they are very inexpensive when compared to other knives. You may have seen Mora fish fillet knives at the hunting/fishing departments of box stores; these are excellent. Carbon steel needs to be washed and dried immediately after use, or the blades rust. Stainless steel knives hold their edges longer and don't rust, but are much harder to bring to a fine edge than carbon steel. Get lots and lots of extra knives, because you will use them constantly.

Finally, although Papa Ragnar didn't write extensively on it to my knowledge, there's the option of returning to blackpowder firearms. These can be acquired new without registration or license right now in most areas, and have the same capabilities as standard firearms – with some caveats: you have exactly one shot, and it takes a while to reload. If you're handy with chemicals, ingredient lists, and can follow directions, you can make the gunpowder for it, or buy lots of extra powder while it is still available. Additionally, you can cast the bullets from leftover metals – some practitioners use fishing sinkers, melt them, and pour into forms that are also readily available right now. For the Hang-on phase, blackpowder might be a very viable option

---

Never point your weapon at anything you don't intend to destroy. Treat all weapons as if they are loaded.

Training

The people who act as your primary defensive unit will function most efficiently if they have consistent behaviors to resort to when under duress – basically, each participant must know what everyone else will do if "X" event happens. That awareness comes from training.

For example, say that the OP nearest your front entry gate sends out a radio alert that there are several individuals sneaking around the fence line. Because the team has trained together, each member knows that this alert signals the camera operators to turn on cameras outside the property and monitor for other suspicious behavior. Instead of other team members rushing from their posts to the front gate, they increase their own OP monitoring – the lurkers could be a distraction effort to open up another entry way onto your land.

No one needs to say what they are doing, because every team member *knows* what is happening. The alert from the front gate OP set off a chain of responses among team members. Since they don't have to talk on the radio about what they're doing, anyone outside the property who might be listening in to radio comms to find out how the group reacts to threats, won't get any useful information.

This is but one small part of the entire training spectrum that your people must know in order to defend your ground. Skills with defensive firearms is also a large element with practice in stationary marksmanship, shooting while moving, and utilization of cover. By far the most accessible information you can find on these topics is in the book *A Failure of Civility* (AFOC). Here are just a few points – but don't think you understand this broad topic, until you have read, studied, and internalized AFOC and other books on "home defense":

- Be proactive – make plans before you need them.
- Lock down and control all entry and exit points.
- The Center of Operations (Command Post) needs to be on top of all events and outside sources of information (other people talking on radios, HAMs, public info sources, police bands, etc.).
- Have a group identifier, armbands on *both* arms which are hard for outsiders to duplicate (*AFOC* suggests fabric from household curtains, for example).
- Wear camouflage appropriate to the season and region.
- OP sites are manned 24/7, no more than two hours per person per shift.
- Interior monitoring patrols, at intermittent and unscheduled times.
- Marksmen with overlapping fields of fire, plus ones set up outside the property line.
- Fall back positions within your property boundaries.
- Development of "fatal funnels" to lead intruders into firing zones.
- Reinforce inside perimeters with barbed wire and concertina wire.
- Concealed high position viewing and marksman sites in attics, high trees, well concealed hillsides, etc.
- Emergency bug-out procedures, BOB always packed and ready to go.
- Emergency relocation plans, training, practice.

Matt Bracken makes excellent points about the importance of "night training", practicing moving around your property and it's features at night, becoming familiar with the terrain, and discovering the differences in day versus night lighting, sound, and movement. This should be printed and practiced.

Night Fighting 101
https://westernrifleshooters.wordpress.com/2012/08/19/bracken-night-fighting-101/

Firing Positions and Fatal Funnel

These are important basic concepts for defense, so I will touch on them here. When your OPs are set up, the ideal is to have **fields of fire** – that is, directions in which the people in the OP can shoot – that overlap with another OP. The overlap – such as an X-shaped field, with the target in the center of the X – gives your group better access to the target, and fewer means for the targets to hide from the shots. Ideally, again, each OP would have a specific area over which they can shoot – say, a 45-degree view of an entrance road. The edges of their field may be marked with a touch of paint or bit of fabric, so that the excitement of the moment is less likely to have your group firing wildly. Limited and overlapping fields of fire helps prevent "friendly fire" accidents, and keeps the focus on your targets.

A **fatal funnel** is any means that directs would-be interlopers into an area that is difficult to leave, where they are centered in the fields of fire. For instance, wrecked cars "stalled" so that intruders must slow down to travel around them or stop at a roadway blockage, might constitute a fatal funnel – particularly if on a cliff or riverside that gives no easy cover or means of escape. A "game trail" path that "sneaks" into your property might lead around a couple bends into a deadend canyon or directly into the field of fire of a concealed and covered OP, creating a fatal funnel for intruders.

When you are out after things have turned ugly in society, be conscious of your own potential escape routes – at the post office, in movie theaters, at the supermarket or mall. Even when stopped in traffic. Make a point of leaving a full car length between you and the car in front at all stoplights, and be in either the right or left hand lanes – so you can turn quickly and hit the gas if something goes strange. Being stuck in traffic with no way to get out is the worst kind of fatal funnel, and one that we can see taking place all over the nation every day.

Subterfuge

Sun Tzu (ca 500 BC), the Chinese general and philosopher, wrote:

> "All warfare is based on deception. Hence, when we are able to attack, we must seem unable; when using our forces, we must appear inactive; when we are near, we must make the enemy believe we are far; when far away, we must make him believe we are nearby."

Survival in extreme social circumstances is also based on convincing unpleasant people that there's *nothing to see here, move on.*   Or that there might be something here, but there no way to be sure and it's going to be too much trouble to find out. This reduces your target value and improves your resilience and security.

There's many ways to do this, all reliant on your own creativity and understanding of human nature.   Effectively, ask yourself what would discourage *you* from checking out any location. Does it look ransacked, like the good stuff is gone already? Does it look risky or dangerous? Does it smell bad? Are there strange sounds? Create those experiences in anyone who views your property.

Years ago, I read an article about wealthy people living in large cities. A number of them had taken a remarkable step: they bought run down empty industrial warehouses near the downtown areas. They had the buildings gutted, and the interiors refitted with the fancy construction they wanted: indoor pools and spas, game rooms, multi-level cathedral ceilings, bowling alleys, sun rooms and grow spaces, huge fireplaces, gourmet kitchens, large theater and dance halls, whatever they imagined. Outside, the buildings still looked scroungy and worn out, with just a chain-link fence and industrial guard shack keeping out trespassers – with a near-invisible high tech security system watching the surroundings as well.   Passersby had no idea that inside that shabby old structure was an actual palace.

I believe it was either Selco (https://shtfschool.com) a survivor of the Bosnian war, or Ferfal (http://tspwiki.com/index. php?title=Fernando_%22Ferfal%22_Aguirre) survivor of the Argentine financial collapse, who reported another interesting example. One resident of a town during the calamity went out and dragged dead human bodies – casualties, murdered people, diseased -- in front of his property. Then he posted a sign that read something like, "Mess with me, and this happens to you." The story was that nobody bothered that house or family.

Signs can tell a story and discourage intrusion:

- Quarantine
- Police "do not cross, crime scene" tape
- Biohazard: chemical spill
- Biohazard: medical waste
- Danger: radiation
- On a truck: "Septic Cleaning" or "Manure Spreading"

Notice that none of the preceding signs indicates that there's anybody home – just that the site is dangerous in some way. Compare that to these:

- Trespassers will be shot. Survivors will be shot again.
- Keep out. Private property.
- Nothing here is worth your life.
- You are here (showing a view from a rifle scope with cross hairs)
- Looters will be shot.

As entertaining as these can be, every one of them screams, "Good stuff here, armed, use a sneak attack."

Any residence or business that looks like it's been ransacked has a reduced chance of being entered by intruders – not a zero chance, but a reduced chance. Dump trash in the yard, weeds growing everywhere, break a couple windows, pull curtains out to blow in the breeze, spray paint flat black above windows and doors to look like soot suggesting the place has been on fire.

Consider decoy residences that look like someone is there – perhaps a small green garden patch in the front. Site a viewing post so that you can watch the place. Intruders can then be managed from a safe distance.

Use your good sense. No one in their right mind wants to face a firefight or harm another human being.

Even Sun Tzu knew that:

> The supreme Art of War is to get the better of the enemy without fighting.

Forced Off Your Land

Fire, incursions by raiders, avalanche, landslide, onerous taxes, repressive regime, weather becoming unlivable – there may be unanticipated events that compel you and yours to leave the home and land you have developed for the cold times. The reason for having to leave will dictate *how* you leave, as well as what you plan for your group's future. There are two basic conditions with many variations, of course: Running away; and Moving on.

Running Away

During WWII, a middle European farm family at the edge of the fighting heard cannon fire approaching – they knew it was only a matter of time. The father told his teenage and adult children to milk the cows, put the milk in portable containers – then, slaughter the cows, and pack the meat. While that was going on, he harnessed the horses and prepared their wagons, gathered some basics and farm tools as sharp potential weapons, loaded coats and blankets, and drove the wagon to collect the family. They evacuated, and survived.

In many ways, that old farmer's response was brilliant – as hard and painful as it must have been to kill the animals that had been their life and lifestyle, and to leave their farm without looking back. He not only provided food for his family, he deprived the invaders of food as well. I don't recall whatever location they headed off to – apparently it was good enough, since one of the young daughters lived to tell it in her old age – but, given the old farmer's strategic decisions, I suspect he had a destination in mind already. Obviously, it was a safe one.

The primary survival strategy of a fast-getaway is having a place to get away *to*. That means planning, mapping, and forming alliances who won't be surprised if you show up at midnight, with your family and worldly goods in a wagon. The go-to place should be decided in advance, with all the critical details worked out well ahead of any possibility of need.

Depending on how far you'd have to travel, placing food, water, and security "caches" along the way will make your escape significantly safer than doing without. A *cache* (pronounced: *cash)* is a collection of items you might want or need, usually placed in a hidden spot such as buried, in a cave or outcropping, or in a collapsed building. A cache can contain pretty much anything you might think of – boots, blankets, knives, ammo, freeze dried food, bottled water, and so forth – that could assist you if you had to leave quickly or without your usual supplies. You'll need to mark your cache location in a way that stands out to you but doesn't scream "it's here!" to everyone else. Bent or broken branches might be one way. Or a landmark, such as "two large trees east of the broken oak" could be used.

If you're on foot, a cache every ten miles would be about right. If you are riding a horse, every twenty miles or so would give a day's travel between caches. If you are driving and roads are good, space them a tankful of gas apart.

Then, if you "hear the cannons", or maybe if you even think the cannons might be heading your way, you move.

Moving On

During the Maunder Minimum, farmers in Switzerland reported glacier ice descending onto their land at the rate of *150 feet in a day*. That means, in the course of a week, a wall of ice might cover over 1000 feet – in 5 weeks, it would be covering more than a mile of land.

Hopefully, you've sited your location below the edges of past glaciations, below 40° latitude, and never have to see those kinds of effects in person. Having three or four bad crop years might be a reason to seek a warmer climate, or if rivers rise so much that you become an islander for part of the year, or if the area you're in becomes too droughty, or chaotic and unsafe – perhaps, then, it's time to move on.

In these scenarios, there are a few concepts that apply to both:
   ▪ The time of day/night and season will need to be considered – summers may be too overly hot to spend time in the sun; winter blizzards will impede any movement outdoors.

- Number of people involved – whether it's dozens of adults and newborn babies, or merely a lone married couple -- will affect equipment, ability to move quickly, and transportation.
- Distance and time away from your property – short temporary trips versus long or permanent ones. If you expect to have something to come back to, you'll need someone to watch or take care of the place.
- Available transportation methods: vehicles, their ability to make the drive, fuel, tires, and your capacity to make impromptu repairs will affect how quickly and how far you can go. Extra gas or diesel may be needed, along with extra spare tires, "flat-fix", tire plugs, or other means of repairing damaged tires
- Would you plan to move on horseback or with horse-drawn equipment? If so, make sure you have sturdy working horses that will pull and ride, plus the kinds of tools needed to make repairs to bridles, harnesses, and wagons.
- If your vehicles breaks down or the roads become impassable, make sure you have backups – bicycles or motorized trailbikes, plus good pairs of hiking boots might be your best option.
- Always move in a group, and don't stop for hitchhikers or the equivalent.
- Always send out an advance scout who can check out the terrain unobtrusively.
- Maintain an "outrider" who watches the main group and looks out for problems.

If you are heading to a Bug Out Location (BOL) that you have set up in advance, don't approach it directly. If you're not there, someone else may have moved in, and it wouldn't be prudent to walk up to the door and tell them to leave. Scope the place out from a distance -- plan good locations for viewing when you secure the arrangement -- and watch the site for a day or two before attempting to move in.

Becoming Nomadic

This is probably a low-likelihood situation, at least for the initial years of the Zen-slap. Depending on the severity of the coming Cold Times, it may become a lifestyle for a portion of the population at least.

Effectively, nomads will be following the weather, animals, and the plant growth, moving along with wild game and harvesting fruits and wild crops as they go. Some may be nomadic from city to city, scavenging locations that are accessible in summer and leaving to sell their goods further south as the winter comes on. Much depends on whether this Cold resolves in a few generations, or if it progresses to a full-on Ice Age.

Many groups of American Plains Indians migrated through their region with the seasons, camping beside rivers to fish, then following herds of animals, and finally to another area harvesting nuts and berries as they returned to their original campground. Some planted corn and other crops, then travelled to another area to hunt or fish, and returned in time to harvest the crops.

We are not that distant from the nomadic lifestyle as we like to imagine. People routinely travel from the major northern cities down to warm southern locations as the seasons change right now – "snowbirds" who migrate in RVs to enjoy the warm weather. Some people still migrate from place to place following jobs, too.

The nomadic lifestyle will require housing such as tents, RVs, "covered wagons"; transportation like horses or oxen, bicycles, motorbikes, RVs, cars or trucks; backup food sources including buckets or barrels of basics such as salt, sugar, flour, beans; backup water and water purification. If livestock will go with you, you'll need cages for the smaller ones like chickens, rabbits, baby goats, and so on; or a means to herd, protect and corral the larger ones – sheep, goats, cattle.

A nomadic lifestyle with large livestock will spend more time camped than it will actively moving, because the animals need time to eat and drink. If you stop for a while, make sure it's not on private land – a landowner would be justified in running you off or holding some of your livestock in exchange for land use. Consider sending someone ahead to negotiate a stay-over and what the landowner would take in return? A calf? Two lambs? Labor?

Nomads still need currency, that is whatever is being used for money or trade at the locations they frequent, good manners for dealing with established towns and cities, something to sell to the people who have currency, perhaps meat? Vegetables? Salvage? Skills? Ideally, one to several outriders move around the group and verify locations are safe to travel into. Security remains a concern, and the old cowboy concept of "circling the wagons" is a valuable consideration. All members of the group should be proficient with defensive firearms or other weapon use.

Travelling Safely in Cold Times

Travelling in the cold, particularly snowy and icy cold, requires a good deal of advance planning and extra care – because cold can kill you. It's not just slippery roads and the risk of a wreck, it's the fact that without the protection of shelter and the warmth required to keep your body temperature up, you simply can't survive.

Even if all you plan to do is hop in the car and buzz around to the nearest supermarket for a loaf of bread, you may be at risk. An accident that blocks your travel, another driver who is erratic, or an unexpected snowstorm could stop you right where you are – and stick you there for an unforeseen period of time. In the spring of 2017, drivers in Japan were buried – literally *buried* – in their cars during a sudden heavy snowfall. It came down so fast, they couldn't even get out to walk to safety.

Too many people are so expectant of "normal" conditions, that they leave their homes without jackets and cold weather clothing when they drive in the winter. They might do it a thousand times and never have need of any gear, but that *one time* is all it takes to become a statistic. When we are into the full-on effects of the coming little ice age, there won't be any second chances. You'll have to be ready every single time you go out.

Ready in this case means: warm clothing suitable for walking a long distance in the cold, good boots, hat, emergency water; lightweight food like granola bars, peanut butter, sardines, dried pineapple for a day or two; matches and fire starter plus kindling; flashlight, firearm, and currency of whatever people will take at the time.

That's enough supplies that you'd be wise to get a sturdy but nondescript backpack. Make that a plain, non-tactical, everyday sort of thing, so that it doesn't stand out as loaded with goodies. That will make it easier and more convenient to move your emergency pack from the house to the car each time you leave.

Take it often enough, and it's a habit. Refill the gas tank when it's half-empty. Don't wait until you are running on fumes; stations may not be open, have fuel, or have grid power to run the pumps.

If you still have the ability to travel by motor vehicle, you will need chains for the tires. Outside of the northern parts of the US, the use of chains is unusual. Here in the Midwest, our local car-repair supplier would have to special order them. Perhaps that will change in a few years. Chains help the vehicle navigate on slick and snowy roads; it is asking for problems to drive on bad, unplowed roadways without chains. You might be a great driver, but the next guy coming at you head on may not be. Keep a folding shovel and some sand or ice-melter in the trunk. Always take your emergency backpack. Always.

If you must go out in snow, consider snowshoes for any kind of cross-country trekking. These smaller size ones pictured on the next page are for young adults. Bigger folks need bigger snowshoes. The one on the right is where you'd strap your boot. The one on the left is upside down so you can see how it's designed to grip snowy and icy ground. The front tips bend up slightly, and when you walk you drag your heels a little. Snow that's more than a few inches deep will require snowshoes. Without them, you'll sink and have a difficult time making any progress.

You can make snowshoes by bending a sapling into a similar shape, something like a tear-drop, and lashing the ends together at the heel. The pointy end acts as a rudder. Cross and crisscross lacing over the foot bed. This will act as your grippers.

Traditionally, snowshoes were made with leather strips, but you might try paracord or any other sturdy cording (except for nylon, which is too slippery). You'll have to replace cordage over a season, but it's not hard to do.

In Nordic countries, the cross-country ski trek is a winter sport, plus a way to get around when the snow is deep. If you've already got skis and experience, hang on to them. If you don't, you can generally find used pairs at thrift stores. You'll need ski boots that fit the skis you have, or you can modify the skis so that your existing boot will fit. Basically, the ski will need a boot tip sized lip or strap to hold your boots in place as you push forward through the snow. Additionally, you'll need a pair of ski poles to help with the forward effort. This is very physically demanding exercise, by the way, and uses muscles you don't use the rest of the year.

Carry your backpack with your emergency supplies when you go out on show shoes or skis, too.

12 WHAT IF....?
THE BIG PICTURE

What if it doesn't happen? What if it is worse?

Throughout this book, we've looked at multiple ways to respond to a cooling and chaotic physical world. We've discussed where to live, what to live in, how to keep warm, storing and growing foods, adapting your water supply, adapting to lower power sources, staying healthy, managing your resources, and providing a secure environment. Each of these elements is an essential human need; each is vital to your survival no matter what the future brings.

Hopefully, by this point, you've put together how location works *with* how your home is built, the livestock that will feed you, the food you're able to grow in your garden, how you'll keep warm and dry, and how to set up defenses for all that. An extended family or like-minded group would be able to settle in to a situation like that, and prosper whether hard times come upon us, or not. You're no more separated from the rest of the world than you choose to be at this time.

Modern technology is likely to survive simple Cold Times – there is high technology already used in the extreme cold of both Polar regions and in Siberia, so technology won't just disappear. Cold tolerant retrofits may be required, though, and that may put some tech offline during the transition.

If an EMP or solar CME decimates the grid, high technology will go with it, but simple gasoline engines will continue to work as long as stored fuels last. Technology is a fragile master – better to be in a position where you don't absolutely *have to* depend on it.

Dropping overnight into the 18th century, or going full Mad Max is not a high-level risk...although we can't discount it entirely. Our population has never been as dependent on the continuous flow of electricity, or food delivered by JIT, as it is now. We just don't know what might take place in a worst-case situation...or even a moderate situation.

We little people, we worker bees, do have reports that the wealthy and elite are building survival bunkers and super-hardened homes at a furious pace....but they are not telling us why. The rich may merely be responding to the same sense of urgency that affects the rest of us, and reacting in a grand style. Or they may be privy to information that isn't shared with us wee folk. But they are preparing, and that tells us something.

So, if the Cold Times don't arrive with ferocity, or don't come at all, are you worse off or better off for taking the steps to prepare for hard times and more self-sufficiency?

That's a question only you can answer.

On the other hand, if the Cold Times are more intense – instead of a century of harsh winters, poor growing seasons, and stifling summers, the mini ice age converts to a full-on glaciation that lasts for a thousand years – you will have a running head start on readiness. You already know, ahead of the herd, that times will get more difficult, and you've made plans to make it easier on you and your family. That gives you an enormous advantage, one that will benefit your descendants into the far future.

The Big Picture, here, is thinking ahead beyond your children's children's children – into a future we can perceive only dimly. We can say without hesitation that there are some things your descendants *will absolutely need* – the same things you do: shelter, food, water, defense.

They will also need knowledge. The best way to pass knowledge along to people who are not yet born, is in the form of books. We don't know what the future will bring, so if we want our descendants to have the mental skills and aptitude they might need but won't be able to access from the internet or YouTube, we must keep books:

- how-to's
- biography
- mathematics
- classical novels
- astronomy
- building
- cooking
- archeology
- religious
- cartography
- agriculture
- history
- art
- medical
- geology
- reference
- metallurgy
- geography
- music scores
- biology
- paleontology
- languages
- architecture
- physics
- ship building
- formularies
- encyclopedias

– a thousand books would barely scratch the surface of what our descendants may need to know.

Don't count on public libraries to do this. They are rapidly moving to electronic media. Even the truly great works of the past, Descartes, Plato, Aristotle, Aquinas, Jefferson, Shakespeare, are all but lost already. It is the rare person today who has read any of Western Civilization's finest thinkers...and there will be few to no readers in the future, if someone doesn't value, save, and pass along their works.

New books are often prohibitively expensive, but used books aren't. Do not store your books in one location – you could lose all of them if something happened to the site. Spread your repository among families, so that each household becomes a Keeper of

Books.

Then, share and pass around volumes.

Stay Informed

Although existing trends indicate that the Cold will be obvious in just a few years, we simply cannot be sure what additional effects may accompany the weather changes.

Major institutions have damaged their credibility with the public so efficiently, that little trust remains – mainstream media, insurance companies, the word of politicians, all cratering in a pit of their own digging. Will governments admit that they have misled their citizens? Will the media trade their bias for factual reporting? Will insurers be able to cover hundreds of thousands of new damage claims – especially after paying out for the hurricanes, fires, and floods of 2017?

On the personal safety level, there are questions as well. Are there enough FEMA and local agency supplies and cold-weather equipment stored up to handle emergencies on a wide scale? What backups exist for sudden grid-compromising events? How will oil and energy and food cross the Mississippi to take care of the Eastern Seaboard if the New Madrid fault lets loose and destroys roads, bridges, and barge traffic? What recourse do the citizens of Seattle and Portland have, if the overdue Cascadia quake levels the entire coastal Pacific Northwest region?

Finally, what happens to a national financial system that is suddenly thrust into that kind of pressure – one in which the average citizen cannot raise $400 in cash for an emergency? That is a financial system that is already teetering, with major retail chains failing weekly.

We won't know what happens, until it happens. In the meantime, we must watch the signs that we can find, locate media that *is* trustworthy (it's not on the mainstream), and then **take action.** That's the only way you and yours will live through these times.

COLD TIMES

COLD TIMES

RECIPES

This is the way that I cook, and recipes that I routinely use. There's nothing magical about them – a good cook modifies recipes to suit their taste and that of their family. Use your own preferred recipes, and be sure to store extras that are unique to your tastes (specific spices, for example).

STARTER

This can be used for raising bread. Everything made with a starter is a living, creative effort – you will have failures, but if your starter is healthy, it will all be perfectly edible.

Simple Starter
- 1 tsp active dry yeast, more or less
- 1 cup clean water
- 1 cup flour

Mix all together, more or less of water to flour so that you end up with a slurry like pancake batter. Set in a clean bowl or mason jar, covered with cheesecloth to keep out gnats. Leave at room temperature overnight or perhaps a bit longer. It will get bubbly and develop a tangy aroma. Stir it a couple times if desired and let it bubble up again. It's ready to use.

Hold back a half-cup of this, add 1 cup of water and 1 cup of flour, mix well, and ferment as before. You can keep your starter going indefinitely (literally for years), and the flavor will just keep getting better and better.

Natural Starter
This can be made with juniper berries (I've used cedar berries), or

even fresh organic grape skins that still have the white powdery residue on them. That white powder is actually naturally occurring yeast organisms.

- 2 or 3 tablespoons of fresh juniper berries
- 1 cup flour
- 1 cup clean water

Soak the berries in the water for an hour or two, then remove and dispose of the berries. Add the water to the flour until it is like a batter, then culture as *Simple Starter*. It will take this one several days to begin to ferment and bubble up, and it raises bread a little more slowly. The flavor is a little bolder and perhaps with a slightly stronger undercurrent. Keep the starter going the same way.

Beer Starter

This is ideally done with a homemade beer, or a Trappist ale that has yeast residue at the bottom of the bottle. If you make beer or even wine at home, you can use the fresh dregs (yeast) at the bottom of the fermenting vessel.

- 1 cup beer or fermenting dregs
- 1 cup flour
- Water sufficient to make a batter

Culture as *Simple Starter*. This has a nice nutty tang, and just gets better with aging. Keep it going using just water and flour.

Potato Starter

- 1 small potato, boiled in the skin until fork-tender
- 1 cup water from the boiled potato
- 1 cup flour

When the potato is partially cooked, mash it slightly in the water. Finish cooking. Let cool a bit. Pour about a cup of the water, more or less, into the flour – it's okay if there's some potato bits in it, but I like to remove the skin. Mix with the flour to a batter consistency, then continue as *Simple Starter*. This starter raises bread slowly, but to me it has a smoother tang. May continue the starter to future batches.

Doughball Starter

By far the simplest of all, in terms of ingredients, but takes a little longer to be ready.

- Water
- Flour

Mix "some" flour and water together until it forms a slightly damp paste that you can gather into a baseball sized ball. It should be damp but not sticky. Put the ball into a bag or container of flour, and let it sit there for a couple days – check on it every so often. Once it smells a little tangy and become somewhat "resilient" to the touch, it's ready for the next step – add water to batter-consistency, let it bubble up over a day or two, and treat as *Simple Starter*.

Yogurt, Kefir, or Raw Milk Starter
- 1 cup yogurt, kefir or fresh raw milk, thinned with a little clean (boiled or filtered) water
- 1 cup flour

Proceed as *Simple Starter*. This one cultures a bit more readily if it's kept in a warm location, say around 95F degrees. It will smell pleasantly sour when bubbly. If it smells musty or unpleasant, toss it and start over. Continue this starter by adding a half cup to a cup each of flour and water – no additional milk, kefir, or yogurt is needed.

QUICK BREADS

Flat Bread
These are the simplest breads – basically flour, water, and salt – patted or rolled into a very thin pancake shape and then fried in a hot cast-iron or other heavy-bottomed pan with a little oil. It can also be cooked on a hot flat rock, if needed. This makes a nice flour tortilla. Can also be made with corn flour such as masa harina into a corn tortilla.

Corn Cakes, Corn Bread, or Hush Puppies
The essentials are like flat bread: corn, flour, water, salt. The eggs and fermented liquids can be used to raise the bread if you have no baking powder or baking soda. Sweetener gives it a pleasant flavor and brown crust, but it's perfectly tasty without it.
- 1-1/2 cup fine corn meal
- ½ cup flour (optional)
- ¼ cup sugar, honey, or syrup, more or less to taste
- 1 cup buttermilk, milk, sour milk, kefir, yogurt, beer or water
- 1-2 eggs
- 1 tsp salt
- 1 tbspn baking soda or baking powder

- 3 tbspns oil, butter, or bacon grease
- Optional: any or all of chopped onion, black pepper, boiled corn kernels, jalapeno, bacon or cracklins

Mix together. For corn cakes, add enough liquid to make it the consistency of pancakes. Fry in oil until crisp, then turn over and fry until toasty brown. Serve with jam, honey, syrup, dusted with powdered sugar, or with sausage gravy.

Make corn bread using the same recipe, by placing the batter in an oiled or greased pan and baking for 20 minutes or so in a 325-350F degree oven. You can also stove-top bake in a covered Dutch oven over low heat or in a fireplace.

Hush puppies are the same batter, but dropped by tea spoonsful into hot oil. Fry until browned and floating.

Sweet Breads

The essential ingredients are flour, oil, and sweetener with eggs and baking soda or powder to raise it. The flavor of the sweet bread is determined by the added ingredients – grated zucchini, bananas, chopped apples or apple sauce, grated carrots, walnuts, and spices. Once you have the basic recipe, you can make any kind of sweet bread you like. This recipe makes 2 loaves, and makes a rich dessert or snack. Use rehydrated freeze-dried or dehydrated ingredients if you've got them.

Basic Sweet Bread Batter
- 1 cup oil, butter, or lard
- 2 cups dark brown sugar, or 1-1/4 cups honey, or 2 cups sugar and 2 tablespoons molasses, or 1 cup sorghum or molasses
- 4-6 eggs
- 1 tsp salt
- 2-1/2 cups flour (mixed wheat, corn, oat, bean or other may be used)
- 1-2 tbspns baking soda or baking powder

For zucchini bread: Add 2 cups grated zucchini or other squash, 1 tsp cinnamon, 1 tsp vanilla, 1 cup chopped nuts and/or raisins or other chopped fruit.

For banana bread: Add 2 to 4 very ripe bananas, 2 tablespoons lemon juice or vinegar, ½ tsp vanilla (or omit), 1 cup chopped nuts.

For pumpkin bread: Add 2 cups cooked pumpkin or other

winter squash, 1 tsp cinnamon, 1 tsp ginger, ½ tsp nutmeg, 1 tsp vanilla, and 1 cup chopped nuts and/or raisins or other chopped fruit.

For apple bread: Add 2 cups peeled, chopped tart apples, or 1-1/2 cups applesauce, 1 tbspn cinnamon, 1 tsp vanilla, 1 cup chopped nuts and/or raisins.

For carrot bread: Add 2 cups grated carrots, 1 tsp vanilla, 1 tsp cinnamon, ½ tsp ginger, ½ cup grated or chopped pineapple, and 1 cup chopped nuts and/or raisins.

Directions: Mix all ingredients well, starting by mixing the oil with the sweetener, then adding the eggs and flour. Add the rest and stir until well combined. Grease and flour two loaf pans, or a 9x13 cake pan, or 2 round cake pans. Fill and bake for 35 to 55 minutes at 350F degrees, or in a slower oven for longer. Done when a toothpick inserted in the center comes out clean. Let sit in pan 10 minutes, then turn out on a rack to cool.

These breads all benefit by a light frosting – a drizzle of powdered sugar mixed with a little water or yogurt and dash of vanilla is nice. A regular cream cheese frosting is ideal.

YEAST BREADS

Yeast breads are typically made with fresh or dried powdered yeast, but that's a modern convenience that merely replaces the traditional "starter" discussed here earlier. Making a good yeast bread is truly a lost art – it takes practice and skill to turn flour into a well-risen and tasty loaf.

If you've never made bread by hand before, this Awakening phase is the best time to learn how. There's many recipes out there, many YouTube teaching videos, and other resources to show you how. Even so, your best learning tool is to simply grab a recipe and give it a shot. The five-pound "bread" flour bags in the supermarket usually have a recipe on the package – follow it to the letter to get your hands powdered up and into the game. Success will be a delight, and failure will be a chance to learn. After that, you can begin to experiment with wheat berries and home-grinding.

If you make one single loaf by hand once a week for 52 weeks –

you *will* be an authority on home bread making in less than a year.

This recipe will make 2 loaves.

Ingredients
- 6 cups, more or less, of fresh ground wheat flour
- 2-3 cups water or fresh scalded and cooled milk (the bacteria in raw milk will affect the "rise" if it hasn't been scalded)
- 2 tablespoons butter or lard or other fat
- 2-3 teaspoons salt
- ¼ cup honey, molasses, sorghum, or packed brown sugar (not vital but adds flavor and "rise")
- 1 teaspoon cinnamon powder (optional)
- 2-1/2 teaspoons active dry yeast OR 1 cup starter culture
- If you have it, 1 tablespoon of potato flour (not "starch"), or ¼ cup finely ground dried potato flakes or ½ boiled cooled peeled mashed potato can be added to help keep the loaf moist.

Directions
Warm the liquids to lukewarm (slightly warm to the touch, like baby's milk would be). Place in a large mixing bowl. Add the honey or sugar to dissolve. Add the melted lukewarm butter or lard. Add potato if you have it. Mix in about 2-4 cups of flour until you have the consistency of thick pancake batter. Stir well for several minutes to help develop the gluten. Mix in the salt, cinnamon, and yeast or starter. Stir well again for several minutes. This saves you having to do the first kneading of the bread.

Set this aside, covered, in a warm kitchen to rise about double in size. If using yeast, this could be an hour or two. If using starter, perhaps several hours or overnight.

When risen, beat in remaining flour again, this time mixing until it forms a ball of dough. Add extra flour if needed – this is art rather than science. Grease your hands well. Place the dough ball on a floured surface and knead vigorously until it springs back when you push a thumb into it to "dent" it and the dough surface is smooth. This will take about 10 minutes of kneading.

Kneading is merely pushing and turning the dough, pulling the sides in and pushing and turning again. Use your body weight and upper body strength to push, pull, turn, and fold the dough. Keep pulling the outside edges into the center, pressing down, and turning again. This is great exercise!

Divide the dough into two equal balls, knead slightly and form into loaves. Place in a greased loaf pan, and cover with a clean kitchen towel, and let rise to the top of the pans – an hour to several hours.

Bake in a 350 degree oven for about 30 minutes, or a hot solar oven for 40 minutes (loaves will rise a little more). Watch the loaf – it is near done when it browns and becomes golden. The loaf is cooked through when it makes a "hollow" sound when tapped. Tip out of the pan, and rub all over with a stick of butter to soften the crust a bit. Cool on a wire rack for at least 15 minutes (hot bread will burn your mouth!). Slice with a serrated knife, but don't press down – that will crush the loaf. Butter and enjoy!

CURE ALL CHICKEN BROTH AND SOUP

This is the chicken soup known for its healing properties, that grannies throughout the ages have foisted on their ailing families – and it does actually work! The method of making it extracts easily digested proteins, calcium, enzymes, minerals, vitamins, and trace nutrients, as well as potent antibacterial and antiviral elements. It can also be used as a tasty meal or stew base.

Broth is usually the colored liquid, strained from the thicker loaded soup. Both are highly nutritious.

Ingredients:

1 whole chicken (excluding head) but including the thoroughly scrubbed scaly legs and feet, as well as skin, liver, heart, and gizzard
Salt, Pepper, Bay Leaves, Allspice
1 whole bulb of garlic
1 – 2 onions, chopped
2 large carrots, sliced and/or grated
3 stalks of celery, chopped
Handful of fresh or dried parsley
Cup each as available:

Potatoes, diced
Sweet potatoes, diced
Broccoli, cabbage, kale
Tomatoes
Wild greens
Squash
Anything else on hand

Directions

Place the chicken and parts in water to cover. Add a bay leaf or two if you have them, a tsp or so each of salt and pepper, and three whole allspice. Bring to boiling and slow boil until the meat is cooked. Let cool a little, take the bird out and remove all the meat. Set the meat aside. Return the bones to the water, bring back to a boil.

Add all the vegetables and garlic. Add enough water to cover everything. Simmer, covered, for an hour or longer until all the vegetables are mushy to create a rich bone broth. Strain through a sieve, saving all the juices. Press the veg and bone to extract any remaining juice and return juice to the pot. The mushy remains can be fed to chickens or hogs.

Now, the broth can be pressure canned at 10 pounds pressure for 90 minutes for later use at a moment's notice. Or, the fresh broth can be provided to the ailing person, adding extra salt and pepper (1 tsp salt per quart of broth).

Alternatively, for soup: add back the reserved meat, more chopped vegetables as desired (onions, carrots, celery, potatoes, peas, etc), and cook until the vegetables are tender. Add noodles in the last 10 minutes of cooking or dumplings or whatever you prefer. Salt and pepper to taste.

PICKLING EGGS

Select relatively fresh eggs – but not newly laid ones because they are harder to peel. Place eggs in a pan in cold water to cover, add a teaspoon of salt or baking soda; this will make shelling them easier. Bring the pan to a boil, and gently move the eggs around with a wooden or silicon spoon. Continue at a rolling boil for 3 minutes. Turn off heat and cover the pan. Let the eggs sit in the hot water for 10-12 minutes. Pour off hot water, and put eggs immediately into very cold water (snow would be fine); the sudden temperature change makes them easier to peel.

While eggs are cooking, prepare the pickling solution. This amount is sufficient for 3-4 quarts of pickled eggs. Adjust accordingly.

3 cups vinegar (any flavor)
2 cups water
1/3 cup sweetener (sugar, honey, maple syrup, etc.)
1 tablespoon salt
1 tablespoon mustard seed
1 tsp whole black pepper
1 tsp pickling spices (optional)
Chopped onions (optional)
Sliced jalapenos (optional)
Bring all to a boil and simmer until eggs are ready.

When you can handle the eggs comfortably, shell them out, placing eggs into hot, clean canning jars (12 to a quart jar); jars should be on a towel or wooden cutting board, not a tile surface to avoid cracking them. Pour the vinegar solution over the eggs in the jars to ¼" of the top – you can leave all the spices and flavoring in it, or strain them out.

Clean the jar rims and place a canning lid on, then tighten a band securely on each jar. CAUTIOUSLY, using oven mitts on both hands and a towel wrapped around the jar, invert each jar and then set back down upright. Let cool – the lids should click when they seal. Any jars that don't seal can be kept in cool storage and used first. The rest will keep for a year. Best after about 2 weeks of aging.

FREEZING EGGS

I used to crack eggs, gently whip together whites and yolks, and freeze in ice cube trays. This works if you have a deep freeze, and plastic bags for the egg cubes. Each cube is equivalent to one egg. Thaw in a cup or bowl in the refrigerator or cool spot, then whip and use as fresh – makes good scrambled eggs and quiche, too. You can also separate the whites from the yolks, mixing each gently in separate containers and freeze in different bags

More recently, I have been freezing eggs whole in their shells. The shells will crack, usually from "pole to pole". You can leave them this way and pack into freezer bags or use a vacuum food saver bag (better). When you are ready to use an egg, take it out, place in lukewarm water for a minute or so – twist the shell off. Let the egg thaw in a cool covered dish, then it's ready to use. Alternatively, you can place the shelled frozen egg in a fry pan with plenty of oil on low heat – it will thaw as it cooks, and comes out with a lump in the middle.

Another option is to freeze the eggs (shells will split). After a day in the freezer, take out, dunk in lukewarm water, and twist the shells off. Put the eggs back in the freezer to firm up. After several hours, bag in freezer bags or in food saver bags. Then, back into the deep freeze.

Eggs stored in a vacuum sealed bag will keep for a year (or longer) in the freezer. Thaw before use, or cook as above.

CANNING MILK

The combination of high heat and pressure alters the milk and develops a cooked flavor in the end-product. It's just like fresh milk in texture, but nothing like fresh in flavor – it's better! Perhaps the closest flavor approximation is caramel, or the European cheese known as Gjetost or Mysost. Canned milk can be used for cornstarch-based puddings, in coffee, or where you'd use fresh milk, but simply will not set up for cheese or yogurt.

Prepare canning jars and lids by washing and boiling. Get your pressure canner set up according to manufacturer's directions, having one to two inches of very warm water over the rack in the bottom. Bring milk directly from the barn and filter as usual. No need to pasteurize since canning will do the job for you. While milk is still warm, pour into hot canning jars to one-half inch from the top. The milk must be warm to start with (even if you must reheat it), or the jars will burst under pressure. The milk also must be super-fresh, no more than 48 hours old and refrigerated – or you'll end up with canned curdled chunky milk. Clean jar rims, apply lids and seal.

Place jars in the canner so that no jars touch. Close and clamp canner according to manufacturer's directions. Allow steam to escape vigorously for several minutes before closing the vent. Heat canner to 240 degrees, ten pounds pressure (or appropriate for your elevation), and hold quarts and pints at that level for 25 full minutes, counting from after the temperature and pressure are reached. If the pressure drops below 10 pounds, you must reheat and restart counting the time – 25 full minutes at 10 pounds pressure.

Turn off heat and don't move the canner until the pressure has dropped to zero. Carefully open the steam vent. Do not try to rush the cooling process – it may take an hour or so. When you can handle the lid, undo the canner top and remove with great care. Let the canned milk rest for 15 minutes or so in the canner before removing – the jars may still be bubbling internally for a while. Set the jars aside to cool completely. Check for lid seals. When cool, label and store each jar.

A use for pressure-canned milk is a variation on plain vanilla cornstarch pudding – it's a caramel delight which makes a light and nutritious mid-winter treat. Mix 1/3 cup brown or white sugar (or ¼ cup honey or maple syrup), ¼ cup cornstarch, and 1/8 tsp of salt in a saucepan. Stir in 2-3/4 cups of cold canned milk and gradually bring to a boil over medium heat, stirring the whole time to prevent burning. The pudding will thicken considerably. Boil for a minute, stirring gently, then remove from heat and add two tablespoons of butter or bland oil. Cool or chill. The recipe can be readily doubled or tripled, and it's especially nice with a dab of whipped cream or swirl of chocolate syrup on top.

CANNING MEAT

Any type of meat may be pressure canned by the same process. For smaller pieces, such as chicken legs or sections of rabbit, you can leave the bones in or out – the method is the same. For larger animals, you can chunk the meat into uniform 1" square pieces, or coarsely grind the meat or make into sausage. Remove visible fat – it can gum up lids and cause lid sealing failures if the pressure drops too quickly in the canner. Freeze or process the fat separately, don't throw it away. Fish should be canned in smaller jars, half pints are considered the 'correct' size so that the meat is fully processed.

You can add spices or small ingredients, such as slices of onion, for flavor. Leave out all garlic, whether fresh or granulated – under pressure canning, garlic becomes rather bitter.

Method
Wash and boil or hot-water rinse jars and lids. Set on a wood surface, such as a cutting board, or place on towels laid over a tile or stone countertop. Put meat into the jars, but do not pack overly tightly, within 1" of the top rim of the jar. Add 1 tsp sea salt (or other non-iodized salt) to each quart jar, and ½ tsp to each pint or ¼ tsp to half-pints. Pour boiling water into each jar to cover the meat, up to 1" from the top jar rim. Clean the rims and put on lid and band and tighten. Fill pressure canner with lukewarm water a minimum of 2" of water above the bottom rack, or according to canner directions.   Place jars into the canner so that they don't touch.   Close and seal canner according to manufacturer's directions.

Turn up heat and continue until steam vents from the canner for a couple minutes, then place the weight on the vent to close. Let pressure build to 10-pounds, 240 degrees (or whatever is appropriate for your elevation).   Hold at 10-pounds 240 degrees for 110 minutes for quarts, 90 minutes for pints and half-pints. If the pressure goes below 10-pounds 240 degrees, you must reheat and restart the timer – it must maintain that temperature and pressure for the full continuous time.

When the time is done, turn off the heat and do not move the canner. Let it cool until the vent weight can be removed without any hissing – it could be an hour or so. Remove the weight, then carefully remove the lid so that steam rises *away* from you. Leave the jars in the canner for a while so that all bubbling inside the jars stops – lids may seal during this time with a clicking sound. Remove the jars to the cutting board or towels, and let rest until cool. Label with type of meat, date, and then store.

MAKING FRESH CHEESE

The perfect use for that extra milk; double or triple or multiply the recipe as needed. A gallon of milk makes about a pound of cheese.

1-quart whole goat's milk
¼ cup vinegar or lemon juice

Bring the milk almost to a boil – there will be tiny bubbles around the edge of the pan. Turn off the heat. Immediately add the vinegar or lemon juice. Stir once or twice. The milk will separate into curds and whey. Let this sit and cool off until you can handle it with ease.

Pour the curds and whey through boiled cheesecloth resting in a colander so that you catch the curds as the whey drains into a collecting dish. The whey can be consumed if you wish, or fed to the chickens, pigs, cats or dogs.

Take the curds in the cheesecloth, twist slightly to drain, and then put the curds into a bowl. Add ¼ teaspoon of salt per half pound of fresh cheese – or other spices and flavorings as you like (chives, garlic, pepper, sugar, strawberries, etc).

This fresh cheese can be used exactly as it is as a spread over toast. Or, you can treat it like cottage cheese, ricotta cheese, or use it in any recipe that calls for cream cheese!

BUTCHERING, GENERIC STYLE

An amazing thing about animals is that they're all basically the same underneath. All the critters in this book have livers, kidneys, similar heart and blood vessel systems, lungs, brains, stomachs and digestive tracts. The birds have a couple additional little attachments – one is called a crop (located in the neck where it joins the body) and a gizzard (inside the body) that do the work of teeth.

So, basically, butchering is the same work, no matter how big or small the carcass you're working upon. For this reason, I've written rather general instructions on butchering that could apply to almost any edible critter.

Let me suggest that you not overly concern yourself with producing "supermarket" cuts of meat – although you certainly can – because those specialized cuts are prepared using high speed electric meat saws on partially frozen pieces of meat. Home-raised meat can be any size, shape, or thickness – and still cook up into a mouth-watering treat.

Head: Earlier chapters on individual animals have instructed you how to stun and bleed the animal or bird; and to remove the animal's head. There are two main reasons for this: (1) once the head is off, it's emotionally easier to do the work; and (2) you don't usually eat the head (though some people do boil down pigs' heads for "head cheese").

Hanging: Tie loops of twine or rope around the animal's hind legs at the ankles, and suspend the animal from a strong support at a height that is comfortable for you to work at. The animal's neck and shoulders will hang down, and will continue to drip fluids.

Skinning: Chickens can be skinned by pulling the skin off like a glove, inside out. However, the skin is a good source of fat, so if you're able to leave it on, do so. You can pluck the feathers from a chicken immediately (it does take some effort), or you can dunk and swish the headless bird in a near-boiling kettle of water for a minute or so – that will loosen the feathers, and you'll have an easier time pulling them out. Immediately after plucking, dunk the bird in cold water to stop the skin-cooking process.

For larger animals, carefully lift the skin away from the muscle at the back of the animal's thigh, and insert a sharp knife beneath the skin. Cut the skin ONLY (!), from each rear hock to the anus, then mid-abdomen all the way to the neck, then outward toward the end of each front leg -- lifting with one hand so that you don't puncture the muscle or gut. For very young rabbits, you may only have to separate the skin from the rear legs using your knife, and then peel the hide down inside out like pulling a glove off of the carcass. For male animals, cut to one side of the scrotum and penis.

For larger animals, begin "folding" the skin backwards from the cut line, using a dull knife this time to peel and separate the skin. It's okay if you accidentally cut a hunk out of the muscle or poke a hole in the skin, but the fewer cuts like this there are, the more attractive the results will be. For goats, some owners actually just cut a small slit under the skin near the anus and insert a garden hose – turn on the water and pressure separates the skin from the carcass without too much effort, as well as cooling the meat quickly.

Continue until you have completely removed the skin. You may wish to remove the front feet at this time, rather than trying to skin them out. Garden clippers work on rabbits. For goats and pigs, fold the foot forward and cut the tendons, then bend the foot backwards and cut the inside tendons – then, you can twist the foot off. Cut the tail off flush with the body.

Lay the skin down, fleshy side up, and coat with a layer of salt if you plan to tan it.

Gutting: For sheep and goats: with your sharp knife, cut a circle around the anus, and pull the rectum out slightly. Tie a piece of twine around it and close up the anus so no bowel contents spill onto your meat. For chicken and rabbits, this is unnecessary.

Now, again using the sharp knife cut directly down the center of the animal's belly with the knife blade's sharp edge facing OUTWARD, not inward. *Keep one hand immediately behind the knife inside the animal's gut, to prevent accidentally cutting into the bowels.* If you do, the meat is still salvageable (wash cavity after degutted with a solution of one part bleach to four parts water, or lots of running water if you don't have bleach), but your life will be easier if you avoid cutting the bowels in the first place.

Cut down the rib line – you'll hit bone. At this point, the bowels, and stomach and will try to fall out of the open gut. Make sure you have a collecting bucket to drop these into. The rectum should slip out as a whole piece with the twine still on it. If not, make a few more cuts around it until it does. The lower bowels and stomach may now rip loose from the rest of the chest contents, or there may be some bits still connecting them.

For birds, just reach in now, and pull all the remaining guts out – no need to cut down the chest.

For other animals, cut down the centerline of the chest. You may need a heavier knife to cut through the cartilage where the rib bones join in the center of the chest. This is the animal's thoracic cavity, in which you'll find the liver, kidneys, lungs, heart and throat. Go ahead and pull these out, and place in your gut bucket.

If you wish, save the kidneys (which are shaped like giant kidney beans), liver, and heart. The liver has a small dark green finger-shaped gallbladder attached to it. Cut this out by removing liver from around it and being exceptionally careful not to cut the gallbladder. The greenish bile is very bitter and will make anything it touches inedible.
Rinse or wash off the carcass now, which should be clean of all guts, organs, and windpipe. What you've got here is a nice, muscular piece of meat. Trim any bruised-looking sections, and cut off jagged sections of neck.

Cutting: With smaller animals such as rabbits or very young goats, you can section the carcass into portion-sized pieces. It's easier to section a carcass if you cut at joints. Cut the rear legs off at the ball-and-socket joint where they meet the hip. Cut the hips off where the first vertebrae (backbone) meets it. Cut the mid-back (loin) off where it meets the rib cage. Cut the ribcage down the middle so you have a right and left "breast" section. You can also separate the foreleg at the shoulder at this point if you wish.

Larger animals can be cut into the same pieces, and then cut into smaller serving sizes if you wish. In addition, you can de-bone meat (completely remove the bone from a piece), roll the meat up, and secure with butcher's twine, so that you end up with a lovely boneless roast.

On your first new butchering jobs, you may end up with a bunch of little chunks of meat from various parts of the body. No problem! These are the pieces sold in supermarkets as "stew meat" and "stir fry" for exorbitant prices. Consider yourself blessed!

Remember to cut the back feet off at the ankle joint, and remove the twine.

Each section of meat should be individually washed in running cool water, patted dry with paper towels or air dried for a few minutes, and put in a covered container or plastic bag in the refrigerator to age. You can also age meat by hanging the entire

carcass in a cold, covered area that doesn't quite get to freezing –
an unheated garage in winter, a shed, or even off the limb of a
large tree. The goal is to get the carcass to cool quickly, then
tenderize as it hangs. Avoid hanging where predators, dogs, or
cats, can get at it. Pigs and goats can be eaten the same day they
are butchered, but the goat will be tough if it isn't aged. Birds and
older rabbits must be aged or it will be like eating leather. Young
fryer rabbits up to eight weeks old can be cooked immediately
after they have cooled.

Notes and Cautions: If meat should drop and hit the ground, it is
unfortunately contaminated with microbes. With a very clean
area, you may be able to get away with using that meat – as long as
you saturate it with one part bleach to four parts water, or rinse
thoroughly in clear water, and it is well cooked (not rare) when
you eat it. If the meat falls on manure, you're risking a good case
E. Coli-caused diarrhea if you eat it. Keep your butchering area
clean!

TANNING HIDES

Here's a low-cost and low-labor method for turning those hides
into useful items – I've used this on goat skins, sheep skins, rabbit
hides, and even deer skins, but it can be used on any mammal hide
when you want the hair to remain on the leather. An average goat
pelt takes about an hour to process and a couple days to dry; it
costs only a couple dollars per skin (really) if you're doing several
at a time; and it results in a soft, workable hide that can be used
as-is or cut up for sewing projects.

Handling the Skins: The quality of hides you begin with will make
a big difference in how your pelts tan out. Fresh hides, right off
the animal, should be cooled immediately. Trim off any flesh and
scrape visible fat from the hide. You don't have to scrape it
completely, though – that will take place later and be much easier
at that point. Place the skin in the shade, lying completely flat
with the fur side down, preferably on a cold concrete or rock
surface.

When the skin feels cool to the touch (a half-hour or so),
immediately cover the fleshy side completely and thoroughly with
plain, non-iodized salt. Use three to five pounds per two
goatskins. Three pounds of salt costs less than a two dollars, and

this is the first treatment for a hide that makes the next steps possible. If skins aren't salted within a few hours of removal from the animal, you might as well forget it – they will have already begun the course of decomposition and will probably lose their hair during the processing.

At this point, because you're probably busy dealing with the animal carcass and don't need to worry about the pelt, you should leave the skin in a protected spot to dry. You may tack it lightly to a tree, fur side down; or to the side of garage, or lay it flat wherever is handy. Add salt again if you've lost a lot in moving it; the salt will draw moisture from the skin and liquid may pool in low spots. Just add more salt. Transport the skin flat – you can stack several, if you keep a good layer of salt between them.

We've had trouble with neighborhood cats and other predators gnawing the edges of skins that were too easy to get at. Put the hide so it is out of reach, even if that means laying it in the bottom of a cage and locking the troublemakers out! You don't need to stretch the skin yet, just make sure that it is completely flat, with no curled-up edges. Let the skin dry until it is crispy. This may take a few days to a couple weeks. When completely dry, the skin is very "stable" and won't change or deteriorate appreciably. We've found salted goatskins that we'd forgotten in a barn for a couple years – they tanned up as nicely as if they were brand new.

If you're able to tan within a half-hour of taking the hide off the animal, you may skip the "salting" step.

Equipment: You'll need two large <u>plastic</u> trashcans, about 30-gallon size, and one lid. In addition, have on hand measuring cups, a wooden stirring stick about four feet long; staple gun and staples OR hammer and small stainless nails; wire bristle brush; and a wood rack (or stretcher) to tack the animal pelt for drying.

For a sufficient quantity of tanning solution to tan four to six goatskins or 10 rabbit skins, use these ingredients (cut the recipe in half for fewer skins):

7 gallons of water
16 cups plain salt (not iodized)
2 pounds (16 cups) bran flakes
3-1/2 cups battery acid (from auto parts store)

One box baking soda
Can Neat's Foot oil

Mixing the Solution: a couple hours before you plan to tan, take three gallons of water and bring to a boil. Pour this over the two pounds of bran flakes. Let this sit for an hour. Strain the bran out, saving the brownish water solution. Discard the bran flakes (or save to feed to critters).

Next, bring the remaining 4 gallons of water to a boil. Put the 16 cups of pickling salt in your plastic trashcan. Pour the water over the salt, and use the stirring stick to mix until the salt dissolves. Add to this the brown bran liquid. Stir.

When this solution is lukewarm (neither hot nor cold, comfortable to the touch), you are ready to add the battery acid. Keep the box of baking soda right next to you with the top open. Very, very carefully pour the battery acid along the side of the trash can into the solution – don't let it splash, if you can help it.

CAUTION: *If you get battery acid on your skin, use plenty of cool running water to rinse it; then apply the baking soda; rinse again. If battery acid splashes into your eyes or mouth, immediately run cool tap water on the spot for AT LEAST ten minutes. You should see a health care provider right away. If battery acid splashes on your clothes, it will eat a hole into the fabric – flush with water and cover with baking soda.*

Stir the battery acid in thoroughly. Keep the trash can lid tightly on this whenever you move away from it, even for a couple of seconds. It's a good safety habit. Kids and cats move fast.

If you have dried skins, soak them in clear fresh water until flexible. At this point, you can peel off the dried inner skin from the hide fairly readily. If you have fresh skins, use as-is. Add the skins to the solution. Stir the hide or hides, pressing down carefully under the liquid until fully saturated. Leave them to soak for 40 minutes, stirring from time to time to make sure all parts of the hide are exposed to the solution. After 40 minutes, the soaking tan is complete.

During the soak, fill your other trashcan with lukewarm clear water. When the time is up, use the stirring stick and move the skins one-by-one into your other trashcan. This is the rinsing process, which removes excess salt from the skins. Stir and slosh the skins for about five minutes, changing the water if it gets very dirty looking.

At this point, some people add the box of baking soda to the rinse water – there are pluses and minuses on this decision. Adding the baking soda will neutralize some of the acid in the skin. This is good because there will be less possibility of residual acid in the fur to affect sensitive people. However, this may cause the preserving effect of the acid to be neutralized as well.

Remove the hides from the rinse water. They will be very heavy. Let them hang over a board or the back of a chair or other firm surface to drain. If the pelt has tears or holes, you can mend them at this point. Use waxed thread (run a wax candle along the thread after it is in your needle) and a whip stitch (the kind you see on moccasins) to make a secure and relatively invisible mend. If the hole is large, you can cut a piece of the leg ends and sew it in place.

Now, using a sponge, rag, paper towels, or a paintbrush, swab the still damp skin-side of the hide with about an ounce of Neat's Foot oil. It should be absorbed fairly quickly, leaving only a little oily residue. That's okay.

Drying: Tack the hide up, skin side down, to your "stretcher"... we use salvaged wood pallets. Gently pull the hide as you tack it so that there is some tension in the skin – no need to exert excess pressure or over-stretch. Try to put your tacks around the edges so that the marks won't show later.

Cleanup: Your tanning solution can be neutralized for disposal by adding a couple boxes of baking soda to it. It will froth and bubble vigorously and release a potentially toxic or irritating gas, so give it plenty of ventilation and get away from the bucket while this is happening. When all the bubbling has stopped, about five minutes later, you can pour the mix out. Your town may have ordinances preventing you from pouring it down the drain – and all that salt would be hard on metal pipes and septic systems. I've heard of people putting this salty mix on driveways and paths where they wanted to stop weeds from growing.

Final Steps: Check the hide every day. When the skin-side feels dry to the touch in the center, but still flexible and somewhat soft (before the skin is crispy-dry), take it down from the rack. Lay the hide fur-side-down and go over the skin with a wire bristle brush. This softens the skin and lightens the color. Don't brush heavily or excessively in one spot – just enough to whiten it and give it a suede-like appearance. After this, set the skin where it can fully dry, a day or so longer. When fully dry, the skin is finished. Lay it on a chair; fit it onto your car seat. Doesn't that look and feel great?

Care: Skins processed by this method can't be washed without some loss of quality. Washed skins get very crisp and uneven when dried. However, you can thoroughly brush the fur side, shake out the skin, vacuum it, or wire-brush the skin side to touch up any very dirty spots. Depending on how well you rinsed the hide after tanning, there may be some residual salt in the fur – this can be drying to human skin, and may leave little white flecks around, and might even absorb moisture from the air if your weather is humid. Other than being uncomfortable or making a mess, this shouldn't be a problem – the salt eventually works out of the hide.

A Gentle Caution: Once your friends know you can tan hides, be prepared for them to bring around THEIR hunting trophies and livestock hides for treatment. If you decide to do this, take my advice: don't do it for free. Commercial tanners get $50+ to tan a single hide, and you should price your work accordingly – even if your return is just a case of good beer. Otherwise, you'll find yourself left with no time for anything else.

FRUIT JUICE

The original recipe came from Helen and Scott Nearing, the "first back-to-the-landers". You can use any fruit, or any combination of fruit. Try plain grapes or just blackberries – or combinations such as peaches and strawberries. If you use grapes with seeds, you may wish to remove the seeds first, but it's not necessary.

1 cup fruit, crushed or uncrushed
½ to 1 cup sugar or honey to taste
Boiling water to fill a clean quart jar

Put the fruit in the jar, add the sweetener, pour the boiling water over it and cap immediately. When the lids have popped down and the jars are cool enough to handle, give them a good shake to dissolve the sweetener.

Set the jars aside for several weeks to let the flavors develop. If you like clear juice, filter it through cheese cloth or a sieve before drinking. If you like your juice to have some body, you can shake before using and mix it all up, or run through in a blender or use an egg beater to whip it well.

GENERIC WINE RECIPE

Adapted from *How to Develop a Low-Cost Family Food-Storage System*

Wines are shrouded in mystery – and there is a kind of charming element to grape wines that taste as though they are actually blackberry, or oak-aged, or loaded with sweet cherries. That's "the magic of the grape." Although wines produced from specialty grape varieties and grown in grape-enhancing soil can be delightful, there's more to wine than just grapes. Historically, wine has been made from almost every vegetable substance known to humans – it's an alternative method of storing the harvest, a pleasant relaxing drink that can be enjoyed with a meal or by itself, and an outstanding barter item.

Grape wine connoisseurs shudder at the thought of using any yeast but one made specifically for wines, and there are a dazzling array available for home use. Unless you have specific wine variety preferences, a Montrachet (pronounced: *mon tre shay*) yeast makes a good all-purpose beverage – many health-food stores carry this type of yeast. Even so, a perfectly acceptable vegetable or fruit wine can be made with ordinary cooking (bread) yeast from the supermarket.

One tool you will need for home wine-making is an air-lock. Air-locks can be found at beer and wine-making supply shops, or you can construct an air-lock container fairly simply. The idea is to exclude outside air from the fermenting wine liquid, while allowing the beverage to expel excess carbon dioxide and other fermentation gasses. Some home vintners have used a glass gallon juice jar, fitted a cork tightly in the top, and punched a narrow hole through the cork from top to bottom. Through the cork, a two-food section of aquarium tubing is carefully inserted so that a couple of inches extend below the cork bottom, and the top edge of the cork is then sealed melted with wax around the tubing.

After the jar is filled, the cork-and-tubing is fitted firmly in place, and the long end of tubing is submerged in a jar filled with water. As the wine ferments, gasses will escape through the tubing, and bubble up through the water – but no air will be able to enter and contaminate the jar.

I've had good results using plastic gallon vinegar jugs, punching a hole through the plastic screw-on cap with a leather punch, and inserting aquarium air-line tubing. It fits so snugly that wax isn't needed. As a plus, the cap is easy to attach and remove from the jug.

The Process
Wine-making from flowers, herbs, fruits and vegetables is not complicated. Like all fermentation-based food, such as cheese or bread, it requires adherence to cleanliness and attention to detail. In each of the recipes that follow, the steps are the same:

- Wash the vegetable thoroughly. "Garden Dirt" wine is not appetizing. Chop or cook and mash as directed.
- Add veg/fruit/etc to the water; put in dissolved sugar and other chopped ingredients, except yeast.
- Cool or warm the water and added ingredients to room temperature, or even a shade warmer. Add the dissolved yeast and mix thoroughly. Cover container with lid or clean towel held in place to keep out gnats.
- Set in room-temperature spot for about 2 days.
- Strain off the liquid into an air-lock container(s). You can still consume the remaining "soup"-- chickens and pigs enjoy it as a treat. Close and set up the air-lock in a room-temperature location.
- Let continue fermenting for one to two months, until all bubbling ceases.
- Transfer the liquid to a clean holding container by siphoning – that keeps the clean upper liquid free of the "dregs" that have settled to the bottom. Use aquarium tubing, or special winemaker's tubing, moving it as little as

possible. Leave sediments at the bottom of air-lock as much as possible, but don't agonize over it. Taste the wine while siphoning – it will be quite strong, probably have a terrible astringent quality. Don't despair! Once the wine has aged and matured, the flavor will be completely different.

- Add clean eggshells (wash them before cracking the eggs), and leave some egg white clinging to the shells. This sill draw any remaining sediments to the eggshells, so that the wine clears naturally over several hours or days. Cover this container tightly with cotton wool or several layers of cheesecloth.
- When the wine has cleared, siphon into the final storage bottled and cork them (don't use canning jars, although commercial "screw cap" wine bottles are fine). Leave behind the eggs shells and sediment. If you taste the wine now, you'll notice that the flavor has already changed a little. It will continue to improve. Label each bottle with the date of bottling, type of wine, and winemaker.
- Store in a dark, cool place. Don't bother to try the tomato or pea pod wines for at least a year – they are nasty until they've aged. Begin sampling the other wines after 2 months. Set a few of each type back and try them after 5 years, then after 10. Surprises are in store for you!

<u>Recipes</u> *Can be doubled, tripled, or more.*

Carrot Wine
(Sweet, potent, and a dark orange shade – like a sherry.)
1 gallon and 2 cups water
5-7 pounds fresh carrots cooked and mashed
4 pounds white sugar or 1 quart honey
2 whole sliced oranges
1 lemon rind, plus all the juice (leave out the white pith)
½ pound raisins, chopped
1 package yeast

Onion Wine
(Delightful, pale golden and intense – but no oniony taste.)
1 gallon water
½ pound peeled, sliced onions
1 potato, washed and sliced thinly
2 pounds sugar

1 pound raisins, chopped
1 package yeast

Pea Pod Wine
(Use the empty pods, after harvesting your peas. Makes a bright, white, earthy wine.)
1 gallon water
3 pounds of pea pods, boiled until soft in some of the water
3 pounds sugar or quart honey
1-1/2 cups lemon juice
1 package yeast

Tomato Wine
(Let the mashed tomatoes rest in the liquid during the entire period of fermentation, about 21 days. Stir every second day. Results in a blushing golden wine, with a complex, distinctive flavor – no hint of tomatoes.)
10 pounds of chopped, mashed tomatoes
1 gallon water, poured boiling over tomatoes
4 pounds of sugar
3 slices fresh ginger root or ¼ tsp powdered ginger
1 tablespoon salt
1 package yeast

Zucchini or other Squash Wine
(White, sweet, mild wine.)
3-4 pounds peeled/unpeeled, diced squash
1 gallon water, poured boiling over the squash
1 cup lemon juice
3 pounds sugar or 1 quart honey
Spices to taste: cinnamon sticks, ginger slices, a few whole cloves

Fruit Wine
(Any fruit or combinations, makes a sweet, fruity dessert type wine.)
1 gallon water
4 pounds crushed fruit, more or less
2 pounds sugar or 2 cups honey
spices to taste: ginger, stick cinnamon, lemon juice, raisins as desired
1 package yeast

MAKE AN HERBAL SALVE

These directions are specific for *comfrey salve*, but can be used with any skin-healing herbs or combinations. Typically, I'll add a teaspoon of menthol or camphor or even bergamot essential oils, to give a little extra oomph to the salve. This is made from oil so it will be greasy, and most herbs will discolor clothing and sometimes skin....which is normal.

Ingredients
3-4 fresh large comfrey leaves, or a fist-sized chunk of root
OR 1-1/2 cups dried leaf and root
2 cups virgin olive oil, or home-rendered lard, or beef suet (don't use store variety, unless free of preservatives)
1-2 ounces shredded or chopped bees wax

Directions
Place the oil in a pot, and bring to a gentle boil. Add the herb carefully to avoid splashing. Turn the heat down low, and let the mix simmer until the herb is blackened – perhaps 20 minutes or so. Let it cool so it is easy to handle but still warm. Strain the oil mix carefully through a cheesecloth in a sieve, saving the oil in a clean pot. Now, add the beeswax and mix thoroughly – if it doesn't melt readily, you can gently heat the oil until it does.

Once the beeswax has melted, you can add any essentials oils you plan to use. Now, test the texture of the mix by dipping a clean teaspoon in it, then letting the mix cool on the spoon. Feel the salve texture – it should be firm but not hard. If it's not firm enough, add a little more beeswax to the mix. If it's too hard, add a little oil/fat. Test again.

When the texture is right, poor the liquid oil into clean 4 oz canning jars or smaller containers. Cover and let cool with the lids off. When cool, put on lids, label with date and contents, and it's ready for use.

COLD TIMES

RESOURCES

Food and Supplies

Check local sources first. There are many, many internet sites; this is a sampling.

Amazon (Amazon.com): everything, books, food, DVDs, supplies

Baker Seeds (rareseeds.com): One of the best sources for non GMO open pollinated heirloom seeds. Their annual beautiful full color big catalog includes an outstanding section on growing plants and saving seeds, as well.

Emergency Essentials (beprepared.com): #10 cans of storage foods. Good quality, shipping has taken weeks to months if there is a "run" on.

Food Storage Planner (https://www.foodstorageplanner .com/five): useful software to keep record of home food storage. Online download or CD version.

LDS Self-Reliance (https://store.lds.org): Home -> Home and Family -> Self-Reliance -> Food Storage. Good quality, excellent prices, shipping in a few days. Box clearly marked storage food.

MREDepot (MREDepot.com): storage foods, good MREs, #10 and #2.5 cans, first aid kits, other goods. Prices are typical, ships next business day, plain brown box. Outstanding service.

Painted Mountain Corn Alpine Varietal (Rockymountaincorn.com). Outstanding hardy variety that can stand some cold and comes to harvest quickly. Non GMO, organic source.

Med-Vet Supply (shopmedvetsupply.com). Medical supplies, some pharmaceuticals (must have state license for prescription meds), equipment.

Southern Exposure Seed Exchange (Southernexposure.com) Source for Gourdseed corn which grows in humid hot environments.

Thrive Life (www.thrivelife.com): freeze dried foods, excellent quality, pull-top cans, organic and some GMO-free and gluten-free; can storage shelves of variable sizes. Online shopping list and delivery setup. Prices are a bit higher than average.

COLD TIMES

INFORMATION RESOURCES

Atomic Corn
The World's Worst Corn Crop
http://calteches.library. caltech.edu/1235/1/Corn.pdf

Corn
Taking Genetic Stock
https://agresearchmag.ars.usda.gov/2000/jan/corn/

Castration
Very good info on 3 methods for sheep and goats, prepared
for Third World use. Download this now for later reference.
http://www.esgpip.org/PDF/Technical%20bulletin%20No.%
2018.pdf

Cold Climate Greenhouse Resource: *A Guidebook for
Designing and Building a Cold Climate Greenhouse* available
at: http://www.extension.umn.edu/rsdp/community-and-
local-food/production-resources/docs/cold-climate-
greenhouse-resource.pdf

Night Fighting 101 – Matt Bracken
https://westernrifleshooters.wordpress.com/2012/08/19/bra
cken-night-fighting-101/

YouTube.com
Adapt 2030 – outstanding site with info on the coming solar
minimum
Ice Age Farmer – innovative, low and high tech, low cost
solutions, lots of useful hands-on material and links
Oppenheimer Ranch Project – wonderful resource with
frequent updates

COLD TIMES

ABOUT THE AUTHOR

Anita Bailey has a diverse and unique background – starting with arts and literature, then to alternative health care such as reflexology and herbal remedies, through commercial livestock raising sheep and goats, then organic homesteading, and now to a cow-calf operation. Along the way, her family lived without electricity for two years. She became a registered nurse, then a Master's level nurse practitioner working in primary care and urgent care, and earned her Doctorate in the field. Between canning and preserving the various foods grown in a large garden and earning her SCUBA card, she trained and utilized dogs of different breeds for search and rescue operations, and completed a second Master's degree in Disaster Preparedness and Emergency Management. She's the author of hundreds of articles on small farming, peer-reviewed scholarly works in Alzheimer's and nursing research, and popular how-to books. She is married and living the dream in the rural Ozarks. This is her fourteenth book.

Made in the USA
Las Vegas, NV
03 February 2022

43042189R00225